GULF
WAR
ONE

HUGH MCMANNERS

GULF WAR ONE

REAL VOICES
FROM THE FRONT LINE

EBURY

3 5 7 9 10 8 6 4 2

First published in 2010 by Ebury Press, an imprint of Ebury Publishing
A Random House Group company

Introduction © General Sir Rupert Smith 2010
Text copyright © Hugh McManners 2010

The Random House Group Limited Reg. No. 954009

Addresses for companies within the Random House Group can be found at
www.randomhouse.co.uk

A CIP catalogue record for this book is available from the British Library

The Random House Group Limited supports The Forest Stewardship Council (FSC),
the leading international forest certification organisation. All our titles that are
printed on Greenpeace approved FSC certified paper carry the FSC logo.
Our paper procurement policy can be found at www.rbooks.co.uk/environment

Mixed Sources
Product group from well-managed
forests and other controlled sources
www.fsc.org Cert no. TT-COC-2139
© 1996 Forest Stewardship Council

Designed and set by seagulls.net

Printed and bound in Great Britain by Clays Ltd, St Ives PLC

ISBN 9780091935986

To buy books by your favourite authors and register for offers visit www.rbooks.co.uk

CONTENTS

FOREWORD

In 1990 I was the Commander of the British armoured division sent to the Gulf, as part of the coalition force in Saudi Arabia, which would ultimately fight Saddam Hussein's army and liberate Kuwait. As Commander, my view of the events of the war was influenced particularly by three factors. First, there was the need to acquire, organise and train the forces I was allocated into a fighting formation, capable of defeating the enemy in such a way that we played to our strengths and guarded our weaknesses. Second, was that being located in the desert I was to a large extent isolated; from the rest of the British Army, Whitehall, UK politics, and from the reporting in the media – and so the British public's perception of the crisis and what we were doing. The last factor was my position in the chains of command. I was firmly linked and subordinate to the US chain of command as far as the tactical battle was concerned, and at the same time part of and dependent upon the British Army for logistical support and direction as to the part we were to play and the risks we were to take, all the while being responsible for leading my command of some 15,000 men and 7,000 vehicles to achieve our specific objective.

Reading the accounts in *Gulf War One* from some of those who were engaged in this great endeavour has been informative and given me pleasure. They give a consistent picture of the rapid scramble to find the necessary manpower, equipment and sufficient spares to deploy a viable force, the uncertainty we experienced as to what this force was to achieve, and how, and our growing confidence as we realised we could do it.

Although on arrival in the Gulf we had a great deal of training and organising to do before we were ready for battle we were not poorly trained – we could not have accomplished what we did if this had been the case. However, our training had become too narrowly focused on the anticipated defensive battle in north-west Germany that was part of the Cold War deterrence. To keep expenditure on defence as low as possible, the quantity and nature of our equipment had also become centred solely on acquiring only what could be justified against the requirements of the anticipated battle in Germany. So those deployed at the end of 1990 suddenly found that their training and experience was scarcely relevant and the inadequacies of their equipment became increasingly evident.

To their great credit, the men and women deployed rose to the occasion. Considerable initiative and imagination was shown, old lessons were re-learnt and adaptations made. The professionalism and resourcefulness of the vast majority of those I saw was of a high order, as is illustrated in this book. As we began to work together in the desert so the confidence within the team grew. This was largely as people saw the array of our own and allied forces, and were assured that our organisation and logistics did work and were improving all the time. In this regard the Royal Engineers, the logisticians and the Royal Electrical and Mechanical Engineers were absolutely critical to our success whether in the field or at the port. We were supported by them wherever we went. We also had the Royal Navy standing by, and if, at any point, our overland communications had been broken by enemy action I would have relied on their support.

I understand why the Navy appears little in these pages, but I would like to give them special mention as their considerable part in this combined endeavour is not generally and fully recognised. It was the Royal Navy who led the combined fleet based on the US Navy Carrier Battle Groups up the Persian Gulf towards Kuwait. It was they whose armed helicopters sank about half of Iraq's navy and defeated the missile attack on the US battle-ships. And, not long after I had established my HQ to the north of the city, the first ship to dock in Kuwait was a Royal Navy frigate; a lucky few of the divi-sion had their first hot show for weeks. The artillery is the other organisation that I would like to highlight. Their effect on the enemy was not anticipated by many before the event, and I do not think it is widely understood even now. When forming the force that was to take on the Iraqi army I asked for and was given a substantial artillery component. My US Corps Commander reinforced the division further, allocating me a US artillery brigade. The weight of high explosive we were able to bring to bear on the target was thirty times more artillery power than a commander of a Second World War armoured division would have had at his disposal. That I could use this great force as I wished was a considerable advantage, and I could always call for more firepower, from our artillery or via air attack if needed. The Royal Regiment of Artillery did an outstanding job. For example, one unit was re-equipped with the M109, a medium gun, and another received the new MLRS rocket system only days before the land battle began. They learned how to use these weapons as they deployed, whilst at the same time working out the tactics of their use with the Americans. They would lead us into battle, with shattering effect.

The different view points that exist between the commander or his staff and the soldier on the ground has been a characteristic of command in battle ever since armies were bigger than a few hundred men. Indeed, if people at different levels do *not* have different points of view – or see things from different perspectives – then someone, usually the superior, is not doing his job properly; he should be seeing a bigger picture. To have this disparity work to advantage requires a strongly-held, common aim or objective, and absolute confidence in each other's judgment.

In our modern multinational military endeavours the difference of perspective extends from the man on the ground back to the individual capitals of the allied states. This makes it very difficult to align the different perspectives to the required advantage. The politicians and senior military commanders in each capital are concerned about their *national* contribution to the operation, balancing the political reward they expect from committing the contribution against the political risk at home if things go badly. Each capital will have a different balance of reward and risk.

On the other hand, the multinational commander in the theatre of operations is concerned with the achievement of the aim of the operation itself, which is whatever all the states can agree on, balanced against the threats presented by his opponent – rather than the risks to particular national contingents. Subordinate to him, each national contingent commander in the field has to achieve the objective set him by the multinational commander in such a way that he puts his nation's interest at least risk. The difficulties of aligning these viewpoints are aggravated because the multinational commander is often an unknown quantity in capital cities other than his own and his judgment is questioned as a result.

In the circumstances of this war in the Gulf, and as described in this book, we can see it took some time for the judgment of commanders in the field, both multinational and national, to be trusted and for objectives to become sufficiently aligned. Given the evidence of the more recent operations in the Balkans, where I was a multinational commander with many of the capitals showing a marked reluctance to allow their contingents to be risked in a fight, or Iraq and Afghanistan, we, Great Britain and our allies, have yet to work out how to function collectively so that this inevitable difference in perspective is not a source of friction and sometimes confusion.

Would the UK be capable of conducting an operation such as that of the first Gulf War in the future? Our forces are at least a third smaller than they were in 1990 and, as I write this, we face a defence review that promises swingeing cuts to both manpower and equipment. We do not have and will not have the supporting organisations and logistical reach to maintain our equipments in the field. We should also remember that while we defeated Saddam's army and liberated Kuwait we did not end his rule. The conflict may have ended, but the fundamental confrontation with Saddam Hussein continued until 2003, involving humanitarian operations in Kurdistan, UN Sanctions and inspections and the enforcement of the No Fly Zones established over North and South Iraq, which some argue continues to this day, albeit in another form. Could we sustain such a thirteen-year deployment in the future?

I am always conscious that retelling events is not the same as living them. There is a certainty that creeps into recollection, whereas in fact at the time nothing was certain, especially the outcome. This is particularly the case in war and battle – times of great uncertainty where facing the unexpected becomes routine, and a mixture of excitement and apprehension are the dominant emotions. But despite my mistrust of my own memory and that of others, there is much to be learned – and enjoyed – from these memories. Of course, for some of our number and their relatives, the operation of 1990–91 has not ended. Mercifully we had few killed and physically wounded; although for those who are bereaved or incapacitated the loss is no less just because few have suffered it. But, as this book tells, there are others whose memories of these events are as disturbing, uncertain and shocking as the event itself. Memory being so personal it can be difficult to share these thoughts with others, particularly because in modern warfare we operate in small groups dispersed over a wide area. So I hope this book is a help to all who have yet to reach the end of Operation Granby.

For my part I wish all those who served with me at that time all the best of good fortune.

General Sir Rupert Smith KCB DSO OBE QGM
September 2010

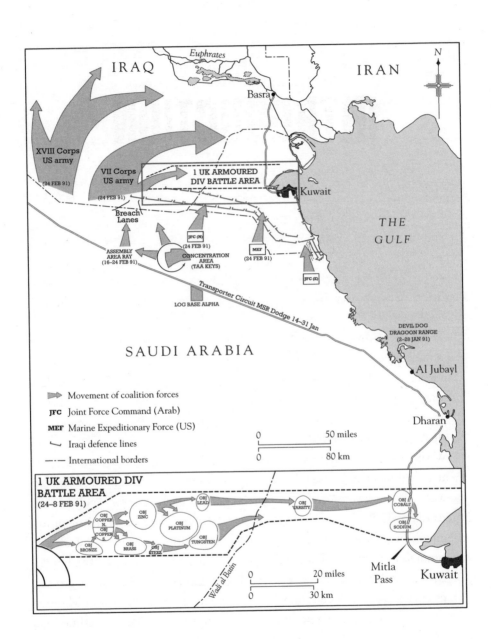

IRAQ

IRAN

Euphrates

Basra

N

XVIII Corps
US army

(24 FEB 91)

VII Corps
US army

(24 FEB 91)

1 UK ARMOURED
DIV BATTLE AREA

Kuwait

THE
GULF

Breach
Lanes

JFC (N)

(24 FEB 91)

MEF

(24 FEB 91)

ASSEMBLY
AREA RAY
(16–24 FEB 91)

CONCENTRATION
AREA
(TAA KEYS)

JFC (E)

Transporter Circuit MSR Dodge 14–31 Jan

LOG BASE ALPHA

DEVIL DOG
DRAGOON RANGE
(2–28 JAN 91)

SAUDI ARABIA

Al Jubayl

Movement of coalition forces

JFC Joint Force Command (Arab)

MEF Marine Expeditionary Force (US)

Iraqi defence lines

International borders

Dharan

0   50 miles

0   80 km

1 UK ARMOURED DIV
BATTLE AREA
(24–8 FEB 91)

OBJ
LEAD

OBJ
VARSITY

OBJ
COBALT

OBJ
COPPER
N.
OBJ
COPPER
S.

OBJ
ZINC

OBJ
PLATINUM

OBJ
TUNGSTEN

OBJ
SODIUM

OBJ
BRONZE

OBJ
BRASS

OBJ
STEEL

Wadi al Batin

Mitla
Pass

Kuwait

0   20 miles

0   30 km

INTRODUCTION

Iraq president Saddam Hussein invaded the sovereign Arab emirate of Kuwait in August 1990. His Soviet-equipped tank army was the fourth largest in the world. But Saddam failed to predict the enormous and unprecedented military response that would ensue, from a remarkable and surprising coalition of Arab and European nations and military forces under United States command.

The US Marines landed fully equipped forces into Saudi Arabia with remarkable speed, and within a month, supported by coalition air force squadrons, felt able to contain further Iraqi attacks into the Saudi oilfields, although heavily outnumbered. Concurrently, the rapidly-forming coalition armies were despatching heavy armour by sea for the Gulf, taking up most of Saudi Arabia's considerable port and airfield facilities.

With coalition armoured ground forces still arriving and training in theatre, and Saddam Hussein having reneged on many withdrawal offers, the six-week air war began. Aided by Special Forces on the ground, coalition air forces removed the threat of Saddam's air defences and aircraft, many of his chemical, nuclear and biological weapons facilities, and reduced his ability to command his troops. Then before the coalition forces crossed the border for the ground war, artillery and strike helicopters attacked Iraqi ground forces in Kuwait. A deception plan, by which the US Navy and Marines were poised to make an amphibious landing along the eastern coastline into Kuwait City, diverted tens of thousands of Iraqi troops, and succeeded in persuading the others to expect attacks from the wrong directions, digging less effective defensive positions. These highly coordinated preparations, and then the high tempo, unprecedented concentration of artillery, rapid movement and deep strike of the eventual ground attack, routed the Iraq army, which Saddam withdrew once he realised he would otherwise lose them.

In researching this book, I was very surprised at the lack of understanding and appreciation by senior politicians of the way this war had been planned and fought. Some senior military people, not directly involved, were equally ignorant. Their general thesis was that this was 'the war that never happened', with modern forces rounding up huge numbers of hapless, ragged, ill-equipped troops – 'old men and young boys'. This was, in fact, the first war of the technological era, and possibly the last tank war, in which the coalition fielded and fought the largest armoured formation in military history with some 400 more tanks than the German Expeditionary Force which fought Operation Zitadelle in the Kurst salient in 1943, which is generally considered history's largest tank battle.

As with Iraq's earlier eight-year conflict with neighbouring Iran, Saddam's generals had used largely static First World War tactics; these were totally ineffective against extremely rapid British and American deep-strike attacks using the world's most advanced artillery, followed up by fast-moving tanks destroying targets day and night at ranges greater than 3 kilometres. The Iraqi troops who remained, by the time the infantry arrived to clear their positions, were indeed rag-bag and inadequate; but that was due to the coalition's text book application of the air–land battle doctrine developed over decades of Cold War in Europe.

Generals do not plan wars intending to fight; if they can, in an ideal world, they achieve the result they require *without* fighting. Part of the job of a general is to shape events, the enemy and the battlefield to that end. General Schwarzkopf, and his corps and divisional commanders, of whom Generals Boomer and Smith feature largely in this book, achieved exactly that – which is how all wars should be fought. One might feel sorry for the journalists involved, who complained they'd covered far more exciting and hard-fought campaigns.

In telling this enormous and complicated story, I've had to limit the scope of my book, deciding for two reasons to tell it from the British point of view: at time of writing (2010), it seems that a British cost-cutting defence review will divest the British Army of most of its heavy armoured capability;

tanks are incredibly expensive. Gulf War One was the largest tank battle in military history, with more tanks on both sides than at Kursk (7,818, as opposed to the 6,528 which fought at Kursk). Far more significant was the intensity of the Gulf War, in which the tank battle lasted only one hundred hours, as opposed to the Soviet's six week slog for victory at Kursk. Secondly, Britain was determined to be the lead support nation to the might of the USA, even though its armoured forces were not up to this task; and in some aspects (getting the Arab dimension of the coalition together, and providing troops with prophylactic drugs against chemical and biological weapons, are examples) led the way. Indeed, the British armoured force was to have led the way in the US Marines' coastal attack, but was moved to the US Army 7th Corps after predictions of extremely high casualty figures in the US Marines' operation.

I therefore sought reliable, perceptive witnesses, who'd occupied key places at the various levels in the planning and fighting: from Whitehall, down the command chain to the front line. Most are officers and senior officials, because, at this point in the telling of the history of the conflict, it is perhaps the 'bigger picture' that is most useful. With twenty years' distance, it becomes possible to talk about the intricacies of decision making. Some interviewees even now feel sensitive about talking about certain events: Squadron Leaders 'Phil Smith' and 'Dave Brown' are aliases for that reason.

The background to the Kuwait invasion is complicated and stretches back a century to various British political and military involvements in Iraq; and, of course, various American alliances in the oil region. Indeed, six days after Kuwait's full independence from Britain in 1961, the then Iraq President Brigadier Kassim announced Iraq's ownership of Kuwait. The prompt arrival of 42 Commando, then the 24 Infantry Brigade (Operation Vantage) prevented an Iraqi invasion.

Saddam Hussein's secular Ba'ath Party had taken power in Iraq by *coup d'état* in 1968, Hussein himself rising to become vice president, and in 1979, president and head of the Army and Revolutionary Command Council. The USA supported Iran until 1979, when the West-leaning Shah of Iran was deposed and the Shi'a Muslim ayatollahs took power in Iran. The USA then abandoned Iran believing the Islamic state threatened American national security. The USA preferred Saddam Hussein's secular government, and so supported his 'Mother of all Battles' – Iraq's 'First' Gulf War, a very bloody

12-year stalemate with Iran, on the grounds that it prevented Iran dominating the oil region.

So for the previous decade before invading Kuwait, Iraq had enjoyed the support of the United States of America, as well as receiving trade and military support from other world powers, particularly Russia and France, who had both supplied equipment to Saddam's 260,000 battle-hardened troops. Saddam's MiG fighters were modern, able to outmanoeuvre for example the Royal Air Force's Jaguars. His regime possessed biological and chemical weapons, which he was ready, able and very willing to use, and his nuclear development programme was very close to producing results. Saddam was warned by the USA and Britain that, if he used these weapons, to expect a nuclear response. Western missiles are more sophisticated, accurate and reliable, with controllable kilotonnages which, being more useable, are more of a threat. This proved a textbook nuclear deterrence. Nevertheless, in 1990 Iraq's armed forces were by far the oil region's dominant military power.

Saddam's invasion of Kuwait bore similarity to his war with Iran. In 1980, following a series of border disputes but without warning, Iraq invaded Iran, hoping to take advantage of its internal chaos following the revolution. However, after several months of fighting, Iran took back its lost territory, then went on the offensive. Half a million people were killed in battles resembling the First World War: large-scale trench warfare, human wave attacks and the extensive use by Iraq of chemical weapons.

Throughout this earlier war, the US had played down Iraq's use of chemical weapons, preventing the United Nations from condemning Iraq, despite the deaths of thousands of Iraqi Kurdish civilians and militia. US President Ronald Reagan formalised the USA's policy of support for Iraq in a National Security Decision Directive in June 1982. The war had serious adverse effects on shipping in the Gulf, as well as the economies of the whole region and also western nations. The land war declined into a stalemate as neither side was able to bring to bear overwhelming amounts of armoured artillery or air power, with the well-equipped and more professional Iraqi army cancelled out by Iran's huge numbers of infantry.

In 1987 the UN presented a US-sponsored peace plan. At Iraq's acceptance of the plan, Iran attacked the south of Iraq. Iraq recaptured this territory, then attacked northern Iran, the Iraqi air force using cyanide in a bombing attack on the northern Kurdish village of Zardan. Following this attack, Iran accepted the UN peace plan. The Iraqi air force then supported an attack by the Iranian mujahideen – a leftist, militant anti-government group – into western Iran, but following American pressure then withdrew. The mujahideen were left to be massacred by Iranian paratroopers, and the First Gulf War ended.

Emboldened by continuing American support and funded by oil revenues, Saddam and his all-powerful Ba'ath party developed the idea that Iraq could become the leader of the Arab world with, for example, a seat on the UN Security Council. The Ba'ath movement is secular with Marxist origins, preaches Arab unity, is especially strong in Syria where it's named the 'Socialist Arab Rebirth Party', and is split into factions. The Iraqi branch, particularly, is strongly anti-Persian.

Iraq's national aspirations were on a very large scale, including leading an alleged coalition to dismember Saudi Arabia, with the southernmost parts going to Yemen, and King Hussein of Jordan re-inheriting the Hejaz, the region from which his Hashemite dynasty originated, and which includes the holy cities of Mecca and Medina; plus a financial pay-off to Egypt because there wouldn't be any territory to offer the guardian of the Suez route to the Mediterranean. The remainder, including a hefty slice of the oil fields, would go to Iraq. A senior government figure told me that he couldn't verify that this was Saddam's intention; however, 'for a number of years a very strong and long-standing bitterness was held by the Saudis toward Jordan over allegations of Jordan's relationship with Iraq, as the Saudis believed Jordan had been party to this grander scheme.' He didn't want to be quoted by name, as he said the subject was still 'too sensitive'.

Aspects of this plot, which is one of many plans over the years to dismember and reallocate various Arab states (and Israel), with equally as many authors including Britain and the USA, were to continue after the Gulf War, with Jordan helping Iraq with sanction-busting trade routes through her north-eastern border.

During the eight-year war with Iran, Saddam Hussein had run up huge debts – $17bn from Kuwait's ruling al-Sabah family – and felt pressurised to settle up. By 1990, even Iraq's substantial oil revenue could no longer service this debt. Kuwait refused Saddam's demands to cancel the debt and instead was party to agreeing lower oil prices, further disadvantaging Iraq. With the dissent of northern-based Kurdish separatists causing internal problems, and his country's economy crippled by an annual inflation figure of forty per cent,

Saddam felt he had to do something. He accused Kuwait of stealing $2.4 billion of Iraqi oil by slant drilling from across the border, which they were apparently doing using very sophisticated American equipment, whilst Iraq could not drill.

Kuwait and its ruling al-Sabah family, now incredibly rich – to an extent from undercutting other oil states and selling oil cheaply to Japan and the USA, then investing heavily in American stocks and shares – was not well regarded by other Arab states. There are stories from this time of a US ambassador telling Saddam that if he invaded the less-than-democratic state of Kuwait, the US would not interfere. The conspiracy-theory rationale for this conversation was that America was losing its influence in the Persian Gulf, and so wanted a crisis from which it could 'rescue' the oil states. Saddam Hussein concluded that the Americans and other Gulf states might at least acquiesce to his taking over the emirate, and so amassed his troops on the border.

According to King Hussein of Jordan, the ruling Kuwaiti families privately agreed to Saddam's terms. They would forgive Iraq's debt and each pay $10bn in war debts to Iraq in return for its fighting the Shi'a on behalf of Sunni Arabs. However, the Saudi foreign minister Sheikh Sabeh Ahmed al-Jaber al-Sabah announced publicly that Saddam would be offered only $500,000, and Saudi Arabia would call in the Americans. Two days later Saddam invaded.

CHAPTER 1

ALLY TO ADVERSARY

Iraq's invasion was condemned by the United Nations within hours – before dawn on 2 August. The US Marines and 82nd (US) Airborne Division were despatched to defend Saudi Arabia. US Secretary of State James Baker began months of travelling, gathering political, financial and military support from the international community. When on 14 September Britain pledged an armoured brigade, President Bush described it as 'the icing on the cake'.

But fighting a war in the Middle East was the last thing any British or American defence secretary or military commander was expecting in 1990. Throughout the 1980s the NATO member countries had continued to fund expensive air and armoured land forces aimed at countering the perceived Cold War threat of Soviet Union expansion westwards. At the turn of the decade, the decline and dissolution of the USSR led to NATO governments cutting defence spending, and thus also reducing the military capability of their armed forces.

The American military was still haunted by the loss and humiliation of its defeat in Vietnam, while Britain was governed by a prime minister who had led her nation to remarkable and resounding victory eight thousand miles from home in the Falkland Islands.

However, despite Prime Minister Margaret Thatcher's enthusiastic war leadership, Britain's armed forces were a very long way from combat readiness. After four decades of increasingly unrealistic pretence of being ready to fight off the hordes of the equally notional Soviet Third Shock Army, British forces in Germany were too narrowly focused on a battle with the Soviets that nobody expected to actually fight, what General

Rupert Smith called 'the ritual dance of deterrence', and under-equipped for actual fighting. The Thatcher government was deeply unpopular, and was in the process of claiming back military savings in the so-called 'peace dividend' after the collapse of the Soviet Union, by severely axing the defence budget.

The British Gulf effort was codenamed 'Operation Granby' – as part of the more descriptively named US 'Operation Desert Shield'. Within a week, the Royal Navy sent ships, and the RAF Torndao F3 fighters, and Jaguar ground attack aircraft, followed by Tornado GR1 to defend Bahrain.

Hashim Ali
Iraq freedom fighter

Saddam Hussein had made many threatening speeches against our neighbouring countries for not supporting him in the war against Iran. His speeches, and the line of the Iraq government, was that they'd fought for eight years against Iran on behalf of all Arabs, losing many men and much equipment, and that all the money was lent by Kuwait for this purpose. Saddam Hussein said the Arabs should be supporting Iraq and giving them this money, rather than demanding the paying back of this huge and odious debt.

There is much background to the invasion of Kuwait, and an accumulation of grievances. In the early 1970s, when the British Army withdrew from the Gulf and the Emirates emerged, the Shah of Iran decided this was the right moment to capture three islands in the centre of the Gulf – Abu Musa and the Greater and Lesser Tunbs. I'm sure Britain was aware of these tensions.

In 1975, Saddam Hussein signed a humiliating agreement with the Shah of Iran, in which he conceded sovereignty to half of Shatt al-Arab – Iraq's big river – so that the Shah would withdraw support from the Kurdish movement in the north of Iraq. The price of the collapse of the Kurdish movement in the north was paid for by the loss of water and land in the south.

At that time, we considered Iran to be weak. But we ourselves had no real government, only a few people led by Saddam. Having just one person at the top of the pyramid was a great weakness for Iraq. This person decides everything, without consulting even his closest advisers.

I was a freedom fighter, but I was not fighting against Iraq. I'm not Kurdish, but Arab. My group thought we could fight the Iraq regime to make it collapse from within. The majority of opposition to the Saddam regime were Kurdish parties, forces and militias. But there were also many Iraqi parties, several communist, democratic parties and Arab nationalists – a broad spectrum of opposition against the regime and its claims that there was no other party in Iraq apart from its own Ba'ath party.

Theirs was a stupid attitude – that there was no other leader than Saddam, all said in the same way as there is no other god but God! – a typical total-itarian system.

Our freedom group was a proof that Iraqi people were not all clapping and applauding the regime, as it claimed we were. We wanted people to know that there was a diversity of opinion inside Iraq. But unfortunately, at that time, the Arab intelligentsia, and the majority of Arab countries, sided with the Saddam regime.

The Rt Hon Tom King
UK Secretary of State for Defence

When I became Secretary of State for Defence in 1989, the world was chang-ing under President Gorbachev, but our entire focus was still on the Warsaw Pact. In November the Berlin Wall came down, and things began to change very rapidly. The Soviet Union had been held together by military coopera-tion and Soviet Union-wide conscription, so we watched with great interest as that started to crumble. Lithuania went first, with young draft dodgers in Vilnius no longer prepared to serve in the brutal Soviet army which was deployed in Afghanistan, and the Lithuanian government no longer prepared to force them. Next was Latvia and the rest of the Baltic states, and that was the start of the break-up of the Soviet Union.

Hashim Ali
Iraq freedom fighter

I'd been an activist since 17 July 1968, after the Ba'ath party *coup d'état*. After finishing university, we were taken into the military service, people with Ba'athist inclinations as officers – the others made to be the ordinary soldiers, with the most ridiculous basic training in marching and to shoot a rifle. After nearly two years of this, I was sent to work in the central command, a large camp forty kilometres from Baghdad called Al Haji, with rockets, chemicals and lots of other regiments.

It had become very dangerous by this time. Anyone with any political background other than the Ba'ath party was liable to be executed. A few of my good friends from university were Ba'athis. They weren't allowed to say anything, but I sensed they were not happy about this. A lot had brothers, relatives and friends in the Ba'ath party, and had learned bits of the secrets of what was going on in the Party's closed rooms; mainly in-fighting, which was scandalous and horrific. There were many sexual and other scandals within the Party and the government, with people being punished in a military way. They punished their own members as well, imposing totalitarian, military rules.

I was approached many times to join the Ba'ath Party, but said I wasn't interested in politics. I had to sign documents to say I wasn't a member of any other parties. I was under huge pressure, with my closest friends being arrested and detained. We heard about what was happening to people detained in the 'boxes' as we called the detention centres, located throughout Baghdad. You never knew where they were – maybe in your neighbours' house, or in the next road. Then my brother was missing for two weeks, and we couldn't find him anywhere. When he was released, he was a broken man.

What he'd been through was horrible. He said some people came to the laboratory where he worked, he was blindfolded and driven round and round so he didn't know where he was, until they led him into a house. There he said he could hear the screaming of girls and women – he didn't know if this was recordings or torture. He went through an interrogation procedure which ended with a rod being put up inside him, into his seat, then static electricity discharge being put into that rod. The usual joke of the security forces was to threaten to make you do something 'Or we make you sit on a bottle'. My brother said he felt that he was dying and his body exploding, and he was forced to sign something.

He was a member of the Ba'ath Party, so I don't know why he was taken. But then after two weeks of detention he'd been released. But ten months after he was released, he was taken again and we never saw him after that. Then much later we heard he'd been executed soon after his second arrest.

So in 1987, a few days before Saddam took full power, I left Baghdad. Later that year, I was in the north of Iraq, helping to run a radio station broadcasting messages to the Iraqi people against the regime. We were in a place near Kirkuk beside the triangular area between Iran, Iraq and Turkey, at a headquarters of the freedom fighters. One evening in June, two aeroplanes bombarded the area and people recognised the smell, like garlic, and discovered it was chemical weapons. People's skin and sensitive areas became irritated and swollen, they couldn't open their eyes and were literally crippled; more than forty people [suffered from] different levels of contamination, and three people died in the actual attack.

We were fifty kilometres over the other side of the mountain from this, where many of the people escaped by walking over the hills. Their voices were just whispers, like only breathing, because of what had happened to their throats. Many others, being Kurds, had gone across the border to Irani Kurdish villages to get treatment. Another area was attacked called Melkhan, but there was only villagers there – no freedom fighters.

Dr Mary McLoughlin

I'm a hospital doctor from Ireland, working in hospitals abroad. In 1989 I was recruited by an Irish medical contracting company to work in a hospital in Baghdad.

In September 1989, with the war with Iran ended only the previous year, there were still very few goods in the shops. But we could see, month by month, life getting better for the people. It was much easier for us to get around, to rent a car, and we were able to drive to Mosul, even fly to Basra and stay in the Sheraton hotel. We had a great time. Iraq was a beautiful country, and we were not in any way prepared for what happened. Iraqi people were delighted the fighting was over, and that their country was coming right. They were spending money again, and seemed to be loosening up and beginning to enjoy their newly found peace after a very hard eight-year war.

Hashim Ali
Iraq freedom fighter

After the coup, Ba'ath party membership had increased rapidly. But it was oil money that really made the difference. After nationalising our oil – or at least one year later when the oil money began to arrive in Iraq – was when the Ba'ath party made themselves really powerful. They bought the people, and this was the beginning of Iraq's decline.

Everything else was going right for Iraq. We had previous unbelievably high levels of land development, and plenty of money. Iraq was to become the 'Switzerland of the Middle East'. But without wisdom, money is nothing.

Dr Mary McLoughlin

We never discussed the Ba'ath party. Even discussing the Ba'ath party in private would usually mean instant death of any Iraqi, so we didn't do that. We would have been putting their lives in danger.

But in the meantime the Ba'ath party kept good order. There were very few security problems, banditry or local hostilities, although I wasn't there during the Iran–Iraq war, when travel was not possible. Foreigners were extremely well regarded by the Iraqis, and we all had a great time.

Hashim Ali
Iraq freedom fighter

I am opposed to the Ba'ath party, but I hope I will not be biased about them. Their name means 'Resurrection'. Coincidentally, the Shah of Iran had a party with the same name; both looking backwards towards a return of better days. There's nothing wrong with this, and it has a very good side, representing good values. I'd say that the Ba'ath party's political position began as a way of thinking about society, people and ideas, to be pan-Arab before being Iraqi.

But in reality the Ba'ath party were purely Iraqi, concerned with seizing power and keeping it. I used to read their newspaper, and I was very confused by all the propaganda. I read some of their books too, and tried to understand, but it was all gibberish, like contemplation and wishing, rather than a clear plan for developing a society with roots, like schools and universities, that can grow. But as is inevitable when you have money, eventually they did start to move things forward, but with a lot of corruption and fraud.

Their central message was to build Arab power, so when in 1970 that great Arab figure Egyptian President Gamal Abdel Nasser passed away, the Ba'athists saw themselves as providing the replacement. They had this idea of there being one Arab history and one Arab land. There was never such a unity, so this was like dreaming about a glorious past that never existed.

The Rt Hon Tom King
UK Secretary of State for Defence

I'd been four years as Secretary of State for Northern Ireland, the ideal training for a defence secretary, working with some of the army's best commanders. I'd also been a National Service officer, and served four years in the TA [Territorial Army]. Some politicians think military people are a strange breed apart, but I was able to cut through the usual 'bloody politicians' and 'bloody civil servants' attitude of the military.

As the two Germanys came together, the Warsaw Pact crumbled, removing the need for us to maintain so many troops out in Germany. The rest of 1989 was taken up with our 'Options for Change' defence review, adjusting to the new situation in Eastern Europe.

Lieutenant Colonel Charles Rogers
Commanding Officer, Staffordshire Regiment

In the 'Options for Change' defence cuts, the Staffordshire Regiment was to be axed – amalgamated with the Cheshire Regiment, who we thought were from the wrong side of the hill: northerners, of a different character to ourselves. They thought they were rather a smart regiment, so it didn't work for them either. The *esprit de corps* of county infantry battalions is built up over time based on geography, so disbanding or amalgamating is very painful. When I told the sergeants' mess, they burst into tears and demanded to know why, only I didn't know. I had no way of leading them through this, and felt a bit of a twit.

Dr Mary McLoughlin

I was working in the renal transplant ward of the Ibn al Bitar private hospital, funded by Saddam Hussein, granted to the people during the Iran–Iraq war when nobody had been allowed to leave the country. Through public tender, an Irish company had the job of managing the hospital, so half the staff were Irish on long and short contracts, and all the rest were from other countries. Our patients were Iraqis and a few Kuwaitis. The director was Iraqi, but we had little to do with him.

The patients were not from the Iraqi elite, but every walk of life; from the hills or villages as well as the city. The kidney transplant unit treated a lot of people who lived in the desert and had been living under very poor conditions, particularly children. The hospital was a truly socialist organisation, and right up until the end, the treatment people received there was completely free. We were mostly humanitarian aid workers, and would not have worked in a hospital which catered only for the elite.

There were a number of practices in our hospital that wouldn't happen elsewhere, for instance the buying of kidneys, which was done extensively. Rich Iraqis bought kidneys from Egyptian workers and suchlike, for themselves or for their relatives. Although many of the medical staff queried the ethics of this, I didn't consider this particularly a problem. In fact, I decided that kidney-buying was *more* ethical because it overcame another, rather more unwholesome, practice by which the women of a family would be ordered to donate their kidneys to other family members.

The Rt Hon Tom King
UK Secretary of State for Defence

In July 1990, intelligence reported a developing row between Saddam Hussein and Kuwait. The Iran–Iraq war had caused terrific casualties, but was now in the background. Saddam accused Kuwaitis of slant drilling from their side of the border into oilfields on the Iraqi side of the border, stealing the oil. There was also ill-feeling over Kuwait lowering the price of its oil. Kuwait owned the Q8 chain of garages selling their own petrol in Europe, so could profit downstream from low oil prices. It wasn't just Iraq complaining about this, but also the region's other oil-producing countries.

Major General Alexander Harley
Assistant Chief of Defence Staff (Overseas), Ministry of Defence, Whitehall

In April 1990 I was posted back to Whitehall from Germany, where I'd been chief of operations in the old Northern Army Group Headquarters, to be ACDS (Overseas), the man who had to deal with any overseas crisis. My boss was the Deputy Chief of Defence Staff (Commitments), an air marshal – Ken Hayr.

Soon after I took over, Iraq was looking pretty untidy. Fortunately, I'd already done a job in the MoD as the Director Commitments (UK), when on my second day at work I'd been told to set up a crisis centre to manage the soon-to-occur Falklands War. I didn't get home for the next four days, and managed the crisis centre for the rest of the Falklands War. So I already knew quite a bit about MoD crisis management.

There'd been a number of scares regarding Saddam and Kuwait, but nobody really believed anything would happen until it actually did – a bit like the Falklands, and not very clever. The Iraqis kept moving troops forward, then back again. It was too easy for them to move suddenly into Kuwait. The whole thing happened very quickly.

14

Dr Mary McLoughlin

I'd left Iraq at the beginning of July, for Turkey, with my partner on a month's holiday. Just after we returned to Iraq, Saddam invaded Kuwait. I was due to fly home at the end of my contract. In fact I went down to the hospital office to collect my flight ticket, but the head of personnel said to me, 'Didn't you hear?' And I remember saying, 'Hear what?' It was five months before I was finally actually able to collect that ticket!

Saddam had invaded Kuwait the previous night, all the border crossings and the airport were closed, so no one was flying anywhere. I was absolutely gobsmacked and totally dying to get home, plus I didn't have a job as my contract had finished, so I had no purpose for being there.

Once the crisis started, people suddenly realised that we were in somebody else's country, our fate determined by people with whom we had no relationship. Our people were saying 'They can't do this … we have rights'. But after four days of being glued to the radio and television, trying to find out what was going on, we realised that we had no rights at all.

Major David Potts
SO2 Army Logistics, Quartermaster General's Department

In January 1990, after finishing Staff College, I'd been posted to the Quartermaster General's department in the MoD. This was a massive source of disappointment and confusion to me, as I was an artillery officer, and didn't know anything about logistics. But it turned out that sixty per cent of his staff were in a similar position – infantry, artillery or cavalry officers.

The Quartermaster General himself was a wonderful, avuncular three-star Green Jacket called Sir Edward Jones. His one-star was my boss, Brigadier Roland Notley, who I loved to bits, the bane of the life of the logisticians, as he didn't take shit from any of them, operating in typical cavalry fashion, as if from the turret of his tank. The logisticians found this horrific, which in some ways it was, but they were too immersed in process. In the Cold War, it was all about managing stockpiles and strategic readiness, hardly a stimulating day's work. So, with Roland Notley away a lot of the time, and me living in a flat in Fulham – apart from the work being bloody boring and so, like many of my friends, considering resignation – I was having a cracking time in London. Then in August, with Parliament in recess and everyone on holiday, Saddam Hussein invaded Kuwait.

Lieutenant General Walter Boomer
General Officer Commanding, 1 Marine Expeditionary Force,
United States Marine Corps

When I heard of the invasion, I was driving to Camp Pendleton to take over the post of commanding the US Marine Corps Expeditionary Force. Hearing the news on my car radio, I pulled over to listen. I took over command the next day, but unlike my predecessor, I didn't yet know General Schwarzkopf or some of the other army generals I'd be working with, so I had a lot to do. Nine days later, I left the USA for Riyadh.

Dr Mary McLoughlin

Kuwait was weak and had always been a part of Mesopotamia. Plus, Iraq had always wanted more ports in the south, so invading Kuwait made sense from the Iraqi point of view. But then, in one fell swoop, Saddam fell out with all his neighbours. The Saudis suddenly realised the Iraqis could walk in there too, so they decided they needed the Americans to come over and protect them. Syria, having just changed from being a 'pariah state', also felt vulnerable. Jordan and the other countries were too poor to be of importance.

So suddenly, through Saddam seeming to be so dangerous, America had the whole of the Middle East eating out of its hand again – or at least scared enough to cooperate once more with them. So whereas in 1990, America had been moving towards irrelevance in the Middle East, it was suddenly once more very important. We totally and utterly believed that, and I still believe it. In fact we thought that an American spokeswoman at the time, Margaret Tutweiler,* passed on the message to Saddam that it was OK to invade Kuwait. We discussed that while we were in Iraq, and that's what we believed.

The Rt Hon Tom King
UK Secretary of State for Defence

I'd noticed intelligence reports of Saddam moving troops down to the Kuwait border, and commented [to senior officials] that this looked rather sinister. But nobody seemed very excited about it. Then I was shown a supposedly 'utterly reliable' intelligence report said to be 'from the horse's

---

* Margaret Tutweiler was a US State Department spokesperson who told reporters on 26 July that the USA was not protesting Saddam's sending 30,000 troops to the Kuwait border.

mouth' – i.e. Saddam in private – saying that although he intended to give the Kuwaitis a good fright, to force them to agree to his demands over oil and national boundaries, he wouldn't actually do anything. [But in retrospect] our intelligence just wasn't very good, especially on the capabilities of the Iraqi army. I think there are still uncertainties about that. But then, bang, he did invade. It all blew up in a very short time.

Hashim Ali
Iraq freedom fighter

In August 1990, I was with two friends as refugees in Pakistan, having finally left Iraq. My friend woke us up very early one morning to tell us he'd heard on the radio that the catastrophe had happened, that the Iraqi army was inside Kuwait. We hadn't expected this, even though over the previous years Saddam Hussein had made many threats.

The Rt Hon Tom King
UK Secretary of State for Defence

Saudi Arabia was wide open. Its eastern province had most of the oilfields, and the Iraqi army was a much more powerful force than Saudi's. One of the first casualties was a British Airways jet which landed in Kuwait and was captured, with the passengers taken as hostages.

Major General Alexander Harley
Assistant Chief of Defence Staff (Overseas), Ministry of Defence, Whitehall

The Chiefs of Staff were terribly bothered about where the crisis would be handled: from the Royal Navy base at Northwood or RAF Strike Command at High Wycombe, the only two places with command bunkers. They also argued for a long time, very privately, over who was to be the Joint Force Commander, and the chain of command. Saddam invaded Kuwait in August, but these discussions continued until towards the end of the year.

The Chiefs of Staff had to decide what to do, send plans over to the Cabinet Office for comment, then instruct the Joint Commander to carry them out. But until the Chiefs of Staff decided the chain of command, the rest of the process couldn't take place. I was designated as the MoD's Deputy Director of Joint Operations.

MoD crisis management operated from offices at one end of the fifth floor. The navy had an operations room further down the corridor, and the army set one up in the Defence Crisis Centre complex, a set of rooms flattened and opened out. The intelligence staff were constantly walking to and fro, across Horse Guards Avenue, and, as this was the days before emails, they were carrying highly classified documents, photos and so on. There were also loads and loads of often very long telegrams, and constant telephone calls.

Major David Potts
SO2 Army Logistics, Quartermaster General's Department

Many of the grown-ups were in Hong Kong trying to give it back to the Chinese, so didn't get back for a week or more. I came into work that morning; with the holidays, few others were there. We went straight into a very busy planning cycle, quickly discovering that many people in the MoD didn't know what they were paid to know, while others were seriously fossilised in the Cold War mentality, saying we couldn't possibly go to Kuwait as we haven't got air-conditioned tanks, and it will cost too much anyway.

My job was to muster army resources. If pinstripe-suit chaps with broad braces from Military Operations said we needed to send an armoured battle group, then us five would work out a logistic package to make this feasible.

We immediately worked through all the options; from the UK sending only logistics units, to sending light troops with helicopters, but also the notion that we might actually send armoured forces. This is where the rubber really did hit the road, as our tank was Challenger, of which, thanks to malfunctioning and lack of spares, only twenty-two per cent worked. Our armoured forces were incapable of fighting the Russians in northern Europe, let alone being shipped off to the hostile desert environment to fight.

Hashim Ali
Iraq freedom fighter

In 1990, after invading Kuwait, the Ba'athists believed Iraq had achieved its dream of pan-Arab leadership. With Kuwait's oil wealth giving them the largest oil reserves in the world, they thought Iraq would become a powerful nation, and be given the sixth seat on the UN Security Council. This was all a dream – which is easy to imagine when you are a person sitting at home;

but when you are leading a country and you have such dreams, it leads to the path of death.

Major David Potts
SO2 Army Logistics, Quartermaster General's Department,

We'd work until the early hours of the morning, and then at 7am Roland Notley came in to be briefed, along with General Jones. When they went off to talk to the grown-ups, we went down for breakfast, then returned to be told what problems we had to work on for the next twenty-four hours. By the time we'd answered the latest exam question, it was too late to go back to Fulham, so I'd sleep on Roland Notley's floor for a couple of hours.

We had no IT, and wrote everything out in longhand, then girls in the outer office typed it all. And until later on, it was just the three of us, with nobody else brought in to help.

Major General Alexander Harley
Assistant Chief of Defence Staff (Overseas) and Deputy Director of Joint Operations, Ministry of Defence, Whitehall

Within Whitehall, the FCO, Cabinet Office and so on are very close together, so meetings can be set up pretty quickly, usually around the Cabinet Office table. All the key players know each other, so determining what you're going to do on a national basis can be done very quickly.

Terrorism was, however, quite a scare for us, particularly early on. Saddam Hussein threatened a major terror campaign, especially against Britain and the USA, and there were concerns the IRA might also get involved. So through the Cabinet Office, we took measures like deporting all Iraqi students. Later on, when we sent ships through the Suez Canal, we provided Royal Navy escorts.

Major David Potts
SO2 Army Logistics, Quartermaster General's Department

Roland Notley had right from the start delegated his authority to us, allowing us to take decisions. He'd told me very firmly, 'Do not let anybody make you doubt whether we can take the Challenger to war in the desert. In 1967 I was in Kuwait in a bloody Centurion tank. Our forefathers fought in the desert in Crusader, Cromwell and Sherman tanks. Don't let *anyone* tell you we can't go to the desert in Challenger. We bloody well can. You don't need air conditioning or anything else. You just go there, and do it.' I'd replied, 'Got it, sir.'

There were so many people in senior positions, including senior tank officers, who said how totally impossible it would be to take this crap tank to the desert and fight a war in it. In retrospect, they were probably right.

Quite early on, when all our senior people were away on a big study-day conference, Tom King's office wanted to talk logistics. I went to this meeting, with the Master General of the Ordnance, and other terribly grand people were sitting around this big table, and someone slightly more senior than me from the procurement executive who knew what he was talking about. I was there as QMG's logistic expert. Tom King wanted to know how we could send an armoured brigade with a tank that was only twenty-two per cent reliable. He asked who would talk about the logistics, which I realised was me.

I said in order to support a single armoured brigade, we'd have to put the logistics of a whole division behind it. We'd done a lot of work on this, calculating that we'd also have to strip out all the spares and logistics from the entire British Army of the Rhine. If we managed it carefully, I told him we reckoned the Challenger would be OK. The procurement executive guy then told us what could be done within the timescale to improve the tank.

Tom King then turned to a senior chap from Vickers and said, 'Well, here we are. The nation's thinking of sending an armoured brigade out to the Gulf, and our biggest problem is whether this bloody tank you've sold us is going to work…?' But the man from Vickers was very good, told us what was needed and their plan for a modular upgrade that would sort it all out.

Unfortunately, his timescale wouldn't get our tanks out to the Gulf in time.

The Rt Hon Tom King
UK Secretary of State for Defence

I expressed my concerns about Challenger's reliability to the chairman of Vickers. Various improvements should have been made to all sorts of equipment, not just Challenger, but the Cold War had gone on for so long, becoming less and less urgent as time went on, so these improvements had no real defence priority, so were never made. But when suddenly faced with a serious military challenge, a very serious game of catch-up was required.

Fitting Chobham armour to the Challengers was part of this, plus various new technologies like satellite navigation, and specific desert requirements for Challenger, for example sand filters and larger fuel tanks.

I also spoke with all the major British defence contractors. We'd been buying their equipment all this time and so far it hadn't been much in harm's way. They were trying to sell it around the world, so people would be looking hard at how it performed for us. They got the message. A lot of those companies' staff went out with the troops to make sure the equipment performed.

Major David Potts
SO2 Army Logistics, Quartermaster General's Department

Vickers couldn't make our Challenger tanks sufficiently reliable in time to be used in the Gulf. This was a disaster, so I suggested we should ship them out to the Gulf while working out what to do, then do all the upgrading work out there.

I worked all that night with a guy called Robin Bacon, tabulating how we might do it on to squared paper. This was the sort of stuff we did a lot of in the MoD – producing theoretical schematics that take no account of any of the endless frictions of real life.

We reckoned to muster the vehicles, spares and people, while chartering the ships; put the vehicles on the ships, sail them out to theatre while all the time developing the upgrades to make them reliable; then fly out the upgrade packs, fit them, and drive the tanks upcountry, which we estimated would take sixty-three days.

In the morning, I took our table to my boss. An awful lot of work had been done on all these problems, but after it all went up the chain, our one chart was pulled out of all the other mass of paperwork; and the next thing was ministers announcing we were sending an armoured brigade out to the Gulf, and they'd be there in sixty-three days! This was a blinding moment of realisation for me; that we were absolutely *not* at the bloody Staff College any more. This was for real – serious stuff. Every single thing we did led to people taking real decisions based on our work.

Then followed endless discussions with Germany, in which we were told, 'You don't understand because you're a gunner and he's a cavalry officer. We can't do it like this. Why didn't you talk to us about this in more detail? Where did get your availability statistics?'

We told them we'd used tank availability and reliability figures from live firing training in Canada, then added our own fudge factor. I'd respond to their howls of disbelief with, 'How the hell were we supposed to do something like this? You may not have noticed, but we haven't actually used this bloody tank in the desert lately.' 'Oh well,' the senior Germany people said, 'we don't think this is a very sensible plan.'

CHAPTER 2

OIL TYRANNY

On 2 August 1990, Saddam Hussein's forces had invaded and annexed Kuwait. There was nothing to stop him from continuing westwards, capturing Riyadh and the major Saudi oilfields. But, uncertain of Arab support, he remained at the Saudi border, a line drawn across thousands of square miles of sand through which he could advance at any time. The Saudi military, although seventy-two thousand strong, well equipped with a fine modern air force, had never had to defend its own territory and in the face of a one million-strong army with five thousand tanks and five hundred aircraft. In the face of this serious and unexpected national threat, the repressive nature of the Saudi royal family's absolute rule made the possibility of internal revolution very real.

The Saudi army would need help to defend its own borders, and the distinct likelihood of internal Saudi opposition taking advantage of the situation made it vital that the international community act swiftly to forestall revolution, invasion, or both. At this point, Saddam Hussein controlled more than twenty per cent of the world's oil, so the decision to mount an international operation to defend Saudi Arabia was a race against time. The Saudi government appealed for international help.

Saddam moved swiftly to detain thousands of western workers in Iraq, including four thousand five hundred British, as hostages – or 'guests', 'to prevent the scourge of war,' he said.

The problems of creating an international response to Saddam's threat were enormous, compounded by many tensions between the West and Arab nations, and among the Arabs themselves. From very early on, it was clear the response would have to be military, to defend Saudi Arabia,

23

although intense diplomatic efforts were to continue right up until the very last moment. Furthermore, a military force capable of countering Saddam's army would have to be of massive size. For political reasons it would have to include as many personnel from as many Arab countries as possible, and despite all of this, still needed to be capable of mounting a fast-moving modern armoured campaign.

At this stage only defensive operations were envisaged, hence the name 'Desert Shield'. The major problem envisaged was the logistics of shipping out a tank force large enough to defend against Saddam's Russian tanks. But commanding such a force was also going to be an enormous problem and, more terrifying, there was the spectre of defending against Saddam's use of chemical and biological weapons. Disappointingly, support from some European Union countries – notably Belgium – proved lacking.

Dr Mary McLoughlin

Although many people in Iraq knew tensions were mounting over Kuwait, the actual invasion was a very great shock. Despite the various accusations Iraq was making of Kuwait stealing oil and so on, we didn't think Saddam would actually do anything military so soon after fighting such a long and debilitating war.

And since the end of the Iran war, teams of foreign engineers were working all over Iraq, developing a hydroelectric system and the oil infrastructure. It didn't seem sensible for the government to jeopardise this work. So the idea of anybody planning any kind of war would never have entered my head in a million years.

The Rt Hon Tom King
UK Secretary of State for Defence

Margaret Thatcher was in the USA at the time, to receive the Aspen Institute Medal of Freedom, with President George Bush on his way to Aspen to present it to her.

She very quickly was fully seized that the invasion was an act of naked aggression, of which there could be no appeasement, meeting members of the American cabinet, and urging the international community to take immediate steps to stop it, and put in place a shield to protect Saudi Arabia, with Britain working closely with the Americans. She also made the remark to President Bush, 'It's no time to wobble now, George.'

Major David Potts
SO2 Army Logistics, Quartermaster General's Department
A lowly major is on the bottom rung of the whole MoD ladder. From this position, it seemed to me that the size of the force the UK would commit, and where and how the operation would be commanded, would present very big problems. But I could also see that affordability and logistics would determine the size of the force we were going to send.

The Rt Hon Tom King
UK Secretary of State for Defence
One of the Saudi king's titles is 'Custodian of the Two Holy Mosques'. Inviting in foreign forces was a difficult decision. We needed an invitation, so Dick Cheney, the US Secretary for Defense, went immediately to Saudi Arabia. But the danger was clear, and after a time the invitation was issued, and we went forward.

Martin Bell
BBC Television
Immediately after Saddam invaded Kuwait in August, Tom King went out to Saudi Arabia with a small press pool to schmooze the Saudis. There was a lot of very rapid negotiation of Status of Forces Agreements and so on, to be signed before troops could be sent out. It being the very early days of satellite broadcasting, we flew out to Saudi Arabia with an engineer who had a huge amount of electronic clobber, which was all rather unsatisfactory.

The Rt Hon Tom King
UK Secretary of State for Defence
What was quickly apparent as we started to deploy forces to the Gulf, was that the UK defence budget would need substantial extra funds. We entered very early discussions with Gulf states who felt threatened: Bahrain, the UAE and Oman, as well as Saudi. I visited all of these countries, and they talked with us about making contributions to our costs. We had to move very fast, and so depended on local supplies, particularly water, our people paying directly to use local facilities. We'd either be reimbursed by each government, or conversely we were never charged. Subsequently, at the end of it all, they virtually all honoured the understandings we'd had, and we received very substantial sums from them.

We chartered ships, and obtained permission from the Egyptians to use the Suez Canal. There was some embarrassment at their having been thought to be slightly party to Saddam's great plan, but their relationship with the USA prevented any actual problems.

Lieutenant General Walter Boomer
General Officer Commanding, 1 Marine Expeditionary Force,
United States Marine Corps

We were able to launch the 7th Marine Brigade, our rapid reaction brigade, in very short order out of Twentynine Palms, California on 12 August. The Saudis had never had foreign troops on their soil, so our 7th Brigade's Major General Hopkins had his hands full developing relationships. At first they didn't want him to deploy, concerned that their people be kept calm. The sight of foreigners, especially with weapons, was disconcerting to them. Nonetheless, he got his troops deployed into defensive positions [by 20 August], protecting the border.

At the same time, we'd deployed our maritime pre-positioning ships, loaded with all the gear and supplies we needed for combat. The early decision to launch some of these ships from our base at Diego Garcia [in the Indian Ocean] was a good one. So supplies arrived at the same time as the First Expeditionary Force, and we were fully prepared from the word 'Go'. However, we were facing an armoured army, with only anti-tank missiles and no tanks, which was very daunting.

Brigadier Mike Willcocks
Chief of Staff (Land), Joint War Headquarters, RAF High Wycombe

At the very start, the crisis was seen as a purely air force operation, based on the strategic doctrine that air power can win wars – which is nonsense. The MoD's approach was to do nothing until there was a crisis, and only then select a headquarters to run it. Air Chief Marshal Sir Paddy Hine commanded RAF Strike Command, and his HQ had a huge modern bunker four storeys deep, housing eight hundred and fifty people, and was already operating two shifts as a NATO HQ. He was made joint commander, and Air Vice Marshal Sandy Wilson was sent out to Riyadh with the Air Headquarters South Arabian Peninsula, to be Commander British Forces Middle East.

Amazingly, it took ten weeks for the MoD to decide there might also be a land operation, and bring in expert 'away teams' from the Army's Land Headquarters and the Royal Navy, to start proper joint warfare planning.

Then in October, General Peter de la Billiere was sent out to set up a joint British Forces Middle East HQ in Saudi, and take over from Air Vice Marshal Wilson. Strangely, the air vice marshal remained in theatre for several weeks after this.

Major General Alexander Harley
Assistant Chief of Defence Staff (Overseas) and Deputy Director of Joint Operations, Ministry of Defence, Whitehall

The MoD wouldn't spend money on its own strategic communications, so for each crisis, it was left to the three Services to cobble together something at the last minute, involving very expensive off-the-shelf systems which were inefficient, complex and temporary.

There were huge delays in sending messages – with the emergency 'Flash' system being used for just about everything. It was also very hard for anyone to talk about classified matters securely over the telephone, as the MoD hadn't bought the equipment. The only way we could talk to our opposite numbers in the Pentagon or anywhere else in the USA was by making an appointment with one of the two US liaison officers in the MoD, who'd dial each call with all the security codes for us each time. Usually the person we wanted to speak to was out somewhere, so there'd be a huge logjam of calls to make.

Doing operations with the Americans meant coping with the huge data stream their systems produce, which swamped our systems.

The navy were quick off the mark and moved into RAF Strike Command to organise the securing of Gulf waters. But when we decided to send 7th Armoured Brigade to fight a land battle, we couldn't then shift command to the Army Headquarters Land at Wilton, which didn't in any case have a bunker. So during the initial phases, the army component sent to Strike Command – the 'away team' – was quite small, with a growing army staff at Wilton.

I dealt with Air Vice Marshal Dick Johns in RAF Strike Command. He and I would be on the phone for most of the day, especially early on; and my boss Ken Hayr was talking with Paddy Hine and the official at his level at the

Cabinet Office. It was very close-knit, and had already been rehearsed in Cold War exercises.

Hashim Ali
Iraq freedom fighter

Being in Syria for 1990, we had no contact with anybody inside Iraq as there was severe tension between Syria and Iraq, with Syrian soldiers eventually among the coalition forces. It was a very hard time for us, to see our own people being killed by Iraqi national troops and then by foreign troops; a double tragedy for our people.

People are still people, even when they put military clothes on. They are still our relatives, our sons – our poor uneducated people who couldn't have the opportunity to go to school or to the university, but had to go to the military.

Major General Alexander Harley
Assistant Chief of Defence Staff (Overseas) and Deputy Director of Joint Operations, Ministry of Defence, Whitehall

We put in two air forces from the very beginning: one in Saudi Arabia covering the south of Iraq, and the other at Incirlik in Turkey, covering the northern targets, to remove any threat from Iraqi aircraft and helicopters, and then to achieve complete air supremacy over the whole place.

The key issue with deploying air power is targeting, which is very sensitive – and classified Top Secret. The British government will not sign up to join a coalition without approving *all* of the targets to be bombed – including those being attacked by other air forces in the alliance. We're much better at it now, but in those days, the MoD didn't have proper targeting staff with the right skills, or proper management procedures.

The Rt Hon Tom King
UK Secretary of State for Defence

When I first flew out to Riyadh quite soon after the invitation had been approved, executive jets were lined up beside the terminal building totally ready to fly, engines spinning, indicating the nervousness [of the Saudis] at the time, and the risk of fresh attacks. I met King Fahd, Crown Prince Abdullah, Prince Sultan, the defence minister, and his son Prince Khaled, who was to become Joint Coalition Commander with Norman Schwarzkopf. I first saw them all together with the King, then separately to discuss the various aspects.

Although they wanted us to bring sufficient military forces, so many Christian troops would be testing for a country with Islam as part of its constitution, especially at Christmas. There were also many housekeeping, cost and expense issues. But the Saudis had no doubt that unless there was an adequate response from what became a UN coalition, Saddam would invade Saudi.

Major General Alexander Harley
Assistant Chief of Defence Staff (Overseas) and Deputy Director of Joint Operations, Ministry of Defence, Whitehall

In Whitehall, with our three departments of state located so close together, we can get a national view on something quite quickly. But not so in America; the Pentagon have their line, but don't know the line of the other three departments, let alone what their national line might be. It's therefore extremely difficult to find out what the Americans intend doing.

The White House tends to run everything, but only at the end of their process, when quite suddenly everything shakes together, there's a plan, and off they go. They're very good at this, but it's easy to miss that moment. The British Embassy keep in contact with the process; CDS [Chief of Defence Staff] speaks to the Chairman of the Joint Chiefs of Staff by telephone, and frequently throughout the crisis I sat in. Ministers talked with each other, and once the British Joint Commander was set up, he plugged into US Central Command. I talked frequently with their Chief J3 – my opposite number in the Pentagon – going across to see him several times during the crisis, twice specifically to talk about chemical and biological weapons, a story in itself.

The Rt Hon Tom King
UK Secretary of State for Defence

A key role for me was to ensure we retained public and parliamentary support for what we were doing. We held regular press conferences in Riyadh, London and Washington, which needed coordination, and several debates in the House, plus debates in the United Nations as the situation developed.

During the Falklands, the MoD had stopped the media from communicating any news at all, which would not be possible in the Gulf. So there were lots of lessons to be learned, and journalists had to be treated differently.

Major Rayson Pritchard
Public Information Officer, Royal Marines

I was a public information officer from HQ Commando Forces, and went out to Saudi in August. Unlike the Falklands, this time there'd be journalists running round all over the place, able to communicate freely, which we couldn't control, censorship would not be possible, so we'd have to be proactive, to shape the media's view.

Major General Alexander Harley
Assistant Chief of Defence Staff (Overseas) and Deputy Director of Joint Operations, Ministry of Defence, Whitehall

You can only engage with the press using people familiar with operational thinking at all levels of the MoD which, apart from ministers, means taking hard-pressed senior officials away from what they should be doing. When the actual fighting started, everybody felt the Secretary of State and Chief of Defence Staff together should present to the public.

Lieutenant General Walter Boomer
General Officer Commanding, 1 Marine Expeditionary Force, United States Marine Corps

Iraq had the fourth largest army in the world. We understood this and were very concerned. I was always being asked by reporters, 'If they attack, can you hold?'

I'd reply, 'Yes, we can.' But in our heart of hearts, although we believed we would hold them, we also believed it would be a fight to the death.

If they'd launched a fully coordinated armoured attack in those first days, we would have had our hands full. But every day we got a little stronger, and every day I wondered why they hadn't yet attacked. Our intelligence wasn't giving us any answer to that question. It took ten days to reach the point when I was certain that we were strong enough to blunt any attack which, given the circumstances, was reasonably quick.

Dr Mary McLoughlin

We were still able to travel round Baghdad, although we couldn't leave the city itself. People still had contact with their Iraqi friends, but less so than before, as they didn't want to talk to foreigners at all.

The Rt Hon Tom King
UK Secretary of State for Defence

Saddam's invasion of Kuwait was a source of embarrassment to the French, who had long-standing relationships with Iraq, and had sold them large amounts of military equipment. The French defence minister, Jean-Pierre Chevènement, was also president of the Franco–Iraqi Friendship Society. Initially, Paris was uncertain whether they'd join the coalition, until President Mitterand gripped the situation. The French clearly hoped diplomatic pressures would persuade Saddam to withdraw from Kuwait, so they could resume their very satisfactory defence equipment trading arrangements with Iraq.

When I spoke with Jean-Pierre Chevènement the morning we announced the deployment of 7th Armoured Brigade, he asked me the weight of the tanks we were sending. They subsequently sent their light 14-ton Panhard armoured personnel carriers, rather than [as we did] 60-ton main battle tanks. They also sent an aircraft carrier, but replaced the fixed wing aircraft with helicopters, and ordered it not to go beyond the Strait of Hormuz, seriously restricting its range of activity. They were also never keen about the coalition's military command arrangements.

Major General Alexander Harley
Assistant Chief of Defence Staff (Overseas) and Deputy Director of Joint Operations, Ministry of Defence, Whitehall

Targeting policy is developed jointly with the Cabinet Office and Foreign Office, starting by determining the national aims of the war: in this case, to deter Saddam from attacking Saudi Arabia. Our initial targets were Saddam's forces in Kuwait, without damaging Kuwait itself.

Then, depending on the national aims, targeting policy is developed in line with things like proportionality and legality; do you want to destroy the place completely, or leave the power lines up, the ministry of defence still running? If you destroy a country and all its internal systems, it's ungovernable and can't tell its armed forces to stop, start – or anything.

Targeting is so sensitive that only a small number of people see the lists: the prime minister personally, but nobody else in that office. Every single target bombed was ticked off by the prime minister.

Dr Mary McLoughlin

We'd never heard of smart bombs, and our idea of bombing was like World War Two, falling indiscriminately all over the place, meaning we were *all* going to be bombed. We were hoping these people would have a head on their shoulders and not start bombing *anything*. And another very real fear was that if the westerners started bombing Baghdad, the Iraqi people would turn against *us*.

One of my friends was an anaesthetist and lived in a third floor apartment. So we got ourselves some anaesthetic drugs, for if we were to be caught in the apartment, with the rest of the building on fire, we could commit suicide rather than have to suffer dying through being burned to death. But our greatest fear during this time was of a misplaced invasion by the Allies.

Major General Alexander Harley
Assistant Chief of Defence Staff (Overseas) and Deputy Director of Joint Operations, Ministry of Defence, Whitehall

The targeting framework has to be agreed by Cabinet, then shared with the Americans, incorporating their aims and objectives. You then start to work on the actual targets: which are to be attacked and destroyed, what are you specifically going to leave? In Iraq's case, we decided to leave all the ministries and oilfields, their infrastructure – at least initially – whilst bombing armoured formations, headquarters and airfields. The target lists were developed every day, and of course all of this was top secret.

Lieutenant General Walter Boomer
General Officer Commanding, 1 Marine Expeditionary Force, United States Marine Corps

There are a lot of radical religious folks in Saudi Arabia. We were anathema to them. We took over all their bases, airfields and ports – everything. But it was done with very little strife. We tried to respect what was important to them. I recall only one incident, which I don't think even turned into a fistfight – and nobody shot at each other. Not having alcohol was fantastic from my perspective.

Dr Mary McLoughlin

We never discussed what was going on with anybody Iraqi. Nobody said anything at all to us. It was too dangerous – one word could get them and their families killed.

But you could see they were horrified at Saddam having invaded Kuwait, from the looks on their faces, their sudden withdrawal from foreigners, and their not talking to us. But otherwise they were kind and supportive to us. In fact I cannot remember any time when any Iraqi was unkind to us.

Lieutenant General Walter Boomer
General Officer Commanding, 1 Marine Expeditionary Force, United States Marine Corps

The mission we'd been given by Central Command was 'To protect the critical oil and port facilities of Al Jubayl, its area, and Saudi Arabia, and the island state of Bahrain, destroying and delaying enemy forces as far north as possible'. This was of course far more than one brigade could accomplish.

General Hopkins began to create a defensive position on the fly as each of his units arrived. We immediately began deployment of the rest of the division, with the air wing and logistical force, in a continuous flow on the heels of our 7th Brigade, which didn't stop until I'd got everyone there.

Dr Mary McLoughlin

I sat around in the apartment for a few days, then attended several meetings in the hospital. We expected Saddam to withdraw, but after a week or so, it looked as though his army was settling in, with the other nations preparing for a long siege. We also talked amongst ourselves about conspiracy theories – that the Americans had encouraged Saddam Hussein to take over Kuwait. We were sure he'd realise he'd made a mistake and pull out.

There were now rumours of engineers being rounded up and used as human shields at oil installations and infrastructure points around the country, especially around Baghdad. I went to ask the hospital HR people to give me another job, as it was very dangerous to be an unemployed foreigner in Iraq, and so ended up looking after the psychological and medical needs of the hospital staff. This was very suitable because by this stage, members of staff were beginning to have nervous breakdowns and need counselling. I was older than most, and having worked before in Africa, was more used to violence and sieges, and the lack of rights all round.

Saddam and his cronies were now the boss, with no going crying to the United Nations demanding to be got out. We might have our rights, but they weren't doing us any good.

Major General Alexander Harley
Assistant Chief of Defence Staff (Overseas) and Deputy Director of Joint Operations, Ministry of Defence, Whitehall

During a crisis, Whitehall's daily routine starts with the MoD Chiefs of Staff meeting at 8.30am, to deal with a host of papers prepared by their night staff, driven by the Deputy Chief of Operations – me – taking decisions on issues within their purview. This passes across to the Cabinet Office, who deliberate from 10.30 until 12. Their instructions came back to the MoD for me to collate, and if necessary the chiefs met again in the afternoon. The Joint Commander, Paddy Hine, was part of this process, constantly travelling to and from High Wycombe, mostly by helicopter to Battersea.

Brigadier Patrick Cordingley
Commander, 7th Armoured Brigade

My military career was coming to the end. Most of my brigade had been together for two years and were very well trained. I was looking to the future; maybe as a general, maybe not, but it had all been bloody good fun. But then, in August 1990, there was this invasion of Kuwait. It never occurred to me that my brigade would get involved.

Dr Mary McLoughlin

Various things happened to increase the tension and make us extremely nervous and unhappy. International sanctions were clamped fairly tightly on Iraq, which included stopping the importation of pharmaceuticals and chemicals, so we couldn't get any resupply of drugs for the hospital.

Fairly soon, we were running out of specialist heart, lung and cancer drugs. My close buddy ran the kidney transplant ward. We not only ran out of the chemicals that prevented the rejection of the new kidneys, but also the chemicals needed to run the kidney dialysis machines. So with kidneys being rejected, we had to refer them to Iraqi hospitals; but if *we* didn't have the required drugs, the run-down Iraqi hospitals certainly wouldn't have them, so we knew we were referring them to certain death. This was very distressing.

Lieutenant General Walter Boomer
General Officer Commanding, 1 Marine Expeditionary Force, United States Marine Corps

To be frank, we were the only force available on the ground ready to fight. The army were bringing everything in as quickly as they could, but it was coming in by air, whereas we'd landed complete with all our supplies and equipment. We had a huge amount of combat supplies, enough for something like thirty days' fighting – a really huge amount.

Lieutenant Colonel Charles Rogers
Commanding Officer, Staffordshire Regiment

With the Staffords being axed and merged with the Cheshires in the 'Options for Change' defence cuts, we were talking to them about badges, buttons and so on, plus preparing for a tour of Northern Ireland. I was on leave, listening to news of the invasion from a beach at the Isle of Wight. The media opined it most unlikely that a UK armoured brigade would be sent. But when we returned to our barracks at Fallingbostel [Germany], it was clear that this had become *the* most likely option.

Dr Mary McLoughlin

Within a couple of weeks of the invasion, the Iraqi secret police started a roundup of the thousands of foreign engineers working in Iraq, beginning with the Americans, then the British, leaving engineers from former Soviet countries like Yugoslavia until the very end. At the same time, the Iraqis began bussing in westerners from Kuwait, many with families; buses full of western people and children passing us in the street going to God-knows-where as human shields, or to concentration camps, which was particularly distressing.

Lieutenant Colonel Arthur Denaro
Commanding Officer, Queen's Royal Irish Hussars

We were on exercise on the Soltau training area with our Challenger tanks, during one of the hottest German summers for years. It was a total dust bowl.

The Corps Commander, General Charles Guthrie, flew in by helicopter, and I joked to him that we were doing ideal desert training. Four weeks earlier I'd had a really bad polo accident, splitting my skull in four places, with a metal plate inserted. Charles Guthrie was very cross with me for being out at all. But because my regiment had just arrived in Germany, this exercise was incredibly important. The other two battle groups in the brigade, the Scots Dragoon Guards and the Staffords, had both taken part in intensive live firing training at BATUS in Canada, which we hadn't.

Dr Mary McLoughlin

We were swimming one afternoon at the hotel we usually visited, when a bus stopped outside and some western women came in saying they needed milk and water for their children. We ran the short distance back to the hospital and got as much fresh water as we could from the shop, but when we got back, the bus was gone. It was fifty degrees in the middle of the day – it's hard to imagine the extreme heat of the place. These women and children could not have survived very long without fluids, so we were terribly upset.

This really brought it home to us what was happening to the others, and how privileged we three hundred hospital and embassy staff were, still to wander freely round Baghdad. At this stage, any of the engineering staff who hadn't been arrested were being extremely careful and were certainly not wandering around as we were.

Lance Corporal Roy Sellstrom
Pioneer Corps

I was in Northern Ireland, with 187 (Tancred) Company, 23 Group, Royal Pioneer Corps, guarding the logistic base that supports the whole of Northern Ireland. We're nicknamed 'Chunkies', as we do all the man-intensive labouring jobs that no one else wants to do – like road construction, digging trenches, putting up tentage, mending airfields. The Royal Engineers do more technical tasks, with us doing the labouring.

Dr Mary McLoughlin

You knew the walls had ears and eyes, but not who the ears and eyes were. Officers came to the hospital who were clearly members of the Iraqi authorities – people we'd never seen before the war. We were told quite clearly that if we didn't work in the hospital, we too would be sent out to the institutions as hostages. I had to make home visits, to see people who hadn't turned up for work, then make a report on them. People were very much keeping an eye on us. We kept our noses out of this aspect of it as much as possible. But I never felt threatened inside the walls of the hospital.

There was, for a brief period, talk of us going on strike. But we were told going on strike was punishable by death, so we never raised that one again. Going to work each day was our only form of protection, and so that's what we did.

Lieutenant Colonel Arthur Denaro
Commanding Officer, Queen's Royal Irish Hussars
Generals and MoD officials had been declaring 'Never again will we fight operations with tanks'. Then General Richard Trant mentioned that we might well be going.

Dr Mary McLoughlin
We were listening to Maggie Thatcher and George Bush, both on the radio non-stop, insisting that they weren't going to let the fate of a thousand or so hostages in Iraq affect what they were doing. But in reality there were more like eight thousand hostages; but the fate of these hostages wasn't going to interfere with their implementation of world democracy! This of course was a load of nonsense, as democracy had never been operating in Kuwait anyway.

Sergeant Major Johnny Muir
Regimental Quartermaster Sergeant Major,
Queen's Royal Irish Hussars
My job as Regimental Quartermaster Sergeant Major was to procure everything we'd need, but my only experience of the desert, apart from reading books about it, was a holiday in Tunisia in an air-conditioned coach visiting the various ancient ruins used by the German army in the Second World War.

Major David Potts
SO2 Army Logistics, Quartermaster General's Department
Nobody had thought that the army in Germany might be used anywhere else, especially in the desert – and why should they? It was most unlikely that

a crisis would develop requiring armour, and that the rest of NATO would agree it was worth the strategic risk of removing armoured forces from Europe. But was there risk to Germany? Margaret Thatcher had been more worried about the reunification of Germany, for goodness' sake!

Brigadier Patrick Cordingley
Commander, 7th Armoured Brigade

The next morning, I went off to Corps HQ at Bielefeld to be ordered to war, an extraordinary sensation. Most of the Falkland veterans had moved on, so none of us had any combat experience. Doubts flooded into my mind: are we capable of doing this? Are we properly trained? The people who get to the top of the army are enormously self-confident, and tell everybody they know all the answers. I'm not one of those. I'm quite quiet, not naturally self-confident, and tend to think that I might *not* know all the answers.

The Corps Commander, General Guthrie, said we *were* going, that we'd be reinforced, that I'd go on a reconnaissance with Corps Headquarters Chief of Staff Mike Walker, then tell them who I'd be working with and where.

Sergeant Major Johnny Muir
Regimental Quartermaster Sergeant Major,
Queen's Royal Irish Hussars

I started measuring everyone for desert combat kit and other personal equipment, while the squadrons sorted out the tanks they'd taken over from the regiment we'd just replaced – lots of mechanical work and spare parts, before firing them on the ranges.

We also needed to increase our numbers from peacetime strength of around four hundred up to six hundred. People were drafted in from other regiments, like the Royal Tank Regiment, from Germany and the UK, in a gradual process. We knew most of them, especially people of my rank and status, so this trickle process went very smoothly.

Dr Mary McLoughlin

The BBC started broadcasting programmes about what we should be doing in the event of a nuclear attack. These programmes were so completely stupid that if they hadn't made us cry, they made us laugh: things like we should fill the bath and get in before the bombs dropped. Of course in Iraq, because of the shortage of water, there aren't any baths and all the houses have showers. And nobody said how long we were supposed to remain under the water when these attacks allegedly took place, so we had the choice of either being drowned or nuclear poisoned.

And it wasn't very clear who was supposed to be nuclear'ing who either. Maybe this was based on the thought that the Allies' reaction to the Kuwait invasion might involve this sort of thing. At this stage there was no allied military response taking place, so goodness knows what this was all about.

But we had absolutely no faith in Maggie Thatcher or George Bush senior. Rather than being worried about what Saddam Hussein would do, to be honest we were more worried about what the loonies in the West were going to do. We just wanted them *not* to attack, and to leave us alone.

Brigadier Patrick Cordingley
Commander, 7th Armoured Brigade

In Riyadh, the American build-up was very obvious – aircraft everywhere. We were briefed at the British Embassy, including a three-course lunch with wine and all the rest of it with the ambassador. Mike Walker and I then flew to Al Jubayl to meet the Marine commander who was to be my boss, Lieutenant General Walt Boomer.

Lance Corporal Roy Sellstrom
Pioneer Corps

A Pioneer company was to deploy straight away to Saudi Arabia. Paddy Haddock, our platoon commander and staff sergeant, listed everyone for this deployment, but told a group of us to stay behind, as the OC had a different task for us. In our company, everyone and his dog was trying to get to Saudi, so we were wondering whether we'd be going – or what was happening. Eventually Paddy Haddock came over to us and told us we'd been tasked to go to the Army War Graves Team.

Dr Mary McLoughlin

By the end of August, Baghdad shops were completely empty. You couldn't even buy bread flour. It's amazing how hard it is to feed yourself if you don't have bread. It all seemed to have been bought up for the army, and there was none left for the likes of us. Then, having been used to fantastic food in the hospital canteen, they announced the canteen would feed us just once a day. From that moment, things suddenly became much worse.

Lieutenant Colonel Charles Rogers
Commanding Officer, Staffordshire Regiment

Our preparation was split into training, sorting out equipment and making sure one's families were sorted out. We'd been due to go to Northern Ireland for six months so although our casualty reporting and family support was well sorted, we began to worry that with the very high levels of casualties being talked about for the Gulf, our own battalion system would prove inadequate, especially if the officers' and sergeant major's wives who'd be running the system were themselves bereaved. By the time we left for the Gulf, a much larger scale system for handling deaths and casualties had been created.

Lance Corporal Roy Sellstrom
Pioneer Corps, Army War Graves Unit

I'd never heard of the Army War Graves Team, so I said, 'What, fucking grave diggers? You can stick that!' Staff Sergeant Haddock said, 'No, no. You're not *volunteering* for this. You're going – you're actually doing this.' I was quite taken aback – not what I joined the army to do.

I had another reason: in my first army unit one of the guys had been a member of the Falklands War Army War Graves Team. By 1986, he was completely blown away, in the bar every night pissed out of his head. He seemed completely fucking mad. I didn't know what he was going through, but I definitely didn't want to end up like that. However, I was a lance corporal. And like any serviceman or woman given a job, you get on and do it the best you can.

Brigadier Patrick Cordingley
Commander, 7th Armoured Brigade

You'd expect a Marine commander to be a huge, hunky bloke chewing tobacco. Instead General Boomer turned out to be lanky, wiry, six foot three, very bright, easy to get on with, and very pleased we were joining him. I hadn't realised the US Marines are larger than the British Army, with more aeroplanes than the RAF – a hugely powerful outfit.

US Marine mentality isn't like that of the huge amorphous US Army, but small-army just like us, and Boomer was genuinely excited to see us, for two reasons: our hundred and fifty Challenger tanks, and our armoured engineers. We were going to have to lead through the Iraqi minefields, and his tanks were the older M60s. So even though you mightn't have thought it credible, the arrival of our little British Army brigade gave a huge and very significant increase to his order of battle.

Lieutenant General Walter Boomer
General Officer Commanding, 1 Marine Expeditionary Force, United States Marine Corps

The British brigade commanded by Patrick Cordingley was very important to us, as the Marine Corps is not a tank-heavy organisation. They dramatically increased my combat power and were truly welcome. From Day One we clicked, were very focused, trained realistically, and there was no bullshit – a marriage made in heaven. Patrick took part in everything we did, and, in every training conference we held, always put forward good ideas. We were very content with the relationship, and with the force as well.

Brigadier Patrick Cordingley
Commander, 7th Armoured Brigade

The Marines were blocking Saddam Hussein from coming out of Kuwait and taking the oilfields along the eastern side of Saudi Arabia. We were to enter this defensive line, but the chain of command and the levels of command and what sort of command we'd be under were not at all clear. Whether I had the authority to say what we *shouldn't* do wasn't clear either.

We suggested to Walt Boomer that we needed to come out and train in the desert, after which we could join his line wherever he wanted us – but that should be decided later. This was a purely defensive deployment, and there was no thought of us making an attack.

Lance Corporal Roy Sellstrom
Pioneer Corps, Army War Graves Unit

At the end of the summer, I was sent to Kineton near Bicester, where this new Army War Graves Service was to be formed. But then the Saudis said that no Christian bodies were to be buried on Saudi soil, so clearly 'War Graves Service' became a bit of a misnomer.

Then in late October, Captain Ralph, who was supposed to be in charge, told me to report to Northampton for a day of training. Only Phil Gill and I could make it that day, and were told to report to the Scene of Crimes Officer at the police station. He took us to their 'Black Museum'. After a couple of hours of grim reading, we were told to report to the hospital morgue, where a lad in his mid-thirties, eating lunch, gave us hospital uniforms, a white plastic bib, face mask and yellow Marigold gloves. There was this strong chemical smell. He told us we were there to observe what the pathologist does, to ask any questions, but not get in anyone else's way. He then motioned us through these heavy plastic-sheeting curtains, where we saw a row of six bodies lying naked on these slabs – like on a conveyor belt.

Brigadier Patrick Cordingley
Commander, 7th Armoured Brigade

We were ordered back to UK to brief Air Marshal Paddy Hine, in a VC10 with typists on board so we could dictate the huge amount of orders and instructions we needed to produce before landing. This special aircraft didn't arrive, so we flew to UK in a Hercules, which has webbing seats and is impossibly noisy. Mike and I took turns to go on to the flight deck, where at least we could work, but when we landed at RAF Brize Norton, we were knackered.

Everybody at High Wycombe was completely agog. They developed my camera photos at amazing speed. My bit was to talk about the US Marines, how we'd fit in with them, the desert, then Mike Walker talked about our logistics. Our deployment would be called Operation Granby, as part of the overall operation Desert Shield. I detected a general feeling that people thought we needed to be slightly independent of the Americans.

Major Rayson Pritchard
Public Information Officer, Royal Marines

I joined the embryonic Riyadh headquarters, which at this very early stage was run by hundreds of RAF staff officers. We set up a Joint Information Bureau – the JIB – in the Hilton Hotel, our job to make sure the media painted the forces in a positive, favourable light. This wasn't easy to do; we had very little experience, and if the media saw flaws in our story, or thought we were trying to hide something, their intelligence network would find us out.

Lance Corporal Roy Sellstrom
Pioneer Corps, Army War Graves Unit

The pathologist had a small buzz saw, which, after a few scalpel cuts and pulling the face down like a glove, he used to cut round the skull of the first body, popped off the top with a chisel, pulled the brain out and put it into a silver metal bucket. He then cut from the throat all the way down, using the saw to cut through the whole of the rib cage. This was like being in a fucking horror show. I was dumbstruck – totally shocked. Nobody had told us what would happen in here. I was horrified.

I was twenty-six, and Phil Gill was married with young children. These people were doing this like it was a normal day's work. They got everything out, took very small samples from each organ, after which they scooped it all up and literally poured it all back into the empty body cavity. The smell was horrendous.

I asked the pathologist why he needed to do all that to these bodies, just to get such a small sample. He just said that's what they had to do. This was serious wake-up time for me.

Phil was a father, and when they got to the last body, which was a teenager, he told the pathologist, 'I've got kids. There's no way you'd do this to one of my kids.' The pathologist replied, 'I'll tell you now, son, if one of your children dies of unnatural causes, they'll end up in the mortuary.'

'Now that I know what you'se people do,' said Phil, 'I wouldn't allow it.'

'It wouldn't be up to you.'

I could see Phil was very upset and getting vocal, so I said we should both go. All I could smell were these fucking dead bodies, and couldn't breathe. Everywhere I looked was blood, a horror video, but everything was for real. We dumped the clothing and got out of there as fast as we could.

The next I knew, we were back in Simpson barracks, sitting in the cook-house eating our tea. It was totally surreal, and I realised I'd just had one of the worst days of my life – up until then, at least.

Major Rayson Pritchard
Public Information Officer, Royal Marines

Eighty or so British journalists were all over the Dhahran airbase – aircrew taking photos from the air for them, invitations out to restaurants, lots of over-friendly relationships, with all sorts of unguarded comments being published.

Their Scottish Reservist squadron leader press officer's media experience was working for Glasgow local radio, so he was rather out of his depth. I was told to sort out the security leaks. I got the station commander to ban the socialising. For a time, the illicit relationships continued, the journalists trying it on with 'covert' requests like pleading to store rolls of shot film in the pilots' fridges, saying they had no fridges themselves.

So to keep the press onside, we had to feed them stories, which meant setting up proper press facilities to control what they saw, and so influence what they printed.

Without any access to military briefings and HQs, journalists could turn snippets of information into stories – one little detail from talking to some-body's driver, to which they added something else, until they'd got enough to fly a kite. Sometimes they got more than that, to make a story that could be more incisive, and maybe an embarrassment to the military. And as soon as they've filed, it's old news and they're out there again prodding, looking ahead, twisting and poking for the next story. They're bloody good intelligence gatherers, although not one hundred per cent accurate, or getting the whole story.

Lieutenant Colonel Charles Rogers
Commanding Officer, Staffordshire Regiment

None of us had done desert warfare, so we organised talks from people like an infantry officer who'd commanded thirteen battalion attacks in the Second World War. This made far more sense than reading text books.

There was a huge PR focus, and people like the Duke of York, the colonel of our regiment, turned up on visits to see us. I'm not saying this was a *waste* of our time, but it did take up valuable time.

Squadron Leader Phil Smith
Royal Air Force

In the early days of the RAF's Gulf deployment, we lost three crews in quick succession during training: one Tornado crashed into the sea, and two on land, which focused everybody's attention.

Back in UK, a group of aircrew and ground staff were designated to be battle casualty replacements, to fly out immediately people were killed and injured in the fighting. The replacements were continually on standby, going to work each day not knowing whether they'd be back home in the evening, or going to war. At least in theatre, we knew where we stood.

Major General Alexander Harley
Assistant Chief of Defence Staff (Overseas) and Deputy Director of Joint Operations, Ministry of Defence, Whitehall

Deciding the size of a military force to be sent on operations is a very fractious debate between the Chiefs of Staff and Ministers, the latter always wanting to restrict the force level to an absolute minimum. The MoD make a *recommendation*, but the government make the decision, and are very mindful of the total cost. As force levels increase, costs rise astronomically, needing more shipping to carry everything, and so on.

But Ministers don't understand how the army must tailor its units according to terrain, prevailing weather, the enemy's quality, capabilities, forces and equipment, adding ancillaries like electronic warfare units. Nor do they understand combined arms operations – the army working with the navy and air force.

Lieutenant Colonel Charles Rogers
Commanding Officer, Staffordshire Regiment

For Operation Granby we increased from peacetime to a special war establishment of seventy-five per cent more people: medics, mortars and anti-tank, plus more infantry soldiers in the backs of our own vehicles.

Normally these extra people would be provided by Reservists and the TA, but the TA wasn't called up for Granby, so we had to go to neighbouring armoured infantry regiments like the Grenadier Guards. We were given a platoon of guardsmen, and some twenty or so others. Some other infantry regiments needed entire companies from other regiments.

Brigadier Mike Willcocks
Chief of Staff (Land), Joint War Headquarters, RAF High Wycombe

The command and control of the operation back in UK was 'not fit for purpose', even though in the best British traditions it was made to work. Also, there was a great churning-through of people at High Wycombe: I was to become the third Chief of Staff (Land) for the operation. The first had left on posting, and the second wanted to get out to the Gulf. I was lucky to be in post for the good bit.

When I did arrive in the High Wycombe bunker, I rapidly discovered that the RAF weren't doing things the way one would expect. The headquarters had a very soggy feel to it, even though everybody worked bloody hard. My goodness, we made things difficult for ourselves.

Lieutenant Colonel Mike Vickery
Commanding Officer, 14th/20th King's Hussars,
4th Armoured Brigade

I was the Commanding Officer of the 14th/20th King's Hussars, a cavalry tank regiment, based in Munster and part of the 4th Armoured Brigade. I had three squadrons equipped with Challenger 2 tanks, plus a squadron in Berlin with older Chieftains – some fifty-seven tanks.

When Saddam Hussein invaded, we were told there wouldn't be any fighting, but that after six months of hanging around in the desert, 7th Armoured Brigade would have to be relieved. We were warned to take over from them in June 1991.

Lieutenant Toby Masterton
A Squadron, The Life Guards, 4th Armoured Brigade

Had I not been sacked as the Recce Platoon commander, I wouldn't have gone out to the Gulf. Our Commanding Officer was due to leave, but when he learned that armoured units were being sent to the Gulf, had attempted to extend his command and take our whole regiment. He'd also tried to extend his command into a Guards-only battle group with a squadron of Scots Guards. However, all this had failed, apart from any other reasons, because of the rest of the army's dislike of the 'Guards Mafia'.

The end result of my own prolonged and unhappy experience as his Recce Platoon commander was during armoured training at BATUS, in appallingly cold weather conditions, when I was summoned to the Commanding Officer, and in our usual behind-your-back regimental manner, without warning was sacked. Major James Hewitt commanded our A Squadron, warned for the Gulf with the 14th/20th Hussars. I was sent to him, to be his Liaison Officer.

Second Lieutenant Alistair Watkins
1st Battalion Grenadier Guards, 4th Armoured Brigade

In the summer of 1990, I'd been just about to pass out of Sandhurst. A friend came running down the corridor shouting, 'We're off to war, Saddam Hussein has invaded Kuwait.' I wasn't very serious about soldiering, regarding the army as challenging but fun.

I passed out of Sandhurst and, after leave, joined the first battalion of the Grenadier Guards in Munster. I drove over to Germany, arriving at eight on a Sunday night at their old Wehrmacht barracks, to a dark and empty Gothic officers' mess. Three officers watching television completely ignored me, so I found my own room and settled into battalion life.

Lieutenant Colonel Arthur Denaro
Commanding Officer, Queen's Royal Irish Hussars

It became official in the middle of September. The press were there, and it was all incredibly exciting. We hadn't had a war like this since Korea. The weight of this only started to weigh on the shoulders of we Commanding Officers when we actually deployed in October.

But we had one hell of a lot to do. Those units not going were told to give spare parts from their tanks to ours – pretty pissed off but hugely helpful. We worked twenty-four hours a day, with kit arriving, equipment being serviced, spares procured.

Lieutenant Colonel Charles Rogers
Commanding Officer, Staffordshire Regiment

We knew Saddam had a large, experienced, war-fighting army, so both soldiers and families were nervous. We discussed people being killed; whether as in the Falklands, bodies would be flown home. There were also worries about Saudi being a Muslim country and their not allowing bodies to be buried there, and what would happen if there was chemical warfare and the bodies were contaminated. But I didn't have the answers to these questions.

The medical side suddenly became of much greater interest – which had, I hate to say, not been practised with due diligence on our previous exercises.

Brigadier Patrick Cordingley
Commander, 7th Armoured Brigade

We had serious logistic challenges, the worst being the unreliable Challenger, particularly its TN37 gearbox. Also, after eight hundred and fifty miles, the engines had to be replaced. Although we knew the total number of miles each tank had done, we hadn't kept records for the individual engines. This meant some tanks might be capable of eight hundred miles, whereas others might be just about to break down. Many of the other vehicles were in a similar state. It just hadn't been done properly.

Major David Potts
SO2 Army Logistics, Quartermaster General's Department

If a Challenger's engine conked out, you didn't repair it, but replaced it with another. But as we'd bought a tank that wasn't reliable, what we needed was loads and loads of spare tank engines; but when we tried to muster the engines, nobody knew where they all were, or how many. This shows how truly bonkers things were.

Major General Alexander Harley
Assistant Chief of Defence Staff (Overseas) and Deputy Director of Joint Operations, Ministry of Defence, Whitehall

The CGS was summoned to see Margaret Thatcher, who demanded very specific and absolute reassurance that we wouldn't end up with broken-down tanks everywhere. So in order to provide the number of tanks we'd agreed to send, and fulfil the prime minister's requirement, every single tank engine we possessed had to go, leaving Germany for years afterwards with empty hulks.

We also sent 155mm artillery guns, for which we had nowhere near enough ammunition. I don't know how we'd been going to fight the Cold War... The Americans needed all theirs and couldn't help, and the Belgians refused to sell us any of theirs, so we had to go to the open market. The Cold War used quite a bit of shop-window dressing.

Major David Potts
SO2 Army Logistics, Quartermaster General's Department
We had similar problems gathering together everything else we needed; and the army had nothing for fighting in desert.

We compiled, in longhand, a huge list, with a time chart of how long we thought it would take to locate each item, buy it, get it out to the Gulf, then issue to the troops – an amazing chart!

After several weeks, more staff were brought in to help, and this process became much more formal and detailed. But this really brought home how totally focused we'd been on the Cold War in north-west Germany.

Brigadier Patrick Cordingley
Commander, 7th Armoured Brigade
I had this nagging worry in the back of my mind about whether we'd be able to do it, and more to the point, was I up to it? There was nobody to look after me when we were out there; I couldn't go to the Americans and say, 'I need help.' General Peter de la B's headquarters was six hundred miles away. So instead of being hugely excited, I was very concerned.

At my first briefing in the bunker at High Wycombe, I was told the enemy army was four million strong, equipped by the Russians with A-10 anti-tank missiles which would go through the frontal armour of a Challenger tank at four kilometres range. The Republican Guard had T-72 tanks, with a gun they said could penetrate the frontal armour of Challenger at a thousand metres. The chemical and biological aspect was particularly concerning. They'd used it during the Iran–Iraq war, so intelligence said there was no reason why they wouldn't use it now. They'd got anthrax, and we'd have to fight in our NBC [Nuclear, Biological, Chemical] suits.

Major General Alexander Harley
Assistant Chief of Defence Staff (Overseas) and Deputy Director of Joint Operations, Ministry of Defence, Whitehall
Although we had NBC suits, respirators and atropine pen injectors to counter chemical attacks, we didn't have any pre-emptive vaccinations for biological weapon strains. However, we knew that the appropriate tablets could protect our troops prophylactically from biological strains.

Porton Down [the UK's Defence Science and Technology Laboratory], together with our intelligence services, were working flat out to find out what biological strains the Iraqis were developing: was it anthrax, plague or what? I believe a strain of anthrax was eventually determined. Our view was that we should develop vaccinations as part of our duty of care to the troops.

Sergeant Major Johnny Muir
Regimental Quartermaster Sergeant Major,
Queen's Royal Irish Hussars

We knew that apart from its unreliability, Challenger was not designed to fight in desert conditions. I also knew that the high nylon content of our European combat kit and tank suits would make them very hot and unpleasant in the desert. Proper desert combat kit was made of different materials and was very much more comfortable. We were sent the desert cotton undergarments, but were to be very disappointed when desert combat clothing failed to arrive before we deployed.

Lieutenant Colonel Mike Vickery
Commanding Officer, 14th/20th King's Hussars,
4th Armoured Brigade

Everything was focused on getting 7th Armoured Brigade ready. We lost all our later Mark 2 Challengers to 7 Brigade, and then in October were ordered to remove the large and important parts of our remaining tanks to be used as spares. People took everything from us – literally *everything*.

By the end of October my tanks were bereft of engines, gearboxes and final drives, up on chocks with no tracks. You could see right through each tank from front to rear, from one end of the tank park to the other. I was presiding over a scrap yard. Very soon, thanks to my absolute insistence on not giving utterly *everything* away, we had just the one working tank.

They then removed our fire-control computers, and the next thing on the list was to remove the gun barrels – a very serious business, as you had to dismantle and remove the commander's cupola, dismantle the turret, then remove the heavy breech block before removing the barrel from the back through the crew compartment. The Technical Quartermaster's department was being sucked dry of all spares, and by November we had pretty well nothing.

Lieutenant Toby Masterton
A Squadron, The Life Guards, 4th Armoured Brigade

After I was sacked, back at Athlone barracks in Germany, panic preparations were under way. In utmost secrecy, with strict orders that the press were not to know, our vehicles were cannibalised. There was such a rush, that instead of undoing all the cables and connections to remove engines and starter packs, the REME fitters were cutting all the connections, or burning through them using thermic lances. It was organised panic. Our Challengers were gutted, and with all their top-secret armour and so on, were soon the most expensive and highly guarded scrap-metal skips in the world.

The Rt Hon Tom King
UK Secretary of State for Defence

The political strategy of those months wasn't to fight a battle with Saddam Hussein, but to stop his aggression. We had also to rally the Gulf states, via the Gulf Cooperation Council, and see what contributions they could make; rally the United Nations to get the right resolutions approved to authorise the actions we were taking; then to organise sufficient international pressure, diplomatic and military, to persuade Saddam Hussein to get out. And, right up to end, we were still doing that. Regime change was never an objective.

Operation Desert Shield was the first part of this process – to protect Saudi; then we had to turn it round as the forces built up, to create a credible attacking force – not to fight, but to make him realise that if he didn't get out, it would be a fight he'd lose.

Brigadier Patrick Cordingley
Commander, 7th Armoured Brigade

I'd come out of my first intensive intelligence briefing thinking, 'Bloody hell, not only are they battle-hardened after ten years of war, they've also got impressive kit, and been trained by the Russians.'

But then I realised, as was to happen a lot when I asked questions, people were telling me everything they knew, imagining it made them seem clever and efficient. They didn't think through what I actually *needed* to know.

In retrospect, I don't think our Army Intelligence Corps had any real intelligence on the Iraqi army, but just pulled out their old dossiers and used that. MI6 didn't provide me with any sensible information, either. I was more realistically briefed out in the Gulf by American intelligence.

But regardless, numbers were very much on the Iraqi side, and throwing around chemical and biological weapons would give them a huge advantage too – always assuming we didn't use tactical nuclear weapons to stop them. I asked Peter de la Billiere whether we were likely to use tactical nuclear weapons. He said he didn't know the policy on that. I did hear, later on, that the Americans had said to the Iraqis, 'Don't use chemical or biological weapons against our soldiers, or we'll use nuclear weapons against you.'

Major General Alexander Harley
Assistant Chief of Defence Staff (Overseas) and Deputy Director of Joint Operations, Ministry of Defence, Whitehall

Saddam had said very clearly that he would use his biological weapons against the coalition. We could see he had the facilities, and were very worried. When one talks about the reasons for having an independent strategic nuclear deterrent, avoiding being blackmailed is an important use for it. Before the ground war, Saddam was sent a joint USA–UK message, that if you use either chemical or biological weapons against us, you can expect the very, very gravest response. This was code for 'You'll get a nuclear weapon'. That very clear message was sent to the Iraqis, but nevertheless we continued preparing for chemical and biological weapon use.

Lieutenant General Walter Boomer
General Officer Commanding, 1 Marine Expeditionary Force, United States Marine Corps

I was always asked by reporters what we'd do if he used chemical weapons. I'd talk about how well prepared we were with chemical suits, etc., but also say that Saddam knows if he uses chemical weapons we will obliterate his nation. Now that was bullshit on my part because nobody had ever said that to me, but I liked the way it sounded – and I also believed that was what would happen.

But the second thing that gave me comfort was later, when we captured an Iraqi chemical weapons officer. He told us that even though his unit had chemical weapons, he had no intention of firing them if ordered, as he believed that would mean the end of his family in Bagdhad [from nuclear retaliation]. He was speaking only for himself, but there were certainly others like him. I interpreted this as meaning it was very doubtful even if Saddam ordered a chemical attack, that his chemical units would obey him. But I don't actually think the Iraqi chemical units were ever ordered to launch, because I believe Saddam had been warned. In the end, we attacked wearing chemical suits, which in the heat you just don't do.

The Rt Hon Tom King
UK Secretary of State for Defence

We knew Saddam already used chemical weapons to kill thousands of Kurds. The [US] president was prepared to suffer large numbers of casualties in the process of liberating Kuwait, and we'd been warned to expect significant casualties. I was asked fairly regularly what would happen to Saddam Hussein if he used chemical weapons. I never made any specific threats, but stuck to saying that if he did that, he would be very, very foolish. I intended that remark to make it quite clear that the comeback for him would be disastrous. I thought it important not to specify what means would be used, but make it quite clear that we would not tolerate the use of chemical weapons.

I heard that Saddam was warned by the Americans that the response to his use of chemical weapons could be nuclear. The Americans were in the lead, and we were quite clear that any use of chemical weapons would receive a very, very significant response, and he was in no doubt about this.

The Rt Hon John Major
Prime Minister (from 22nd November 1990)

What frightened our troops, and us back in Whitehall, was the prospect of chemical and biological weapons being used. We knew the Iraqis had them, and that Saddam Hussein had used them in the past against his *own* people. Their possible use in battle was the principal apprehension of both soldiers and military commanders. And so the Iraqis were warned by the United States, in no uncertain terms, that they should not resort to biological or chemical warfare. Thankfully, they did not.

Major General Alexander Harley
Assistant Chief of Defence Staff (Overseas) and Deputy Director of Joint Operations, Ministry of Defence, Whitehall

The Americans had decided not to provide their troops with biological weapon vaccinations. I went over to Washington to tell them that we *were* going to protect our troops, and that we were already busy deciding how we would do it, how long it would take, and how we could get it ready in time.

I met with my opposite number in the Pentagon and was told that the Americans didn't like what we were doing, and that us doing it put them in a very difficult position but that if we insisted on continuing, they wanted to be kept more closely in touch – which was quite clearly a stalling tactic.

So, back in London we had to decide whether to stop developing the vaccinations, as this issue was quite clearly going to be outside our partnering arrangements with the USA.

Lance Corporal Roy Sellstrom
Pioneer Corps, Army War Graves Unit

No one at Kineton knew how we were to be trained, so we were put to shift work in the ammunition labs, fitting some special new type of fuses to 155mm artillery shells.

There was such a demand for us to get these shells ready for the Gulf, that the Royal Army Ordnance Corps ammunition technical NCOs told us to do the critical processes of the fitting they were supposed to do. We refitted thousands of these massive shells – a recipe for disaster really, leaving it to the Pioneers.

Lieutenant Colonel Mike Vickery
Commanding Officer, 14th/20th King's Hussars, 4th Armoured Brigade

At one brigade conference, my friend the 17/21st Lancers' Commanding Officer was tearing his hair out at being sucked dry. I offered to send one of my troops – three tanks, twelve men and one subaltern, to the Irish Hussars, as I didn't think we'd be going anywhere for six months. The Irish Hussars' CO, Arthur Denaro, told me he didn't want a troop, just a sergeant here, a couple of drivers, some soldiers, etc., but I told him he could have a complete troop, my best, with my best troop leader and sergeant, or nothing. People work better with those they know. I wanted them to fight together, not just be bums on seats.

But Arthur didn't want them, so I made the same offer to the CO of the Scots Dragoon Guards, John Sharples, who nearly bit my hand off for them. He added rather cheekily, 'Could I also send a captain to keep an eye on them?' So he also got my Signals Captain.

Lieutenant Colonel Charles Rogers
Commanding Officer, Staffordshire Regiment

The Grenadier Guards sent a platoon, which stood in front of me and would only say 'Sah!' From Queen's Company, they were huge, *monstrous* young men, six foot four to six foot seven. Their Warrior vehicles weren't designed for people like that. I couldn't see how they managed to fit in. They were charming, excellent soldiers – completely immaculate.

We also received some very nice young men from the PWO [Prince of Wales's Own] and Royal Green Jackets. But we didn't have any personnel problems, although others did – like the artillery regiment whose second-in-command was moved on.

Sergeant Major Johnny Muir
Regimental Quartermaster Sergeant Major,
Queen's Royal Irish Hussars

The Irish Hussars like a good party and have never been teetotal, but alcohol was banned from Saudi Arabia. Ingenious methods of smuggling were devised, for example in the tanks themselves, up the barrels, which were sealed by the breech at one end and with a muzzle cap. The charge containers are a good refrigeration unit. Even if customs were to check the tanks at any time, they wouldn't know where to look. Shampoo bottles were also used. This was obviously banned, but soldiers will always be soldiers.

Lt Colonel Arthur Denaro
Commanding Officer, Queen's Royal Irish Hussars

Quiet days left time to think, making us nervous, and we needed to know when we were to leave, so I rang round Brigade HQ and the other units. Somebody must have complained about this, as a little later I received a rocket from the Commander, which was very unfair! Next day I held a mammoth movement conference in my office with brigade staff plus representatives from corps. The problems and procedures for arrival in the Gulf were explained, and tempers cooled.

On 1 October, the secret people from BRIXMIS [British Military Liaison Mission] brought us a Russian T-72 tank – in great secrecy, hidden in the gym so that the officers, senior NCOs and tank commanders could see an enemy tank; it was fast, robust, very well protected with good frontal armour, and a very good gun, easy to operate, which suits Arab forces, who, in my various experiences of working with them, will often forget how to do the more difficult bits, rather like me with my digital camera – I just take the easy option.

At a battle group trainer session the next day, my headquarters was very poor. I was unamused, and showed it. We eventually sorted things out, but this was not good for confidence and self-esteem!

Sergeant Major Johnny Muir
Regimental Quartermaster Sergeant Major, Queen's Royal Irish Hussars

Some people didn't live up to our expectations, and some came forward on sick parade with mysterious and previously unknown medical conditions. Others were left out for other more understandable reasons.

As you can imagine, there was name-calling and mickey-taking, but this problem was potentially far more serious. A tank troop is a tightly knit little group; one person suddenly dropping out creates a big problem. I felt sorry for the ones with genuine medical reasons, who really could not have gone. We were pretty hard about people's weaknesses.

Those who were left behind, regardless of the reason, were responsible for the extremely important job of looking after our two hundred families. Most of the families were very young, from the UK when we moved to Germany.

Maggi Denaro
Commanding Officer's wife, Queen's Royal Irish Hussars

When you marry a man in the army it's understood you'll take responsibility for the wives of the men he commands. All the commanding officers' wives in Fallingbostel had been nurses, so we knew how to deal with people in difficult and upsetting situations, plus we'd already been squadron leaders' wives, so we had an innate understanding of what other women might need.

Because I obviously had the ear of the Commanding Officer, I tended to be the one to whom they came if they needed things, but in reality we were just all wives together, with our husbands away – looking out for each other.

Sergeant Major Johnny Muir
Regimental Quartermaster Sergeant Major,
Queen's Royal Irish Hussars

If I was captured, I thought about how my wife and fifteen-year-old daughter were going to feel, and how would I feel. Things like personal letters and photographs, if found on your person, could be used by your captors in a psychological way. I decided I'd destroy anything like that once we deployed into the desert. I didn't speak to anybody else about this – certainly not my wife. My family had been through the uncertainty, measuring the possibilities and probability against the unknowns of service in Northern Ireland, so this wasn't entirely unfamiliar to us.

Our QM [Quartermaster], Captain Phil Nunn, went out to the Gulf early, leaving me to ensure the Regiment and its stores were loaded and got off properly. I went on the last flight out, on the anniversary of the Battle of Balaclava and the Charge of the Light Brigade. I wondered if those boys had felt the same as I did, riding off into something completely unknown. But then I thought that they'd also left their families behind as well.

I looked out through the French doors of my quarter toward the woods, where a little deer was grazing. I wondered if I'd ever see that sight again. I really didn't know if I was coming back from this, for the first time in my army career. My daughter came downstairs for school and said, 'Well, I'll see you Dad.' I said, 'I'll see you too,' then as I hugged and kissed her, I lost control and became very emotional. Ten minutes later the same thing happened when I said cheerio to my wife Jackie.

I walked the hundred yards to the square, getting myself into a soldier frame of mind. My wife walked round the corner on her way to work, so I winked at her and shouted some orders just to keep control of myself. Then as the buses arrived, I said something quite foolish. The wife of one of the staff sergeants was there with her two sons. I'd known her husband ever since he joined the regiment, was at their wedding and knew their sons. As I ordered everyone on to the bus, she looked me straight in the eye and said, 'Look after him for me. Make sure he comes back.' So I replied, 'I'm coming back on the last flight, so they'll all be back before me, each and every one.'

It was only once we were en route to Hannover airport that I realised this was a commitment I could never fulfil, for which I could be held to account. Saying it had made me feel important, and I could only hope it was going to work out like that.

Major General Alexander Harley
Assistant Chief of Defence Staff (Overseas) and Deputy Director of Joint Operations, Ministry of Defence, Whitehall

To get our convoys through the Suez Canal, we needed Egypt on side, which was difficult. Aircraft had to fly through various national airspaces, which had to be agreed. There was antipathy between groups of Arabs and the Saudis. But Saddam's act of invading Kuwait was considered too outrageous, plus there were general Arab fears of where it would stop.

I went round the Middle East with Tom King's party, building the coalition. In Saudi, we sat in an incredible tent structure and met the king. We also went to Bahrain, Oman, Qatar, the Gulf States and so on. They were all distinctly nervous, but after a lot of hard work came round to the determination that this boil had to be lanced. The Syrians even provided a division – although they didn't actually do very much.

The Rt Hon Tom King
UK Secretary of State for Defence

Warsaw Pact countries joined the coalition like absolute lightning: Hungarian and Czech chemical defence units, one of their particular specialities; Polish hospital ships, plus another from Japan. The Americans were very keen that we and the Dutch provide minesweepers – one of our niche areas of expertise, against the possibility that Saddam might mine the Gulf.

Coordinating all this was a terrific strain for the Americans. The Saudis fortunately had amazing infrastructure: Dhahran airfield with huge runways, and the enormous port facilities at Al Jubayl. Even then, there was also terrific strain on the Saudis, and some material had to be diverted to other places. The extraordinary coalition was finally completed by the arrival of Taliban Mujahideen infantry battalion, who arrived late from Afghanistan –

a symbolic expression of gratitude to Saudi Arabia for being supportive to them in their fight against the Russians.

Something like forty-two different countries were involved, although some contingents arrived without the means to support themselves, which gave us difficulties. Although it was important that as many other nations as possible were involved, it was also very important that they didn't take resources away from other nations.

Major Rayson Pritchard
Public Information Officer, Royal Marines

One of our biggest problems was created when the Saudi government refused to allow British soldiers to be buried in Saudi soil. In the Falklands we'd initially buried the bodies in mass graves on the islands, and in previous wars, the bodies were buried in the countries where they died. The usual casualty process had to be completely changed, replaced by a whole new administrative machine. The bodies would all have to be flown home, requiring steel coffins, body bags, flags to drape the coffins, a reception organisation back in the UK, with people dealing with families, arranging funerals, and so on.

Following on from this, the logisticians considered what would happen when the field hospitals were set up and casualties were being treated. Usually there's a huge incinerator site down-wind of each hospital, to burn all the fouled dressings, theatre disposables, amputated limbs and body waste. However, the Saudi authorities ordered that the ashes of infidels could not be allowed to blow across their soil. So support ships with incinerators had to be lined up offshore, with all the waste hermetically sealed in bags then flown out by helicopter for incineration.

This was very emotive to us, and many people were extremely annoyed. Being here to help the Saudis, people felt there should be more give and take.

The Rt Hon Tom King
UK Secretary of State for Defence

The Saudi leadership understood we were coming to their defence, so it wouldn't be fair for our people to be treated according to their rules. They accepted that we would wish to observe our customs and religious practices, but requested that this not be flaunted – for example by celebrating Christmas with fireworks.

There were also internal security tensions within Saudi, and serious concerns as to what this situation might lead to. In addition to their feeling of betrayal by Jordan, they were also very concerned about the Yemen; there were large numbers of Yemenis labouring and in domestic service in Saudi. Most were expelled as a fifth column of unreliable loyalty.

Major General Alexander Harley
Assistant Chief of Defence Staff (Overseas) and Deputy Director of Joint Operations, Ministry of Defence, Whitehall
Foreign Office contacts were extremely helpful, especially places like Oman and Jordan where we already had very strong links. Some Arab nations feared once we were there, we'd stay, and needed persuading that we wouldn't march into Iraq, and only stay as long as it took.

Some nations provided money rather than military forces – the Saudis did both. We went round getting the money together beforehand, in the form of taking pledges to pay for the military effort.

The Rt Hon Tom King
UK Secretary of State for Defence
It was a clash of cultures. In Saudi Arabia, women can't even drive cars, while US National Guard air-to-air refuelling tankers were being flown by female pilots. The Prince Governor of Eastern Province complained to Schwarzkopf about busty American girls at Dhahran, wearing tight T-shirts, unloading American Globemaster aircraft in hot weather, which [he said] was having a bad effect on Saudi men working at the airbase. There were incidents.

CHAPTER 3

DESPERATE REINFORCEMENT

American President George Bush had ordered the US Marines to defend the Saudi ports along the coastal part of the Saudi–Kuwait border, whilst the US Army's Central Command, CENTCOM, under General H. Norman Schwarzkopf made ready to move to Saudi Arabia to command some half a million troops from various nationalities.

The UK had decided to send an armoured brigade from Germany, beginning on 8 October. Because this had never been done before, the move was beset by various and many problems of logistics and ill-preparedness, including the difficult decision over how many troops to send, which units and how the operation should be commanded. The main body departed on 15 October, and eleven days later over half were in Saudi: one hundred Challengers, seventy-four Warriors, eight Scorpions, twelve Scimitars and other vehicles. But it soon became clear that even *more* troops would be required than initially thought and so, with great political reluctance and damaging hesitation, the UK government agonised over sending its entire German capability to the Gulf.

Russia was strongly opposed to this American-led rescue operation, especially as it might conclude with military action being taken against Iraq, which Russia regarded as within its sphere of influence, supplying vast amounts of military equipment to Saddam. Russian President Gorbachev, himself trying to stay in power and prevent the break-up of the former Soviet Union and Warsaw Pact, needed any kind of leverage he could find. The enormous outflow of military capability from northern Germany lessened NATO's ability to defend home soil, a weakness which might make it worth Russia's while to oppose the Saudi rescue plan at the UN. With this intention, the Red Army's main intelligence directorate, the GRU, was ordered to discover if the UK had replaced the tanks and artillery it was sending to the Gulf, from its war maintenance reserves.

Major General Alexander Harley
Assistant Chief of Defence Staff (Overseas) and Deputy Director of Joint Operations, Ministry of Defence, Whitehall

The Americans keep everything they need already at sea. We'd considered doing the same, but couldn't afford it. We hadn't even got a hospital ship. As in the Falklands war, the UK government relied on a legal instrument to 'take up' UK merchant ships. However, in 1990 we suddenly discovered the UK merchant fleet was so reduced it hadn't got enough ships. But then, because political decisions were being left too late, *any* available ships were booked up. The price of our paying the shipping companies to break these contracts was astronomical. Nobody had kept an eye on this, another aspect of the typically 'shop-window' Cold War approach.

So we ended up putting our highly secret, expensive tanks, missiles systems and other equipment, into the charge of Chinese, Indonesian and all sorts of other crews. At the time when 7 Armoured Brigade was sailing, Egypt was pretty anti the whole operation, plus we were worried about terrorists, and so had to put troops on board to defend these ships, and give them Royal Navy escorts. It was pretty gimcrack.

Major David Potts
SO2 Army Logistics, Quartermaster General's Department

For a while, getting everything together was being done entirely by me. I wasn't allowed to talk to anybody, so started out by guessing, then decided I'd phone people who'd worked in desert environments, and very rapidly ran up a huge list. But once the funding valve was turned on, Roland Notley extended what we were doing into an MoD-wide operation, and the full range of MoD agencies became involved.

Brigadier Mike Willcocks
Chief of Staff (Land), Joint War Headquarters, RAF High Wycombe

I'd been the Commander Royal Artillery of 4th Armoured Division at Herford in Germany during the summer of 1990, when the whole thing kicked off. The process of deciding what to send for a Gulf operation was a real nightmare. General Peter de la Billiere was made incandescent at how the 'bean-counters', as he called them in the MoD, crabbed their way incrementally from the sending of 7th Armoured Brigade, towards deciding to send an armoured division to Saudi Arabia.

Major General Alexander Harley
Assistant Chief of Defence Staff (Overseas) and Deputy Director of Joint Operations, Ministry of Defence, Whitehall

The MoD was awful. I used a camp bed in my office, most of the loos didn't work; first thing in the morning serried lines of people in suit bottoms shaving at scruffy basins, no showers, with only a couple of bathrooms in the whole place. The Second Permanent Secretary had one, so I used to borrow his key. We ate in a dark 1940s canteen downstairs, the 'Greasy Spoon'.

The night staff were vital; a hundred or so military officers and civil servants, led by my Central Staff Operations Group, working through the night to prepare plans, reports and papers for the Chiefs of Staff Committee at 0830, before being sent across the road to the Cabinet Office. Another hundred or so Defence Intelligence Staff people worked across Horse Guards Avenue in the Old Admiralty Building. My boss and I had to make sure this mass of work achieved coherence. The Chiefs also met at weekends, so the process never stopped.

Continuity was vital; people couldn't just go home, so most worked twenty-four-hour shifts, then came back in after having a sleep. By the time I'd had my final meeting with key staff, it was around 2am, so I'd take a couple of hours' sleep before assembling it all for the Chiefs of Staff.

Some things were time-sensitive and needed very fast work, others gradually building until decisions could be taken. Anything could be rejected and bounced back down to us, and with so many other countries in the coalition, was immensely complicated.

The central staffs were also talking to NATO headquarters, which weren't in our command structure but were providing other coalition members and United Nations operations, plus General Peter de la Billiere's HQ out in the Gulf, and the whole UK diplomatic structure.

Major David Potts
SO2 Army Logistics, Quartermaster General's Department

The Minister summoned the Chief Executive of the Defence Clothing and Textiles Agency to give him grief about why there wasn't any desert camouflage clothing.

He gave the Minister both barrels back, telling him it was because there'd been no funding, and British industry wasn't delivering, so he was having to get the trousers made in Morocco, the jackets in Algeria and other totally bonkers things. The funding taps were turned on too late for a lot of things to be ready in time – which was rather shameful.

Major General Alexander Harley
Assistant Chief of Defence Staff (Overseas) and Deputy Director of Joint Operations, Ministry of Defence, Whitehall

The American five-star headquarters Central Command, CENTCOM, commanded by General Schwarzkopf, normally looks after Europe and the Middle East. Comprising more than three thousand people, it was flown out of MacDill Air Force base in Florida, to Saudi Arabia.

Below that level, thirty nations were involved, including British and French divisions, Syrian and Egyptian divisions – all with their own headquarters. There were also Special Forces headquarters, the various operational fighting headquarters and maritime and air headquarters. One of our most important negotiating cards was the British signals monitoring and intelligence facilities in Cyprus, and GCHQ – not that we needed actually to 'play' these cards. But they certainly helped ensure our seat at the table, and that we would be privy to American intelligence, which no other coalition members were.

It took a very long time to string together the command chain for this operation, and for quite a while, we didn't know how Schwarzkopf was going to organise the coalition command structure and, more specifically, would we be on the inside track or not? Who would the command structure reach back to? It was a very involved process.

This operation needed a properly formed headquarters with trained staff, and masses of communications with huge bandwidth and satellites. The

Americans with CENTCOM are the only ones with all this. The Brits and French can do it up to a point, but not to this level.

Lieutenant General Walter Boomer
General Officer Commanding, 1 Marine Expeditionary Force, United States Marine Corps

This was the first operation in a long time to be commanded as a joint force, run by Central Command. This meant that the [US] Service Chiefs were now in the role of *supporting* the operation, giving their operational commanders the troops and logistics they needed. But that pretty much formally ended their role; which is not to say they didn't take an interest operationally, but it no longer *belonged* to them.

The Commandant US Marine Corps at that time was General Alfred Gray – an interesting personality, but one of those guys who find it difficult understanding that he's no longer calling the shots. He had ideas about operational planning, which I chose to ignore. He wanted to come and visit more often than the other Service Chiefs. Colin Powell, Norman Schwarzkopf and I collectively said, 'Your visits are disruptive and time-consuming. So no, you can't come.' He said, 'I'm not going to cause you any trouble. I just want to talk to the troops – and cheer them up.' He got the message, but wasn't happy.

As you can imagine I was consumed every waking minute; there wasn't time even for much sleep. I didn't need any more on my plate.

General Gray thought he was helping, but actually created unnecessary tension – which I didn't need.

Dr Mary McLoughlin

Quite abruptly, around 8 September, Saddam released elderly women and children. This was a huge relief to everybody. The female doctors and nurses weren't allowed home, irrespective of whether they had children at home or not. Only the wives of the top consultants who had family with them were allowed to leave.

At the same time, very strangely I was granted an exit permit; this was because I was thought to have been at the airport when Saddam Hussein invaded, in an aircraft that was grounded at that moment. So, along with all the people who'd been in transit coming into Kuwait or into Baghdad on flights that were refuelling, I was also to be flown out.

I told the hospital authorities I didn't want to go. My partner was still there and I was coping a lot better than many other people. I asked if they could shift my exit visa to someone else. However, after a few days, I was told I'd have to go home. But they asked me to tell everybody back at home of the very serious situation we were in. Well, of course I agreed to do this.

I had my birthday on 9 September in Iraq, then flew home with a group of about fifty people.

Major Rayson Pritchard
Public Information Officer, Royal Marines

Initially the Americans were gung-ho about being the saviours of Saudi Arabia, but after the issues of the bodies and surgical waste and other problems, the Americans reverted to becoming cultural Butt-heads, refusing to see the Saudi point of view, insisting they fall in with all our requests.

A sauve young Saudi captain served in the HQ, had been educated in the USA, spoke excellent English and normally wore combats; one day came in wearing Saudi traditional robes. His *dishdash* and cloak were silk of the finest quality, with gold braid around the outside; clearly one of the royal family. People started listening to him more than the senior Saudi lieutenant colonel, as he explained the Saudi point of view in an urbane, sophisticated way.

A US Navy captain took charge of the JIB [Joint Information Bureau]. Known as 'Hollywood Mike' from his previous job liaising with the film industry over use of US Navy facilities, he'd organised the classic video of Cher in stockings and suspenders grinding around on the twelve-inch guns of a US battleship. 'Hollywood Mike' was very quick to adapt to Saudi sensitivities.

Dr Mary McLoughlin

In late September, I was back home with instructions to tell the Irish government how serious the situation was in Iraq. Senior Austrian officials had gone across to Iraq, bringing back the entire Austrian contingent, so I was told to get the Irish government to send over somebody senior as Saddam Hussein had asked, to bring all our people back. Some of the other people who came home were trying to do the same thing as well, but for some reason people were complaining and pestering me more than others – probably because I was a doctor.

But our foreign minister Gerry Collins never went to Iraq, and did not meet the likes of me. The Iraqis would reward the seniority of ministers sent with the return of larger numbers of foreign nationals. Junior Irish officials returned home with nothing.

It seemed to us at the time that the Irish government considered it more important not to break ranks with the British or the Americans, than saving Irish lives. We did say this a lot of times, but we might as well have been talking to the dog for all the good it got us.

Major General Alexander Harley
Assistant Chief of Defence Staff (Overseas) and Deputy Director of Joint Operations, Ministry of Defence, Whitehall

The decision to send more than just 7 Brigade was taken in September, when it was quite clear Saddam Hussein was going to have to be kicked out of Kuwait. Deciding whether we should invade Iraq was also a huge debate, especially over which Arab nations might be offended to the extent of not joining, and the legality of invading. But very quickly it was realised that invading Iraq was not to be the game, and the operation was restricted to the recapture and handing back of Kuwait.

I was quite scared that this might develop into a world war.

The Russians had a really major stake in Iraq, having provided military equipment, and Russian engineers to help build nuclear facilities (as did a lot of European industry as well), so MoD was monitoring the Russian response to our deployment, and any potential knock-on effects around the world.

The security of Europe was also a very worrying aspect, although the fall of the Iron Curtain had made things difficult for the Russians. However, the formation of our coalition was sending strong messages to Russia – for example Syria's very definite joining in, having been a Russian puppet throughout the Cold War.

Captain Miloš Stanković
Parachute Regiment, Russian interpreter,
Joint Arms Control Implementation Group (JACIG)

At the end of September 1990, the Soviets called a snap inspection for no discernable reason, very unusually sending over three GRU colonels. After a couple of days, we realised they were on an intelligence misssion, but couldn't work out what it was.

They kept ordering the helicopter to fly around Luggershall, where the UK's strategic reserve of tanks and heavy weaponry is kept, talking to each other about whether the railway lines to the depot were rusty or shiny. The moment we realised this, our Colonel surreptitiously ordered the pilot to fly nose up.

If the Russians could be sure that the British sector in Germany was no longer defended by the tanks and artillery that they could also see being shipped en masse to Saudi, the whole balance of forces that had underpinned the Cold War in Europe would be removed. This knowledge would help determine whether Russia could risk supporting Saddam Hussein in anti-American diplomacy, at a time when demonstrating international authority might just mitigate the break-up of the Soviet Union.

But it can't have taken them long to realise that all BAOR's remaining tanks and artillery were gutted hulks standing on wooden blocks.

The Rt Hon Tom King
UK Secretary of State for Defence
I don't think we replaced the tanks we'd sent from Germany with tanks from our UK war maintenance reserve, the Soviet Union at that stage being so inward-looking that the risks were minimal. But the Americans weren't stripping down Germany to go to the Gulf, the French remained in position in Europe, as did the German army itself, so our judgement was that this didn't seriously create new risks for what was hoped would be a short campaign.

Dr Mary McLoughlin
At one public meeting, a very senior member of the Irish Department of Foreign Affairs read out an official letter from Iraq saying that Saddam Hussein would release members of staff from the hospital if they were replaced by people from Ireland, so I immediately put up my hand and said I would go back.

Major David Potts
SO2 Army Logistics, Quartermaster General's Department
We eventually took over the surrounding offices, bringing in watchkeepers [officers who would monitor radio traffic, plot movements and incidents and

keep operations staff alerted] to work round the clock, and over twenty people doing what I'd previously done, with me as *de facto* Chief of Staff .

The scale of resolution was amazing; we had to do *everything* – for example, the British Army didn't have any sunglasses! One of the generals asked did we really need *sunglasses*? Well, actually we do. We bought big tortoise-shell jobs, for sixty pence a pair. We didn't have bergens, and our boots were made of cardboard with nothing resembling a desert boot. All this was because the risk calculation in the Cold War was very different to that of actually fighting a war. Our forces in Germany were there as a trip-wire in case the Russians attacked. Nobody seriously imagined we'd actually have to fight them – just *deter* them.

Dr Mary McLoughlin

When I landed at Baghdad airport, I felt immensely relieved. I had a one-way visa – allowed to come in only, with no mention of leaving. The hospital authorities met me at the airport. I don't think anybody was released, but I didn't really care as I was so happy to get out of Ireland. It was easier to deal with the Iraqi authorities than with our Ministry of Foreign Affairs and the hysterical people ringing me up from Iraq demanding to know what I was doing.

There was now a more clearly defined social life, particularly around the various nations favoured by the Iraqis; for example, the Yugoslavs and their social club. I don't think the French were locked up, either.

But the British and American embassies were both absolutely full of refugees; some eighteen hundred men had quite literally run into the British Embassy on hearing that the Iraqi authorities were locking people up. Several of us ran clinics at the various embassies. Some of their people were quite old and infirm, with heart, diabetes, cancers and other conditions.

Lieutenant Colonel Charles Rogers
Commanding Officer, Staffordshire Regiment

While we waited for our equipment to arrive, we lived in very large sheds at the port. The US Marines looked after us really well, and we ate their rations – MREs [Meal, Ready-to-Eat], which were reasonably inadequate. We emphasised discipline and water-drinking, plus running and exercise, so by the time we went into the desert, we were reasonably acclimatised. There wasn't much to do.

As commanding officers with no soldiers to command, we made a nuisance of ourselves, driving round the desert and getting bogged in.

Dr Mary McLoughlin

We were driving out of the hospital twice a week, to treat people at the embassy, bringing drugs with us from a hospital for local people that was well known to be already running out. The Iraqis absolutely had to know that we were doing this, but I have to say that they never stopped us. They knew that there was a shortage of drugs, but we were never stopped.

Lieutenant Colonel Arthur Denaro
Commanding Officer, Queen's Royal Irish Hussars

I went to meet the Commanding Officer of the Marine Corps tank battalion, Lieutenant Colonel Buster Diggs: a real character, very black, very amusing, and very good. Their divisional headquarters was a vast empire under cam [camouflage] nets about one hundred and twenty kilometres north of the port.

The brigadier was very worried about low morale, whereas I was pissed off about the delay of the ships! Another endless conference discussing the arrival times of boats and personnel; a nightmare, and so frustrating. Another eighty-three men had arrived, making a total of seven hundred of us in the hangar, but more delays in the arrival of our tanks.

Dr Mary McLoughlin

We couldn't imagine that people would now be released, and were settling in for a long siege. We didn't believe that anybody outside was going to act too crazy; for example, we didn't believe the Americans and British could be planning to drop bombs on our heads.

Brigadier Patrick Cordingley
Commander, 7th Armoured Brigade

We'd prepared a booklet entitled 'Living in Saudi Arabia', about Arab customs like eating with the right hand, not showing the soles of your feet, but apart from this we weren't very jacked-up on the cultural side. But we did know that we had to respect their religious customs. It was, however, slightly surprising to us that they didn't want to respect *our* religious customs. We weren't, for example, supposed to hold church services outside, but we did it quietly undercover; padres came with us, but had to black out their crosses and be called 'welfare officers'.

The only top secret document I saw throughout the whole time was from the Saudis, after an American army all-women football team was seen playing on television. They were very upset about this.

Major Rayson Pritchard
Public Information Officer, Royal Marines

We provided a press facility for the 'First British tanks to arrive in the Middle East since the Second World War'. We'd been told in no uncertain terms, from Tom King's office, that when they lowered the ramp from the LSL [Landing Ship, Logistic], every tank was to start first time and drive off without any problems.

This was ensured by flying out crews of REME mechanics with spare batteries, jump leads and everything else, to meet the ships at Doha and UAE, to start up every tank several times each day, then switch off just as the ships docked. The heat and fumes on the tanks' decks were appalling.

We put cameras on an American coastguard harbour boat, and in the rear tank deck of an LSL, the photos and film available to everyone. Brigadier Patrick Cordingley was standing by on the dockside ready for interviews, the press arranged on the quayside, with us running round like arseholes to give them what they'd told us they wanted.

Lieutenant Colonel Charles Rogers
Commanding Officer, Staffordshire Regiment

The Portaloos were some distance outside the hangars. When the soldiers used them, they had to take their rifles and gas masks with them, wearing shorts, military T-shirt and a floppy hat. Pictures of a couple of REME guys going to the loo were hardly a story. I don't know how everybody got so excited about this.

Major Rayson Pritchard
Public Information Officer, Royal Marines

But on the day, *The Times*'s photographer Chris Harris decided to slide off away into the roped-off areas. Two soldiers were walking back to the accommodation, wearing T-shirts and one with Union Jack shorts, carrying their respirators, with rifles slung over their shoulders. He asked them to walk towards him carrying their rifles as if they were on patrol, between the lines of Portaloos. These two clowns did this, Harris took the photos, transmitted them back to his editor in London, and despite everything we'd laid on, *The Times* published them on the front page with the caption 'British soldiers on patrol in the Gulf…'

The flak that then rained down on us was incredible. Brigadier Dutton was the first, demanding to know why we hadn't kept 'this … what's he called – Harris – under control … that's why you people are there'.

Then Tom King's outer office phoned, demanding a back-briefing detailing exactly what we'd done, the measures we'd had in place for the day, how the photos were taken, etc., which we sent back by fax (no emails in those days). Then eventually letters were sent by the government to the editor of *The Times* complaining about their printing that photo.

Lieutenant Colonel Charles Rogers
Commanding Officer, Staffordshire Regiment

Nothing was happening except our equipment arriving, but Patrick Cordingley was being phoned up and blamed by the MoD for everything they didn't like; he was being winged every time, with no top cover from Riyadh. We could see he was under terrible pressure.

Because he's quite an emotional man, we worried that this might take his eye off the ball – although he didn't. But he was made to look as if he was tripping over his own feet, one after the other, whereas actually people in the MoD were not helping him as they should. We had confidence in him and knew he'd be all right, but at the worst times we were definitely worried that he might be relieved, which would have been a disaster.

Major General Alexander Harley
Assistant Chief of Defence Staff (Overseas) and Deputy Director of Joint Operations, Ministry of Defence, Whitehall

I held twice-weekly non-attributable briefings for the press in a little room downstairs, showing them maps and giving a really good insight to what was going on; some of it was quite sensitive, which they were told they mustn't publish. Most of them behaved very well with this, but a couple of newspapers did not: like the *Sun* and *Daily Mirror* who came to these meetings asking lots of questions, in order, it appeared, to get some sensational quote out of it. We could see the serious press getting seriously fed up with this, as it screwed up the process.

Lieutenant Colonel Charles Rogers
Commanding Officer, Staffordshire Regiment
The port became rather uncomfortable, especially when the Scud missile threat began, so once our vehicles arrived, we moved west an hour and a half into the desert, and took over a huge unused migrant workers camp, which became known as 'Camp Four', for R&R and as a staging post. We were about one hundred and fifty miles from the enemy, so felt fairly safe, but moved around all the time just in case.

In November it was hot – dry heat inland, humid on the coast. People had to get to know the realities of using our equipment in the heat; for example if the smallest amount of sand got into our rifle – the SA80 – it jammed. Oiling it, the sand got stuck in the oil, making it worse, and we were to discover further problems with SA80 as the hot weather increased.

Sand was also a problem for the LAW 80 anti-tank weapon, jamming it so the rocket didn't always come out, sending the whole thing whooshing off down the range. We were also given things like CLAW [close light assault weapon] grenade launchers for the first time, which we had to learn how to use.

We had to learn to conserve water, and carry huge amounts of it. We eventually received desert combats, body armour, desert boots and sunglasses which had to be issued, and the soldiers had to get used to it all.

We did early-morning runs, plus some battalion attacks on foot, marching overnight with our kit in case everything went wrong and we were required to operate without the vehicles. We also did that wonderful British Army thing, 'Stand To'; getting up half an hour before dawn every day – traditionally considered the best time for an attacker to attack.

Major Rayson Pritchard
Public Information Officer, Royal Marines
A couple of days later, we held another press facility. The journalists were incensed with Harris. As they lined up to get on to the bus, I said to him,

'Chris, you're not coming.' He went incandescent with rage. 'You mean to say you're not going to let *The Times* report this ... my editor will have something to say about this.'

I replied that his editor should speak to Tom King about it, as the orders had come directly from him. 'Fuck off Chris. You're not getting on the bus.'

The other journalists were very supportive, having seen us rushing around like idiots laying on what they told us had been the perfect press facility. However, we couldn't exclude *The Times* indefinitely, so once it had all died down a bit, we let him back in. But he'd needed that little smack on the bottom to say, 'Don't mess us around.'

The Rt Hon Tom King
UK Secretary of State for Defence

Norman Schwarzkopf showed me a Middle East edition of the *Herald Tribune*, with a photo of two US soldiers wounded in some training exercise on the front page, saying this photo had been published before he in Riyadh had been told about the accident. We had the same problem.

This sort of thing is in the nature of the media. Despite nothing happening, the journalists were being chased for stories by their editors, to justify their presence out there. But the nature of the Gulf conflict made it difficult for seasoned war correspondents to give it any of the colour they wanted. For example, the pilots were flying dangerous, testing missions, then spending the afternoon lying beside their hotel swimming pool in Bahrain. It wasn't like the Western Front!

I took a lot of interest in press coverage, particularly to ensure that silly stories didn't undermine our troops out there.

Major Rayson Pritchard
Public Information Officer, Royal Marines

Tom King's outer office phoned us a lot, especially when things went wrong. I don't know how they got our phone numbers, but they ignored or couldn't be bothered with the military chain of command, and would ask us directly, 'How the fuck did you get that wrong, or let that happen?' There was no email, all faxes and phone calls with a four-hour time difference.

If there's a security breach which reveals future plans, that's serious. But if it's someone having a bit of fun with a playful caption – like *The Times*'s photograph, it's just not important. The politicians seemed to be suffering from paranoia.

Lieutenant Colonel Charles Rogers
Commanding Officer, Staffordshire Regiment

I stopped doing 'Stand To' after overhearing some US Marines talking in their Humvee [large four-wheel drive] next door to me. One was asking, 'What time do the Brits get up?'

'Oh,' came the reply, 'half an hour before dawn.'

'Why on earth do they do that?'

'It's some hang-up from their colonial past.'

I thought there was probably something in that, so I stopped our soldiers doing it.

Lieutenant Colonel Arthur Denaro
Commanding Officer, Queen's Royal Irish Hussars

We commanding officers of 7th Armoured Brigade – John Sharples of the Scots DG [Royal Scots Dragoon Guards], and Charlie Rogers of the Staffords – were inseparable when we were together, if that doesn't sound too Irish.

We were very close friends, but also very competitive, from the 'Best Barracks Garden in Fallingbostel' prize, to how many vehicles we had on the road every day out in the desert. I think Patrick Cordingley knew he could trust us, but that's not to say we were easy guys to command, and I know Patrick found *me* particularly difficult at times.

But we worried about Patrick as he was worrying so much. But he had a brilliant way of handling us – and delegated mostly everything – and when he interfered and we told him not to, he stood back. But he had clear ideas, and his command worked very well. We respected and liked him enormously, teasing him quite a lot, and he only gave us a hard time every now and then.

Brigadier Patrick Cordingley
Commander, 7th Armoured Brigade

After a visit from our Joint Commander Air Chief Marshal Sir Patrick Hine, I drove CDS's Chief of Staff for a more detailed look at logistic operations.

I was in my new Range Rover, presented to me by the Rover Group after Toyota had given us free Land Cruisers. Al Jubayl's roads were designed at right angles to each other, with traffic signs at crossroads determining rights of way, exactly as in America – the only difference being that the locals preferred to put their faith in Allah as opposed to the signs.

We'd just left the field hospital for the port. As we approached a cross-roads doing thirty-five miles an hour with four of us in the back of the Range Rover, a blue car was clearly going to hit us. We ended upside down, having been rammed backwards, skidding along on the roof. There was then a farce, in which our military police escort, assuming this to be an assassination attempt, rammed the blue car. The driver of the blue car ran over and looked at us upside down, shouted 'Oh shit', then ran off into a nearby bank.

The military police followed the driver into the bank with pistols drawn. One forgets life was operating normally, so the bank was full of customers. But somehow the mayhem was resolved when it was realised that the driver was telephoning for an ambulance.

It took a while to get out of the Range Rover, some of us with whiplash injuries, and although I knew I was in trouble, as the commander, one felt that you *don't* make a fuss.

The military police took us back to the field hospital we'd just visited. The medics were sucking their teeth and saying, 'Yes, you're probably all right… There's no real damage,' but with me knowing my back was hurt, and that very soon I'd be in trouble.

Sergeant Major Johnny Muir
Regimental Quartermaster Sergeant Major,
Queen's Royal Irish Hussars

We were the last of the QRIH to arrive, our TriStar landing in the early hours of the morning on Balaclava Day, to unbearable heat. Some lunatic-buffoon of a movements major told us to wear our wide-brimmed camouflage cloth hats 'All the way down, *all* the way round, *all* of the time.' We were going to war, so who cares how we wear these stupid hats. Immediately we left the assembly area, they were shaped into cowboy hats, beanie hats, fishermen's hats, sou'westers – you name it; everything but 'All the way down, all the way round, all of the time".

We found the regiment in a huge hangar at the port, just getting up. It stank, the horrible sweet smell of Portaloos. They took us for breakfast,

American rations produced in an American field kitchen: creamed beef or porridge, which looked like pig swill. What would I have given for a box of British Army compo [standard ration pack] to make my own breakfast. Flies were everywhere; you'd no sooner got a slice of American sweet bread to dip into the swill than they were eating more of it than you were.

I thought what my family would be doing now, but I was in a different environment, a long way from home. I wasn't comfortable, nothing was familiar. I wondered how I was going to handle it.

Lieutenant Colonel Charles Rogers
Commanding Officer, Staffordshire Regiment

Our training began with platoon operations, working up to company and battalion training, manoeuvring in the desert, and studying the Iraqi tactics.

But this early training was all done in glorious isolation to anybody else, whereas for real we were going to be surrounded by twenty other battle groups, plus artillery and so on. I think the tank commanders had the most difficulty adapting. With everyone else running on the same playing field, an armoured battlefield gets very tight if you're not careful.

Brigadier Rupert Smith
Deputy Commandant, Army Staff College, Camberley

I was the deputy commandant at the Staff College when the Iraqis invaded Kuwait. I knew I was to take command of the First Armoured Division in Germany.

In late October, it became clear, politically, that the level of this fight meant that any country wishing to have a say was going to have to provide military forces of at least a division. France did the same. Although I was still in Camberley, I knew this, and that our 7th Armoured Brigade was likely to be reinforced.

Major General Alexander Harley
Assistant Chief of Defence Staff (Overseas) and Deputy Director of Joint Operations, Ministry of Defence, Whitehall

A force designed for Germany needed to be very seriously reconfigured if it was to fight in the desert. But it was very hard to get consensus on what that should be.

As Deputy Director Operations Army, I had a whole series of very difficult meetings with Tom King and the Armed Forces Minister, Archie Hamilton, trying to agree this. I'd take along the army recommendation of what the proposed force should consist of and why, but they'd say, 'You can't send more than thirty thousand people.' But what's the logic for saying thirty thousand? Somehow, within that totality, we were expected to fit in whatever we needed to do the job. But this wasn't going to be like the Cold War. We were actually going to have to *do* something.

We'd started out wondering could we get away with sending just one brigade, or maybe an enlarged brigade? We then decided to send a second brigade with its artillery, for which we needed a divisional headquarters, which comes with long-range divisional artillery and other things.

People would have liked to have sent a third brigade, to provide the force with a reserve. But political capping [of numbers] made sending a third brigade impossible, plus I don't think we could have sent another brigade within the time available. We didn't have the logistics in Germany for any more than two armoured brigades; all our spare tank engines, for example, were taken up by the two brigades, and Challenger was an unreliable tank, and not desert-worthy.

As we went down the track towards committal, new requirements emerged – for example, electronic warfare. Ministers hated the idea of us adding electronic warfare squadrons, or specialist fuel delivery units, or anything else that would take us over what they'd already decided the final number was to be.

Brigadier Patrick Cordingley
Commander, 7th Armoured Brigade

My back was seized up and despite taking painkillers I wasn't sleeping. I felt I needed to crack on, but after four days of not sleeping I realised I wasn't making decisions properly. I told my Chief of Staff, Euan Loudon, that if it went on much longer I'd have to ask to be withdrawn. I smile when I think of it now, but my staff said, 'Hang in there. It's going to be all right. We really don't want a change of command at this stage.'

This was a real lesson about command on a battlefield: that any change in a well-organised unit causes enormous disruption. Having people you know is one of the huge advantages of a professional army. Had I bowed out, I knew somebody else was waiting in Riyadh to take over. At the time I hoped they'd urged me to stay because they liked me, but I now wonder whether I was the devil they knew, preferable to somebody else with different ideas who didn't know them?

Lieutenant Colonel Arthur Denaro
Commanding Officer, Queen's Royal Irish Hussars

We knew Patrick was pretty shook up by that car crash, on only Day Four when we hadn't yet deployed from Al Jubayl. There was huge pressure on him, plus lots of silly bad press.

But as brigade commander, you're completely by yourself. If I'd been bollocked by Patrick I could ring up John Sharples and say, 'What do you think – was that fair?' Poor old Patrick had nobody to lean on. It was very tough. You forget how young we all were. He was forty-three, coming on forty-four, commanding ten thousand troops on the ground. We didn't want anybody else – for sure. We were very happy with Patrick.

Brigadier Patrick Cordingley
Commander, 7th Armoured Brigade

My immediate staff – Euan Loudon, the artillery CO Rory Clayton, Moore-Bick the sapper and my Deputy Chief of Staff – knew I was in trouble, and had clearly talked about it. They told me in no uncertain terms what they were going to relieve me of, to keep things going. They were hugely competent so this was very comforting.

This cemented our relationship, and we became very fond of each other. We were looking after twelve thousand people, and the logistics alone were extremely difficult. We also had to make sure that people did what was required to be ready, rather than what they thought they should be doing.

Major Rayson Pritchard
Public Information Officer, Royal Marines

After Brigadier Patrick Cordingley made himself accessible to the press – as he thought was necessary – he became very worried about their reactions. His problem was being too honest with them; then once it became obvious we were going to war, of baring his soul. His concern was over casualties, and doing what he thought was right to prepare the British public for people getting killed – which got him in hot water. But there was probably a bit of the loneliness of command about it too; that there wasn't anyone else he could talk to about his fears.

Lieutenant Colonel Arthur Denaro
Commanding Officer, Queen's Royal Irish Hussars
General de la Billiere came to visit us, and was pretty gloomy, with pessimistic predictions as to what might happen. I got very angry with my officers about not visiting our sick guys in hospital.

Maggi Denaro
Commanding Officer's wife, Queen's Royal Irish Hussars
We didn't think anything was actually going to happen. But then some senior people came to visit us from Rheindahlen [the headquarters for British forces in Germany], to tell us that if we went to war, thirty-three per cent would be killed and injured, which we thought alarmist, and made us grumpy. They said trained people would come from HQ and give us counselling; whereas we thought that if people were to die, we didn't want strangers coming in from outside, and that us wives with our fantastic padre, who all knew each other, should do it. But I don't know if this feeling was shared throughout the regiment.

I talked about this with some other wives and the welfare people in Rheindahlen, who said that if the predicted third of casualties came in, we'd be overwhelmed, so things would be taken out of our hands. This feeling of loss of autonomy was undermining and made us angry. But once we got into coping with all the day-to-day activities, this anger slowly dissipated and we calmed down. Staying positive was the most important thing.

Major Rayson Pritchard
Public Information Officer, Royal Marines
One of the journalists asked me, 'What is an armoured infantry battalion?' So I gave a series of impromptu lectures on the British Army; rather ironic, my being a Royal Marine. We then provided press facilities covering all the units, then tracing a letter from UK to the front line with the Royal Engineers, the logistic set-up, a facility on water and sanitation, minefield breaching.

Martin Bell
BBC Television

I was reduced to covering total trivia, like an RMP [Royal Military Police-man] directing the traffic with a little rat sticking its head out of his pocket. We did 'Mail Delivery' to 'Fraternal Visits to US Marines' – who had a completely different culture. With Patrick Cordingley's accent and so on, he was the absolute image of what they thought a British Army officer should be, so we enjoyed that.

Maggi Denaro
Commanding Officer's wife, Queen's Royal Irish Hussars

We put a bubble around ourselves to avoid things we didn't want to hear, for example the media coverage of the high casualty predictions. The media did seem to misinterpret a lot of what people said – especially Patrick Cordingley.

Our German wives stopped listening to German television and radio, which was full of doom, gloom and body bags, switching over to British Forces television. The all-day television coverage was pretty overwhelming.

There were German demonstrations against the war in the various towns around our barracks, but our own local community was very strongly support-ive of us, putting on children's parties for us at the schools, taking us out, and so on.

Brigadier Patrick Cordingley
Commander, 7th Armoured Brigade

On 28 October we were visited by the American Under-Secretary of State for Defense Policy, Paul Wolfowitz, who asked me what I felt we should do. I said a left flanking attack into Iraq, coming round into the Iraqis from the side. But I also said that this would probably be impossible as we only had a UN resolution to kick the Iraqis out of Kuwait, not to enter Iraq. I was rather fascinated to be the most junior commander, yet be asked for my view by an American under-secretary.

Afterwards I reported what I'd said up the British chain of command, and of course everybody was frightfully worried that I'd overstepped the mark, and said I should be monitored in the future, or forbidden to speak to these people! I thought this absolutely barking. I was part of an international coalition army, so why was my allegiance supposed to be so strongly attached to Great Britain's MoD, and why did they feel the need to control me? I never got away from the feeling that this was a silly way to go to war.

Lieutenant General Walter Boomer
General Officer Commanding, 1 Marine Expeditionary Force, United States Marine Corps

We spoke pretty freely to Wolfowitz and Secretary Cheney about the whole campaign. Cheney had his own ideas, which weren't what Schwarzkopf and I wanted. Cheney wanted to get his ideas out on to the table, but was fine about it once we'd sorted it all out. Colin Powell was always included in these conversations, which were very frank. There was a lot of give and take, and they listened to us. I don't remember Patrick overstepping the bounds in any of this. If there'd been any sort of dust-up, we would certainly have heard *all* about it.

Brigadier Patrick Cordingley
Commander, 7th Armoured Brigade

7 Brigade had now grown to almost the size of a division, so I was given a deputy commander – John Milne. We gave him accommodation, welfare and various parts of the logistics chain: we for example needed to set up 'Camp Four' to give the soldiers a recreational break from the desert. We kept him away from the actual command chain, which was already being run by my normal staff, a restriction that a lesser man would have found difficult – but he was a very good bloke.

My posting [as Commander] was due to end in December, with a staff officer in Riyadh, Tim Sullivan, already appointed to take over from me. Although I was too busy to think much about this or discuss it, I really did hope it wasn't going to happen. Had I needed replacing, it should have been by my deputy John Milne who by that stage knew everybody, and not Tim Sullivan. With the complexity of the operations we were developing, and the relationships with all the other nationalities around us, a totally new commander coming in would have been a real problem.

Lieutenant General Walter Boomer
General Officer Commanding, 1 Marine Expeditionary Force, United States Marine Corps

I learned a long time ago that I wasn't smart enough to do something like this by myself. I couldn't lock myself inside my trailer, then twelve hours later come out with a brilliant scheme to attack Kuwait. But I do understand how to get the best from my folks.

I always asked for ideas, e.g. gathering my senior commanders around a sand table and talking through operations. It was ultimately my decision and they all knew that, but I'd gather their best thoughts, and that's what would go into the plan. I'd then spend private time ruminating, then hold another session and in another week we'd have a couple of refinements, and a plan evolved. Although everyone's ideas weren't included, they'd been considered. We had the luxury of time to do this; but if you've got smart, combat-tested commanders working for you, not to listen to them is stupid.

I also spent a lot of time with my G2 [intelligence officers] trying to understand what we were up against. At night, I would try to think through what the enemy might do, particularly with chemicals. Up until the time we attacked, I'd work pretty late but was able to get a little sleep most nights.

Brigadier Patrick Cordingley
Commander, 7th Armoured Brigade

Things gradually got better for me; I began to get sleep, but still had problems getting in and out of my tank, and was more ratty than normal. Apparently I was pretty ratty anyway.

But there wasn't anyone I could pour my heart out to; I was pretty close to my Chief of Staff Euan Loudon, but he was younger and a major and I was the boss. My three Commanding Officers, Sharples, Denaro and Rogers, were very close indeed and could always go into an Arabic *fuddle* and chew the cud between themselves. They'd come along and have a chat with us, which was very good of them, but as I certainly couldn't pour out my heart to anyone in Riyadh, I did feel pretty isolated at times.

Lieutenant Colonel Arthur Denaro
Commanding Officer, Queen's Royal Irish Hussars

We had a brilliant chaplain, an Irish priest who'd been with us before. Everyone loved him and he was such good fun. More and more people came to his services, whether they were Catholic or not. I was able to talk with him, and he'd ask me how I was personally.

Sergeant Major Johnny Muir
Regimental Quartermaster Sergeant Major,
Queen's Royal Irish Hussars

For their long sea shipment, our tanks, vehicles and equipment had been put into care and preservation to prevent seawater damage, smeared with grease and so on, which had to be cleaned off, then everything serviced and prepared for action. Where there's oil and grease, sand finds it and sticks to it, so this was very uncomfortable.

And amid all this, lo and behold, our desert combats arrived! This meant I had six hundred men to measure then issue with three sets of this vital kit. I'd already worked out a plan for doing this, but the sudden delivery took away my remaining feelings of self-pity and uncertainty. The regiment was beginning to deploy out into the desert, so I created a mobile tailoring shop called 'Burton's Mobile Service' on a truck, and we fitted everybody out in the desert.

Major Rayson Pritchard
Public Information Officer, Royal Marines

About five days after the Queen's Royal Irish Hussars tanks arrived at Al Jubayl and were fitted with sand filters, their first squadron was moved by low-loader into the desert. We laid on another press facility for this, for the press go out to the desert, see the tanks arrive on the transporters, then film them whizzing up and down.

Literally as the first tank arrived, belching smoke with sand swirling everywhere, a herd of camels walked along on the ridge behind them, led by a local. The television crews and clickers were beside themselves at this, running around getting all the angles as the skylined camels moved slowly across the middle distance and the tanks came thundering past up close. After this had been going for ten minutes, one of the journalists asked, 'How the hell did you organise that?'

I told him, 'Don't ask. You do your job, I'll do mine.'

4 Platoon, of Number Two Company, 1 Grenadier Guards preparing their Warrior armoured personnel carriers for firing of Rarden cannons, at Munsterlager ranges in Germany. Lieutenant Ruadhri Duncan on turret

Preparing newly arrived Warrior armoured personnel carriers at Al Jubayl

Second Lieutenant Alistair Watkins, Number Two Company, 1 Grenadier Guards

Dr Mary McLoughlin (right) with Chris Duckling, her partner, and Iraqi friends, at a New Year's Eve party in Baghdad on 31 December 1990

Major General Alexander Harley

The Commanding Officers of 7th Armoured Brigade: Lieutenant Colonels Arthur Denaro QRIH, John Sharples Scots DG and Charles Rogers of The Staffords

Lieutenant Toby Masterton of The Life Guards

Hashim Ali, standing, with a friend and fellow freedom fighter Ehsan, taking their turn as bakers for their resistance group in 1983–84 in the high mountain area of Lolan in Iraqi Kurdistan

The Staffords briefing

Platoon runners from
Number Two Company
HQ, 1 Grenadier Guards
waiting to carry the
order to enter the
minefield breach back
to their platoons

A Warrior of Number Two Company,
The Grenadier Guards driving to
main assembly area

CQMS Paul Ladd, Number Two
Company, 1 Grenadier Guards
replenishing the Warriors with
GPMG ammunition

Sergeant Shaun Rusling, Parachute Regiment resus medic

Major Ray Pritchard making the first satellite telephone call, testing the new equipment on its arrival in the desert. He phoned home

© ALISTAIR WATKINS

Number Two Company, 1 Grenadier Guards, stood to wearing NBC equipment early in the deployment before desert camouflage suits were issued

13 Squadron detachment to Dhahran. *From left to right:* Flight Lieutenant Mike Stanway (Pilot), Flight Lieutenant Tom Perham (Navigator), Flight Lieutenant Andy Tucker (Navigator), Squadron Leader Brian Robinson (Pilot), Group Captain Glenn Torpy (Pilot and squadron commander), Squadron Leader Roger Bennett (Navigator), Flight Lieutenant Gordon Walker (Navigator)

© CHARLES ROGERS

The Staffords battlegroup lined up
'Dover docks' style, ready to pass
through the minefield breach

A burning Iraqi oil well
near the Basra Road

© CHARLES ROGERS

Martin Bell
BBC Television

We were courted by the military in their preparatory phase – an expectable attempt to get us onside. There were lovely little acts of stage management, for example when we first visited the QRIH. We were greeted outside a large tent by the adjutant, Captain Cuthbert, who treated us to a huge spiel about the traditions of the regiment, the history of Balaclava, the Charge of the Light Brigade, Winston Churchill and the whole shooting match, before being ushered into the presence of Colonel Arthur Denaro. It was choreographed, but they were nevertheless very forthcoming.

Lieutenant Colonel Arthur Denaro
Commanding Officer, Queen's Royal Irish Hussars

In the desert, I imposed very strict discipline, to the extent that some people asked if I wasn't being too strict – or over-keen. But we needed to become operational.

We'd 'Stand To' every morning and evening, even though the enemy were hundreds of miles away. We'd never emerge from under our cam nets unless fully kitted with body armour, helmet, weapon and gas mask, or show lights or make noise at night.

This discipline was difficult to achieve, as the regiment was spread out over fifty miles of desert. In the troop positions, the tanks were twenty to fifty metres apart, under cam nets.

It was also a personal discipline for me, getting up every morning at four, to walk round all the HQ and battle group positions to see everyone as they were standing-to in their trenches. I'd talk to the boys every morning and evening, until it became second nature to us all. But there was a real sense of pride that we were good and getting better, especially driving past other units, with no cam up, or lights on all over the place.

Brigadier Patrick Cordingley
Commander, 7th Armoured Brigade

The area commander was a delightful Saudi admiral who gave us permission to set up ranges [which were called 'Devil Dog Dragoon Range' after the US Marines' nickname, and Cordingley's regiment the 5th Royal Inniskilling Dragoon Guards], but said we had to liaise with the Saudi air force which controlled the airspace. At a meeting with two Saudi air force officers, who both spoke perfect English, one asked me the ricochet height of a 120mm tank gun. As you can imagine, I had absolutely no idea, and guessed something like five thousand feet. Afterwards I did quietly ask our liaison officer, Rod Trevaskus, to find out what it really was – some enormous height like forty-five thousand feet!

They gave us permission to fire for a couple of hours in the morning and again in the evening. We needed to do very realistic fire and manoeuvre exercises, with artillery, tanks, and infantry, but we didn't have any safety staff as we would in Germany, so this was going to be very dodgy. The desert had undulations, so the tanks would be driving fast round corners, firing on the move through thick dust and so on – not to mention the infantry's weapons and the artillery. I remember thinking, 'We're going to kill people here.'

Lieutenant Colonel Arthur Denaro
Commanding Officer, Queen's Royal Irish Hussars
Because the desert is so strange and different, with no roads, rivers or woods, learning to survive and work effectively is very important. I was the only person in the regiment who'd been in the desert before – as an SAS officer in Oman. It took everybody that first month just to get used to it, especially the young soldiers, and the discipline provided something on which to lean when uncertain or bewildered. Apart from a couple of very early contraventions, which resulted in my sacking one crew commander and removing a couple of others, the boys were utterly disciplined throughout – which being an Irish regiment was remarkable!

Brigadier Patrick Cordingley
Commander, 7th Armoured Brigade
The only time I talked to Peter de la Billiere in Riyadh, I told him I was worried we would kill people during the training. He told me that was to be expected. I also said I was concerned about the media saying the inefficient British Army can't even train without killing its own people, but General de la Billiere told me he would take responsibility for this aspect of it, which I thought very good of him.

In the end, we didn't kill anybody, but we did wound six people, mostly from throwing grenades. On a German training range, there's always a safety trench to jump into if somebody mishandles or drops a grenade – not here. Also, some people weren't lying down flat enough after throwing them and took shrapnel wounds, which taught them a lesson or two.

Lieutenant Colonel Arthur Denaro
Commanding Officer, Queen's Royal Irish Hussars

Being dry was very helpful to us. I'd come from teaching at the Australian staff college. Their hard-drinking roughnecks simply didn't drink on exercise, so I thought if the Australians can do it, so can the Irish Hussars. So, *mostly*, we were dry.

Brigadier Patrick Cordingley
Commander, 7th Armoured Brigade

Devil Dog Dragoon Range provided twelve miles to manoeuvre and fire the tanks, plus another ten miles' safety distance. Camels were a real problem, as they all belonged to somebody, and if we killed one we had to pay compensation. Of course, every dead one was a hugely valuable, racing camel.

We started off with low-level training, then company and squadron training, progressing as quickly as possible into our battle groups. The artillery was used throughout, bringing it down as close as possible so people could get used to it. Not having safety staff added to the danger – especially at night; but it was realistic.

Lieutenant Colonel Arthur Denaro
Commanding Officer, Queen's Royal Irish Hussars

A and D squadrons fired on time at 0815 hours, and then made an extremely fast exciting run over nine kilometres with each tank firing forty rounds, standing still and on the move. The firing was very accurate and very sharp. We did the same thing in the afternoon, but this was not as good, with several interruptions when camels and aircraft came on to the range.

Brigadier Patrick Cordingley
Commander, 7th Armoured Brigade

We were now driving round, fully bombed up and ready to fight. One of my major problems emerged at this stage, when Master General of the Ordnance Jeremy Blacker rocked up, seeming very discreet and awkward, saying he needed to talk to me. They'd discovered the Challenger bag charges for the fin-stabilised APDS [armour-piercing discarding sabot] rounds were 'rather volatile, that if a tank got a direct hit, piercing one of the bag charge containers, there could be a spontaneous reaction, the whole tank detonating.'

'Thank you very much for telling me that,' said I. 'But what do you expect me to do about it?'

He said, 'You've got to re-store all your tanks, separating the volatile charges, so that in theory they're less likely to spontaneously detonate. But you can't tell your soldiers why they're doing this.'

In other words, ordering one hundred and twenty-one experienced crews to change the way they've always stored up their tanks, but without any explanation. They're not stupid and would want to know why, with all sorts of stories going round.

'OK,' said I. 'But supposing I don't do that?'

'That's your call,' he replied.

So I decided not to do what the Master General of the Ordnance had told me.

Lieutenant Colonel Arthur Denaro
Commanding Officer, Queen's Royal Irish Hussars

Unlike our poor ancestors in the Second World War, whose tanks had petrol engines, a modern diesel-engine tank doesn't 'brew' ['brew up' is army slang for a tank catching fire] like that, so on the eve of going into battle, being told that they would was very bad news. The UK scientists did this from time to time.

We discussed whether to tell our people, and decided not to. There were enough frightening things going on with Saddam talking about 'trenches of fire' and 'the Mother and Father of all battles', without setting off all sorts of other hares.

Brigadier Patrick Cordingley
Commander, 7th Armoured Brigade

From that moment, for me the fire and movement exercises were a rack of worry. I knew from studies of the Second World War that seeing a tank brew up is very depressing for other tank men. If one spontaneously brewed, I'd have my people not wanting to get into their tanks. MoD were developing non-volatile bag charges, so I hoped this problem would be resolved before the fighting began. But this added to the pressure the media were creating for me, and of the training and keeping my soldiers up to the mark. I could have done without it.

Lieutenant General Walter Boomer
General Officer Commanding, 1 Marine Expeditionary Force, United States Marine Corps

Our intelligence was mostly what we generated ourselves, or obtained from captured Iraqi prisoners who'd given up then walked across the line, tired, dirty and hungry. This trickle increased, and although it never became a flow, I grew confident that the Iraqi force had pretty low morale and wasn't being supported properly by Baghdad.

The prisoners we were taking didn't understand why the hell they were in Kuwait, although they knew they'd moved into somebody else's country, and were being asked to defend it – as contrasted with the last war [the Iraq invasion of 2003], when we were moving into *their* country.

Lieutenant Colonel Arthur Denaro
Commanding Officer, Queen's Royal Irish Hussars

Brigade headquarters told us that a second brigade might be coming out with a divisional headquarters – which we thought a nightmare!

We cancelled training because we'd exceeded our tanks' permitted track mileage before even starting. I had fifty-seven out of my fifty-eight tanks still on the road, after using only twelve engine packs.

Brigadier Patrick Cordingley
Commander, 7th Armoured Brigade

When an American tank needed a new engine, their huge new engineering factory in Saudi Arabia would make one. Ours had to be flown back to Germany, repaired, then flown back out again. Tank engines are very heavy, so this took up a lot of aircraft space. There was a continual battle deciding what actually needed to be flown out of Germany: ammunition, spare parts, normal replacement kit, plus the mail – which in itself was a huge problem.

To start with, our mail was mostly 'blueys' – free airmail letters – going backwards and forwards until towards Christmas, when the British newspapers got behind us, creating a huge surge of parcels. The army postal depot at Mill Hill, and our transport into the desert, couldn't cope. At this point I was asked what my priorities were. I opted to have all the Christmas parcels, rather than a couple of extra tank engines.

Lieutenant Colonel Arthur Denaro
Commanding Officer, Queen's Royal Irish Hussars

Our families went through a very testing time. A nineteen-year-old trooper was likely to have a seventeen-year-old wife with a baby on her knee and quite possibly another one in her belly, very young and bloody frightened, a world away from their families and home communities in the depths of Belfast, from where many of our soldiers come.

But I'm lucky that I've got a brilliant wife, the widow of an SAS officer herself, who knew what it was like for her husband to be away on operations – not just with Mike, but with me as well. She knew what care the families needed. I had a very good QM who was a bit too old to be out in the desert, so I sent him back to administer the families, which he did brilliantly.

But we also had two hundred individual reinforcements from other regiments. I personally met them on arrival and shook each by the hand, to make them feel warmly welcomed and part of our team right from the start. Maggi would write to their families, even if they were from England or anywhere else, so they felt part of a unit that really cared for them. This word 'care' has now got sloppy connotations through overuse, but that's what was required. The people joining at the last minute were coming into a very, very tight team.

Sergeant Major Johnny Muir
Regimental Quartermaster Sergeant Major,
Queen's Royal Irish Hussars

As the regiment deployed into the desert, I was posted away to run the newly established brigade base camp – Camp Four – promoted to be its Regimental Sergeant Major. I didn't want to leave the regiment, but although I hadn't been ordered to do it, I accepted the job. I was working under a Scots Dragoon Guard colonel who I already knew, in the unfamiliar environment of the brigade headquarters. I hoped this wouldn't lessen my chance of being RSM of the Irish Hussars.

Lieutenant Colonel Arthur Denaro
Commanding Officer, Queen's Royal Irish Hussars

We were expecting delivery of hugely secret depleted uranium [DU] rounds – long darts, which being exceptionally dense and heavy would give us increased range, accuracy and penetration. When they finally arrived, each tank was issued with five.

We were told to tell our crews that they were not to enter any vehicle hit by a DU round, but very specifically that we were also *not* to tell them the reason why.*

WO1 Johnny Muir
Regimental Sergeant Major, Camp Four

There were some very different units in Camp Four: a huge field hospital with many TA soldiers, Pioneer Corps, divisional signals, headquarters staff and all sorts of others. In addition, these units had their own very experienced RSMs, who had to accept that even though the new kid on the block, I was in charge of the camp and of saying how it was going to run. I had to be diplomatic, and felt a long way from my own regimental family.

Second Lieutenant Alistair Watkins
1st Battalion Grenadier Guards

We were part of 4th Armoured Brigade. I drove home on leave, but the adjutant phoned my mother to order me to return immediately as we were to go to the Gulf. No one had imagined we might be sent anywhere at short notice on operational duty. The Russians were our big worry. This caused enormous upset with my mother, sister and girlfriend, who thought the end was coming.

This weekend was so full of massive family upset and tears that by Sunday night I'd had enough and couldn't wait to get back to the battalion. I drove back in convoy with my best friend in the battalion, Charlie Allsopp, who'd had the same family experience.

---

* DU or depleted uranium is much heavier, harder and denser than tungsten or lead, and so retains far more kinetic energy. The long darts of DU broke up in the process of penetrating Iraqi vehicles, creating radio-active metallic dust which was dangerous to inhale. Cancers and various other Gulf War medical problems are attributed to this.

Major General Rupert Smith
General Officer Commanding, 1st Armoured Division

After a week commanding 1st Division, the Corps Commander told me we were going to the Gulf. I was told my division was the most mature and worked up in the Corps at that time.

However, this was going to be very different to the predictable, rather nice exercises of the North German Plain, with which most people had become far too familiar. We were going to attack, not defend. All our equipment, tactics and processes had been developed for the defence of Germany rather than attacking into Iraq, so people would have to get used to doing things they'd never done before.

Second Lieutenant Alistair Watkins
1st Battalion Grenadier Guards

The battalion was in full frenzy – having been running down, about to return to UK. We were now being split up to reinforce other battle groups, our CO left without a battalion. I'd been a platoon commander in Number Three Company, but when it was split up to reinforce the others, as the most junior officer in the battalion, I lost my platoon and was assigned as a watchkeeper with Number Two Company. All the platoons were under-strength, sucking dry the remainder of the battalion. Losing my platoon was rather challenging.

Major General Rupert Smith
General Officer Commanding, 1st Armoured Division

I knew my Division's equipment and lots of the people, ex-staff college students, and a high percentage of airborne and Parachute Regiment officers. But I soon identified a group of men who were not comfortable with this new enterprise, promoted through years in Germany. These people knew only the annual BAOR routine, in which everything is known. But in a war, sticking your plan on the wall for all to see isn't very sensible.

So from the beginning, I was deliberately denying people information they were used to knowing. This required them to believe in their superiors, even though things might not make sense to them. Only in late January did I tell everybody what we were going to do. The logistics, supply and mainte-nance problems were also very new, so the need to get people confident enough for all this to work was something I knew I'd have to develop once we got out to the Gulf.

I'd moved into the GOC's house, but because my children were at boarding school, my family hadn't moved in yet.

Major General Alexander Harley
Assistant Chief of Defence Staff (Overseas) and Deputy Director of Joint Operations, Ministry of Defence, Whitehall

When British troops go under the command of a coalition, we always strive for an additional straight-line national command in case anything goes wrong; in the Gulf this was General de la Billiere, in Schwarzkopf's headquarters, holding a red card and authorised to say 'No, that's not consistent with my instructions and we won't do it'.

Peter de la Billiere was very well regarded by Schwarzkopf and, by virtue of our providing a division and other very tight arrangements with Americans, had a seat at the table in Schwarzkopf's inner sanctum. We also had British planning staff throughout the American headquarters, which no other coalition members had.

Major Rayson Pritchard
Public Information Officer, Royal Marines

The live-firing battle runs were a big press facility, to which Tom King came from London, accompanied by the big hitters from London like John Keegan and Robert Fox. Tom King gave a press conference from under a cam net, and, on the night live-firing battle runs, we put camera crews on to the tanks and Warriors; impressive, very high-impact stuff, rehearsed and staged specifically for the media.

Tom King spoke for about fifteen minutes, giving an overview and making some announcements. He also mentioned the American's MRE 'Meals-Ready-to-Eat', repeating their joke of calling them 'Meals Rejected by Ethiopians' which the journalists scribbled down. My boss turned to me and whispered, 'That's five more hours' work for me tonight'.

The next morning, I read everyone's articles to see how they'd reported the same press conference. Each was quite different. I hadn't realised that the stories that make up world news depend on one person's opinion.

WO1 Johnny Muir
Regimental Sergeant Major, Camp Four

A major in the medical unit phoned asking did we have any body bags. I asked why, and was told, 'Don't be stupid – it's to put a body in.' Naively, I asked if this was for a training exercise, and he said, 'No, we've just had a death.'

The camp commandant and I found a gathering of military police at a tragic scene in which a soldier had put his SA80 under his chin and pulled the trigger. This soldier would have showed traits that, if identified, could have prevented him doing this – at least that's what would have happened in the Irish Hussars. All these units needed to start pulling together.

I'd brought a body bag, then a Pioneer Corps NCO delivered a roughly made coffin – not something you'd see in the back of a hearse – making me realise just how basic things were going to be.

Then out in the desert, an officer in the Royal Corps of Transport was killed; two soldiers lost from our brigade before we'd even heard a shot fired in anger.

Brigadier Patrick Cordingley
Commander, 7th Armoured Brigade

We declared ourselves ready and were given a slot in the Marines defensive position on their left flank, next door to the 24th Infantry Division of the First US Army. Their Commander, General Barry McCaffrey, sent a Black-hawk helicopter to pick me up, and we flew over their position. It was staggeringly large. A quarter of a million US troops had arrived by that stage, and amid all their divisional and corps commanders, there was 'little old me'. I quickly came to respect the way they were going about business.

Major General Rupert Smith
General Officer Commanding, 1st Armoured Division

Out in Saudi, the focus, from General Schwarzkopf downwards, was on getting everything out there, rather than what we might eventually do. This didn't worry me, as I had the same problem.

I met the US Marine commander General Walt Boomer, and was well briefed by Patrick Cordingley. I could see how firmly embedded they both were. We flew back to UK on 19 November, for a big meeting with Air Marshal Paddy Hine and his staff. Most I didn't know, but Paddy Hine had known me since I was a teenager, when he'd been my father's adjutant and had tested me for my motorcycle driving licence. This made me feel easier.

To much RAF sucking of teeth, and long looks from certain senior airmen, Paddy Hine gave me command of *all* the helicopters. Their barely muted disapproval stopped when Paddy Hine asked, 'Who else are the helicopters working for?' I was also to have six Hercules transport aircraft: two from the Royal New Zealand Air Force, to resupply us by parachute, and take out casualties.

Lieutenant Colonel Arthur Denaro
Commanding Officer, Queen's Royal Irish Hussars
I visited the field hospital to see Corporal Nulty and others. The large number of medics rather alarmed us: plus I found them a most scruffy, badly led lot. But I heard (and hoped) they were good medics.

Brigadier Patrick Cordingley
Commander, 7th Armoured Brigade
The medics were a problem. 32 Field Hospital, with four hundred and fifty beds, was far larger than most UK hospitals, made up from a huge number of TA and regular establishments, with three full colonels, each thinking they were in charge – a recipe for disaster. Because they were from so many disparate units with nothing to do, their morale was very low and getting worse. My having to deal with the disagreements of these three colonels made me recognise they were affecting everyone further down the line.

So we instituted a programme called 'Love a Little Bit of 32 Field Hospital' which the soldiers much enjoyed – at the thought of getting to the nurses. Each regiment would take a group from the hospital out into the field, practise casualty evacuation, showing them how everything worked and what they were doing. We expected a lot of casualties, so this was important.

Lieutenant Colonel Charles Rogers
Commanding Officer, Staffordshire Regiment
We were very concerned about medical cover. I wasn't worried about my team's ability to treat people, but I was worried about them getting lost. I gave each an infantry captain, an infantry sergeant to get their defence and admin sorted out, plus an infantry corporal clerk to ensure we didn't lose track of where people were.

The biggest nightmare is not knowing where your soldiers are, particularly as the distances we'd be moving over would be so vast. Getting the wounded to the field hospital depended on helicopters being available.

Major General Rupert Smith
General Officer Commanding, 1st Armoured Division

I'd been told our Challengers were to be up-armoured – but the huge number of aircraft flights the heavy armour would take up would delay flying out other things.

I said, 'But what about our other armoured vehicles?'

'No,' they said, 'we're only up-armouring the Challengers.'

So I'd refused to have *any* of the tanks up-armoured unless the other armoured vehicles were up-armoured as well. Tanks can stand off from the enemy and fire at over three kilometres, whereas the infantry, and people like artillery forward observation officers, would be working much closer to the enemy.

It took more than ten days to get the MoD to realise that I wasn't going to put soldiers into battle with the tanks far better protected than everybody else. It was a very interesting row, and a really difficult point to get accepted – all to do with morale.

Brigadier Patrick Cordingley
Commander, 7th Armoured Brigade

Out in the desert, people were sleeping by their vehicles, so when not on radio watch, would be in their sleeping bags for around twelve hours. We realised after a while that they were becoming introverted and worrying too much, so we decided to create dugouts with light-proofed tents where they could meet up, talk and play games. The SSVC [the welfare charity, Services Sound and Vision Corporation] pumped out chess sets, dartboards, television sets, videos and so on. We also tried to provide some centralised cooking so they could eat with the rest of their squadron; but it was still compo, compo, compo with some bread and eggs, but no vegetables.

Lieutenant Colonel Arthur Denaro
Commanding Officer, Queen's Royal Irish Hussars

I insisted that the boys needed a break away from the officers, so, as well as the soldiers' recreation camp 'St Patricks', we created an officers' mess tent 'Zero Hotel' as part of the headquarters, for when we weren't moving. It had a six-foot trestle table, camp chairs, with a fridge and fan in one corner, tattered copies of *Country Life*, and a framed photograph of Montgomery of Alamein. There's no point wearing a hair shirt in war when you don't have to.

Brigadier Patrick Cordingley
Commander, 7th Armoured Brigade

I could visit all my units, but getting in amongst the soldiers was the important bit. I'd say I had twenty minutes to spare, could anybody give me a game of chess? Corporal Smith would be volunteered, and he usually won because I was rather more listening to all the banter going on all around me and joining in. I'd also join people when they were eating: sharing their baked beans, they could ask me questions.

Lieutenant Colonel Arthur Denaro
Commanding Officer, Queen's Royal Irish Hussars

Patrick knew he was always welcome at our respective headquarters, but being a cavalry officer, he inclined more towards the Scots DG or ourselves, than the Staffords, who lived a more austere life: Charlie Rogers lived in a trench beside his Warrior.

Brigadier Patrick Cordingley
Commander, 7th Armoured Brigade

Living the way we did in the desert, I couldn't shut myself away from people, which was a problem sometimes. I'd tell people to push off so I could think something through, and sit in the back of my 432 [an armoured personnel carrier]. I was otherwise available all the time to everybody, which was wearing, but terribly important that people know you're about with their interests at heart. I had great confidence in everyone.

Major General Rupert Smith
General Officer Commanding, 1st Armoured Division

The next two weeks in Germany were a blur of long days and late nights. 3rd Division was to train and despatch all our units, which took a great deal of effort away from me. At some point in November, I went across to UK to say goodbye to my boys at school.

My headquarters was very good. Its Chief of Staff, John Reith, had been a company commander of mine when I was a [Parachute Regiment] CO. He had an enormous grip on the detail and the intelligence and operations side, allowing me to concentrate on thinking about the future. My Colonel AQ was the chief administrator and quartermaster, and between them they ran the HQ, with the chief of staff being *primus inter pares*.

The HQ was split into a main HQ running operations and intelligence, and a rear HQ concentrating on admin, maintenance and repair of equipment, and logistics. Various commanders were in charge of artillery, engineers, medical, transport and so on, with their own small headquarters as part of the main HQ. One doesn't tell them what to do, but gives them missions, leaving them to plan in parallel with me how they're going to do it, speeding things up enormously. The Commander Royal Signals, in addition to being responsible for the communications of the HQ, is also responsible for its administration – feeding, movement, camouflage, guarding and so on. At brigade level, the same structure was mirrored at a smaller scale.

Brigadier Patrick Cordingley
Commander, 7th Armoured Brigade

Now that we were ready, my next problem was what were we going to do with our twelve thousand soldiers day by day, for an indefinite period of time? This was complicated by the British soldier being used to working six-month tours in Northern Ireland.

But once 4th Armoured Brigade arrived, we'd have all the British Army's spare tank engines, but also all the people trained to use them. There *were* no replacements, of soldiers or equipment, so people were realising that they could be here for more than six months.

Major Rayson Pritchard
Public Information Officer, Royal Marines

On Thanksgiving Day, President George Bush came over, to visit an army, marine and air force unit, a ship at sea and an airbase, then fly straight out again.

There were one hundred and twenty American media people already in Riyadh. An additional one hundred and fifty arrived the day before, plus the usual White House media on board Air Force One, with more in a follow-up Jumbo. The JIB was housed in the International Hilton. Normally its putting green was occupied by a couple of foil-lined tents with satellite dishes, and a small cable run into the hotel through the back door, which wouldn't close.

By the time Bush arrived, this area was covered with tents and dishes, with a two-foot diameter cable run back into the hotel. Each visit location facility had live feeds back to a newly erected media tent, with rows of desks, microphones, and images projected on to a huge screen. We sat back and watched this awesome, massive media circus in action – typifying the might of the American media in action.

Lieutenant General Walter Boomer
General Officer Commanding, 1 Marine Expeditionary Force, United States Marine Corps

When the President and Mrs Bush came out to the desert, they couldn't see every marine, so we told each unit to send a certain number of representatives – a lot of people, all armed, carrying ammunition. The Secret Service said nobody was to have a weapon anywhere around the president. I said, 'Wrong.' They then said nobody could have any ammunition, to which I also said, 'Wrong, but obviously none of the weapons will be loaded.'

Mrs Bush was a very attractive lady, a real trouper who, with her grey hair, could have been the mother to most of our troops. They all wanted to say 'Hello, Mrs Bush', and for her to sign the back of their jacket or something. Her handler – a female – told me the marines needed to back off. But Mrs Bush was having such a great time, so I told this woman *she* should back off.

When it came time for her to leave, Mrs Bush got in with me, and as we drove to where the helicopter was waiting, a line of troops formed up spontaneously shouting, 'Goodbye, Mrs Bush, thank you for coming.' It was a very, very touching moment. She had tears running down her cheeks, so I said, 'Mrs Bush, if you don't stop that, you'll have me crying too, which would not be a good thing for the Commander's image.' Somebody took a photograph of her saying goodbye to me beside the helicopter door, which later she signed for me, and is now beside my desk.

CHAPTER 4

FURTHER REINFORCEMENT

Having stripped out the British Army in Germany to send one greatly enhanced armoured brigade over fifteen thousand-strong, the UK government realised that its position in the coalition as the largest non-Arab contributor and the main ally of the US depended on sending a much larger formation – at least an armoured division.

This 'second wave' of units from 4th Armoured Brigade, plus the huge 1st Armoured Division headquarters with its artillery, logistics and other units, which would bring the British contingent to over thirty-five thousand, faced even more problems than 7th Armoured Brigade. There was also a growing realisation that Operation Desert Shield was becoming very much larger and more challenging than anybody could have imagined.

So while the first wave of 7th Armoured Brigade units trained in the desert, in Germany and in the UK, the remainder of the force assembled and loaded, a process made very much more difficult by the British government's continued reluctance to understand the army's force requirements and agree numbers.

7th Armoured Brigade was soon to finish training then join the Americans in the defensive line on the Kuwait border. This necessitated a large move from its desert training area. But before this could take place, politicians and military chiefs had to decide whether the British force would be fighting with the US Marines in their attack up the coast to capture Kuwait City, or in the desert with the US Army 7th Corps, against the Iraqi tank army.

Lieutenant Colonel Mike Vickery
Commanding Officer, 14th/20th King's Hussars,
4th Armoured Brigade

My tanks were now empty hulks, and the soldiers I still had were very tired.
I was then told 4th Brigade was to be out in the Gulf before Christmas, with
our tanks.

This was a real 'Oh shit' moment. How the hell were we going to get fifty-
eight working tanks? I also realised that if they needed to double the numbers
out there so quickly, they must be expecting an actual war very much bigger
than they'd first thought.

All this took place on the day that Thatcher was ousted by the Tories –
two pretty earth-shattering events on the one day.

The Rt Hon John Major
Prime Minister

I'd been Chancellor of the Exchequer – and on holiday – when I first read
news reports of the Iraqis moving into Kuwait. It was clear that unless diplomatic efforts evicted them quickly, the situation could escalate rapidly. I
remember thinking that this was going to cause us a great deal of trouble, and
put us to a great deal of expense.

After we came back from recess, there was the great crisis inside the Conservative Party. In November, Margaret [Thatcher] resigned, we had a leadership
election and I became prime minister. By that time, it was clear that within a
few weeks of my becoming prime minister, we were going to have a war.

The Rt Hon Tom King
UK Secretary of State for Defence

The ousting of Prime Minister Thatcher was a very difficult, distracting time.
I was totally involved with the war, so had to let everything else wash over
me. With Douglas Hurd as Foreign Secretary and me as Defence Secretary
remaining in position and working as usual, we had continuity, so it wasn't
like a general election and a government changing completely.

Major General Rupert Smith
General Officer Commanding, 1st Armoured Division

Mrs Thatcher was suddenly deposed in a coup. Within twenty-four hours the battle group commanders were telling me, 'This man Major had better get out here as quickly as possible as he's no Thatcher and the soldiers all want to know who he is.'

My message back to UK crossed over with a message coming the other way saying 'The prime minister will be arriving tomorrow and is yours for the day'.

I got 4th Armoured Brigade laid out so we could fly over it to show him what it looks like on the move. We landed, he talked with soldiers, and by the end of the day there was no question that he'd sold himself.

The Rt Hon John Major
Prime Minister

Saddam was a wonderful opponent, because he was such a hateful figure. If any war can be popular this one was, in terms of public perception of its desirability and justification. Saddam had invaded a neighbouring nation. Had he not been stopped, he would have continued on, right down the Gulf, which would have been catastrophic to the peace of the Middle East and much else besides. So there was no doubt in my mind that justification for the war was rock-solid.

Saddam's internal repression put many of the people who would normally have opposed the war into a difficult position, and therefore neutered their opposition. Neil Kinnock [the Labour leader] was supportive, although there were dissenters in Parliament: the usual anti-war grouping, predominantly on the Labour side. But many of the Labour Party were as hawkish as any Conservative. As a result, I had no significant party political problems – although, as I recall, Congress offered President Bush only a narrow majority for action. It was very different with the Northern Ireland peace process.

The Rt Hon Tom King
UK Secretary of State for Defence

John Major was a very quick learner and backed everything we were doing. But I'd been travelling round the Middle East reminding everyone of Mrs Thatcher's unwavering leadership in the Falklands campaign. So three weeks later, I had to go back to the Middle East and say, 'Well, whatever I told you before, don't think anything has changed; the new prime minister is behind everything we're doing.'

It wasn't the ideal time to change prime minister, put it that way.

Lieutenant Colonel Mike Vickery
Commanding Officer, 14th/20th King's Hussars,
4th Armoured Brigade

All sorts of equipment was rolling in. Worn-out power packs were being rebuilt and sent to us. 7 Brigade had taken my Mark II Challengers, so we had to take all their discarded, older Mark I's and get them working for us.

You have to do a lot of things to a tank to get it exactly how you want it, for example five different sights to be zeroed on the turret, hours of painstaking work on the ranges. Our first shipment of tanks had to sail on 9 December, giving us two weeks to reassemble the hulks, zero at Bergen-Hohne firing ranges [NATO firing ranges in Germany], followed by a firing camp at way beyond the usual standard. When we'd done that, we repeated it all at night, which we'd never done before.

I was given a squadron of Life Guards, commanded by James Hewitt. I went to see them, out in the freezing bloody cold of Bergen-Hohne ranges. I hopped out of my tank, wrapped up nice and warm in my parka, to see lots of guardsmen looking terribly smart, but wearing only overalls. They were cutting about with great efficiency, but were all absolutely bloody freezing as it was minus five. I grabbed the first few I saw and asked them why the hell they weren't wearing parkas.

'We're not allowed to wear parkas, sir.'

'Why not?'

'Because the boss says so.'

I then got hold of James Hewitt, who told me, 'No, this is a Life Guards thing; they've got to look smart.'

'James – actually, this is not a *good* idea. If people's hands get cold, they can't work the electronic controls. They need to be warm. Never mind about being smart. Get them into their parkas now.'

If you really want to be a good tanker, you've got to get dirty and oily and keep warm. There's no use trying to look pretty. And thus began a sort of 'de-Guardsman-ification' of the Life Guards.

But this took nothing away from the Life Guards. They were bloody good tankers – just had too much of an eye for how they looked. I didn't give a stuff about how shiny their boots were, and quietly persuaded them to spend the time working on their tank – and avoiding getting cold.

Second Lieutenant Alistair Watkins
1st Battalion Grenadier Guards

The grand setting of our *Wehrmacht* barracks adding to the surreal, old-fashioned feeling of 'going to war'. We had a Ladies' Night, everyone in mess kit with all the wives, which kicked off down one end of the table with the subalterns throwing soup and spraying each other with champagne.

There was some very bad behaviour: mad piss-ups, people smashing things up, one platoon commander losing his command. People were going downtown and buying themselves pistols like Walther PPKs, which they took with them. I can't imagine now that people could behave like that.

We were also told that nobody would be allowed to go back home for Christmas, so my girlfriend flew out to see me a few times. Christmas hanging around the mess in Germany was rather bizarre. I couldn't wait to get on with it.

Lieutenant Colonel Mike Vickery
Commanding Officer, 14th/20th King's Hussars,
4th Armoured Brigade

4th Brigade Commander [Christopher Hammerbeck] went out to the Gulf on recce, and while he was away, I was very nearly sacked. The problem occurred when the Divisional Commander, an infantryman, came flying in unannounced to the ranges, expecting we'd be whizzing all over the place firing off rounds on the move, like the tactical exercises he'd seen other regiments doing. It didn't help that he talked with one of the sergeant majors before talking to me, who'd told him we'd only fired six rounds all morning.

But we were zeroing the guns; firing a shot, adjusting the sights on to the target, then firing again until totally accurate, each shot exactly the same, with a cold barrel each time. It takes an hour for the barrel to cool down, so this process can't be speeded up.

He was furious. I tried explaining, but he told me not to blame my equipment!

It's a wonderful and easy 'Generalish' thing to do – putting people on to the defensive then stomping all over them, and once on the defensive I was lost. So to allow the boys to get on with the job, I had to absorb all this crap.

When my Brigade Commander returned from his recce I told him, but I don't believe he told the General he'd got it wrong. In any case, if he did, it made no difference, as afterwards, the General wouldn't change my report. I later learned Rupert Smith was told I should be replaced. He had decided I should remain in command, but the incident really pissed me off and the feeling that I was under a cloud was no way to start a wartime command.

Lieutenant General Walter Boomer
General Officer Commanding, 1 Marine Expeditionary Force,
United States Marine Corps

There were only two ways for us to liberate Kuwait: to attack straight up through the prepared Iraqi defensive positions, or attack from the sea – the latter proving too daunting.

I believed the straight-up attack would ultimately be successful, with reasonable numbers of casualties, but people were looking at every other option. As we 'worse-cased' the casualty figures, everyone became very concerned, particularly as 'worst-case' involved the Iraqi use of chemical weapons. I'm sure this influenced de la Billiere and others in their thinking.

Brigadier Patrick Cordingley
Commander, 7th Armoured Brigade

The American Marines were thinking very carefully, determined not to lose lives, to avoid another Vietnam – even though they didn't mind how many Iraqis died. But they were also determined not to do it until they were ready, and at that stage 'ready' meant bringing in more soldiers.

Lieutenant General Walter Boomer
General Officer Commanding, 1 Marine Expeditionary Force,
United States Marine Corps

After a while it became clear to Schwarzkopf and me, there was a move afoot to take the British brigade away from the Marines and give them to General Freddie Franks and the US Army Corps. Both Patrick Cordingley and I felt this would be a mistake, because even then we knew, despite some obstacles being thrown into our path, that we were going to be the ones to liberate Kuwait.

From a publicity perspective, it would have been ideal for us both to do this. The Marines had an important mission for the British, but we also knew that once they went over to the US Army Corps, they'd be small fish in the big pond and we'd never hear of them again. We both hated that this move took place.

But General de la Billiere believed the Marine Corps intended to take Kuwait regardless of the casualties. This did the Marines and me a disservice, and isn't what we intended, as we were planning to fight it very smartly. But on the other hand, especially initially, we were facing very tough odds.

Brigadier Patrick Cordingley
Commander, 7th Armoured Brigade

I was told privately, the Marines' operation was thought unnecessarily risky for us, as we'd be leading their advance with our armoured engineers. I'd thought this is what we were there actually to do.

The Marines were hugely upset. We'd trained with them for three months and were a key element of General Boomer's force, and the logic of our removal was as unclear to him as it was to me. He certainly didn't know of the MoD's rationale. The Americans were so determined to avoid a repeat of Vietnam or the Korean War disaster that he'd have been very angry had he known that his operation was considered the most dangerous – and the reason for our withdrawal.

Lieutenant General Walter Boomer
General Officer Commanding, 1 Marine Expeditionary Force, United States Marine Corps

When the decision was taken to give the British brigade to the US Army, the odds we faced on the coast were still pretty high, so my supposition is that in London they thought the Challenger tank would have a better commercial showcase as part of a heavy armoured force, sweeping around through the desert from west to east.

From the very beginning, Schwarzkopf did not want to move the British [from us]. He told me, 'You would not believe the pressure I'm getting to move the British 7th Armoured Brigade.'

I understood this pressure. Eventually he told me, 'I can't resist this any more. I'm going to have to move them.'

I said, 'OK. I understand. Give me a US Army armoured brigade of the same capability and we'll say goodbye. We have no choice.'

He did give me an army armoured brigade, but they weren't as large as the 7th Armoured Brigade, nor did they have the same capabilities; but they did a fine job and I was very glad to have them.

This is what I would call 'the politics of war', and a purely commercial decision. If you've been around long enough, you understand how these things work. Challenger is a great tank – not as good as the Abrams. But I was pretty philosophical about it all.

Major David Potts
SO2 Army Logistics, Quartermaster General's Department, MoD Whitehall

The casualty estimates for the US Marines' slog up the coast were truly horrendous, and there were great concerns in MoD about 7th Armoured Brigade being a part of that. 7th Armoured Brigade represented what our army could put into the field. To subject it to a battle of attrition up the coast was thought unwise. But the decision to take them away from the Marines wasn't in order to give Challenger a more sensible role, but because of fears that this move wasn't a sensible use of British forces.

Brigadier Patrick Cordingley
Commander, 7th Armoured Brigade

This redeployment epitomised the silliness of how we went to war, because the MoD didn't want us involved with the dangerous slog into Kuwait, preferring us on the US Army's supposedly less dangerous flanking operation. Their decision was bonkers, with no military or political sense.

If the United Kingdom was to benefit from the rebuilding of Kuwait, we needed to get to Kuwait City.

Major General Rupert Smith
General Officer Commanding, 1st Armoured Division

The poor old Americans were going to have to attack up the coast, and putting us in the middle of their formation would have created impossible logistic spaghetti. We needed to go on a flank, and the eastern flank had the shortest distance for resupply.

But our relationship with the US Marine formation was a different issue. Patrick Cordingley was quite sure we should stay with them. But even though I didn't share his emotional commitment to them, I certainly wasn't careless of that point of view and commitment.

Major General Alexander Harley
Assistant Chief of Defence Staff (Overseas) and Deputy Director of Joint Operations, Ministry of Defence, Whitehall

We did consider leaving 7 Brigade with the US Marines, replacing them with an American brigade, but the Americans didn't want one of their fighting units under British command. But also, 1 (BR) Division hadn't trained with an American brigade, which has different equipment, ammunition, communications, food – everything; and although NATO procedures are the same, inter-operability is fine on an exercise, but not if you have to fight. You can either make it difficult or easy, and until the very end, this looked like it was going to be very difficult indeed.

Major David Potts
SO2 Army Logistics, Quartermaster General's Department

Talking to Americans about all this afterwards, they sometimes tell me that de la Billiere's view that the coastal attack was too dangerous, and his representing this point so forcefully to Schwarzkopf, was actually a good thing. De la Billiere could say things like this and be listened to, whereas the Americans would tell one of their commanders to get on with it.

1 (BR) Division did end up doing the right job. We had a tank about which we had concerns, so we were given a discreet task, with less mileage than the American tanks. The same thing happened a decade later when we were given the discreet task of biting off Basra – a nice little job for the Brits.

Brigadier Patrick Cordingley
Commander, 7th Armoured Brigade

Women proved to be an unexpected problem; there weren't many in 7th Armoured Brigade so they became an object of undue interest. The assistant adjutant of 40 Field Regiment, for example, was a very pretty girl and the only female in the regiment, and we had to place her somewhere else. The

Queen's Royal Irish Hussars' doctor was a very slight girl, but although very good, the soldiers didn't think she'd be strong enough to lift casualties.

One totally unexpected issue was at Camp Four, when I was asked if there could be an area set aside for 'people to hold hands'. No there couldn't. Could husbands and wives share a tent if they were in the same location? No. These things were very obvious, but people still asked.

Robin Watt
War artist

I thought the Gulf operation would involve a lot of British casualties, so I asked if I could go out and do some pictures to sell for the Army Benevolent Fund. At the end of November I went out to the Gulf, going to 7th Armoured Brigade, visiting all their units, winding up with the Irish Hussars. I already knew Arthur Denaro, as we'd been in the same platoon at Sandhurst.

Lieutenant Colonel Arthur Denaro
Commanding Officer, Queen's Royal Irish Hussars

We held a conference at brigade discussing tank engine availability: we were told to expect to lose one engine every five kilometres. Driving back, my own tank broke down.

Major General Rupert Smith
General Officer Commanding, 1st Armoured Division

I wanted to be able to drive the whole division to the Euphrates without leaving a tank behind – some five hundred miles. 7 Brigade's experience thus far had told us we had serious vehicle reliability problems: Challenger tanks, Warrior, and the old AFV 432s were really struggling. Helicopter engines, particularly the Lynx, suffered from sucking in the sand.

We had long meetings with REME staff, working out how to manage this, leading to the deployment of an extra field workshop purely to rebuild engines. Challenger's turret system was particularly problematic, such that when one part went down, the whole thing failed. Automotive failures were even more frequent – all due to fundamental design inadequacies. Although we learned how to keep the Warrior going, Challenger remained fundamentally flawed. The American Abrams tank had its own problems; its gas turbine burned fuel at the same rate regardless of whether it was moving or not – even at rest, just to run the radios. This gave them very large fuel consumption and so serious logistic problems. These days they've been fitted with a much smaller second engine to charge the batteries.

Lieutenant Colonel Mike Vickery
Commanding Officer 14th/20th King's Hussars, 4th Armoured Brigade

Our barracks was located in the middle of a large Munster suburb, our 24/7 preparations causing local protests. I had to visit the local sub-burgermeister, who spoke with our neighbours. With Germany boycotting this war, we also had some twenty anti-war protesters camped outside our barracks gates. Having the previous year had two soldiers shot by the IRA on the road outside, we wore civilian clothes outside barracks and took other counter-terrorist precautions.

But now there wasn't time for any of this, so we wore uniform, and didn't worry about the protesters. This got me into my first bit of trouble with our Brigade Commander, who got caught up in a bit of a disturbance with the protesters when coming to visit us. I got it in the neck for not calling out the Guard. He was a cross person.

Major General Rupert Smith
General Officer Commanding, 1st Armoured Division

I'd not been given a division, but it was certainly a fighting force, with only two brigades not the usual three, plus a large artillery brigade. I also had a brigade of engineers, and the better part of 1 (BR) Corps' Ptarmigan communications system; plus two logistic brigades – one building up the port and the other out in the desert. There was also an aviation group of some seventy-six rotary wing aeroplanes from all three services – my own aviation regiment, two squadrons of Royal Navy Sea King helicopters, plus two RAF squadrons.

With no replacements or reinforcements available, I needed to create my own reserves to get myself out of difficulties. While I might be under US command, I was responsible for my own maintenance and supply, unlike my American colleagues, who would be re-supplied by 7 US Corps. The more we succeeded, the longer [would be] my logistic links and the bigger my problem. Unless all of my logistics could be applied to my division, I'd lose all flexibility.

And as there was no ground of any tactical significance that I could locate in the whole theatre, my objective was certain to be the destruction of the Iraqis, rather than taking any ground. So movement was going to be critical, playing back into the logistic problem.

The developing American plan was for an attack, with me protecting the Corps flank against armoured mobile Iraqi formations, plus the Republican Guard held in depth behind them. To do this, I favoured attacking the enemy positions first, retaining the initiative, thus definitely allowing the Corps attack to take place.

But the problem was a bit like trying to find the man who's got the ball in a game of rugby – determining which enemy units to attack. Furthermore, our attack would be through a breach in the Iraqi minefield.

I therefore decided to fight in depth not width; as deep as possible. I also decided I'd fight my brigades one at a time, with the non-fighting brigade being resupplied. I'd switch them over very quickly, like a boxer punching with two fists, with very fast changeovers so the enemy wouldn't realise I was doing this.

We needed to carve the opponent up into bite-sized bits, each objective achievable by a brigade. The deep attack, which I thought would be done by my artillery and aviation, was to compartmentalise the area before splitting the enemy into bite-sized chunks.

Lieutenant Colonel Arthur Denaro
Commanding Officer, Queen's Royal Irish Hussars
Our exercise was dominated by track mileage, until eventually I had to stop. As fourteen tanks broke down on this one day, I was worried.

Dr Mary McLoughlin
We were downtown, when suddenly the Iraqi people around us started cheering and waving at us. Some actually came over and hugged us. We asked them what was going on. They said, 'Haven't you heard that you're going to be released?' I remember thinking how amazing that they were actually happy that we were being released – extraordinarily generous.

With thousands of people to be flown out, our company scrambled to charter an aircraft, while we faced the dilemma of what we were going to do about the hospital and our remaining patients.

Lieutenant Colonel Mike Vickery
Commanding Officer, 14th/20th King's Hussars,
4th Armoured Brigade

Our first squadron of tanks were painted desert colours, then shipped off to the Gulf, leaving us with three weeks for personal training. We still had no idea what we might actually be doing out there, although the huge scale of it was becoming apparent. We'd obviously learned the lesson of the Falklands fuck-up, where there hadn't been anything like enough artiller. Now very serious amounts of artillery were being pushed out.

Dr Mary McLoughlin

Now that Saddam had agreed to let all the hostages go, we felt sure he would also withdraw from Kuwait, maybe over Christmas or possibly in the New Year. We still had patients at the hospital, and we felt they were probably better off with us than at the Iraqi hospitals. So our hospital authorities made plans to keep our hospital open. We were offered money to stay beyond the deadline, which was 15 January.

I was quite convinced that Saddam would pull out of Kuwait, and remembering the horror of the weeks I'd spent back at home in Ireland, was in no hurry to return. So with my partner and about thirty others, a total of about two hundred and fifty people, we signed to stay on.

Lieutenant Colonel Mike Vickery
Commanding Officer 14th/20th King's Hussars,
4th Armoured Brigade

My wife Susie was six months pregnant with our third. She and my new second-in-command's wife became very firm friends and, with the RSM's wife, they got it all together. She wasn't an army person, having married me when I was a young major, but she took over and got everyone going. The Quartermaster gave them a building with a telephone, they painted it – my pregnant wife up a ladder – but the more they did, the less they were thinking about what might happen.

Dr Mary McLoughlin

Day by day the flights took people home, and work at the hospital continued. I lost my nice staff care job, so was clerking-in patients, doing the bloods and other very menial junior doctor jobs. They hired in doctors from places like India, and by about the third week in December, everybody that wanted to go had left.

Major General Alexander Harley
Assistant Chief of Defence Staff (Overseas) and Deputy Director of Joint Operations, Ministry of Defence, Whitehall

Our search to obtain a suitable biological weapon strain from which to make plague vaccinations finally succeeded – I think from Russia. Porton Down then began to grow the strain to the right quantity from which the vaccinations could be developed. This was terribly secret, because from the moment you've discovered which weapon strain the enemy are using, it takes time to grow enough for your own use, whereas if the enemy learns what you're doing, they can immediately change the strain to something else.

Lieutenant Colonel Charles Rogers
Commanding Officer, Staffordshire Regiment

As winter came on, it got cooler, then absolutely pissed with rain. The ground became boggy, at times like the trenches of the First World War, with green patches of grass appearing overnight. I was bloody cold at night, and wore a tracksuit in my sleeping bag, with a liner and a US Marine duvet. We swapped kit with the Americans; their camp beds and duvets were real winners. The Americans particularly liked our woolly pulleys which they didn't have, and our NBC suits; theirs were not very good. Of course, soldiers shouldn't be swapping NBC suits.

Major General Rupert Smith
General Officer Commanding, 1st Armoured Division

7 US Corps was arriving at the same time as us, so I now had a Corps Commander. The long discussions about what the British division was to do had started before we arrived, over how we could deploy secretly into the desert, train, then fight.

There wasn't enough time for this to be done serially, so everything was done in parallel, which would be risky if Saddam decided to attack before we were ready.

Every battle group went through the Devil Dog Dragoon Range, firing as they would in an attack, right down on the safety limits with occasional injuries, so they understood exactly how it would all work and what it looked like. When the artillery's MLRS [Multiple Launch Rocket System] and larger equipment arrived, they also fired.

Maggi Denaro
Commanding Officer's wife, Queen's Royal Irish Hussars

Our husbands were asking for vests and warm clothes as it's jolly cold, which made us feel rather disjointed. Then people came home, mostly with injuries, who were able to explain what the husbands weren't telling us. Some hadn't really wanted to be out there, but it was very good to have them back.

We weren't told how the regiment was training to fight or what they might be going to do – and speaking for myself, I don't think we actually wanted to know about this. We were getting on with the practicalities of our everyday living, and were concerned about theirs – but not the rest of it.

Major General Rupert Smith
General Officer Commanding, 1st Armoured Division

There were no dates for the war to start. But in order to be ready, I knew I'd have to put my hospitals and logistic units into the desert first, long before my fighting formations could be ready. This wasn't sensible tactically, but that's what we had to do.

I'd asked for scientists from the Defence Research Establishment at Farnborough to crunch enormous amounts of logistic data, routes, loads, consumption – which allowed us to predict the effect of cutting corners, or suggest safe alternatives for lessening the numbers of fuel dumps, and so on. My Chief of Staff, John Reith, then produced what the Russians would call 'Norms' – yardsticks – we could all use as planning data.

We planned to operate for months over long distances. As space was the problem, we needed to establish the size of our unit frontages in relation to our fire power. And by the end of the battle, we were likely to be dispersed over a huge area.

Brigadier Patrick Cordingley
Commander, 7th Armoured Brigade

My couple of nightmare weeks after the traffic accident had taught me a huge lesson about sleep deprivation; that it just wasn't clever to push people too hard when we might to have to do something in a hurry.

When General Rupert Smith arrived, he scheduled a string of divisional exercises to get us working together, many of which were at night. I was quite bullish with his divisional chief of staff, insisting we limit the exercises to just the one night on each occasion. You may think that's a bit wet, but we were living out of our vehicles, in a continual nomadic life with no washing or other creature comforts, so we had to husband people.

Lieutenant General Walter Boomer
General Officer Commanding, 1 Marine Expeditionary Force, United States Marine Corps

The waiting did become heavy on our hands once we had everybody in place. We'd had time for training, which in the beginning was a blessing – specifically in breaching minefields of the types the Iraqis had put up. But after a time I told my commanders to back off, as I was worried the troops would be worn out before the actual attacks. But this was a good problem to have.

WO1 Johnny Muir
Regimental Sergeant Major, Camp Four

American vehicles were parked all over Camp Four, coming down from where they lived, two blocks up. There were some interesting situations, with females from our medical units being found at night in the watch towers with American soldiers. I told my American equivalent, 'We are allies, but as Camp Four is becoming a car park for American vehicles, could your soldiers please stop showing such interest in our nurses.' They took the point.

Brigadier Patrick Cordingley
Commander, 7th Armoured Brigade

We would at some stage become the aggressor, so we had to get people psychologically prepared to kill, and to have them understand it's all right. Christmas was going to be interesting.

There was a definite tension associated with this, and we spent quite a lot of time understanding how people had coped with this problem in the past. We had very few people with operational experience in the brigade – the Falklands warriors had all left, and in Northern Ireland you were always responding to being shot at.

Sergeant Shaun Rusling
Medic, Parachute Regiment

I was a medical nurse, working in a hospital in my home town, Hull. I'd been in the TA Paras, but had a parachuting accident. After recovering from my back injuries, I'd trained really hard, eventually managing to return to my Para unit. I was mobilised and sent to Plymouth to join 3 Commando Brigade's Medical Squadron.

We deployed wearing European combat clothing, and when we did get desert clothing, it came like in dribs. We were never issued desert boots, despite our European black-soled combat boots being unbearably hot. In the end, I bought a pair of desert boots from our NAAFI manager. They were expensive, and the price increased the more people needed them. He'd bought them from an Arab in Saudi.

Brigadier Mike Willcocks
Chief of Staff (Land), Joint War Headquarters, RAF High Wycombe

My battle management group had to coordinate many, and usually conflicting, demands. The MoD were either giving us orders, or constantly bleeding us of information to brief ministers and the press. Theatre, on the other hand, were asking us for decisions on all kind of things. So we had to get in all the up-to-date information and demands, determine what decisions we needed to make, then phrase them so the Commander could deal with them.

There were all sorts of problems: for example, the Poles sent out a hospital ship, and the night they arrived they held a party. But with no alcohol in Saudi Arabia, they drank surgical spirit and seventeen of them died. The hospital ship had to be casevac'd.

Major General Alexander Harley
Assistant Chief of Defence Staff (Overseas) and Deputy Director of Joint Operations, Ministry of Defence, Whitehall

There was a terrible incident when Paddy Hine's military assistant had a laptop stolen from his car boot. This was ghastly – a major shock. An MoD security team took twenty-four hours to confirm that the entire war plan was on it. CDS had to telephone the American Chief of the Joint Staffs, who thought it was just pathetic. But then MoD went bananas and started telling everybody what they could and couldn't do.

Fortunately the laptop was handed back in; but although everyone heaved great sighs of relief, one didn't know that copies hadn't been taken. Joint planning with the Americans is always difficult, but after the laptop incident it became *tortuous*.

The Rt Hon John Major
Prime Minister

Just before Christmas 1990, I flew to America to meet President Bush. When we landed in Washington there was terrible fog, and helicopters couldn't fly, so we drove up to Camp David.

In the car, the president and I discussed risks and options with our respective foreign policy advisers, Brent Scowcroft and Charles Powell. We agreed that hostilities would start on 16 January 1991.

Lieutenant Colonel Arthur Denaro
Commanding Officer, Queen's Royal Irish Hussars

The new, hugely secret Chobham armour finally arrived. It was bloody hard work for the boys to fit, in pouring rain, hundreds of incredibly precious, Meccano-like parts lying on very soft sand, and highly classified instructions. We also received extra fuel tanks to fit on the back of the tanks, 'desertised' anti-sand filters, and a fantastic new CRAV [Challenger recovery tank]. Suddenly we frontline toffs realised how totally dependent we were on our loggie friends. Our REME fitters always worked 24/7, constantly covered in oil, grease, diesel and sand. We could not have moved, or even survived, without them.

Sergeant Shaun Rusling
Medic, Parachute Regiment, 32 Field Hospital

Our equipment had been made in 1972: stethoscopes and sphygmomanometers, with no Dinamap machines to monitor blood pressure, pulse and everything else via an arm cuff; nor did we have oximeters that go on a finger to measure blood oxygen. The 1990 stuff was very simple, electric, not expensive, and totally standard in any UK hospital at that time, but we didn't have *any* of it.

Lieutenant Colonel Arthur Denaro
Commanding Officer, Queen's Royal Irish Hussars

This was the first time that I personally realised how much for the preceding twenty-five years we'd been playing at it. We were complete amateurs. Soldiering all that time in Germany, we never, ever really thought we'd fight the Russians. We were very lucky, having four months' work-up time in the desert; not just a physical work-up, but a tactical and also a psychological work-up as well. When finally we went in, we were bloody good, but we were nothing like that when we first arrived.

Sergeant Shaun Rusling
Medic, Parachute Regiment, 32 Field Hospital

The aero-medical nurses were given wood and canvas stretchers left over from the Second World War, but soon discovered these wouldn't fit into the frames of the Hercules Aeromed aircraft. They were given wood rasps and files to cut them down to fit. When a casualty got to the other end, before being loaded into the ambulances, they'd have to be tipped off on to another stretcher so the girls could have their 'modified' ones back. How tragic was that?

We didn't have proper Lacon boxes with drawers and trays; instead we set up piles of cardboard boxes beside each treatment trolley. We didn't have modern drugs either. When we asked for them, the MoD said, 'No – you're not scaled for that.' The MoD's lists of equipment and drugs was dated 1972, which the MoD hadn't bothered bringing up to date. But to make matters even worse, when the problems were pointed out to the MoD, they still wouldn't change the lists and send us what we needed. They'd got large war stocks of all this stuff, which they wanted us to use up first. If it weren't so serious it would have been funny.

Lieutenant Colonel Arthur Denaro
Commanding Officer, Queen's Royal Irish Hussars

I had a huge crisis of personal confidence in my ability to command an armoured battle group in a high-tech, high-intensity war. Communications and other technology increased one's span of command so radically, to the extent that I thought it questionable whether one guy was capable of commanding fifty-eight tanks – plus possibly a company of armoured infantry.

Sergeant Shaun Rusling
Medic, Parachute Regiment, 32 Field Hospital

The US general in charge of American medical services came to see us. Afterwards he said that because of our lack of modern equipment, he didn't want US casualties brought to us. So we never received any US casualties. It was a very poor show really – and we were the resus team, not a field ambulance or regimental aid post.

I took myself on a visit to the US Army resus, and they *were* equipped correctly: like any UK accident and emergency hospital.

Lieutenant Colonel Arthur Denaro
Commanding Officer, Queen's Royal Irish Hussars

There was also a much more personal question mark in my mind. Apart from the time I'd spent with the SAS at Hereford, where we were bloody professional, over the preceding twenty years as a soldier, I'd *personally* played at it: shirking off from Staff College to play polo at Tidworth, sleeping through lectures, feeling dreadful during courses at Bovington having been up all night socialising in London; we as an officer corps and an army had been playing at it.

I would hasten to make the exceptions – the people who went to the Falklands, or took regiments to Northern Ireland. But being an Irish regiment, we didn't go to Northern Ireland, so we'd never been even close to serious, tough operations in armour for forty-odd years, and it was a very sobering thought.

Major General Rupert Smith
General Officer Commanding, 1st Armoured Division

We invited the press to one of the night attack runs. The artillery was firing very close, producing a lot of really good film footage, which was broadcast.

A couple of days later, my American corps commander appeared with a fist-ful of angry signals from the Pentagon demanding to know why it seemed as if the Brits were the only ones fighting the war! So to avoid damaging the alliance, I had to close down the press access to our training.

With Brigadier Dutton – the Director of Army Public Relations – I'd agreed that provided the press would accept what we meant by 'war correspondents', we'd embed journalists with frontline troops, who'd be told everything that a platoon commander would know, but not until the fighting started. Come this magic day, we'd only deal with the embedded war correspondents.

Major Rayson Pritchard
Public Information Officer, Royal Marines

'Media Reaction Teams', or MRTs, were to be formed to report the actual fighting. But the MoD told us not to tell the journalists, despite them needing to make plans for covering the progress of the war without being killed, getting lost or dying in the desert. We hinted this to journalists, who went straight back to their editors who called the MoD press office demanding to know what was happening. We got a slap on the wrist, but we'd forced the issue, which then had to be dealt with.

So back in London, Tom King and Brigadier Dutton told the editors there'd be a writer, clicker, a television front man and cameraman, and a radio journalist in each team, with people to drive them around, which would pool all its material for the others to use; one team with each armoured brigade. We told the media to work out between themselves who should be in each.

Martin Bell
BBC Television

The deal we worked out seemed quite reasonable: giving up journalistic freedom in return for access. We had to wear desert combat uniforms, including military flak jackets, NBC protection suits and respirators, and were given our own tent.

Sandy Gall
ITN television reporter

We all thought there'd be a war, but couldn't get visas from the Saudi, who didn't like the press very much. When the media reporting teams were formed, the BBC got the desirable 7th brigade, the 'Desert Rats'; whereas ITN ended up with 4th Armoured Brigade. We had a camera team and reporter with them, but wanted to get other correspondents out there, only visas were like gold dust.

Martin Bell
BBC Television

'Embedding' had never been done before, and there were two concerns: operational security, and casualty reporting. We understood operational security, because if we went forward knowing the entire battle plan, we wouldn't want to endanger our own safety, let alone anybody else's. Casualty reporting is another problem, as it's grievous for the families of the dead to first discover what happened from the news. If it's reported that there have been casualties before the families have been told, then there's a long period of deep anxiety for every family in the units involved; so I was never worried about not being able to report casualties or deaths.

But the agreement did allow us to report any foul-ups, and the consequences. Of course, this was never tested.

Major General Rupert Smith
General Officer Commanding, 1st Armoured Division

I considered myself as Commander to be a media asset, but one only to be deployed when there's an audience that needs to be addressed for some specific reason – and this audience was *not* the reporter. The essence of handling the media is to let them have reliable information for free, including a telephone and coffee machine, with briefings, but none done by the Commander.

Major Rayson Pritchard
Public Information Officer, Royal Marines

The non-MRT journalists were busy working out how they were going to get their stories; hiring four-wheel drive vehicles on which they strapped water jerrycans. Later, when Special Forces abseiled on to the roof of the embassy in Kuwait, journalists were already there, having crossed from Dhahran into Kuwait City, where they drove around unescorted and totally free.

Lieutenant Colonel Mike Vickery
Commanding Officer, 14th/20th King's Hussars,
4th Armoured Brigade

My family held an early Christmas on the 22nd, and I went out on the 23rd – a real morale-boosting day to go. Farewell days can drag on; I was very keen to get going. I made all my goodbyes and left home early, to the office where I wrote all my letters to wives, mothers and so on – in case of need. Everyone else was frightfully busy, but I found I had time on my hands, so I got out our regimental history, where I discovered we'd landed in Basra in 1917, where it rained so relentlessly they'd many horses drowned in the night through camping in wadis which flooded; then in the Second World War they'd gone to Iraq with Ferret and Dingo scout cars, when night temperatures had dropped to minus four.

I immediately raced out of the office and ordered the RSM to make sure that everyone took their parkas and poncho raincoats on the plane as hand luggage. He looked at me and said, 'Yes Colonel.'

I replied, 'No, RSM, this isn't a "Yes Colonel", but the real thing. Please ensure they do it.'

Coincidentally, Arthur Denaro then phoned me from the desert to say, 'For God's sake, bring warm clothing…' Later in the desert, I had great pleasure going round the sentry positions at three o'clock in the morning asking the soldiers if they were warm enough. They all said, 'Thank God the RSM ordered us to bring parkas and wet weather gear.'

Brigadier Patrick Cordingley
Commander, 7th Armoured Brigade

Christmas is when people think of home and feel sad they're not there. The British public were pouring stuff in. We weren't supposed to put up decorations or display cards, but as we were out in the desert, we did it discreetly. I think in reality, the Saudis couldn't care less. In fact the shops in Al Jubayl had Christmas cards for sale!

Lieutenant Colonel Mike Vickery
Commanding Officer, 14th/20th King's Hussars, 4th Armoured Brigade

As I was climbing the steps on to the plane at Hannover, I was called to take a phone call from Corps Headquarters. I thought how kind of them to wish me luck, to discover a staff major on the line, 'Colonel, the Secretary of State has put another rate cap on the numbers of people who can go over there, so I need you to take twenty-four people off your regimental manifest.'

I said, 'Well now, that's very easy. Five tanks plus my tank is twenty-four men. If they don't go that's twenty-four men. How about that?'

'Hey, come on, colonel. You're not taking this seriously.'

'No, no. On the contrary, I am taking this very, very seriously. I'm commanding an armoured regiment, and each tank must have four men.'

'But what about your logistic support?'

'I'm taking exactly the right number of men to handle the ammunition I've been told to carry, so just where do you want me to make savings?'

'But you have to reduce by twenty-four men.'

'Oh … fuck off!' I slammed the phone down, then thought, 'Oh God I'm going to be in such shit now.'

We shared a plane with the Royal Scots. I sat with their CO, who I knew from Staff College – a lovely man, but hard and a little dour. At Cyprus, we went to the bar for a final beer, where the Royal Scots CO told me all his soldiers had been dry for months. I asked 'Why?'

'Well, they like to drink.'

'So do mine,' I said. 'But they'll stop drinking when we get to Saudi.'

In fact, the Irish and Scottish regiments found it extraordinarily difficult to stop the drinking, suffering withdrawal problems, so they had to wean them off it. Whereas unlike the Celtic regiments, the Staffords, 14th/20th Hussars and the Fusiliers had no such problems. The difference was quite startling.

Anyway, I told the Royal Scots CO that my soldiers were going to carry on drinking, and if he wanted to take a half-drunk can from a soldier, I wasn't going to help!

Lieutenant Toby Masterton
A Squadron, The Life Guards, 4th Armoured Brigade

With A Squadron, I deployed to the 14th/20th Hussars battle group. B and C

Squadrons went out later as battle casualty replacements. I think they remained in camp, with their tanks only moving out on low-loaders in case they were needed. I don't think my former recce troop ever even left Blackadder Camp.

Lieutenant Colonel Mike Vickery
Commanding Officer, 14th/20th King's Hussars, 4th Armoured Brigade

Our Caledonian Jumbo showed the film *Pretty Woman*. Coming in to land, when the pilot switched it off the whole plane groaned, so it was kept on until the very last moment, the pilot telling us that he'd take the long route to the terminal to give us a chance to see the end, eventually slowing down to virtually walking pace. When the film ended, he got an enormous cheer.

We were driven straight to Blackadder Camp on the outskirts of the oil port, in a large area of sand bounded on four sides by roads. There were many such squares, some with nothing in them. Everything was named after something from the Blackadder television series, the logistics units with a Blackadder logo on their sleeves.

Later that day, I remember sitting in the tent on my bed, unpacking to find all sorts of little presents hidden away in there from the kids, my wife and friends: the *Snowman* tape and so on. Didn't do my tear ducts much good. Next morning, the new life began.

Maggi Denaro
Commanding Officer's wife, Queen's Royal Irish Hussars

We learned how to run our lives without husbands – but there were all sorts of attractive things about not having a husband around, like not having to cook supper for them or iron their shirts. We had several grandparents die, so had to get people back to UK, and there were lots of babies born; but amazingly not a single car crash or any major drama in the Fallingbostel area in that six months – a blessing, with everyday life continuing.

Brigadier Patrick Cordingley
Commander, 7th Armoured Brigade

I tried to visit as many people as possible at their Christmas meals. There were extra rations, and nice things being sent out, but it was a lonely time.

Christmas Eve was a very clear night with stars shining, and I remember thinking how close we were to where it all happened, on a night much the same as this, a few hundred miles away. On Christmas Day, the officers took over all the nasty jobs the Pioneers usually did – burning out the latrines and so on throughout the day. But Christmas was a sombre little affair.

Lieutenant Colonel Charles Rogers
Commanding Officer, Staffordshire Regiment

For Christmas, we had a film night, plus getting people back to Camp Four to make phone calls. But unlike the Irish Hussars' St Pat's [their recreational camp named 'St Patricks'], we didn't create a tented camp for ourselves, as the boys were very happy in their little lean-to tents beside their Warriors, with their company all around.

WO1 Johnny Muir
Regimental Sergeant Major, Camp Four

Christmas Day was like any other day, although I spoke to my wife and daughter that morning, which was quite a low point for me. They'd gone to UK to stay with her parents, and I'd just sent her father a letter explaining how if anything happened to me she'd be looked after, and requesting he take care of them both.

Major Rayson Pritchard
Public Information Officer, Royal Marines

Kate Adie wanted to do a carol service link-up between the families in their homes, and the troops in the desert. Some of it was pre-recorded, interviews with wives at home and kids on their knees, but was mostly live from a garrison church in Germany, and from the desert. The BBC brought a big satellite truck out into the desert, and even got some live interviews going between soldiers and their families, carols around campfires and so on; a feel-good event, at a time when there was nothing positive going on.

Brigadier Patrick Cordingley
Commander, 7th Armoured Brigade

The media were around us the whole time, poking their noses into things, which to be honest was unwelcome at Christmas. I really didn't want to have to bother with them. You always slightly act, so even things like a church service become rather unnatural. But the television linked up with Falling-bostel and somewhere else in England, so we had the QDG's Welshmen singing *Silent Night* and I'm told it all looked rather splendid.

Lieutenant Colonel Mike Vickery
Commanding Officer, 14th/20th King's Hussars, 4th Armoured Brigade

The brigade padre held a rather surreal church service in Blackadder Camp, with a Christmas tree and prayers. There'd been all sorts of rumours about Christians and Jewish members of the American forces not being allowed to pursue their religion out here; that padres couldn't wear their crosses or stars of David. There were complaints from the locals, but everybody ignored this, and there wasn't a problem.

On Boxing Day, it was straight back to work on our tanks, doing upgrades in special marshalling areas, our teams working alongside teams from Vickers. Desert air filters had to be fitted very carefully, on both the air intakes and the gearboxes, as sand rapidly destroyed them.

I arrived at one of the special marshalling areas, to hear an almighty explosion. One of my REME fitters, Corporal Wakeham, had been pumping up a tank's hydrogas suspension with inert nitrogen. The nitrogen cylinders had been purchased locally, with all the correct nitrogen markings, but were filled with liquid oxygen that had exploded. Luckily Corporal Wakeham had been shielded by one of the road wheels, so although his arm was badly burned and fingers smashed, his head and body were OK. Another soldier had been blown off the back of a truck.

I knew Corporal Wakeham's wife and her family very well indeed – a smashing girl. I visited him in hospital, got a report on his injuries from the doctors, phoned Susie to tell her, then phoned Mrs Wakeham to give her a first-hand report on what had happened; that he'd probably be casevac'd back to UK, but I didn't know when. Four days later I was summoned for a most imperial bollocking from our brigade commander Christopher Hammerbeck, for 'not going through the proper channels'.

Apparently, the 'proper channels', an officer and a padre, had turned up to Mrs Wakeham's house and told her he was very badly damaged, likely to lose an arm and all sorts of other nasties. She, bless her heart, told them

'Bollocks, I've talked to the Commanding Officer, who's talked to the doctors, so eff off.' All that had come back up the system, so the Brigade Commander had decided to give me a bollocking.

At this point, I severely disagreed with my Brigade Commander, and told him I'd continue doing this kind of thing until we'd deployed in the desert with no communications. I could see they were trying to practise the notification system, and it was good to have that system, but they'd got the info very badly wrong. We agreed to disagree, as I couldn't see any other way of doing it.

Dr Mary McLoughlin

We worked through Christmas, and had a wonderful New Year party at an Iraqi friend's house – hoping for the best, with my partner and me the only foreigners invited. None of the Iraqis were saying anything disapproving about what was going on, but they were always saying to us things like, 'Well hopefully peace, hopefully it'll be all right.' So we knew what they were saying, even though they didn't say it. And of course their support for us all along showed us how much they disapproved of all that was going on.

WO1 Johnny Muir
Regimental Sergeant Major, Camp Four

After six weeks in charge of Camp Four, Colonel Denaro came in from the desert and asked me if I'd be RSM of the regiment. This was what I'd wanted all my life. If I could have kissed him I would, but he wouldn't have thanked me for that, so I just accepted.

Lieutenant Colonel Arthur Denaro
Commanding Officer, Queen's Royal Irish Hussars

With my Technical Quartermaster returning to Germany – to become a really marvellous Families Officer, I decided to promote my RSM into that job, who was a hugely competent technician but less certain as RSM. This rearrangement also enabled me to bring in the guy I'd always wanted as my RSM, particularly in a war – RSM Johnny Muir. So on Boxing Day I told the RSM he was to be commissioned, then went into Camp Four and told Johnny Muir that he was to become RSM.

RSM Johnny Muir
Regimental Sergeant Major, Queen's Royal Irish Hussars

I'd missed out becoming RSM three years earlier when I'd thought I was ready. Colonel Arthur had told me at the time I'd be next. Being RSM in war was a very, very special opportunity – a very great privilege and honour for me.

Lieutenant Colonel Mike Vickery
Commanding Officer, 14th/20th King's Hussars,
4th Armoured Brigade

To get the regiment as I wanted them, I had to juggle with key people. I had a squadron leader, Peter Garver, who proved brilliant. I needed a really good second-in-command, so asked for a staff major due with us the following May to come early. It was probably thoroughly nasty of me, but I made the incumbent second-in-command my training officer. He wasn't happy with this, but I needed him doing that, plus a brilliant second-in-command who knew a hell of a lot about what we were going to have to do. Even though my ops officer was very bright, I wanted a major to run my HQ, which would get much larger when artillery, engineers and others arrived – so I put in my excellent second-in-command.

I put the regimental gunnery instructor sergeant major into the 2ic's tank, to follow and keep me safe when I whizzed around the front line. I put the adjutant into my loader's seat, a job *supposed* to be done by a bright staff sergeant, so he could talk to the squadron leaders or brigade HQ when I was too busy – as he did back in barracks. This took a huge amount off me, and he was brilliant. He was also a gunnery instructor, but had to learn to cook and make sarnies. I also asked for my *next* adjutant to come to us early from a helicopter tour, as an alternative HQ operations officer.

Lance Corporal Roy Sellstrom
Pioneer Corps, Army War Graves Unit

We were called back in from leave on 2 January. I went to the barber's and had all my hair shaved off, then after not being able to get my wife Deb on the phone, got on the coach to RAF Brize Norton and the flight out.

The Get-You-In Centre for Saudi Arabia was in Shed Three of Al Jubayl docks. Even though the middle of the night it was boiling hot, and we were given bottles of water. Our escorts were guys I knew from 187 Pioneer Company, who'd been erecting a huge tented area at Baldrick Lines. They were armed, they told me, with orders to shoot the Saudi coach driver if he deviated from the planned route. 'You're joking surely,' I said. 'You couldn't just shoot the driver, could you?'

'Well, the threat is supposed to be serious, and that's what we've been told to do.'

Second Lieutenant Alistair Watkins
Grenadier Guards, 3 RRF Battle Group, 4th Armoured Brigade

Guards are a fairly arrogant bunch. We weren't melding with the Fusiliers, although there was good communication between our Company Commander and their Commanding Officer. We thought it rather beneath us to be mixing with Fusiliers – which is outrageous really. They probably thought we were toffs and should be back guarding Buckingham Palace. The army is so tribal – which is why it works.

Lance Corporal Roy Sellstrom
Pioneer Corps, Army War Graves Unit

There were lines of incomers in front of what looked like airline check-in desks. An Adjutant General's Corps clerk brought you into theatre on the computer system, checking your next-of-kin details, asking if you'd made a will, and so on. We were given a Get-You-In pack containing rations, water, and second set of NBC clothing and respirator filter canister, then sat down – for ages.

People of every imaginable cap badge were in this hall; colonels, majors and privates all together, being messed about. It was quite enjoyable, as usually it's us junior ranks being messed around; watching them whingeing and whining, 'Where's my transport. Why do I have to wait? I want to be out of here.'

As it got light, we heard car horns sounding outside; Tommy Halls, Jock McKane and Alan Shaw with three Land Rovers and trailers to pick us up. Tommy held up a large notice like taxi drivers at airports, saying 'Army War Graves Unit', making the officers complain even more.

Brigadier Patrick Cordingley
Commander, 7th Armoured Brigade

We had one man who went absent – but how can you go absent in the middle of the desert? He'd received a bad letter from his girlfriend and wandered off, and it took twenty-four hours to find him again. The lack of alcohol was an absolute winner.

RSM Johnny Muir
Regimental Sergeant Major, Queen's Royal Irish Hussars

I phoned my wife in UK, to tell that she was now the RSM's wife, and that she should return to Germany. She was very supportive, but my appointment was a huge responsibility for her, and I felt for her. She'd known Maggi Denaro for years, and they were to become a very tight-knit team. So on New Year's Eve, after handing over Camp Four, I deployed with my kit bag into the desert, as my regiment's RSM.

Lieutenant Colonel Charles Rogers
Commanding Officer, Staffordshire Regiment

Many of the families who'd decided to leave Germany and go back to UK came back again as they found their own people didn't understand what they were going through. Fallingbostel, despite not being the epicentre of the social world, contained a sympathetic corps of friends and kindred spirits.

Lieutenant Colonel Mike Vickery
Commanding Officer, 14th/20th King's Hussars,
4th Armoured Brigade

Many of our young wives returned to UK as soon as their husbands left for the Gulf. But as the situation developed, realising nobody in their little home villages around Preston gave a bugger about the war, many floated back to Germany, where their letters came, and there was information about what was happening out in the desert. When a general came to visit them, or John Major and so on, the wives organised everything. Princess Anne stayed late, and on being hurried up, made the arch comment to her lady-in-waiting, 'Don't the RAF fly at night?'

Maggi Denaro
Commanding Officer's wife, Queen's Royal Irish Hussars

When the Under-Secretary of State come to visit us, we wore regimental T-shirts with 'Deserted Rats' written on the back.

Lance Corporal Roy Sellstrom
Pioneer Corps, Army War Graves Unit

At Camp Four we had a refrigerated plant to store the bodies before flying them back to UK, plus pre-fab bedrooms with bunk beds up long corridors, communal showers and toilets. This was great, and we met our platoon commander Lieutenant Andy Parry. Our OC, Captain Ralph, a very seasoned old ex-ranker, gave us a briefing. Lieutenant Parry was new out of Sandhurst, but turned out to be a really fantastic officer.

We had two staff sergeants but no sergeant major, and our proper sergeant had left with a chit from the med centre over his dodgy knees. But this was fine, as we'd been pretty wary of him anyway.

Now all together, we realised none of us had actually done this job. Apart from rough notes from the Falklands War operation, and a few telephone calls to the now-retired guys who'd been involved, that was all we knew.

RSM Johnny Muir
Regimental Sergeant Major, Queen's Royal Irish Hussars

The regiment was about thirty kilometres from Al Jubayl, where I reported to Colonel Arthur. He took me for a stroll, and we talked about disciplinary matters – soldiers with outstanding charges that he wanted dealt with before we went into action, so it wouldn't be hanging over their heads.

I had to get used to living out of a vehicle, a Mark 1 Ferret scout car, manufactured in the year I'd been born. It had no turret, and was driven by a man I'd known as a four-year-old child in my village in Ireland.

Everyone had very high expectations of me, and I needed to be sure I was meeting those expectations. D Squadron's Sergeant Major Billy Parkinson was a lifelong friend (and was to take over as RSM from me), and became my leaning post. With him I could be myself. Every RSM needs somebody like Billy. He knew I wouldn't give him any favouritism, and I knew he'd tell me what he thought and keep it to himself. Billy, sadly, died shortly after his time as RSM and leaving the army.

Lance Corporal Roy Sellstrom
Pioneer Corps, Army War Graves Unit

Captain Ralph told us that once fighting started, the MoD had calculated we'd have to deal with at least two hundred dead per day. We were told to start building a framework of wooden trestles, three-high inside this huge refrigerator, but we didn't have chippies or timber. We quickly realised every ship was getting rid of timber used to nail down the cargoes, so although we didn't really know the basics of carpentry, we constructed ourselves a very large morgue.

RSM Johnny Muir
Regimental Sergeant Major, Queen's Royal Irish Hussars

The colonel was receiving briefings he couldn't share with anybody else, and we talked about what we were going to do if we suffered casualties and loss of life. We were quite emotional about this, but came to terms with the probability of this. For all the right reasons, he was making me doubt whether I could keep the promise I'd made back in Fallingbostel. This was going to be a fight; reality was setting in.

Second Lieutenant Alistair Watkins
Grenadier Guards, 3 RRF Battle Group, 4th Armoured Brigade

We started off using camouflage nets, which looked so obvious we stopped. We debated how far apart to park the vehicles, feeling exposed and vulnerable with nowhere to hide. But once the air war started, the Iraqi air threat was removed.

Every night we dug shell scrapes next to the vehicles – three or four feet down, then filled sandbags to build up the walls, the whole thing covered with CARM (chemical agent resistant material) – a camouflaged tarpaulin which went under the cam nets.

Travelling in the back of the Warriors was disorientating, very hot and mind-numbingly dull. Wearing full NBC kit, body armour and everything else, doing attacks was bloody cumbersome and physically exhausting, so we debussed on the objectives rather than walk to them.

The people with kids found the whole thing horrendous, although most of the young officers and younger guys were rather excited. Our excellent company commander Andrew Ford was a naturally very calm person, which filtered down through the whole company.

Major General Rupert Smith
General Officer Commanding, 1st Armoured Division

I built up each of my formations, including the artillery, to be independent with everything they needed with them on wheels, and able to fight on their own – including my own rover group. We expected to be counter-attacked and I wasn't going to hold ground, so was quite prepared to allow enemy formations behind me, with everyone milling around.

Reconnaissance and surveillance were grouped with the artillery, cutting down chatter on the radio nets and letting the artillery get on with their engagements. The attack aviation was part of my artillery, commanded by my gunner brigadier, Ian Durie, operating well forward in the deep battle.

If we were counter-attacked in large numbers, I'd intended to use the space; delay rather than hold ground, thinning out while building a mine-field or other obstacles; then use the other brigade to attack into an enemy flank. The sappers were deployed forwards clearing mines, and also behind the brigades creating a road 'Route Fox' for our logistic resupply.

Because I had all of the [British Army's] reserve equipment, I needed only four hundred replacement crewmen. I was, however, sent twelve hundred battle casualty replacements, as a consequence of the very high casualty predictions made by the MoD. But I was not intending to suffer any casualties, as inflicting casualties is the business of the enemy.

I couldn't get the MoD to understand that replacing people wasn't the problem, but replacing *equipment* – as there were no replacements. Once the spares were used up, that would be the end of it.

The Rt Hon John Major
Prime Minister

We expected a serious Armageddon, with use of nuclear and biological weapons, and to be fighting a very efficient Republican Guard, expecting [to suffer] a very large number of dead and injured. To minimise this loss, Colin Powell and the British generals were emphatic that we should only go in on the ground with overwhelming numerical supremacy – at least three to one – and only when the Iraqi military capability was sufficiently degraded by bombing.

One additional concern during the build-up was the cobbling together of a sham peace deal, simply to prevent hostilities. But despite several efforts, especially by Russia, this did not happen.

Major David Potts
SO2 Army Logistics, Quartermaster General's Department, MoD Whitehall

The casualty assessments proved greatly excessive, but what else were we supposed to do? We'd never actually attacked a Warsaw Pact-equipped force, well-prepared in defence, with Scud missiles and chemical and biological weapons. We'd lessened the numbers to allow for us having air superiority, then produced a prediction of casualties – of very large numbers.

Crossing that berm into Kuwait was going to be the great unknown, where Saddam could use his chemicals to good effect; people in MoD were very concerned. It would have been nuts to have gone into that war saying there weren't going to be many casualties.

Major General Alexander Harley
Assistant Chief of Defence Staff (Overseas) and Deputy Director of Joint Operations, Ministry of Defence, Whitehall

A couple of weeks after we'd located a suitable biological weapon strain, I returned to Washington and told them manufacturing was beginning soon. Again, they tried to stall us. This was a very difficult area between them and us, and they didn't like us being way ahead of them. But our scientists were sharing information, which I'm sure helped them.

Quite soon after that, however, they suddenly changed their minds and, as the Americans do when they make decisions, very rapidly produced hundreds of thousands of vaccination doses. I don't know where they got their initial strains. But in a coalition sense, this was a very difficult bone of contention between the two of us. They hadn't been going to do it, and really didn't like that we were.

Lieutenant Colonel Mike Vickery
Commanding Officer 14th/20th King's Hussars, 4th Armoured Brigade

Even in the desert, one of my squadron leaders Peter Garver used to wear his 'hats, brown, officers' with a 20th Hussars cap badge and smoke a pipe, looking terribly Second World War. The brigade commander used go utterly spare: 'What's he doing? Why isn't he wearing a beret, and don't you know he's wearing the cap badge of a regiment that doesn't even exist?'

In the end I had to tell him, 'Brigadier, honestly, I'm sure you have a lot more important things to worry about than the dress of 14th/20th officers. Our dress regulations state very clearly that anything that's ever been worn by either regiment is fair game. We're not going to wear dress uniform out here, but it's very good for the morale of the boys.'

Major General Rupert Smith
General Officer Commanding, 1st Armoured Division

I decided to regard myself as being under the direct command of the American 7 US Corps, of 3rd US Army, and do what they told me unless there was a very good reason not to, rather than [as had been agreed nationally] the other way round.

Captain Chris Craig, RN, commanded the naval component, with a hospital ship and four LSLs, which interested me greatly. I could see that we might easily become separated from our logistic tail, with no fuel or ammunition, and lots of casualties. My answer to this potential problem would be to head straight for the coast, clear the beaches of mines then be resupplied across the beaches by the Royal Navy. We therefore made sure we had communication linkages with the ships, and that the LSLs were loaded with the supplies we'd need. Our six Hercules were also to be part of this, and we practised setting up forward airfields and parachute resupply.

RSM Johnny Muir
Regimental Sergeant Major, Queen's Royal Irish Hussars

We moved further into the desert, stopping the R&R runs back to Camp Four as we were getting too far away. The squadrons would laager with the tanks in a box, tents pitched inside the laager, with the insides of the tents dug right down to make a more comfortable space.

Lieutenant Colonel Charles Rogers
Commanding Officer, Staffordshire Regiment

I ended up with the largest battle group that's ever been fielded: twelve hundred men with four hundred vehicles – even after I sent one of my companies commanded by Major Simon Knapper across to the Scots Dragoon Guards to civilise them a bit, two infantry companies, two tank squadrons and REME support at the back, plus a whole squadron of engineers.

The problem with our frontline logistics was that wheeled vehicles got bogged in. We had to get tracked vehicles flown in for the company colour sergeants to resupply us with ammunition and rations. But with the change of scenery from Saudi to Kuwait and Iraq, from soft sand to a more gravelly, stony desert, there wasn't in fact a problem.

Soldiers don't lack initiative. Now completely dependent on the desert for their entertainment, they organised scorpion races – even dung-beetle races. One chap made friends with a snake, which he took with him into his sleeping bag – until it bit him.

Dr Mary McLoughlin

International negotiations were extremely tense. Although Saddam had made a lot of concessions with regard to the foreigners in Iraq, he was making no concessions whatsoever with regard to Kuwait. Around 9 January, UN Secretary General Pérez de Cuéllar came over, and then the United States Secretary of State James Baker, but left Iraq empty-handed.

At that point our hospital authorities decided they weren't going to take chances any longer, and would close the hospital, hire a plane, and get us out of the country. Our Iraqi friends were asking, 'What's going to happen to us?', begging us not to forget them.

Ten patients remained in our hospital when we finally turned off the lights and shut the doors. We were booked to fly out of Iraq on 11 January 1991, on the last civilian plane to land in Iraq before the invasion. It landed and we left.

The Rt Hon John Major
Prime Minister

Five days before the beginning of the war, I flew to the Gulf where our troops were poised for action. I met RAF personnel at Dhahran, including

John Nicol (one of the first of our aircrew to crash and be captured) and the Royal Navy at Port Jubayl. But, most memorably, I remember standing on top of a Challenger tank in the desert, addressing the thousands of troops gathered around. I knew the date hostilities would start. The troops did not. Indeed, one of the reasons for my visit was to discuss final plans with Peter de la Billiere.

I don't have a military background, but what struck me immediately was how young all the troops were – mostly between eighteen and twenty-three. The war was due to start on 16 January, which by chance was my own son's sixteenth birthday. As I looked down from the tank, across the sea of faces before me, my son's face metamorphosed over them all, making me realise in a very graphic way that older politicians may send their nations to war, but it's young men and women who go off and fight them. And they are *very* young. That day, I talked to many of them. They were keen, eager and in many ways tense, but looking forward to the experience of conflict. Most expressed their feelings this way, 'It's our job. It's what we joined for.'

Lance Corporal Roy Sellstrom
Pioneer Corps, Army War Graves Unit

At the beginning of January I dealt with my first body. In the armed forces, the rumour mill tells you within an hour or so when a soldier is killed, and very soon after that *how* he's been killed, so we knew what had happened before we got to 32 Field Hospital to pick him up.

The body was with a male nurse, who didn't want to let us have it, so we started off with an argument. It was wrapped in hairy wool army blankets, inside a body bag. We were going to have to get him out of all this and into our transit coffin. He was quite a big chap, and we really struggled. Then after getting him out, we discovered somebody had crossed his arms, and with *rigor mortis*, he wouldn't fit into our narrow coffin. This medic said we'd have to dislocate his arms. I saw this as brutalising, but this is what happens.

We nailed down the coffin lid, and took him back to our morgue. I thought he'd be put on to a plane as quickly as possible so his family could begin their grieving. But for some reason they kept bodies back until there were other bodies, so he stayed with us until somebody else was killed.

The Rt Hon John Major
Prime Minister

On that same trip to the Gulf, I met the Amir and Crown Prince of Kuwait, together with other senior Kuwaiti figures, who had sought refuge in Saudi Arabia. They were shocked by the invasion, and fearful of the damage conflict might do, not only to their own country, but to the region as a whole. They were grateful for Britain's support.

I also met King Fahd of Saudi Arabia, who confirmed Saudi Arabia would commit troops, and offered a very large contribution towards the costs. As I recall, it was a long meeting which began after dinner, and did not conclude until after four o'clock in the morning. During that meeting, news came through that six Iraqi helicopters had defected from Iraq.

Lieutenant Toby Masterton
A Squadron, The Life Guards, 4th Armoured Brigade

We shook out into an area of desert near the coast, with attractive grassy sand dunes, where we could blat off into the sea. I didn't have a vehicle, so while the squadron were off firing on Devil Dog Dragoon Ranges, I'd sit there twiddling my thumbs. After becoming increasingly frustrated, I was given a Second World War Ferret scout car – which, being wheels in very soft sand, whenever I was sent off to do something, got bogged in.

My tasks were to 'forage' for kit with other units as we had so little – anything and everything, especially from the Americans.

Lance Corporal Roy Sellstrom
Pioneer Corps, Army War Graves Unit

The next was a staff sergeant, who'd had his fingers blown off by a fragmentation grenade, been bandaged up and driven down to 32 Field Hospital, but on the way the driver, who'd been doing too many details, fell asleep and rolled the vehicle, killing the staff sergeant. The rumour mill alerted us, so our search and recovery team went up the main supply route along the coast to Kafaji on the Kuwait border, past lots of American units, then out into the desert to find the British unit.

The roads weren't great; we were stopped at each checkpoint, which passed on our details to the next checkpoint to prevent people getting lost in the desert; so the journey took well over three hours.

It got dark, but nobody had heard of this death, or where the body was. Someone said he was with the Americans, further along the MSR. We dossed with a logistic unit, then next morning asked at every American unit until, in late afternoon, we were taken to a huge refrigerated food truck by a white officer, to meet eight black guys – an American grave registration team. For some reason, all their grave registration teams were black.

The first thing we had to do was identify the guy. The Americans gave us his ID documents, but refused to allow us to open the bag as his face was too badly damaged to identify. We couldn't risk taking the wrong body back, so eventually their major, who'd certified him dead, agreed to us making an identification. The worst bit was always opening the bag. You never knew what you were going to find.

I asked for a bucket of water, as his hair and face were seriously matted with congealed blood. Once we'd cleaned up the body, there was nothing wrong with his face so we matched him with his ID card photo, Lieutenant Parry signed for him and we put him into our transit coffin.

We were flying next morning from an airfield, where the Americans gave us a shed away from everywhere else to spend the night. But the Americans' security patrol hadn't been told we were there, so surrounded the building, shouting at us to come out, arms in the air. This seemed rather a big incident for them. They then demanded to know what was in the box, refusing to believe us when we told them.

Lieutenant Toby Masterton
A Squadron, The Life Guards, 4th Armoured Brigade

We worked hard to break our Ferret; then having succeeded, I persuaded James Hewitt to 'lend' me his unused, brand-new long-wheelbase Land Rover. I had a new driver, a very cheeky Scouser, Trooper Doyle, who with rather more imagination than I'd anticipated, transformed this vehicle: chain-sawing the roof off, mounting a GPMG on the back, sandbags in the footwells to protect from mines, and a frame to create a persistent protection 'tent' underneath a cam net and CARM cover. It was a bizarre-looking vehicle, but rather jolly; 'Mad Max-meets-Noddy-on-acid-wearing-cracked bifocals' We sat on the sandbags, knees to our shoulders, festooned with hand grenades, jerrycans, 66mm anti-tank rockets on SLR rifle clips behind our heads. The trouble was, James Hewitt rather liked it, so would borrow it, driving away in our house and kitchen.

Major General Rupert Smith
General Officer Commanding, 1st Armoured Division

During early January, with all the equipment coming in, I spent parts of most days with 7 US Corps, planning. The Americans were very hospitable and liked having us around, but we were very definitely *foreign* as far as they were concerned.

I was also running map exercises to get my people to understand how we're going to do this – allaying their worries in the process: they'd never seen anything like this before, so couldn't see how it would work. I visited units and talked with their officers about tactics, and how our logistics would work.

We often couldn't find things, which people increasingly interpreted as meaning our logistics system didn't work. This was a big problem. I always took my ADC with me, and whenever somebody told us they were missing some vital item, we'd make a note, follow up that problem, then send them back the answer. By February, although we never got it totally right, people's lack of confidence in the logistics was falling away appreciably.

Dr Mary McLoughlin

Because nobody believed Saddam Hussein was going to remain in Kuwait, we weren't flown back to Ireland, but to Cyprus, where we stayed in a five-star hotel. There were thirty of us, with the idea that once Saddam withdrew from Kuwait, we could quickly return and reopen the hospital. So in Limassol, being able to watch real television for the first time, we were glued to the news morning, noon and night, waiting to see what would happen.

Lieutenant Colonel Mike Vickery
Commanding Officer 14th/20th King's Hussars,
4th Armoured Brigade

I gave the Brigade Commander one of my tanks, with one of my best gunnery sergeants. Although the brigadier was a Royal Tank Regiment officer, he'd never commanded a Challenger, so only now realised what a complex beast it was.

We began tweaking our Challenger's accuracy way above the usual, as we had a very seriously large amount of ammunition – each ordinary round costing about the same as an MGB sports car. We also received, for the first time, the new fin-stabilised, titanium tipped long-dart rounds which could go happily through a T-72 at twelve hundred metres; any further out and we'd need the highly classified depleted uranium rounds, which I was told we'd also be getting.

The Iraqis had so many more tanks than us, that arithmetically, we had to hit each one as far out as we could, and couldn't afford near misses. Two feet off the bull at a thousand metres was going to be a miss at two thousand metres.

Robin Watt
War artist

Once I'd done some two hundred drawings, I began to feel rather a passenger. So the Irish Hussars made me their 'Deception Officer'! This involved doing absolutely nothing, but I did look into the subject for them. We were given diesel smoke generators, and cardboard and rubber dummy tanks. Then before we went to concentration area Keys, we recorded all the wireless messages from our last exercise there, which were transmitted later to create the impression that we were still in the old area.

Lieutenant Colonel Mike Vickery
Commanding Officer, 14th/20th King's Hussars,
4th Armoured Brigade

In Germany we'd always been defending, so had never done long approaches, hence our tanks had never had diesel smoke generators like the Soviet T-55 and T-62s. We knew we were going to have to make several long approaches, so Vickers fitted two forty-gallon auxiliary tanks on to the back, with a tap onto the hot exhaust, which created huge amounts of smoke. I volunteered my 2ic's tank for the trials of this – I never took risks with my tank!

When we did the trials, this system created vast, *huge* pillars of smoke; I got radio calls from the Irish Hussars asking why we'd brought our old Chieftains with us, and the Scots Dragoon Guards, suggesting we sharpen up our engine maintenance!

Second Lieutenant Alistair Watkins
Grenadier Guards, 4th Armoured Brigade

We ate combat rations, with fresh food only very occasionally, often the same menus for weeks on end – chicken stew *ad infinitum*. The one benefit of eating exactly the same thing every day is that you end up going to the loo at exactly the same time every day – useful for planning purposes. The loos –

thunderboxes, as we called them – were simply a box with a circle in the top, placed over a fairly deep hole. Sitting on them at night under the stars you could hear the dung beetles scraping around in the hole below.

Lieutenant Toby Masterton
A Squadron, The Life Guards, 4th Armoured Brigade

We got very hungry, often getting the same menu boxes for several weeks. The boys indulged in the usual head-shaving, so I decided to join them. There's always a soldier who brings a clipper unit; it seemed hygienic and practical, plus the boys thought it fun that I was joining in. But word got back to Germany that 'an officer' had shaved his head, so as our adjutant was coming out to visit, I decided to do it properly, and our medic Jock shaved me down to the wood using a couple of razors.

This all came to a head with one of the officers at O group harrumphing like a fifty-eight-year-old with a monocle that I should resign my commission for un-officer-like behaviour. I was told to hide my head beneath a woollen hat. A mischievous officer knocked this off, to which our new CO merely rolled his eyes despairingly.

Brigadier Patrick Cordingley
Commander, 7th Armoured Brigade

We now had to move westwards with the rest of the US Army 7 Corps, three hundred and forty kilometres north-west, too far to trundle, so our tanks were loaded on to transporters. The one road, the Oil Tapline Road designated 'Route Dodge', was already breaking up with the huge amount of traffic going along it.

7 Corps was the largest corps in history, with a staggering number of vehicles. To get us there, I reckoned one vehicle would have to pass down the route every eleven seconds for three months.

Major Mark O'Reilly
Second-in-Command, Queen's Royal Irish Hussars
(from the battle group briefing)

Route Dodge was chaos, with heavy mud, a B vehicle route with only one lane. Six different nations are now on the move, with breakdowns, accidents, plus frightened refugees. Frequent diversions make it difficult to tell if one is on the correct route or not. There is a need for great patience.

CHAPTER 5

AIR HAVOC

Immediately following Saddam's invasion on 2 August, the US and UK had sent fighter aircraft out to the Gulf, commanded by an air headquarters. Once it was decided that a land operation was inevitable, the UK established an overall land headquarters in Riyadh, commanded by General Sir Peter de la Billiere. The RAF worked as part of the coalition air force which, like the ground forces, was under joint Saudi–American command, commanded initially by a USAAF lieutenant general, Chuck Horner.

The air campaign began in planning on 5 August as a three-phase, purely air operation called Instant Thunder, but became part of Operation Desert Storm with the aim of achieving air superiority, so land forces could operate in the open desert without interference from the Iraqi air force. The air force staffs retained their original belief that strategic bombing might force Saddam to withdraw from Kuwait. The RAF's Jaguar fighters remained doing air defence patrolling, but many of the other air defence aircraft were replaced by bombers, recce aircraft to find the targets, and others like ECM [Electronic Counter-Measure] jamming aircraft and refuelling tankers.

The air war started on the night of 16/17 January after UN Resolution 678 – by which Saddam had to withdraw from Kuwait – expired. US Apache strike helicopters destroyed Iraqi radar sites, bombers attacked airfields, stealth bombers hit Baghdad, Iraqi naval vessels were attacked near Basra, and US Navy Tomahawk Cruise missiles hit targets all over Iraq. In all, over 100,000 sorties were flown, with seventy-five aircraft losses, dropping 88,500 tons of bombs from air bases and six aircraft carriers.

Squadron Leader Phil Smith
Royal Air Force

One month before the 15 January deadline, most of the RAF's experienced people were sent home, their three-month tour having elapsed, replaced by an almost entirely new batch of ground and aircrew, who then fought the war. The second lot, having been warned off for the changeover several months ahead, had plenty of time to get anxious.

Group Captain Glenn Torpy
Officer Commanding, 13 (Tornado Reconnaissance) Squadron, Royal Air Force

We deployed just two days before the war started, on 15 January, to Dhahran, alongside twelve Tornado GR1 bombers of Jerry Witts's 31 Squadron, in a mixed batch of crews and aircraft. We had brand-new Batch 7 GR1A Tornado reconnaissance aircraft, with state-of-the-art infrared sensors. Like our aircraft, they were designed only for low-level flying, between two hundred to two hundred and twenty feet. The sensors recorded on to hard disks, could be replayed in the air, and also be data-linked. Not even the Americans had anything like it.

The Rt Hon John Major
Prime Minister

During my meetings with the military, bombing targets were suggested and, providing they were sound military targets, I raised no objection. My view was – and remains – that if you are receiving advice from professionals, you don't overrule or second-guess them unless there really is a sound reason for doing so.

Group Captain Glenn Torpy
Officer Commanding, 13 Squadron, Royal Air Force

Dhahran was a huge Saudi air force base next to a big town, well designed with hardened shelters. We planned from Portakabins, and lived in expat villa accommodation off-base. The F3 [bomber] Tornados from Bruggen were co-located with us.

There were two other RAF locations: Bahrain with Jaguars, GR1 Tornados and Buccaneers; and towards the end of the war, down at Tobuk in the west of

Saudi with more Buccaneers and, later on, the other half of my squadron. In Bahrain, they lived in the Sheraton and Diplomat hotels but as you went west it became progressively more austere: Tobuk was right out in the sticks, on a very basic air force base. But morale was highest in Tobuk, where the boys had the most difficulties – and seemed directly related to austerity.

Major General Alexander Harley
Assistant Chief of Defence Staff (Overseas) and Deputy Director of Joint Operations, Ministry of Defence, Whitehall

I saw all the targeting data before the air war started – wonderful air photographs taken by U-2s and so on before the first bombing raids. In 1990, Iraq was just *full* of nuclear, chemical and biological facilities. They were near to having nuclear weapons, and having already used chemical weapons on Iran were now making biological weapons.

The facilities for doing this were all there, some still being built, but most were complete – huge nuclear facilities a mile square, as big as Kew Gardens. You could see all the buildings and people moving around, all over Iraq; incredible facilities, storage sheds full of chemical drums and delivery systems.

But I'd been very surprised to discover that the targeting process in the MoD at strategic level was so *ad hoc*, with no trained staff, proper committees or process. My boss was rightly very security-minded with all this, not letting other people know what was being done.

This came to a head when we received a battle damage assessment stating that coalition air forces had attacked a target not approved by the Prime Minister. Number Ten were furious, but we couldn't find a copy of the target list, so had to get the security locksmiths in to break into my boss's security cabinet.

We found the MoD's only copy of the target list in there, to discover that there'd been two spellings for the same target, and they'd attacked the wrong one.

Group Captain Glenn Torpy
Officer Commanding, 13 Squadron, Royal Air Force

This was the first combat air operation since the Falklands War, but used far more of the air force: ninety-five RAF fast jets, plus Chinook helicopters and Hercules. The coalition air force flew about two thousand missions every night. The tanker towlines were where you really saw the scale of it, orbiting 'racetracks' with lines of tankers, aircraft transiting up, and those being refuelled, mostly without lights, wearing night-vision goggles.

We had what we called 'warlords' to run each squadron, allowing the boss to manage higher-level interactions with base commanders, and the crews to concentrate on flying the missions. The warlord's role was absolutely key, as he planned every aspect of the deployment, coordinated everything and liaised with the engineers.

Squadron Leader Dave Brown
Warlord, Royal Air Force

Aircrew shared villas: two in the bedroom, two sleeping on the balcony and two in the sitting room. I give them pills so they could sleep for five hours or so. Even so, people complained about not being able to sleep.

Squadron Leader Phil Smith
Royal Air Force

Some aircrew lived in four-star hotels, relaxing beside the pool between missions on sun lounges, travelling to airfields wearing civilian clothes. Going to war each day from a hotel was generally regarded as a bizarre unreality, which further exaggerated the strangeness of what we were actually doing.

Squadron Leader Dave Brown
Warlord, Royal Air Force

Being grounded aircrew, we Warlords knew the guys, plus had our own [flying] reputations from the past. I tried to prepare myself for whatever might happen. There was no preparation for any sort of battle shock. An air vice marshal actually said, 'Oh, we don't bother with that sort of thing.' We expected to lose an awful lot more men than we did. I didn't think I'd be going home.

Squadron Leader Phil Smith
Royal Air Force

The Tornado is an electric jet, with complicated electronics that don't like water. The desert imposed sand, dust, heat – plus torrential rain. In the first weeks of August, with temperatures between 30°C and 40°C, pilots were unable to walk to the planes wearing NBC kit, and I knew of at least one who collapsed on the tarmac. The heat warped Perspex canopies. Once in the air, the Tornados' air conditioning allows pilots to set any temperature they liked. But when the air war started, the weather had cooled down to something like a pleasant British summer, so heat stopped being a problem.

Very few people knew the locations of the targets: at Tobuk only four. The crews spent the waiting time learning and practising evasion drills and tactics for Iraqi radars and missiles, and flying simulated bombing missions. Everybody had their own ideas as to what was going to happen, but nobody knew anything for certain. There was, however, very little low-level night flying practice, as the computer-controlled Tornado pretty much flew itself.

However, the F3 Phantom air defence aircraft at Dhahran flew from August until the end of the war, twenty-four hours of every day, keeping four patrolling aircraft in the air, all without firing a single shot in anger. Not surprisingly, the F3 crews got very pissed off.

Group Captain Glenn Torpy
Officer Commanding, 13 Squadron, Royal Air Force

My navigator Tom Perham and I wanted to test our aircraft's terrain-following radar over the desert. The computer, radar and autopilot could fly the aircraft automatically, or you could fly manually by following the altitude indicator dots of the head-up display's flight director. The minimum height we could dial in was two hundred feet, and most aircraft settled over dead flat desert at around two-twenty to two-forty feet. But as a SAM 8 could get down to one hundred and eighty feet, people devised different ways of flying lower than this. If you really needed to fly below two hundred feet, you could do it manually, by tracking below the flight director, which is what we did for the rest of the war, but only in particularly dangerous areas – you didn't need to scare yourself the whole trip.

Early one morning fellow recce squadron commander Al Threadgold came in to tell me the war had started.

Squadron Leader Phil Smith
Royal Air Force

A couple of days before going in, aircrew had been told of some targets, and how the strikes were to be made. On Sunday 13 January, the complete air strike plan was revealed to squadrons. Also on that same Sunday, our

Darfur Tornado base lost a crew training in the desert over Oman. In a way this was the best thing that could have happened: it prepared us mentally and when, a few days later, we took losses over Iraq, crews coped with it very well.

The deadline for Iraqi forces to withdraw unconditionally expired at midnight on the 15th – the Tuesday. Everyone was ordered into the squadrons at 0900 that morning. The crews drew their maps, were briefed, read through the intelligence reports related to their routes and target locations, and the planes were prepared. Then the crews were told to be airborne by midnight, then stood down.

Dr Mary McLoughlin

At 0300 hours on 15 January, Saddam hadn't withdrawn from Kuwait, so the United Nations lived up to their threats, and actually bombed Baghdad.

We thought Saddam would surrender very quickly, so the hospital kept us on full pay and we remained at the hotel in Cyprus, in the hope that we could return to Baghdad.

The Rt Hon John Major
Prime Minister

The air raids began at midnight UK time on 16 February, and continued until 23 February, when the ground war began. Throughout this period, I was usually up from midnight onwards, being kept up to date with what was happening with each of the attacks, their successes and our losses. If asleep, I was woken to be told of specific incidents.

Squadron Leader Phil Smith
Royal Air Force

On the night it was a cock-up. Some crews were not due to fly until three and four in the morning. By the time they were stood down it was too late for any of them to take sleeping pills, so the war started with everyone shattered.

The first few missions seemed to take the Iraqi defences by surprise. Their planes were observed crashing and on fire, and some allied aircraft were locked up [by Iraqi radar] but not actually hit by missiles. When some raids arrived at their target airfields, they found landing lights still on, and Iraqi aircraft still on the ground, taxiing. They dropped their bombs, the lights went off and the anti-aircraft fire started. The last aircraft in some raids had light Triple-A [Anti-Aircraft Artillery] coming up at them, but as each of these earlier missions was of only four aircraft, this was minimal. On their return, the aircrew were euphoric, reporting that it was easy.

The second wave went off an hour or two later. By that time the Iraqi air defences were fully alert, so they were shot at and returned to base talking not about how easy it was, but about Triple-A. At first the Iraqi fire was inaccurate, but they learned fast. The next early-evening wave returned saying it was horrendous. Several squadrons noticed a marked difference in attitude towards Triple-A, between the crews who had flown missions and been shot at, and those who had not been exposed.

After three days' intensive flying, tiredness was affecting everybody. On the first day, my boss, after being dragged in at 0900 the previous morning, had flown a straight thirty-eight hours. By the third day he was knackered but wouldn't sleep when he should have done. By the end of the third day I was completely shattered, having flown three missions, with another three aborted.

Major General Alexander Harley
Assistant Chief of Defence Staff (Overseas) and Deputy Director of Joint Operations, Ministry of Defence, Whitehall

Achieving air supremacy meant knocking out airfields and their surface-to-air missile sites – SAM 2s and 3s. Their aircraft were kept in hardened bunker shelters, requiring bombs able to penetrate the concrete, and they hid aircraft in villages and other places.

But we achieved air supremacy without collateral damage to pipelines, electricity and civilian communication systems. Our intelligence people knew largely where their military communication nodes were located, so they were also taken out – some by Special Forces. Some targets were attacked in Kuwait, but Iraqi forces in Kuwait weren't bombed until later, although air power was used against their attack down the coast at Khafji.

Once we'd achieved air supremacy, air power moved against Iraq's weapons of mass destruction, hitting installations all over Iraq. By the time the ground war started, the Iraq air threat had gone completely, although the SAM threat still remained.

Squadron Leader Phil Smith
Royal Air Force

We were pretty experienced working in an NBC environment. Every pilot and navigator had flown in the AR-5 respirator and protection equipment, which is very uncomfortable, like running uphill carrying a sack of potatoes. In some squadron locations, freight containers had airtight 'Porton liners' in which aircrew could live between missions if the site became contaminated by chemical or biological strike.

But the intelligence reports were reassuring. We were told each Scud missile fitted with chemical or biological warhead would take out a tennis court-sized area. As an airfield consists of a great many tennis court-sized areas, we reckoned the incoming threat was not that great.

Lieutenant Colonel Mike Vickery
Commanding Officer, 14th/20th King's Hussars, 4th Armoured Brigade

Our training was now over, so we organised a day off, with a film show and so on. Brigade HQ knew that the air war was about to start, but nobody thought to tell us, so when the NBC alarms went off, Brigade ordered full NBC alert and we spent the entire day masked up. It was a good trial and test of our NBC drills, but all day the soldiers kept coming up to me in their respirators and shouting, 'Thanks for the day off, Colonel. It's epic…'

Group Captain Glenn Torpy
Officer Commanding, 13 Squadron, Royal Air Force

Mission planning took three to four hours, with much dialogue with planners and our own trusted liaison guy, Brian Collins, in the air headquarters; plus we rotated people from flying for a couple of days, to spend a day on the ground helping. As a task came in, we'd allocate each to one of these guys, who'd mark up the maps in advance of the crew coming in, leaving the actual route selection to them. We didn't have too many problems with HQ air planners. If we genuinely didn't like the look of a target, we'd ask them why we were doing it. We never actually turned a target down but, especially with heavily defended targets, people wanted reassurance that their mission would be of use.

We also talked with the tanker guys to ensure coordination. If we thought we'd be low on fuel, or the timings were tight, we'd ask them to tank us up along our route.

The bomber mission commanders had a much more complicated coordination job, working as part of a package, also liaising with their escorts, especially the jammers. For we reconnaissance Tornados, it was reasonably straightforward.

Squadron Leader Phil Smith
Royal Air Force

At the beginning of the planning process, a wing of four aircraft, a 'four-ship', would be given an Iraqi airport as its target. The crew would select their own DMPI [desired mean point of impact] and work out attack tracks for each plane. The Iraqis surrounded their military airfields with concentric rings of Triple-A, their primary defences being around the airfield perimeter some four miles across, with larger, outer rings of Triple-A stations.

As planning proceeded, the intelligence changed, sometimes forcing our plans to be revised. Each member of the four-ship worked on different aspects of the plan, until the final detailed briefing session, to pull the plan together.

Group Captain Glenn Torpy
Officer Commanding, 13 Squadron, Royal Air Force

We carried the maximum amount of fuel in two under-wing tanks, plus two very large under-fuselage tanks, which made the aircraft very sluggish and heavy to fly. We normally tanked at ten thousand feet – the optimum for us given our weight, but you could run out of power. On one night, because there were so many other aircraft, with tankers stacked up in the race-tracks, we had to climb to twenty-three thousand feet, but because of cloud couldn't gain visual contact for long enough to join up. We had to descend to two thousand feet and tanked there. Tanking problems jeopardised timings, affecting time on target.

Air-to-air refuelling was often the most dangerous part of our trips; people damaged fuel probes and tanker baskets. There were many nights of bumpy cloud everywhere, and despite radar it was often tricky finding a tanker.

We ran two shifts: the early shift came in during the afternoon, took off as it got dark, returning just after midnight. The late shift came in around nine pm, took off at midnight, returning home around six am – with their whole day displaced. This took a lot of getting used to. The airfield was very noisy during the day, with building work on our residential compound. A lot of us used Temazepam to sleep; it gave me a good day's sleep, without side effects.

Squadron Leader Dave Brown
Warlord, Royal Air Force

After putting on flying kit, and a last chat with intelligence staff, in most squadrons the final preparation was as they left the headquarters, in front of the warlord's desk. The warlord checked they had their codes, morphine, pistol and ammunition, and tried to draw them in on themselves to concentrate on the mission. There'd be the odd quip, then off to the crew bus. Each aircrew had already memorised emergency rendezvous locations and times for the helicopter pickups, the times of the search-and-rescue satellite passing overhead, and so on.

They were dropped off along the flight line, where they signed for their aircraft from the engineer, checked its weapon load then got in, a full hour before take-off, twice the usual time. They'd then start the aircraft and do the checks. If the aircraft proved faulty, they'd be given a spare plane, so that after forty-five minutes there were four planes running with good weapon loads, ready in every respect to go. On most squadrons there were ten planes for the four that went out on missions.

Then they'd taxi off, reporting up over the UHF radio link with the words 'Target check one, two, three, four', and be gone into the warm desert night. The next anybody at base would hear from them would be at the very end of the mission, when they radioed in saying 'Target check' as they landed.

Squadron Leader Phil Smith
Royal Air Force

The missions started gently, transiting at medium altitude to the tanker, which was flying an hour or so out from the Iraqi border. They'd refuel in mid-air, at the same time moving towards the border so as to be full at the drop-off point, then descend to two hundred feet before crossing the border, having checked their low-level flight equipment carefully. If the terrain-following radar or warning gear failed to work, they'd turn back. In the first few days of the war, the abort rate was very high.

Transit across Iraq to target was quiet, the route designed to obtain regular updates from known points on the ground to ensure the navigation equipment was working accurately once they reached the target. Flying at low level is entirely automatic, the sophisticated autopilot and terrain-hugging radar doing all the work. Pilot and navigator monitor progress and watch for signs of detection or attack. The excitement tended to be over the target.

We'd do four hundred and fifty knots through to the target, then two minutes out, put on the afterburner, accelerating up to five hundred and fifty knots attack speed. We'd then turn it off, so as we approached the target we were just beginning to slow down, then release the autopilot, and for twenty seconds fly manually, straight and level, before bomb release. This is when we got seriously fired at by the Triple-A. The first guy through the target was usually OK, but numbers seven and eight were getting shot at in a bad way.

Squadron Leader Dave Brown
Warlord, Royal Air Force

Designed to slip below enemy radar, the Tornado was flown in accordance with Cold War procedures, very low, so that it would arrive undetected, to drop JP233 cluster bombs. But the required final twenty seconds of flying manually straight and level had been a serious topic of debate in crew rooms and bars over the years.

Tornado's low-level bomb aiming system didn't work unless the aircraft was flown in this way, and exposed the crew to maximum danger at the most vulnerable point of their mission. The crews were frightened fartless by seeing the Triple-A coming up at them, and to an extent it put them off their attacks. But this tracer fire also marked the interlinking of the Iraqi anti-aircraft defences, revealing safe corridors down which they could fly, enabling them to change their approach to target at the last minute.

Squadron Leader Phil Smith
Royal Air Force

The concentration required to drop the bombs meant people had to ignore the Triple-A. The Tornado is actually designed for peacetime, to ensure bombs are not dropped by accident. We called it a 'Greenpeace aircraft', as a hundred and twenty-six switches have to be in the right place before the bombs will come off the rails. In doing lots of practice bombing runs, you've trained not to make that final switch, so when you do for real you've broken a very well-tried routine, and so you stand a good chance of breaking other routines. We were in some ways more worried about getting the switch settings right and successfully dropping the bombs, than we were about the Iraqi air defence or missile alarms. It's a big job getting the switches right.

During that final run-in, you'd be looking out for visual signs of Triple-A, and the navigator would be watching for missiles and indications of radar lock.

Squadron Leader Dave Brown
Warlord, Royal Air Force

One of the main problems with the Royal Air Force in war is that the officers are fighting the war and the boys are only supporting that effort. In the army, the boys are the weapon so must be kept briefed up. Being deeply involved with intelligence and planning, the aircrew were well briefed, but the ground crews were in a very different position, and it was our fault that we didn't pass intelligence down to them as we should have done. We were too worried about the tactics and fighting the air war. Ground crews became very sensitive about not being told what was going on. They thought, for example, one Scud going off at twenty thousand feet would kill them all, which wasn't true.

Squadron Leader Phil Smith
Royal Air Force

Once all the bombers had made the run and dropped their bombs, we'd run away at low-level on autopilot, calming ourselves down as we crossed back into Saudi Arabia, then pulling up to the tanker for a refill. Each sortie worked out as being two and a half minutes of complete panic, surrounded by four and a half hours of calm.

On returning to base, debriefing took some ninety minutes, giving a detailed account of the mission to intelligence staff, right down to the colours of the tracer bullets, strobes and any radar illumination we'd experienced, the guns and missiles fired near or at us, and the locations and directions of fire. We then completed a mission report before going back to the living accommodation to sleep – a total of between twelve and fourteen very intensive hours every day.

Group Captain Glenn Torpy
Officer Commanding, 13 Squadron, Royal Air Force

The officers are the guys who break the aircraft then tell the engineers to fix it 'immediately', with all sorts of banter and friction. But when we started losing aircraft, the ground crew suddenly realised that each time they waved us off, they might not be seeing us again. People's views of aircrew changed quite significantly.

Our relationship with our photographic analysts changed as well. We'd look carefully through all the imagery before the mission, then spend up to a couple of hours afterwards with the analysts. It wasn't just leap into the jet, fire it up, bugger off and come back.

Squadron Leader Dave Brown
Warlord, Royal Air Force

On one Tornado base, the ground crew living accommodation was on the far side of the airfield, with a ten-kilometre commute past the local town. They became worried that regularly driving past a potentially hostile residential area was encouraging a terrorist reaction. In the end we issued them with small arms so they felt better. Compared to the danger of missions, the aircrew in this squadron were unconcerned at the prospect of being bombed or shot at by terrorists on the ground.

We had to be very careful what we said when any of the ground crew were within earshot – no funny asides, or expressions of opinion. Rumours really flashed round the place because of the ground crew guy's constant thirst for information. CNN was on all the time, and while at times it scotched quite a few rumours, it started quite a few as well.

Seven men looked after each aircraft, plus specialist weapon-loading teams to load the bombs. They looked after their aircrews really well, having tea ready for them immediately on landing, then as the war progressed, painting aircraft noses with shark's teeth, names and so on – a forbidden activity in peacetime.

The only frightening thing in war is the unknown – the things that you've been unable to think through; like the noise of the Patriots. We knew the Scuds were a limited threat, but nobody knew what Patriots sounded like coming off the rails, and it made a bloody great bang.

I had two girl operations sergeants who were brilliant throughout. Some of the men, however, were very nervous; for example, our clothing store people would be in their respirators if you slammed the toilet door. We had to split them up after a while.

In the early days, the media had publicised the F3 Phantom aircrews' concerns that their aircraft were older, less sophisticated, and vulnerable to the new Russian MiG fighters that the Iraqis were thought to have. But after the initial four-day blitz of low-level airfield attacks by the Tornados' JP233 mine and bomblet weapons, plus by having electronic counter-measures escort aircraft on each mission, the MiG threat was removed. Similarly, the Iraqis' Russian-made SAMs were revealed as being their less sophisticated versions, permitting our bombing raids to fly at medium and high level.

Group Captain Glenn Torpy
Officer Commanding, 13 Squadron, Royal Air Force
The bomber boys also dropped thousand-pound iron bombs from low level, lobbing them in from a climb a couple of kilometres out – the 'loft profile' – often using an air-burst fuse that was particularly effective against Triple-A or aircraft on the ground.

But after the weapon came off, to recover and escape, you had to go into the very aggressive 'loft manoeuvre' – after pulling up, over-banking to one hundred and forty-five degrees, pulling down into a ten degree dive to low level again, all in some twenty seconds. We were pretty sure we'd lost one aircraft doing this.

Squadron Leader Dave Brown
Warlord, Royal Air Force
After the initial low-level sorties, the battle casualty replacement crews arriving from the UK and Germany were noticeably more prepared to push at a lower level than the guys who had been shot at already.

Care had to be taken to ensure that crews were not exposed to more danger than they were capable of coping with. During the medium-level bombing phase I stood down one crew for a day, after they were twitched by a very close missile.

Squadron Leader Phil Smith
Royal Air Force
The stress of low-level bombing, and the threat to aircrew of Triple-A during the first four days, caused serious morale problems. The guys became obsessed by Triple-A, and after four days needed a rest. If we'd carried on, we'd have had to slow the sortie rate and change our tactics.

The allied HARM shooter and ECM escort aircraft were very effective against the Triple-A. If the Iraqi defenders turned their radars on, they were blasted by radar-seeking weapons, and so were soon firing only at sounds. But nevertheless their fire was very effective. They seemed to have unlimited ammunition, one airfield being assessed as having fired over forty tons of ammunition against four aircraft, using sixteen guns in the middle of the airfield, creating the comic-book 'Wall of Lead' which at night, coming up at you, looks terrible. The Iraqis had listening posts at the border, and so after the first days, planes could find themselves under fire all the way in.

We completely rethought our bombing tactics in case low-level airfield denial missions again became necessary, deciding to go in as ones and twos rather than eight-ships, as well as lobbing thousand-pound bombs into the anti-aircraft sites to keep their heads down. However, by the time we'd thought all this through, they'd stopped us going low level anyway.

The guys were relieved. They'd done around three low-level missions each. The recce crews, however, flew the whole war at low-level, on their own, doing five-hour missions across Iraq. And later in the war, we went back to low-level bombing against some targets.

Group Captain Glenn Torpy
Officer Commanding, 13 Squadron, Royal Air Force

After a week of low-level bombing and high losses, the bomber guys got together with the air commander to look at other options. The Americans did the same. Our intelligence people hadn't realised how heavily the airfields were going to be defended, particularly with Triple-A, none of it particularly accurately guided, but it's easy to be unlucky.

It was good that the tactics were changed – an important adaptation to enemy reactions.

Major General Rupert Smith
General Officer Commanding, 1st Armoured Division

After the air forces went in on the 17th, we heard very little of what they were doing – nor did I expect to hear much. Peter de la Billiere told me that when the RAF had people shot down, the Americans became very concerned. He said they were very sensitive about their allies, especially later when the SAS patrol [Bravo Two Zero] was captured. He also told me that he was experiencing difficulty with London over this – another, added background pressure on him.

The Rt Hon John Major
Prime Minister

We needed the maximum national support for what was happening so I invited the leaders of the opposition parties [Neil Kinnock and Paddy Ashdown] to Number 10 on a regular basis. I wished to do as much as I possibly could to keep Parliament away from controversy, and united behind the troops who were fighting. I also had regular meetings with the Archbishop of Canterbury, Robert Runcie, and Cardinal Hume, as well as the Muslim and Jewish leaders. It was important to keep the churches united as well as the politicians and, generally, they were.

There was no histrionics or posturing at these meetings. Everyone understood the gravity of the situation. It was all rather low-key. I told them what the situation was. They made a few observations, and thanked me for keeping them informed. I offered to keep in touch with developments – and did so.

The Rt Hon Tom King
UK Secretary of State for Defence

Saddam fired Scuds at Israel to bring them into the war. To their, and the Americans', credit, this didn't happen. It was undoubtedly Saddam's objective to bring Israel into the war, then declare jihad and be seen as the champion of the Arab world. He'd already been regarded in this way for fighting the war against Iran, with the support of virtually all the Arab countries, who'd seen him as their protector in this respect.

But we were there to liberate Kuwait. Israel was nothing to do with this problem. Our Arab allies wouldn't want to be used in any way as protectors of Israel. Everything was done to ensure Israel kept out of it. A huge SAS and SBS effort was put into identifying the Scud sites – including the mobile sites. This was a major consideration.

The Rt Hon John Major
Prime Minister

When the first Scuds were fired we had real anxiety that they contained chemicals. We simply didn't know. After one such attack on Tel Aviv, I telephoned the Israeli prime minister in the middle of the night asking him not to respond, as Israel would make matters much worse if they did so. I told him that he should leave it to America and Britain to respond to any attacks on Israel.

I spoke to the Israelis several times during the conflict – as I believe did George Bush. They understood that the situation would escalate if they intervened. They didn't like our message, and their natural instinct was to respond, but they accepted the logic of not doing so. It was not easy for them. They are a warrior nation with a war-like temperament, and were being threatened, so the Israeli government had to keep the lid on public opinion. I admired their restraint on this occasion.

Brigadier Mike Willcocks
Chief of Staff (Land), Joint War Headquarters, RAF High Wycombe

The Israelis made it clear that if any Scuds contained chemical weapons, they would really go for it. We were concerned they would nuke Baghdad – a huge worry, even though thousands of Patriot missiles were deployed, and the Scuds were not very technically advanced.

The Americans had earlier said they didn't want any more Special Forces in the Gulf, which was why the British 5 Airborne Brigade were not deployed. But de la Billiere wanted our Special Forces to have a role in the western desert, so they were transmuted from general intelligence, to Scud hunting. A tremendous focus was given to this, and every Scud launch was identified and transmitted to us.

The Scuds weren't very accurate, some of them broke up in the air, and not everyone was scared by them. I was in Riyadh just before the air war started; nobody was on the streets, but immediately the Scud warnings sounded, I saw thousands of people rush out of the buildings to watch them come in. With Patriot missiles going off and so on, it was completely surreal.

Group Captain Glenn Torpy
Officer Commanding, 13 Squadron, Royal Air Force

One of my pilots, Dick Garwood, found a launcher, more by luck than good judgement as he would freely admit, earning us the nickname of 'Scud-Hunters'. For some ten days we were tasked to hunt Scuds.

We covered a vast area. But Scuds couldn't go everywhere, and knowing they were prime targets, hid themselves wherever they could; for example under road bridges. So we tended to fly low along major roads, off-setting ourselves to one side so we could look under bridges or into culverts.

As the campaign evolved, American F15s became the prime Scud hunters; but even then, very few were found. The Scuds were very elusive. Even in the second Gulf War, when so much effort was put into Scud hunting, few were found.

We were also tasked in support of the Special Forces, working well across to the west as far as the Syrian border, to clear routes they were going to use for ingress. We'd fly these routes for several days before a Special Forces operation, reporting on what was there, to build up an intelligence picture and give them confidence.

Lance Corporal Roy Sellstrom
Pioneer Corps, Army War Graves Unit

Up in Al Jubayl we were used to seeing Iraqi Scuds flying overhead, then the trails of the Patriot missiles as they were launched up after them. It didn't really bother us, as the port was forward of where the Scuds were actually landing. It was very different in Riyadh. On a visit down there, when the warnings went off, I was taking my time getting into NBC gear, which several people commented on. But then there was a fucking enormous explosion, the whole of the hotel moved, and then sort of sprang back again. I ran straight under the stairs, trying to put a rubber glove on to my head, with chunks of plaster falling from the stairs on to our heads. It frightened the life out of me.

The Scuds were targeted to hit the runway, but were bouncing off into houses the other side. Most didn't blow up. The guys said the Patriot missiles could also come crashing down as well – with us in the middle of the impact area. We went straight back to Al Jubayl, which was safer.

Group Captain Glenn Torpy
Officer Commanding, 13 Squadron, Royal Air Force

On my first night in Dhahran, a large piece of Scud landed a hundred yards away from where we were living, the first of many in that first week. During each attack, the Patriot defensive missile systems would fire, but we were never sure if a Scud would get through. But after a week or so, people started to treat these attacks as a spectator sport, going to the tops of buildings to watch rather than the shelters. However, later on in the war, big chunks of a Scud did get through and killed thirty-two Americans near to us in Dhahran.

Squadron Leader Phil Smith
Royal Air Force

After the first four days, during which we flew every day, it was realised that the British Tornados were flying more than anyone else in the allied air force. We were told to back off, going into a comparatively relaxed routine in which crews flew every couple of days, which pleased them because they didn't get shot out so much, but led to the ground crews getting bored.

With flying at night, the aircraft would be serviced by the night shift, leaving the day shift with nothing to do, which they became unhappy about. The ground crews, particularly the armourers, had hard physical work to do in preparing the aircraft between missions. However, when compared to a tactical evaluation exercise in Europe, the Gulf War workload was comparatively light. Boredom forced some squadrons to change the shifts round for the sake of their day shift ground crew's morale, which had not been the original intention.

Group Captain Glenn Torpy
Officer Commanding, 13 Squadron, Royal Air Force

We were pretty respectful of the bomber boys over those first few days. About three days in, I was having coffee with Jerry Witts, the boss of 31 Squadron, and he said to me, 'I'm not sure how long I'm going to be able to keep the boys doing this.' He was concerned about the level of risk night after night, compared to the payback. The Iraqi air force wasn't responding – apart from some air activity over Baghdad, so the risk didn't seem to be worth it.

Squadron Leader Dave Brown
Warlord, Royal Air Force

We'd done hard training in peacetime, losing crews in the process, which had hit me dreadfully hard at the time, but you have to roll with it. We lost friends from the very beginning of the Gulf deployment, and didn't even know how many until the prisoners of war were returned at the very end. While the war was going on, you couldn't dwell on it.

I felt dreadfully bad that I wasn't flying. The crews were feeling hard things without a doubt, so my whole object was to make life as easy as possible for them. If they were being a pain in the arse, the rule was that only me or the detachment commander could tell them – nobody else. Some aircrew took advantage of this, ordering people around, pushing their luck, even being rude. After missions, I'd take such individuals aside and sort them out, but I felt an overwhelming need to take every care of them that I could.

Squadron Leader Phil Smith
Royal Air Force

The second phase of the bombing campaign was from medium altitude, around twenty thousand feet, dropping freefall bombs on to much larger targets. The accuracy was little better than that achieved by Bomber Command in the Second World War. Eight bombs dropped from twenty thousand feet on to twenty square kilometres of oilfield might hit only one part of the objective. The accuracy problem was solved by American-supplied laser-guided bombs.

Group Captain Glenn Torpy
Officer Commanding, 13 Squadron, Royal Air Force

The bomber boys stopped dropping at low level, and moved up to medium level bombing from twenty thousand feet, using a new fuse – the multi-function bomb fuse. On the first or second night of this, an aircraft was fragged by its own bomb and the crew went 'missing in action' – later found to be captured. We never discovered whether this was from the fuse being incorrectly set.

The Tornado was never optimised to operate at medium altitude, so sorting all this out and developing tactics took some time. Only towards the end did we receive designators and laser-guidance kits, so only about nine per cent of the munitions were precision-guided.

Major General Alexander Harley
Assistant Chief of Defence Staff (Overseas) and Deputy Director of Joint Operations, Ministry of Defence, Whitehall

The iron bombs being dropped from medium level were too inaccurate to comply with our targeting policy; for example, of not bombing any Iraqi ministries. We daren't risk attacking targets even anywhere remotely near to such buildings.

We had no laser-designated bombs, so had to get some from the Americans, and with GEC-Marconi we developed a system called TIALD – Thermal Imaging Airborne Laser Designator – with a pod on designator aircraft to guide the bombs.

The development of TIALD was very, very rapid, at Boscombe Down, an existing project, rushed forward during the air war itself.

Squadron Leader Phil Smith
Royal Air Force

To fit in with the Americans' admin, laser-guided sorties had to be planned by six pm on the day before the mission. The work rate went down to flying every other day. People relaxed and actually slept. We knew the targets well in advance and it was an easy regime, plus we were no longer being shot at.

Group Captain Glenn Torpy
Officer Commanding 13 Squadron, Royal Air Force

Certain systems have to be working for aircraft to continue on a mission: our flares and EW [electronic warfare] pod for example were pretty temperamental, but our only means of protection against radar SAMs which shot down quite a few people.

We're paid to decide which failures in an aircraft we can carry, and this changes with the scenario, and what we're doing. But it's always up to the crew to decide if they're going to conform to the strict list. One day, our terrain-following radar display bar was canted off to one side, indicating that the inertial platform was malfunctioning, which means you're not allowed to terrain-follow with it. But I decided as we had reasonable weather, I could see enough to go. Some people, however, did press on unreasonably, risking expensive crew and aircraft – as if they'd got a death wish.

Squadron Leader Dave Brown
Warlord, Royal Air Force

When crews had to turn back with equipment faults, they'd be very fed up, especially when that happened a few times on the trot. But as warlord, I'd find myself wondering if we had a case of lack of moral fibre.

When we started doing the laser-guided bombing, we had guys who kept missing the basket, so you'd wonder if they were actually capable of doing the job. In a discreet survey of all the crews, we found one particular guy suffered bad luck – but three times on the trot. I had also had another guy who kept aborting with aircraft failures, and in the end he went.

Aircraft serviceability records show that on the less dangerous medium-level missions, aircrew entered Iraq carrying more aircraft faults than they did in the low-level phase. Crews were very much more inclined to abort the more stressful and dangerous low-level missions if in any doubt, as low-level flying leaves virtually no margin for error, especially with navigation and terrain-following systems. Medium-level bombing in the company of other aircraft does not require anything like the same system reliability.

We became paranoid about defending the aircrew from our superiors, who analysed where each bomb was falling. Whereas you could have said what you liked in a debrief about your low-level sorties, laser-guided bombing debriefs consisted of watching the actual film of the attack, and seeing exactly where each of your bombs went.

However, despite being able to see exactly where each bomb landed, the process of evaluating actual damage caused by the raids took a long time, and we got no feedback about battle damage, so we didn't actually know how we were doing – which the guys really needed. The freefall-bombing phase from medium level caused spectacular oil fires, which at night were visible to the crews who assumed they'd dropped smack on target. In fact, the fires were often caused by only one bomb hitting part of the refinery, with the other seven missing, across twenty-five-square-kilometre targets. The crews were not prepared to accept that they were as bad as actually they were, and even now many still feel like that.

Group Captain Glenn Torpy
Officer Commanding, 13 Squadron, Royal Air Force
We instil huge amounts of discipline into our aircrew, imposing very careful rules of engagement, and, if in any doubt, people are trained not to drop. But I don't think anyone worries about what CNN might say. In any case, there weren't many of these incidents.

Squadron Leader Dave Brown
Warlord, Royal Air Force
Changing from the intense environment of low-level to laser-guided bombing

was very benign, and we had problems winding the crews up. They became blasé about SAMs coming up at them – until a number eleven [aircraft] got shot down, the nav killed and the pilot captured. This incident did the job for us.

Then, as the ground war approached, winter rain and cloud created difficulties both on the ground and in the air. With laser-guided bombing, if you can't see the target you can't drop. Days of solid rain caused lots of problems, particularly at Dhahran with crews getting bunched up after days of aborted missions. Then at the end, when the retreating Iraqi army set fire to the oil wells, smoke also restricted visibility, causing all manner of flying and target acquisition problems.

The aircrew were very critical about everything, especially quick to pick up mistakes by anyone on the ground – by the engineers or intelligence. They could make mistakes themselves, but it was never their fault and you just had to let it ride. I couldn't bother the OC because he'd got his own war to fight.

I told the guys on the ground that the crews might be rude, difficult and unreasonable, but they had to bite their tongues until they're gone, then curse them all they wanted. They were the ones being shot at, so ground crew had to make allowances.

Brigadier Patrick Cordingley
Commander, 7th Armoured Brigade

We were still near to the port. Our chemical alarms went off fairly frequently, but as soon as the bombing started, we assumed this was the Iraqis getting through to us, and so put on our chemical suits and respirators. My thoughts were somewhat different to those of other people in that I thought, 'Shit, I wish I'd not avoided all the NBC drills training back in Soltau through being too busy.' I didn't know how to drink or eat wearing a gas mask. In the heat, your sweat filled up the gas mask, and unless you knew how to empty it, you could drown in the bloody thing! So I hoped the chemical alerts wouldn't go on for too long.

Squadron Leader Dave Brown
Warlord, Royal Air Force

It took several hours before we could say we'd lost a crew. After crossing the border, they'd call in on the radio. If they said 'Mission successful all aboard' we knew they were all right. At other airfields, there was no radio contact at all with their missions after take-off. Ground staff had simply to count them all back in once they landed. But this time, one of our aircrews reported 'Mission successful, no contact with leader', so we knew something was wrong. When they landed, I isolated this four-ship from the others for a few hours, while we did the casualty procedures.

We worked out where the missing crew had gone down, then waited until the time they would have run out of fuel [had they survived] before alerting the search and rescue cell as to where the fireball had been seen. The admin was equally simple: one phone call to get the NOTICAS [casualty notification] system going. On this occasion our night sortie was cancelled, so we were able to go round to the four-ships accommodation for a few beers, the traditional method of seeing a missing crew on their way. The replacement crew arrived the same day; we had the next missions to plan, so life, and the war, went on.

Sergeant Shaun Rusling
Medic, Parachute Regiment, 32 Field Hospital

After the air war began, we were suddenly ordered to move from the transit camp to where our field hospital was being set up. We crammed into three coaches so full of equipment that everyone was sitting on top of the gear rather than the seats, then drove down the main supply route into the desert. After seven hours we reached a junction where the military police were supposed to guide us off the MSR on to a road to the right. But the lead coach carried straight on, ending up in the newspapers as the first British unit to enter Iraq (almost). The American military police had to chase and physically stop them, two hundred metres short of the border.

Lieutenant Colonel Mike Vickery
Commanding Officer, 14th/20th King's Hussars,
4th Armoured Brigade

With no side armour, Challenger was vulnerable to high explosive anti-tank rounds at the side – and also in the rear. The upgrade pack gave us explosive-reactive armour plates for the front glacis plate [the sloped front section of the hull], three by six inches in size, with special lead Chobham armour plates for the side, in a kit complete with all the tools required. A specialist team drilled the holes in the glacis plates, and took most of a day to upgrade a squadron.

It added a lot of extra weight, but oddly made the tank sit rather better, and serendipitously improved the aerodynamics. It sounds odd to think of a tank having aerodynamics, but the changes made the air push the dust away from the engines and down on to the ground. The 750hp engine was very powerful, so the extra ton and a bit made no difference.

Sergeant Shaun Rusling
Medic, Parachute Regiment, 32 Field Hospital

When we arrived at the hospital the NAIADs went off. Three of us knew where our gear was and got masked up on the coach, but most people didn't, so there was a mass panic in the darkness; women screaming because they couldn't get their equipment on. Then someone told us it was a false alarm caused by the burning of shit from the latrines. I didn't think something like that would set them off. These so-called 'false' alarms were to cause us terrible problems.

Brigadier Patrick Cordingley
Commander, 7th Armoured Brigade

The effect of the air war on the Iraqi army was of great interest to us. Riyadh HQ were sending us the daily American air force summaries of the effect of the bombing, given in percentages of their capability, including who they thought the various Iraqi units were. When later the bombing shifted to the Iraqi frontline positions, we were given more detailed estimates, right down to the actual numbers.

Brigadier Mike Willcocks
Chief of Staff (Land), Joint War Headquarters, RAF High Wycombe

Coalition air force intelligence were fooled by the Iraqis' very clever use of fake tanks, fuel dumps and dummy positions. What they assessed often wasn't real, and at the end their assessments were proved to have been inaccurate.

But the Iraqi air force was unable to interfere with allied ground operations, and the strategic bombing campaign was also successful, knocking out the Iraqi communication nodes, which the SBS followed up in a heli-borne raid to cut the main fibre-optic communication cable from Baghdad.

But against Iraqi army units, American army Apache helicopters, and not strategic air power, did the most damage. It's vital to understand that on its own, strategic air power cannot win wars.

The Rt Hon Tom King
UK Secretary of State for Defence

The real challenge of the air war was evaluating the extent to which the military targets had been damaged or destroyed, and also to assess if there'd been bombing mistakes leading to civilian casualties. One civilian shelter was specifically targeted as being the headquarters Saddam was actually in. Unfortunately, the intelligence was wrong and civilians were killed. On another occasion, a missile went off course and into a market place; tragic errors with significant casualties.

The Rt Hon John Major
Prime Minister

Saddam's attempts to present the allied bombing as attacking innocent civilians wasn't a problem. He was a braggart and a bully and had no traction in the UK. Public opinion and the media were supportive of the government. I also sought – and obtained – church and all-party agreement. I don't recall one single uncomfortable moment in this regard.

The Rt Hon Tom King
UK Secretary of State for Defence

For practically *every* bombing and missile raid, Saddam had some PR story that it had been a school or mosque. The damage assessment people had to deal with this, while trying to determine as good a picture as possible of the effect of the bombing on degrading Saddam's ability to fight. They were a great people for subterfuge and deliberate tricks; plus we had a significant shortage of HUMINT [human intelligence] – from people actually on the ground.

And some very odd things happened. At the beginning of the destruction of the Iraq air force, half of them had suddenly taken off and flown to Iran. We couldn't work out if that meant Iran was going to side with Iraq.

Lieutenant General Walter Boomer
General Officer Commanding, 1 Marine Expeditionary Force, United States Marine Corps

The air war was a magnificent piece of work by all the aviators. They started striking in and around Baghdad, but more importantly from my perspective, were also picking off artillery units. Being an Iraqi soldier deployed near the

Saudi border must have been hell. I always take battle damage assessments with a pinch of salt, but was pleased with what unfolded. The more intense the air attacks, the greater the trickle of Iraqis across to us. We were learning more, which helped us immeasurably with the ground attack.

Lieutenant Toby Masterton
A Squadron, The Life Guards, 4th Armoured Brigade

We'd see aircraft navigation lights coming through Saudi airspace, then lights off as they passed into Kuwait. Then a while later, the whole horizon would flash; a very long pause, then an unbelievable crescendo of noise as the sound reached us. Some time later, the aircraft would return, their lights flicking back on as they regained Saudi airspace.

Group Captain Glenn Torpy
Officer Commanding, 13 Squadron, Royal Air Force

Our aircraft were performing superbly, especially the terrain-following system. Our recce equipment didn't work very well to start with, but field service reps from the company worked hard tweaking the equipment, until by the end we were achieving fantastic results. But it could still only be used at low altitude, but as the only people operating at low level, we retained the element of surprise.

Everybody's different, but I felt that the people coping best with the task and stress were the slightly quieter, steady individuals. There aren't many introverts in the air force, but the really extrovert people quietened down – at least some of them did. It was the thoughtful people who produced the goods at the end of the day.

Squadron Leader Dave Brown
Warlord, Royal Air Force

Towards the end of the air war, crews were complaining that some of the targets were a waste of time, which as we got to the end of the priority target list was inevitable. We did question some targets with headquarters, who told us to get on with it. The crews whinged and complained. By the end we were bombing secondary airfields. But we'd tell the crews that if a few soldiers' lives might be saved by their mission, they should just get out there for four hours and do it.

Group Captain Glenn Torpy
Officer Commanding, 13 Squadron, Royal Air Force

With the other squadrons losing people, people at home were far more nervous than we were. My wife Christine watched the first waves of aircraft going into Iraq on television, and our neighbour had to come round to keep her company. Sometimes it's harder for the families than the blokes doing what they're trained to do.

Lieutenant Toby Masterton
A Squadron, The Life Guards, 4th Armoured Brigade

We moved across to the Royal Scots, who were rather a dour lot. There'd been a lot of banter with the 14th/20th, but I think the infantry thought us a bunch of lounge-lizard cavalrymen.

I spent a lot of time scrambling around vague desert tracks, still scrounging kit from all over the place. I managed to drive off a sand dune and crash into a *sabkha* salt lake, where we spent an uncomfortable night at a forty-five-degree angle, before the armoured recovery vehicle arrived to pull us out – with much mirth and pointing of fingers at us.

Dr Mary McLoughlin

By 21 January, it was clear Saddam wasn't going to withdraw from Kuwait. We were fired from our jobs, our pay stopped, then flown to London, where we were free to go wherever we wanted to go. We were extremely upset for the Iraqis, especially knowing they hadn't wanted that war in the first place.

Brigadier Mike Willcocks
Chief of Staff (Land), Joint War Headquarters, RAF High Wycombe

The Joint Force Headquarters' operation ran to a daily routine: I'd come in at 0530 and gather all the information from the MoD, and from theatre, sift it, ask questions and sort it into context for the commander, ready for the 0700 battle group session, followed by the command group at 0800 when all the work was coordinated; then the same again at 1730 when Paddy Hine was briefed. All desks were manned in two twelve-hour shifts.

All sorts of aphorisms and abbreviations developed as the crisis progressed: 'BOGSAT', for example, was a 'Bunch of Generals Sitting Around Talking'. We had two political advisers, Peter Wallace and Andrew Palmer, ambassadors in between jobs, who knew the Arab world extremely well.

Major David Potts
SO2 Army Logistics, Quartermaster General's Department

Beside my desk I kept a cartoon of tank soldiers in the desert eating chocolate and saying, 'Cheers to the Belgians for their contribution to the war effort.'

We were replacing our depth fire M110 artillery guns with the new MLRS rocket system. Nobody knew if this transition could be made in time for the beginning of the land war. We telephoned the Commanding Officer of the artillery regiment, Peter Williams, who said that if we could buy him some special fireproof oblated panels from the French to stop the rocket's reflux incinerating his launchers, he'd be able to change over from eight-inch howitzers in time. There was a lot of hand-wringing about this, as there was only a couple of weeks to do it. But they succeeded, and MLRS ended up being a really battle-winning element.

Brigadier Patrick Cordingley
Commander, 7th Armoured Brigade

We'd first been given prophylactic injections against anthrax, bubonic plague in January, then when the chemical alarms started going off we took NAPS tablets.

The injections themselves were hugely unpleasant, like having bad flu. Rumours suggested NAPS made your hair fall out or was full of bromide, none of which was helpful. We thought the infantry might not take their NAPS, so they were made to take it on parade every morning; but not the gunners, cavalry or sappers. We thought most intelligent people would take it.

But although intended to save people's lives, these measures also heightened people's awareness of the chemical threat.

Sergeant Shaun Rusling
Medic, Parachute Regiment, 32 Field Hospital

The vaccinations were code named 'Victor', 'Cutter', 'Porton' and 'Biological'. Despite being medical staff, we were never told what was in them, or specifically what they were for.

After two of the injections, I decided they were so debilitating, I wasn't going to have any more. I went to my boss Jim Riley, who said, 'I'm going to have them,' and that as a senior NCO, I should set a good example; so muggins had his third one – and it was even worse than after the first two;

a terrible fever for forty-eight hours so I couldn't even get out of my cot. The guys developed a system of bringing people meals. And when I could get up, I had a very painful limp from where they'd injected it. Others were in exactly the same condition.

Lieutenant Colonel Arthur Denaro
Commanding Officer, Queen's Royal Irish Hussars
It's much simpler, by and large, not to explain the details of difficult things to the boys: for example, the injections. We were pincushions by the end of it all, with the amount of antidotes we were either taking orally or having injected into us.

Lieutenant Colonel Charles Rogers
Commanding Officer, Staffordshire Regiment
The injections began, but nobody knew what the effects would be, and they kept telling us we'd need to have more – in particular another plague injection. I said I didn't want the soldiers feeling ill just when we might have to go in. We weren't badly affected, but in the end I didn't let us have the second injection.

Brigadier Patrick Cordingley
Commander, 7th Armoured Brigade
Before 1 Division arrived, my headquarters had sent a signal back to the MoD in London, asking them if the vaccinations had been properly tested. I never received a satisfactory reply.

Major General Alexander Harley
Assistant Chief of Defence Staff (Overseas) and Deputy Director of Joint Operations, Ministry of Defence, Whitehall
There was an efficacy issue behind the whole vaccination programme. The speed at which the work had to be done left something to be desired in terms of testing. We did obtain UK licensing, but balance of risk – between possible side effects and what might happen if troops were not protected – played a big part in obtaining this.

The overriding motivation was that we knew there was a threat, we knew we could do something about mitigating it with our expertise in this area, and so a duty of care was the overriding consideration, even if the vaccines were not one hundred per cent. This risk may also have either put other nations off, or more probably made the UK wary of offering it to anybody else.

It had been a very great struggle to manufacture enough vaccine for our own troops, especially with the US stalling. We had to work on the threat characteristics as we knew them, we did not want the other side to learn what we were doing, and it was not possible to change vaccines quickly. So we and the USA kept very quiet.

However, late in the day we felt obliged to tell NATO and Old Commonwealth members of the coalition what we were doing, and I think there were offers of sharing info so that they could do something about it. But I don't think we had enough to offer anyone any doses, or if we did, whether anyone took up offers from us or from the USA. Broadly, there was no take up.

Major General Rupert Smith
General Officer Commanding, 1st Armoured Division

The prospect of chemical attack worried other people very greatly, but I didn't realise that until afterwards. I didn't think a chemical attack could be effective, because it required us to remain in the same place, grouped together, with stable weather, plus a lot of artillery and other delivery methods. We were deliberately dispersed over large areas, moving every twenty-four hours, so they'd only get a small group of us. We could drive out of any contaminated areas and the weather was far too windy.

The most likely place for us to be attacked by chemicals was as we grouped together to go though the breach. But this would be an act of last resort, so I thought it less likely than other threats.

Sergeant Shaun Rusling
Medic, Parachute Regiment, 32 Field Hospital

After starting to take the NAPS tablets, I experienced physical symptoms that remain with me today, two decades on [2009]: night sweats, fevers, general joint pain, a pain in my left side, and the feeling that somebody's sticking red-hot needles into my hands and the balls of my feet – big, thick, knitting needles.

The NAPS tablets made us get up every twenty minutes to piss, preventing sleep. Hospital fire buckets were used as bedside urinals. After three weeks I decided to stop taking them, and the need to piss faded. Quite a few others made the same decision.

I also developed a bad chest infection, and on reporting to the duty doctor, found a huge queue waiting to see her, all with the same problem. She'd been sitting there most of the day dishing out tetracycline to everyone in the hospital. You can't go sick in the middle of a war, can you?

CHAPTER 6

FACING ARMAGEDDON

The largest armoured corps in military history was now gathering in the Saudi desert to fight the world's fourth-largest army. With six months to prepare, the Iraqis had created a minefield along the border, behind which their defending brigades were sitting, with tanks and artillery as well as chemical and biological weapons.

Clearing routes through the minefield belt, then funnelling together to pass through, would be the most dangerous part of the operation, offering the best opportunity for the Iraqis to use chemical and biological weapons, and thus cause maximum casualties.

Once all the British formations had finished training, they had to move from their Devil Dog Dragoon training area inland to concentration area Keys, coming together as a division for the first time, joining the American 7th Corps to carry out further training in the tricky 'Passage of Lines' procedure – passing through the American positions then through the minefield breach. Finally, 1 (BR) Division moved to the forward assembly area Ray, from which they'd actually launch the attack itself.

General Rupert Smith had started running a series of map exercises, in which he gave a scenario and problem to his commanders and their staffs, who would discuss their solutions, in the process explaining and developing his concept for the approaching battle. They had a couple of weeks for divisional training: complicated manoeuvring and rapidly regrouping at night, culminating in Exercise Dibdibah Charge in mid February, as part of the division's move to assembly area Ray. General Smith had issued his first working draft of the battle plan to his commanding officers on 29 January, as the Iraqis mounted a major attack at Khafji; and he was certainly not envisaging any sort of enemy collapse.

After much political and military deliberation following the success of the air war against the Iraqi air force, it had been decided that the ground war would start only when the bombing campaign had reduced the Iraqi army's ability to fight to a measurable and significantly diminished percentage. The date by which this would be achieved could not be predicted, but once all the troops' equipment had arrived, and they were trained and in position, the clock could start ticking.

Various diplomatic attempts to prevent the fighting continued, with cancellations and restorations of the operation – with all the inevitable problems these caused coalition troops – taking place right up until the very last minute, as Saddam prevaricated about withdrawing from Kuwait.

Major General Rupert Smith
General Officer Commanding, 1st Armoured Division

Fighting an armoured battle with artillery, we could expect to suffer Second World War levels of casualties, but with more burns. In the Falklands War my regiment had lost a quarter of its strength. If NBC were used, these figures would be very much greater.

Although I wasn't intending to fight the sort of battle that would create those numbers of casualties, we did need to be ready. The field ambulances were reinforced, with a third field hospital behind us, half of it packed on pallets ready to be moved forward. Setting up a field hospital without a source of water is a waste of time, so one of our early objectives was a wellhead, where we planned to put down a fifty-bed hospital.

We planned jointly with the Americans over casualty evacuation – a body is a body rather than any sort of equipment – using the nearest helicopter to take injured to the nearest hospital.

Lieutenant Colonel Mike Vickery
Commanding Officer, 14th/20th King's Hussars, 4th Armoured Brigade

I knew the DERA [Defence Evaluation and Research Agency] scientists who'd brought over our enhancement armour. We calculated that its extra protection meant the Iraqis had to get within twelve hundred metres to knock us out, whereas we could kill them at over three thousand. This over-match decided me to change my tactics, putting all my tanks forwards, firing them all at once in volleys, which I talked over with General Rupert when he visited, pushing different-coloured boiled sweets around the table.

But navigation was a challenge. Our enormous maps had three contour lines and no detail – the 'Gaffa' or Great Arabian Fuck All. You zeroed your mileage trip, then sent a man out with a compass fifty metres ahead to indicate the bearing, then tried to find something on the horizon on that bearing. You pointed the gun at this point and told the driver to follow the gun for the measured distance.

They fitted sun compasses to the tops of our tanks in January, when there is no sun in the desert. However, right at the end of our training, we received six GPS Trimble Trimpak satellite navigation systems, which changed things remarkably, and meant we could at last move bloody fast, even at night, using our excellent thermal imaging night sights.

Major General Rupert Smith
General Officer Commanding, 1st Armoured Division
GPS trackers became a symbol of manhood. I decreed the engineers and artillery had priority as they were with all the forward units, but also because they'd drop the biggest bollocks if they were in the wrong place. Next the logisticians got them so they could resupply the front line, and finally the infantry. There was rather a fuss about this, but in the end we received enough for everyone.

Lance Corporal Roy Sellstrom
Pioneer Corps, Army War Graves Unit
If we were to cope with two hundred bodies a day, which could be chemically contaminated, thirty-two of us wouldn't be enough, so Lieutenant Parry and Captain Ralph went out recruiting people from Blackadder Camp, where there were lots of battle casualty replacements with nothing to do. They'd be paid ten pounds a day extra, and it was a great life…

We ended up with people from every cap badge, but they had to be trained, as you can't just suddenly do this job, especially in a war. After all sorts of objections over us using bodies as training aids, eventually the chain of command agreed this was necessary, but we were told 'it had to be done with decorum'.

Unfortunately, the first batch freaked out on their initial trip to the morgue, when the fridges' massive aero-engine fans unexpectedly came on and inflated the half-opened body bag. Several fled, and one fainted, splitting his head on the trestle – which was exactly what *wasn't* supposed to happen. This training was vital, but with all its equipment and disinfectant, a morgue is clinical. On the battlefield there's none of that, plus you're dodging the bombs and bullets.

Brigadier Patrick Cordingley
Commander, 7th Armoured Brigade

On Go Day, the American 18 Corps and the French were to attack up towards the Euphrates, while the US Marines and Arab coalition forces attacked directly towards Kuwait City. Then on Go+1, the US 7th Corps, including ourselves, the largest corps in history, would attack north bypassing ordinary Iraqi regular army units, then turn east to destroy the Republican Guard behind the main defensive position.

We'd first have to pass through a gap in the Iraqi minefield made for us by the US Army; then, while the rest of 7th Corps crossed the minefield, the Brits were to stop the Republican Guard from moving. 7th Corps would then come up from behind us to destroy them.

The operation's *raison d'être* was to remove the Republican Guard, as once they were destroyed, Saddam would be left without a significant military force to keep him in power.

Sandy Gall
ITN television reporter

I shared a taxi one night in Dhahran with the famous American journalist Colonel David Hackworth, a Second World War and Korean War veteran, now *Newsweek*'s defence correspondent. He wore all his uniforms and old identity passes, and picked up a huge amount of information through people not looking too closely and inviting him into their camps. 'They very rarely rumble me,' he said.

He told me that with all the air pounding, the Iraq army was on its last legs, with its communications structure in very bad shape. He thought when it came to the ground war, the Americans wouldn't have too much difficulty.

Lieutenant Colonel Mike Vickery
Commanding Officer, 14th/20th King's Hussars,
4th Armoured Brigade

It takes a long time to bomb up a tank. The Stalwarts [large-tyred six-wheel trucks] bring huge pallets of machine gun and main armament ammunition tins, which have to be opened up with hammers and screwdrivers to take out a lot of lining and packaging, get the ammunition out, then hump it across for packing into each turret.

Tank ammunition has a detonator cartridge, which remains in the tank after firing and sets off the propellant tube, propellant and the penetrator. When you load a round into the gun, the penetrator goes in first, then the propellant, and the breech is closed. The detonator cartridge fits into the back of the breech like a brass twelve-bore cartridge, and sparks off the propellant. When the gun fires, everything's burned with only the tiny cartridge flipping back into the turret.

Stowing the ammunition safely is vital. HESH [high explosive squash head] projectiles occupy half a storage tube, whereas fin-stabilised rounds are much longer and use up a complete tube. Nothing explosive – like HESH rounds – must be stored above the turret ring, which is less armoured than the main body of the tank. The Russian tanks don't do this, so their turrets blow off when you hit them. There's also a lot of linked 7.62mm machine-gun ammunition, in long belts.

Lieutenant Colonel Arthur Denaro
Commanding Officer, Queen's Royal Irish Hussars

We set off in the Toyota for the long drive to our new concentration area Keys; six hours of ducking in and out of endless columns of vehicles and equipment, nose-to-tail for literally hundreds of miles, 'undertaking' total jams along the edge of the desert; many convoys taking over twelve hours.

Most of it was orderly, although the odd American M1 tank transporter driver went bananas, careering wildly, overtaking other transporters, on a single-lane road, despite empty fuel bowsers hurtling back in the opposite direction. The Italians were, of course, the worst.

Lieutenant Toby Masterton
A Squadron, The Life Guards, 4th Armoured Brigade

The move to Keys was expected to take two days, the tanks on low-loaders.

The soldiers flew out from an airfield in the middle of nowhere in Hercules transporters, and James [Hewitt] put us in charge of bringing up the rear of our low-loader convoy. However, just as James and the squadron departed, an enormous convoy of ammunition, spares, main engine packs and huge amounts of very important kit arrived. They were told, 'You're too damn late. We can't take it.'

'But it's all the engines and ammunition you need…? And we can't take it back.'

'Too late. You'll have to bury it.'

So all this stuff was buried at a grid reference in the middle of the desert, and the Quartermaster told to indent for more.

RSM Johnny Muir
Regimental Sergeant Major, Queen's Royal Irish Hussars
On arrival at Area Keys, I'd been told to expect two Royal Engineers JCB digger tractor units with earth-moving buckets. By the time the Regiment arrived, I had to have dug bunded [embanked] positions for each of battle group HQ's twenty vehicles.

We arrived late on the first night, and during a spectacular lightning storm, a soldier fell and damaged his back. We had to drive him back to a medical unit.

Lieutenant Toby Masterton
A Squadron, The Life Guards, 4th Armoured Brigade
It occurred to me we could quickly drive south to the R&R camp for a shower, burger, ice cream, make phone calls home, then catch up the convoy next day. We arrived at this rest camp, where we got a bunk and made phone calls. Or at least Doyly did, but all mine got answerphone messages. I was a bit depressed about this, so that night we drank the miniature bottles of malt whisky my mother had sent me inside shampoo bottles, and ate a highly booze-soaked fruit cake my father had made. He'd carved the words '*Nil carborundum illigitimi*' [Don't let the bastards get you down], on to the wooden cake board, which next morning we lock-wired on to our radiator grill as our motto.

I tried some more phone calls, speaking only to an ex-girlfriend and my father, but not my mother, who'd just gone out. I felt extremely guilty about this, as if anything had happened to me, I'd condemned her to beat herself up for ever. There's a double-edged sword to making phone calls.

Lieutenant Colonel Mike Vickery
Commanding Officer, 14th/20th King's Hussars, 4th Armoured Brigade

There were particularly large numbers of broken-down American Humvees, bonnets up by the side of the route, crews staring disconsolately at the engines. My soldiers had all wanted to replace their Land Rovers with Humvees, which interestingly stopped after they'd seen this.

Lieutenant Colonel Arthur Denaro
Commanding Officer, Queen's Royal Irish Hussars

We passed the Scots Dragoon Guards tanks on their transporters, before heading west where a Royal Military Policeman gave us the worrying news that the Greeks were just ahead. With the Syrians and Egyptians using the same Russian tanks as the Iraqis, tank recognition was going to be a nightmare.

Eventually, at 1500 hours in a very gloomy, bleak, flat windswept desert, we found the camouflage nets of our advance party at exactly the spot we expected.

RSM Johnny Muir
Regimental Sergeant Major, Queen's Royal Irish Hussars

Hearing the rumble of the tanks some twenty miles away I realised we weren't going to get the positions dug as I'd been ordered by the Commanding Officer. He called me to book: 'RSM, you've not done what I asked. At best, I'm displeased.' I replied, 'Colonel, we were promised two JCBs, but in the end we got just one JCB for half the time. I did what I could.'

'I'm not happy,' he retorted.

'Colonel,' I replied, 'Rome wasn't fuckin' built in a day,' and stormed off. We didn't speak for a couple of days.

Sergeant Shaun Rusling
Medic, Parachute Regiment, 32 Field Hospital

We had to set up resus and two theatres, plus dig in what we called the Porton shelter, a sealed unit equipped to resuscitate chemical or biological casualties. It had never been used on operations before.

We were then told that 32 Field Ambulance was to be the chemical hospital in case of chemical or biological attack. This revelation came as a shock, as it was the first we'd heard of it, and we'd done absolutely no training for what is a very complicated and critical job.

Lieutenant Colonel Mike Vickery
Commanding Officer, 14th/20th King's Hussars, 4th Armoured Brigade

I reached our muster point in the middle of empty desert to the north of King Khalid Military City. We'd driven past our tanks much earlier on the Oil Tapline Road, with no sign of them arriving.

Hercules aircraft appeared from the sky, landed, disgorging all my soldiers, then took off, leaving my entire regiment with no tanks and half a day's food. Then it started pissing with rain, heavily and continuously.

It's very strange for us to be without our tanks – our house, tent and garden shed combined. The soldiers had never been anywhere without them before, or at least in Germany there'd be a camp with some shelter while they waited.

Soon very cross people were poking me in the chest demanding to know why I couldn't bloody well organise for their tanks to arrive on time. They'd have been fine had we said beforehand the tanks might not be there. But they'd believed what we'd told them – and why not?

Morale was very low; we were miserable and bedraggled. And handing out half my bar of chocolate didn't do any good. It was way out of my league; but shit happens, and the sooner my people realised this, plus achieved an elasticity of mind, the better. But eventually the tanks did arrive, everybody got in, and off we went grumbling. I didn't hear the end of it for days.

Sergeant Shaun Rusling
Medic, Parachute Regiment, 32 Field Hospital

If we suffered a chemical attack, we were told there'd be a special ward for contaminated casualties. The people designated to work on that ward were given confidential briefings on what would be involved. I'm glad I wasn't one of them, but with so much toxin in the same place, I think we'd all have been similarly affected.

RSM Johnny Muir
Regimental Sergeant Major, Queen's Royal Irish Hussars

Every day at first and last light, the Commanding Officer and I would walk around the positions – inside the perimeter I might add, checking everybody was all right. For these next few days, the Colonel didn't accompany me. On the third day, a pretty horrible, rainy evening, I walked past his tent saying my usual 'Good evening, Colonel.' He replied, 'Is that you, RSM?'

'Yes it is, Colonel.'

'Is everything all right, RSM?'

'Yes, Colonel, everything's fine.'

'Would you like to try some of Mrs D's homemade fudge?'

Second Lieutenant Alistair Watkins
Grenadier Guards, 1 Royal Scots Battle Group,
4th Armoured Brigade

At Keys, we were within range of Iraqi artillery, so everything became several times more intense. We received our Chobham armour – everyone convinced the big panels were full of water. Our Warriors weren't affected by the extra weight, but our old 432 armoured ambulance couldn't keep up, so we ditched it.

We soon discovered irredeemable jamming problems with our SA80 rifle. Taking cover in the sand, and any other movement, had to be done very carefully to avoid getting sand anywhere near it, which obviously wasn't sensible. Debussing out of vehicles involves lots of sand all over the place. We worried all the time about them jamming. Much later, someone buried a captured Iraqi AK-47 in the sand, dug it up then fired and it worked perfectly. Equally, the American M16 rifle was rock solid.

Sergeant Shaun Rusling
Medic, Parachute Regiment, 32 Field Hospital

The CO of 32 Field Ambulance told us we should ignore the NAIADs alarms because they were set off by aircraft dumping fuel in the air. The RAF guys on the heli-pad, who'd worked on RAF stations protected by NAIADs where fuel dumping happened all the time, told us fuel dumping *never* set them off.

Major General Rupert Smith
General Officer Commanding, 1st Armoured Division

When the bombing started in January, I'd put my main HQ forward, from which we deployed into the main operational area – a huge trucking operation which shifted an enormous amount very quickly. But as we were beginning to move our first battle group, the Iraqis made a very big attack, into a place called Khafji.

I didn't tell my division about this so we could continue moving. But there was nothing between this incoming Iraqi attack and my logistics units.

Lieutenant General Walter Boomer
General Officer Commanding, 1 Marine Expeditionary Force, United States Marine Corps

Khafji was the right place for the Iraqis to make an attack. The geography of eastern Saudi and Kuwait is very restricting. Although the east coast looks like desert, there are very large areas in which a tank will sink right up to its gun. We had enough vehicles stuck to learn this the hard way. To come down the coast road would have meant them being sitting ducks. It wasn't going to work. Coming west through the desert, as they did, gave them a much better chance.

Brigadier Patrick Cordingley
Commander, 7th Armoured Brigade

During our mass move to Keys, we received reports of an Iraqi tank formation driving in our direction. With half of 7 Brigade's units still moving, and the tanks on transporters, we were very thin on the ground. There was only us and 1st Division's forward HQ between this huge array of Iraqi forces and a massive allied supply dump, Base Alpha, to our rear.

Lieutenant General Walter Boomer
General Officer Commanding, 1 Marine Expeditionary Force, United States Marine Corps

We were out-loading our logistic units at the time of the Khafji attack, but by that time we'd [developed] the strength to counter them. I don't think they had the combat power to get as far as Al Jubayl. When I looked back up the Iraqi attacking column, it did look like a standard Soviet attack, but they weren't shooting, moving and communicating as well as they should have done, and you have to do all three together to succeed.

But our armoured vehicles generally confused them and blunted their attack, until we could call in the air.

The Rt Hon Tom King
UK Secretary of State for Defence

When Saddam attacked Khafji, our supply lines were very exposed, as we'd deployed our field hospitals and supply units into the forward areas, and were bringing up huge amounts of materiel. Our fighting units hadn't yet deployed, so this was a very difficult moment. MoD then received reports that our logistic units had been attacked, which turned out to have been a very bad traffic accident.

Major General Rupert Smith
General Officer Commanding, 1st Armoured Division

I flew to my forward main HQ, called in the logistic commanders, my forward reconnaissance squadron commander and the air defence people, telling them that the Iraqi attack hadn't been defeated.

I was also thinking should I stop the out-load, as I was the one who was going to be told I'm a bloody fool for building my hospitals before putting out combat units to guard them. In the end I told the logistic commanders to make sure they could fire their anti-tank weapons.

It was an uncomfortable forty-eight hours, as I sat on my hands and let everyone carry on. The US Marines or Saudis finally defeated the remnants of this attack at Khafji. But throughout I was living with the consequences of my earlier decision, with worse consequences if I fiddled with it, and not a problem I could share with many people.

Lieutenant General Walter Boomer
General Officer Commanding, 1 Marine Expeditionary Force, United States Marine Corps

As the Khafji attack unfolded, I never thought it a full-scale attack on Saudi Arabia. Although I had a regiment ready, we were able to allow the Saudis to (quote) 'defend their own soil'. It wasn't a good time for them, I can tell you. But I've now come to believe the Khafji offensive *was* in fact a full-scale attack on Saudi Arabia.

However, at the time we learned what we'd already suspected; that the Iraqis weren't nearly as good as you'd think judging from their numbers and equipment; and that we were going to be able to defeat them on the ground. Our intelligence was now telling us these guys weren't going to commit one hundred per cent to this battle, so Khafji gave us a lot of confidence. The only dark cloud over all of that, as we approached the time to attack Kuwait, was this whole issue of chemical weapons.

Major General Alexander Harley
Assistant Chief of Defence Staff (Overseas) and Deputy Director of Joint Operations, Ministry of Defence, Whitehall
Saddam took a bloody nose in the Khafji incursion, which greatly boosted Saudi morale. But he didn't have any air, or much armoured infantry, and his attack seemed rather ham-fisted. Our impression [in MoD] was more of a reconnaissance foray than a major attack. Quite a lot of American air power was used on it.

Lieutenant Colonel Mike Vickery
Commanding Officer, 14th/20th King's Hussars, 4th Armoured Brigade
We visited the American armoured regiment through which we were going to have to move, to discuss how we were going to do it. They all came back to us that evening, to see what Challenger looked like through their thermal imaging sights.

The first thing their Commanding Officer said to me when he hopped on to my tank was 'God, your tanks look just like T-72's'.

I said, 'No they don't – but why do you think they do?'

All the Americans could see were our barrel-shaped extra fuel tanks on the back, which Russian tanks also have; so I asked him to look carefully at our smoke dischargers, count the number of road wheels, the angle and size of the turret, and so on [standard means of identification for tankers].

'Aw shit,' he said. 'Our guys don't look at that sort of thing.'

So instead of having the day as a picnic for the Americans, we spent it doing armoured fighting vehicle recognition.

Major General Rupert Smith
General Officer Commanding, 1st Armoured Division

For security reasons, people hadn't been told that we'd left the Marines. The American army themselves weren't clear about whether they should be giving us intelligence; and in any case weren't giving their own divisions much intelligence either. But this was more critical for us than the American formations, as we had the job of protecting 7th Corp's flanks.

Furthermore, the Americans were holding and processing information at a higher level, whereas nobody was doing this for us. Also, we weren't allowed to go out into the desert and get intelligence for ourselves, as that would have revealed our position.

Lieutenant General Walter Boomer
General Officer Commanding, 1 Marine Expeditionary Force, United States Marine Corps

The Iraqis had *some* intelligence of our huge build-up, but didn't seem to pick up on our main move. The assistant division commander of 1st Marine Division was running some serious deception operations, using troops, communications equipment and vehicles, acting like a division in a place where we weren't going to attack – but where they could believe we *might* attack. This was our primary effort, but it never seemed to work.

Our other huge deception operation was for an amphibious feint. Being an amphibious corps, we'd made plans all along for an attack from the south to link up with the army. As we explored that option, we realised that actually doing such an attack would be way too complicated. You've got to be really careful about how complicated you make things in battle.

Major General Rupert Smith
General Officer Commanding, 1st Armoured Division

By early February, we'd stopped believing intelligence assessments. American intelligence believed the Iraqi divisions were deployed in a row with their tactical reserves behind, but the more we analysed our own photography, the more we thought their divisions were deployed in columns backwards, so we worked on the basis of our own assumptions. We later captured seven Iraqi generals – the commanders of the Iraqi divisions we decapitated in our attacks, proving we'd been right.

We'd brought out the UK's entire inventory of redundant 1950s artillery photographic drones – unmanned aircraft which flew off a truck, could do six or so turns while taking pictures, before flying back and landing by parachute. They had a fifty per cent failure rate, and we'd been told not to bring any back afterwards. We discovered the Egyptians had exactly the same drones, so after becoming very friendly with them, persuaded the American security and deception planning people to let us fly them from the Egyptian area. We used modern satnav to determine the drone flight start point and so the locations of the ensuing photographs – an interesting use of old and new technology.

Brigadier Mike Willcocks
Chief of Staff (Land), Joint War Headquarters, RAF High Wycombe

Special Forces had set up a cell in the bunker. I was one of the few people allowed behind their green baize door, into where their Chief of Staff was running the thing – and there was, quite literally, a *green baize door*. The Chief of Staff was required to keep me informed about what he was doing each day, but they operated directly to de la Billiere in Riyadh, who as Deputy Joint Commander had tactical control of our Special Forces. I could *request* them to do things, but they received their actual orders directly from de la Billiere.

Major General Rupert Smith
General Officer Commanding, 1st Armoured Division

I sent people to the air headquarters, returning with a massive cardboard crate of pictures. After much fuss and demand, we were also given an air mosaic of our entire area, but with no interpretation. After hours of work by many soldiers with magnifying glasses, gluing it all together, we were able to follow the tracks of Iraqi resupply trucks in the sand, showing us their unit boundaries, confirming that all their headquarters were indeed back in the rear. Then our Special Forces captured us a prisoner who'd been returning to one of 'our' units after leave in Baghdad, who was able to confirm this.

Sergeant Shaun Rusling
Medic, Parachute Regiment, 32 Field Hospital

Our hospital had a tunnel system of sealed-off inflated tents called 'Colpro' – Collective Protection Equipment. But unfortunately our Colpro wasn't sufficiently inflated to keep contamination out. Sand affected the air pumps inflating the tents, and we'd no spares. Our bosses didn't understand how important this was.

Brigadier Patrick Cordingley
Commander, 7th Armoured Brigade

I decided my nine-by-nine tent was too small for order groups and conferences, so had an ISO container [a standard freight container] moved up from the port, which we lined with maps, creating an office with a table and chairs. But it was so hot we had to keep the doors open, so it funnelled the wind, filling up with sand. Every time we moved, we had to find a trailer then load this bloody thing to follow on behind us. So that idea didn't last for very long.

Sergeant Shaun Rusling
Medic, Parachute Regiment, 32 Field Hospital

As soon as we were set up, casualties started coming from road traffic accidents, especially from the busy, dangerous MSR. Two US Blackhawk helicopters flew up and down the MSR all the time, picking up casualties. There were also lots of the usual stupid accidents; negligent discharges, and one lad whose foot wound we thought a bit dubious.

There'd been a classic accident inside a tent: putting the wrong sort of fuel into a tent heater, and not going outside to light it. It exploded inside the tent, the poor young lad sat opposite inhaling as the flames hit him. By the time he arrived with us, he was in a very poorly state with a brass airway tracheotomy in through his cricothyroid membrane. He swelled up as we infused him. I held his arms as the surgeon made escharotomy cuts to keep his circulation going. I never thought I'd ever do that. We later read in the *Sun* that he died in Bristol burns unit. To be honest, we hadn't thought he'd live that long. But he was a young fit man – only twenty-one. He could take a lot of battering.

Lance Corporal Roy Sellstrom
Pioneer Corps, Army War Graves Unit

Through January and February the bodies were piling up – twenty-three from road traffic accidents alone, plus suicides, illness and so on. All this loss of life was making me angry – it was how I coped, my survival mechanism. With some, I got angry with the blokes themselves: Major X – sorry Colonel X –

arrived in theatre at Shed Four, and despite being seriously tired after the flight, insisted on driving, and didn't bother wearing his seat belt, having a massive car crash at over a hundred miles an hour. Because he hadn't booked into theatre, for ages we couldn't find out who he was, and he'd only been out visiting. We also gave some of them nicknames as another kind of defence mechanism; one Pay Corps guy was 'Rasputin'; we imagined him counting his money.

Lieutenant Colonel Arthur Denaro
Commanding Officer, Queen's Royal Irish Hussars

I'd wander around our huge squadron positions with the RSM, talking to everybody, sometimes also with one of the young RHQ captains taking notes. And every morning possible I'd have regimental 'prayers' – getting the squadron leaders in, often from several miles away, discussing training, our soldiers and operational points. One morning, one of the young captains sent me a note, 'While we were walking round yesterday, you asked me to make a note. I can't remember what about, but I hope this helps.'

I now knew every single one of the six hundred and fifty-three guys in the regiment – their issues and backgrounds. In Fallingbostel, you could never have done it. In the desert, it was one of the great treats. I still know and see them today.

Major General Alexander Harley
Assistant Chief of Defence Staff (Overseas) and Deputy Director of Joint Operations, Ministry of Defence, Whitehall

Around the end of January, as we were deciding to attack, the Chiefs of Staff commissioned a specific study from the Defence Operational Analysis Establishment at West Byfleet, to tell us actually how good the Iraqi army was going to be.

Well, their analysis told us they were going to be rubbish.

The DOAE gurus had traced back as far as Saladin, comparing the performance of Arab armies against other armies over the ages, including the Israelis. But regardless of how well equipped they'd been, over the centuries they'd not done well when the chips were down.

Because this wasn't what Intelligence and everybody else was saying, I had to go down to West Byfleet and talk this over with them. There wasn't exactly a sigh of relief over this in the MoD; in fact, there was general disbelief. We remained thinking they'd be bloody difficult to deal with, well equipped, their T-72 tank a match for Challenger, plus the NBC threat right up front.

But it turned out that these earwigs from DOAE were absolutely right.

Lieutenant Colonel Arthur Denaro
Commanding Officer, Queen's Royal Irish Hussars

The General visited for two hours, and from what he said, I reckoned we'd be here for another week, after which it will be a long drive in our tanks and then into Iraq. He was very confident in the way the Americans were planning it, with heartening news on the radio about the air war.

I got back to our HQ in time to meet *The Times* and the *Mirror* correspondents, plus Martin Bell, who'd all been interviewing Robin on being an artist in the field, which was rather fun.

Martin Bell
BBC Television

These people were under terrific pressure, and trusted us not to breach their confidences. Talking to us was also quite important for them, as with the impending defence cuts, all the regiments were under great pressure, so getting theirs prominent was very important for them.

People like Robert Fox [then *Daily Telegraph* correspondent] and I had seen more wars than the soldiers had, but this was the first time I'd been alongside British forces in a war.

Lieutenant Colonel Mike Vickery
Commanding Officer, 14th/20th King's Hussars,
4th Armoured Brigade

Being a commanding officer can be very lonely; you don't want to be chatting with a twenty-six-year-old adjutant about your innermost concerns and fears. It's traditional to talk to the padre, but mine was a very bright twenty-seven-year-old Catholic lad who very much identified with the soldiers and they with him. So I found Robert Fox a great man to talk to. We used to sit and philosophise, bang-on in fact.

Our brigadier was happier talking to the press than the rest of us. I was happy to talk with Robert Fox, who I trusted, but not with press people I didn't know. One journalist completely shafted me when I allowed him to attend orders, which he relayed to his newspaper. Fortunately this was intercepted by the censors, but I was reprimanded. Before I got to him, Robert Fox had pretty nearly shot him, as this had given the press corps such a bad reputation.

Major General Rupert Smith
General Officer Commanding, 1st Armoured Division

The press were part of our deception plan. I'd directed they be given lots of facilities before the bombing started, always showing the sea in the background to make it clear that we were in the east. Once we'd moved, there were to be no press facilities, and we concealed our geographical locations. Most of the Iraqi divisional commanders we captured later assumed we were still on the coast.

The Americans ran a central press censorship system, which the BBC and ITN television people were very keen to avoid. They worked hard to ensure that our censorship arrangement worked, because we processed everything twenty-four hours faster, giving them a huge commercial advantage, so their footage could be sold all over the world, earlier than anyone else's – it was a symbiosis.

Lieutenant Colonel Arthur Denaro
Commanding Officer, Queen's Royal Irish Hussars

I woke to the battering of rain on my tent roof, and struggled into the wet to tell people not to Stand To in the trenches; but happily the RSM beat me to it. At times I felt so guilty, sitting in my own little warm tent. Poor C Squadron were up-armouring.

Major General Rupert Smith
General Officer Commanding, 1st Armoured Division

Eventually, with great difficulty and expense, we got most of the battle groups up-armoured. We did have to order more drill bits, as we blunted more than had been provided, drilling through the front glacis plates. But I remained very uncomfortable that others, like the REME fitters who had to work right up on the front line, were still not up-armoured.

Lieutenant Colonel Arthur Denaro
Commanding Officer, Queen's Royal Irish Hussars

On Australia Day, John Sharples, Charles Rogers and I flew to see a dug-in Egyptian T-62 tank. We were shown into their commander's tent, a magnificent affair, putting my nine by nine into the shade, with great hanging drapes and an enormous Egyptian eagle on its standard hanging over his bed, with carpets and sofas.

Lieutenant Colonel Charles Rogers
Commanding Officer, Staffordshire Regiment

They were lovely; their Russian-built tanks in a circle with the Commanding Officer's huge tent in the middle. He lived in absolute luxury, and was very generous and nice. They were to be advancing to one side of us, so we were concerned to get to know them, and needed to make contact with them, so as not to have too much contact with them during the battle – if you see what I mean.

Major General Rupert Smith
General Officer Commanding, 1st Armoured Division

The sand was ruining our aircraft engines after only twenty hours, until an RAF corporal designed and fitted a metal block for the air intake, which although degrading the Venturi effect [the constricted flow reducing pressure] greatly extended engine life. I don't think there was any debate about modifying the rest of the fleet.

I urged my staff to get rest, even fly down to the coast for a day or so to see new faces and eat a different sort of meal – not get up for breakfast if they didn't want to. I'd get up early to have time to myself, have breakfast, go to the HQ at 0900 for a meeting, then go round the units, returning around six. I think I'm my best intelligence officer, so I'd spend the early evening with the collators. At eight pm we'd have the final meeting of the day to make decisions, then we'd all have supper together in the now-empty mess tent. Every third day I'd visit the rear HQ, and go back to Jubayl about once a fortnight.

We were now free of outsiders, the division together as one unit, knowing what we had to do, and starting to use the [divisional] machine as a whole. My two brigade commanders were being competitive about who was to go first. I refused to decide until I knew what the battle was to be.

Brigadier Patrick Cordingley
Commander, 7th Armoured Brigade

Hammerbeck and I wanted to know which brigade would be first to go through the minefield. It would be impossible to change halfway through, so this decision was very important.

So from now on, we practised passing our complete division through the American 1st Infantry Division and the minefield gap – all at night. It was absolute chaos. There wasn't even any enemy and still it was a shambles.

This was a very nervous time, only forty miles from the Iraq border, with everyone wanting to get on with it.

Lance Corporal Roy Sellstrom
Pioneer Corps, Army War Graves Unit

As units' training became more intensive, the numbers of deaths increased, but our collection system fell apart. Some of the bodies were really bad, so blokes were beginning to say, 'Fuck that, I'm not doing it any more,' so those of us who were committed to the job were doing it all.

It often took a long time to find them [the bodies], and when we did, they were often hard to identify – faces ripped off from going through a windscreen and along the road. It's fucking frightening looking at things like that. Unzipping the body bag, or unwrapping them, was often the worst bit. If there was nobody else around, we used to line up, stand to attention, do a little bit of a pretend fanfare, then flip a coin for who was going to open the bag – literally flip a coin. No fucker wanted to open that bag … you didn't know what was in there. If the others were like me, their hearts were jumping out of their chests. If it wasn't all smashed up, there was always a gasp of 'Thank fuck for that'.

Lieutenant Colonel Arthur Denaro
Commanding Officer, Queen's Royal Irish Hussars

The big build-up of Iraqi tanks to the north of the border was continuing, so I brought the Regiment to a higher state of preparedness, then sat and relaxed outside my tent. Summoned to brigade headquarters, the Commander and I agreed that the points I'd made yesterday, about which we got so heated, were in fact correct.

I returned to run a short orders session: a trooper was marched in front of me for sleeping on guard, a bad state of affairs; he'd just come in from a long route march.

The next day I drove over to division for the divisional commanders' first briefing on the actual battle plan, arriving just in time, joining that awful gathering of officers that always hang around a divisional headquarters – making one feel insecure, like outsiders. The plan sounded pretty interesting, although the intelligence brief was very poor, with absolutely nothing we didn't know already.

Then the RSM and I went to A1 echelon, who were gathered for their anthrax jabs, so I had mine. They looked like the cast of a third-rate nativity play, *shemaghs* [traditional Middle Eastern head wrapping] on every angle and dangle.

Robin Watt
War artist

We all got colds and flu as the direct result of our second BW [biological warfare] jab, and those bloody nerve agent pills, which we had to take every eight hours. We were told to remind each other, 'Have you taken your NAPS?' and with it being every eight hours, were also woken in the dead of night to take the wretched things.

Major General Rupert Smith
General Officer Commanding, 1st Armoured Division

I liaised with the Egyptians next door, and we settled down, moving each night, with me visiting units every day, lunching with different people so as to be available down to a very low level in case people wanted to talk to me. This was the first time most people had seen the other arms and services *en masse*, seeing for example a regiment of eight-inch artillery guns driving past, or ten helicopters doing something.

We were on radio silence to prevent revealing our positions, although away from the front line, we did some training using radios on low power with shortened antennae. The brigade, divisional and artillery nets didn't open up until we attacked – and thank goodness they worked! Before that, we were totally dependent on our Ptarmigan trunk communications system, which snaked all the way back to the ports using micro-transmitters, with links into the flanking divisions, and through Jubayl to Riyadh.

There was also a telephone link to the MoD in London, then back out to Riyadh, via two satellites and a hand-cranked range telephone, which lived under the seat of my APC [armoured personnel carrier]. Using this I talked to Peter de la Billiere most nights; we'd clip the wire on to this hand set, wind the handle and a woman's voice would say 'MoD London'. I'd ask for Peter de la Billiere, and she'd say 'Very well' and there he'd be.

Brigadier Mike Willcocks
Chief of Staff (Land), Joint War Headquarters, RAF High Wycombe

The MoD spoke directly to people in the Gulf whenever they wanted to know something. Tom King, in particular, had discovered he could dial out from his MoD office through various exchanges, directly into the back of armoured vehicles in the desert.

But unfortunately, the Secretary of State and his staff didn't realise how lethal it was for them to get information without going through the military chain of command. Apart from anything else, the boys on the front line are busy. If you go straight to the back end of an armoured vehicle asking, 'What's happening?' whoever you talk to will give you totally the wrong impression. It's dangerous. Unfiltered raw information can be absolutely lethal.

The Rt Hon Tom King
UK Secretary of State for Defence

I had a direct-line telephone system to Peter de la Billiere, and used to speak with him at least once a week, sometimes more. He really wanted me to leave him alone so he could get on with it. But I wasn't phoning trying to keep him up to the mark, but so I could feed the media frenzy for information back in London. It was important for us as we had a good story to tell, and didn't want to repeat the Falklands mistakes of deliberately keeping people in the dark.

Brigadier Mike Willcocks
Chief of Staff (Land), Joint War Headquarters, RAF High Wycombe

Our headquarters, and Peter de la Billiere out in the Gulf, were absolutely infuriated by MoD people looping past us. We regularly made representations to get them to stop this, trying to persuade them that we had a much more useful, considered, commanders' view.

But in the end, this very serious problem was solved by the boys out in the desert, who simply disconnected the telephones.

Lieutenant Colonel Arthur Denaro
Commanding Officer, Queen's Royal Irish Hussars

I had one outstanding issue: two of my lads had stolen my staff car, then driven it to Hamburg for a night out. The authorities at home recommended they go to jail, whereas I thought they'd had huge courage to nick my car, so would show the same courage in war. So I just admonished them, we cracked on – and of course they were outstanding.

I found one of the troop leaders unshaven. We had plenty of time and enough water, so this guy got both barrels from me. The RSM came along afterwards and cheered him up as over-harsh criticism, when morale is brittle and people are tense, is not a good idea. That was a lesson to me.

Major General Rupert Smith
General Officer Commanding, 1st Armoured Division

I decided to give people laptops, to form networks as people used them – with the help of a Royal Signals systems engineer, beginning with 'frisby networks' in the rear logistic area, as people flipped floppy disks at each other. By the time we'd written the op order, recipients were able to receive it electronically – although not everyone, so the paper still had to flow.

Lieutenant Colonel Arthur Denaro
Commanding Officer, Queen's Royal Irish Hussars

General Rupert spent several hours with us, but even though his was an impressive performance, by the end we all felt slightly depressed because he'd been so matter-of-fact. He talked of a ninety-day war, with twenty per cent casualties for every twenty-four hours fought. But, as we discussed afterwards, the casualties would only apply to every day of actual fighting. We played a few cards in the evening, continuing discussing General Rupert's 'ninety day' idea: 'Was it ninety days from now, ninety days from when the war started, or ninety days from when we arrived?'

Major General Rupert Smith
General Officer Commanding, 1st Armoured Division

If the Big Red One [the US 1st Infantry Division] got the breach head created and there was open space beyond, I decided to lead with my recce screen, then 7 Armoured Brigade and their tanks would drive straight in and out the other side. Everything was self-contained, so the battle groups and brigades could fight on their own, and I could detach brigades and change things around without messing up the spaghetti at the rear.

The second possible scenario was that we might cross the breach head then have to fight an enemy closing with us, leading with either brigades, depending on time and distance. The third possibility was that we'd have to fight our way out of the breach itself, for which I'd need lots of engineers up front, and my infantry-heavy battle groups.

We now needed to close up to the US 1st Infantry Division, then be ready to pass through the minefield, so I pushed forward a regulating head-quarters to begin organising this. I told my Chief of Staff I wanted harbour areas laid out like at Dover docks, where vehicles queue up according to size and type, to be called forward on to the ferries in any order they like. Or in my case, to fight whichever of the attack scenarios I found myself facing.

Brigadier Mike Willcocks
Chief of Staff (Land), Joint War Headquarters, RAF High Wycombe

Much earlier in the campaign, when one of the wing commanders from the bunker had his laptop stolen from his car with the coalition's entire battle plans on its hard drive, General Schwarzkopf had been so incensed, he'd refused to allow the final war plan to be taken out of his headquarters. So a day or so before the attack went in, I had to travel out there myself to bring back the plans.

Major General Rupert Smith
General Officer Commanding, 1st Armoured Division

My HQ was reinforced very substantially to operate indefinitely round the clock, with air cells to task our considerable helicopter force, plus extra communications 'blisters' so we could work directly to the RAF and Royal Navy, but also to the 3rd US Army and Al Jubayl port, and into the US 7th Corps, with liaison officers from all these units.

Main and rear HQs each occupied slightly more than a tennis court, inside a vehicle circle under two large canvas tents – usually protected by a bulldozed sand berm. There were two identical main HQs, to leapfrog forward when we moved, so one HQ was always operating.

I didn't have a smaller tactical HQ, but when on the move used a mobile rover group – a small fighting unit commanded by my ADC, with MILAN anti-tank weapons, anti-aircraft weapons and GPMG SFs].

Brigadier Patrick Cordingley
Commander, 7th Armoured Brigade

I received rough timings for our move up to the 1st US Division and our attack assembly area. We were losing one tank every twenty kilometres the brigade moved, so transporters were supposed to carry us the forty-odd kilometres.

We were given a series of air photographs of the positions we'd be attacking, showing only what looked like worms creeping across sand, but only a very short time to work out our own brigade plans, which was ridiculous, our having been out there nigh on five months… desperate really, as we tried to work out what we might have to attack.

Four hours after the divisional O group, we called our own commanders in. But while we were briefing them, division ordered us to be ready to move twenty-four hours earlier than planned, and without transporters.

This totally broke the sacrosanct 'No move before…' rule. Having been given twenty-four clear hours before any sort of move, we had tanks with their engines out, people servicing vehicles, loading ammunition and re-stowing just about everything. The message got round very rapidly; people could now put an engine back in four hours. But there was no time for Churchillian speeches on the eve of battle or anything like that. It was basically 'Good luck lads, crack on and see you in the assembly area'. And the weather was truly filthy.

Brigadier Mike Willcocks
Chief of Staff (Land), Joint War Headquarters, RAF High Wycombe

In the High Wycombe briefing routine, the air force fell over themselves to impress Paddy Hine, who was their peacetime boss and wrote their confidential reports. Their briefings banged on forever, with far greater detail than he should ever have been exposed. The navy came unstuck one evening, because the Admiral, having delivered the navy briefing on what the fleet were doing, sat back and relaxed. The RAF's air transport fleet were getting really hammered by the constant resupply, and was one of our serious concerns. The Air Vice Marshal Engineering went through all this in excruciating detail, finishing by saying grimly, 'To sum it up, Commander-in-Chief, the fleet's in a hell of a mess!'

The Admiral jumped up, shouting at his Chief of Staff, 'Why did nobody tell me?' Paddy Hine was very amused by this and said, 'Calm down. We're talking about the air transport fleet.'

Major General Alexander Harley
Assistant Chief of Defence Staff (Overseas) and Deputy Director of Joint Operations, Ministry of Defence, Whitehall

Armed Forces Minister Archie Hamilton was nominated to do a press briefing, and I was told to be the military person accompanying him. They could ask me anything, so I had to understand all the dimensions, logistics, what's happening at sea – a terrifying business. People gave me all sorts of advice; to avoid long discussions, and how the press like a straightforward answer.

It was in a huge room downstairs, with a stage and maps. One guy asked a bloody great long question, to which the answer was yes, so I just said 'Yes' which got a laugh. Although I was terrified of letting slip something sensitive, it seemed to go OK. But it took me away from my job for the best part of a day, so I said I couldn't do it any more. My boss, Air Marshal Hayr, extracted me from this.

The Rt Hon John Major
Prime Minister

Throughout the war I made and received regular telephone calls from other heads of government. President Gorbachev, who had initially tried to find ways of preventing the war from happening, urged us to end hostilities as quickly as we could. I think that for internal political reasons, Gorbachev had to be seen to do whatever he could to prevent the war, but I don't believe he seriously expected his calls would have any positive result – and they didn't. In 1990, Russia was a creditor nation to Iraq and, apart from the political considerations, they no doubt wanted their money back.

I spoke to President Mitterrand on a few occasions. France had her own views, and initially there'd been dragging of heels. But once the war was under way, I don't recall any pressure or difficulty from the French that led to concern at my level.

Lieutenant Toby Masterton
A Squadron, The Life Guards, 4th Armoured Brigade

The move to the staging area was done in total radio silence – quite extraordinary. We still had problems keeping up with the tanks, which were long enough to flop across large holes, leaving us and the Scorpions to find other ways around. People wore full NBC Black [respirators and all their protective kit] inside the tanks, and were passing out with heat exhaustion. In our open 'bush', at least we had the wind to cool us down. At night, however, it was freezing, even wearing nine layers plus a Chinese quilted fighting suit, until by nine in the morning, we were back stripped down to T-shirts.

One of the troop leaders, Johnny Wheeler, trapped his foot in the traverse ring of his tank, between two and a half tons of swivelling turret. I helped pass him down to the medics; he was giggling from the morphine, and was ribbed mercilessly.

Robin Watt
War artist

I travelled in a Bedford fuel truck. The driver, Trooper Howell, had driven non-stop all the previous day then worked without pause throughout the night refuelling tanks while their crews slept. The order to move came at three o'clock in the morning. I was standing at the head of the column of vehicles. The trucks moved off immediately, showing minimal light, with dispatch riders threading in and out of the column. I managed to identify my Bedford as it moved past and scrambled into the cab, festooned with all my equipment. A few minutes later I realised my respirator was missing – my most precious possession.

Lieutenant Toby Masterton
A Squadron, The Life Guards, 4th Armoured Brigade

On convoy lights in crap weather in radio silence, we could get lost, or squashed by the tanks. Their drivers were already knackered. We were following the battle captain's AFV 432. It grew dark, we couldn't see anything, were totally freezing cold, and eventually both fell asleep. Our Land Rover trundled gently off to the left, while the rest of the squadron carried on. As Doyle's foot slid off the accelerator, we came slowly to a halt.

I woke up when we stalled, with no idea of where I was – then an awful, awful realisation that we'd fallen asleep, were lost and were in absolutely deep shit. I couldn't even remember what we'd been doing.

I woke Doyle for a heart-to-heart. We didn't know where we were. We couldn't hear anything, with no idea how long we'd been asleep. We couldn't contact anybody on the radio, and were as spare as arseholes, more so than I've ever been in my life, or hope to be again.

Lieutenant Colonel Arthur Denaro
Commanding Officer, Queen's Royal Irish Hussars

We finally arrived in our position at the staging area, to incredible sights as vehicles poured in from every direction, people meeting up who hadn't seen each other for years, or just eyeing each other up, noticing different standards of discipline and professionalism; we, of course, were quite the best.

Lieutenant Toby Masterton
A Squadron, The Life Guards, 4th Armoured Brigade

We ought to be able to hear our squadron's fourteen Challengers and the rest of the battle group. But there was total silence, so we must have been asleep for a while. Then hearing something, we headed towards the sound, keeping the revs down. Then paranoid about being close to the border, and of minefields, I lay over the front of the bonnet, feet hooked round the base of the windscreen, trying to check the ground for mines with my little red-filtered Maglite, crawling along pointlessly towards any sound we could hear, at about half a kilometre an hour. After persevering for hours, we decided to stop.

As dawn began, seeing man-made features facing us confirmed my fear that we were inside Iraq. I crawled forward with binos to see soldiers; which after getting closer I could see were British – Royal Engineers. Their CO was extremely nice – didn't make me feel a complete tit, and said we could move on later with one of his unit packages. When we did get back, having been posted 'missing in action' for two days, you can imagine the ribbing I received.

The Rt Hon John Major
Prime Minister

During the war I held regular meetings with senior military personnel, and chaired a small War Cabinet. On 7 February 1991, the War Cabinet was meeting in the Cabinet Room of 10 Downing Street, sitting at one end of the Cabinet table, when suddenly there was a huge blast.

Someone (Tom King I think) shouted, 'It's a mortar. Everyone get down.'

The windows facing the garden, from which I was some twelve feet or so away, are designed not to shatter, but to absorb an explosion. As they buckled inwards, everyone dived under the table. I remember the whole building shook and trembled.

We waited until the shock and after-shock had subsided before getting out from under the table. I suggested that we should continue the meeting elsewhere, so we went down beneath Downing Street to Cabinet Office Briefing Room A – known colloquially as 'Cobra'. On reflection, given our extraordinary escape, a remarkable sense of calm prevailed.

We weren't sure, as we were in the middle of a war, whether the mortar was from the IRA, or a group operating on behalf of the Iraqis. Either seemed possible. Saddam was a braggart and bully above all else, and we were never sure what sort of capability he had. We knew from his treatment of the Kurds that he had chemical weapons, but we didn't have as much intelligence as we would have liked.

But it soon became clear that the IRA was responsible. They'd been cheeky enough to park a vehicle outside the Ministry of Defence and fired their mortar from there. The bomb did far more damage to Downing Street than was acknowledged at the time. There was a lot of remedial work done later.

Lieutenant Colonel Arthur Denaro
Commanding Officer, Queen's Royal Irish Hussars

Now in our forward position as part of the US 7th Corps, we visited 2/47 Armoured Battalion, part of the US Army's 1st Division, whose job is to prepare the minefield breach. They had some excellent kit, but were not as together as us: mail, for instance, took five weeks, they'd got no integral fuel-carrying capacity, and their food was pretty poor. They did, however, have the most amazing amount of intelligence, including details of the Iraqi trench system.

Returning to Brigade, I found Brigadier Patrick under pressure from the

Divisional Commander; he wanted to get that off his chest, and we talked through slightly more detail of the general plan.

Lieutenant Colonel Mike Vickery
Commanding Officer, 14th/20th King's Hussars,
4th Armoured Brigade

Our final work-up exercises revealed worrying problems with my Grenadier Guards. Their Warriors couldn't move as fast as we did; and they were unwilling to accept and give orders directly over the radio as we did all the time. We hadn't got time for them to stop, get out, and give orders to everyone.

I taught them that when I said, 'Orders in five minutes,' their company second-in-command flicked his set on to rebroadcast so that my orders were heard by everyone. They then had to get their brains round adding the extra bits of information they needed to do *their* jobs.

Whenever possible, I gave the Grenadiers their own tank troop; creating a formation once known as a 'combat team'. It's much easier to walk alongside a tank that's thumping all the things that would otherwise shoot at you.

Lieutenant Colonel Charles Rogers
Commanding Officer, Staffordshire Regiment

We had only unsecured radios, so had to use a terrible coding system called BATCO, which creates meaningless numbers that people had to decode, not always correctly. It blocked up the radio, and could make people lose faith. So instead I tried to stop and get people together, which was quicker, plus I could describe things to them.

We'd always decried the Soviet's unsophisticated procedure of attacking straight from the line of advance – but discovered as we trained, that's in fact what you do. For a battle group attack, all my people needed to know was the location of the Start Line and where they were to sit on it, which could be given over the radio and required no great detail. Orders were pretty darn quick, then we advanced until we hit something.

Lieutenant Colonel Mike Vickery
Commanding Officer, 14th/20th King's Hussars,
4th Armoured Brigade

My two Guards company commanders were both very tall and delightful: Grant Baker, six foot six and skinny, commanding the Queen's Company;

and Robert Ford, nicknamed 'Panzer', six foot, enormous and went on to become the Queen's Equerry. At my O groups, while my squadron leaders were sitting comfortably, doodling, chatting with me before I actually started, these two would sit at attention, looking two feet over my head. If I addressed them they'd bark 'Sah!'

Eventually I had to talk with them privately. 'I know you guardsmen have thirty-two different ways of saying "Sir" when you mean something different. But what I actually need from you, as I'm about to put your soldiers into harm's way, is eye contact – and an arrangement in which you tell me if what I'm ordering you to do is reasonable – and not just saying "Yes Sah!" all the time. I'm not an infantryman. If you have different ideas, please let me know. Do you think that's fair?'

With a slight smile, they both stood to attention and looked over my head before barking 'Sah!' But at the next O group they were noticeably more relaxed; we chatted and their comments and suggestions were well taken. But clearly they weren't used to discussions in O groups, which worried me.

Lieutenant Colonel Arthur Denaro
Commanding Officer, Queen's Royal Irish Hussars
A shrink visited us. He interviewed me, then produced a questionnaire for the soldiers to fill out. It was quite inappropriate and I certainly couldn't issue it out. I was furious. We expected the Warning Order [preliminary notice of an order or action to follow] so it was getting very close.

Lieutenant Colonel Mike Vickery
Commanding Officer, 14th/20th King's Hussars,
4th Armoured Brigade
To stop our fin-stabilised propellants spontaneously detonating, we were told to fit new charge bins into the turrets. We tried fitting the new bins into my tank, which took twenty-four hours, destroyed the zeroing, and they were bulky and sharp-cornered, getting in the way. After one squadron had been done, I stopped it. The soldiers were very happy we weren't buggering about with the tanks any more. But I wasn't able to re-zero my tank, and through-out the fighting my adjutant was constantly cursing as he bashed his knees in the dark on the bloody new bins.

Lieutenant Colonel Arthur Denaro
Commanding Officer, Queen's Royal Irish Hussars

On St Valentine's Day I went to Brigade Headquarters to receive orders for the divisional move to assembly area Ray. I told Brigadier Patrick the move hadn't been properly thought through, which turned into the first real row I've had with him.

When I got back, my regimental headquarters had already left, leaving just me and my tent. Our line-up for the move was pretty chaotic, and I blew a fuse or two. I suppose it was a build-up of pressure, but I'd got cross with Brigade and cross with the boys. This was not terribly good of me, so I sat beside my Land Rover and opened my parcel. The mustard jar it contained was broken, which was maddening and very smelly and such a waste; I'd been so looking forward to it.

Just as I was feeling particularly blue, Major Mark O'Reilly turned up and chatted through the window and I felt a bit better. Three B-52s were glinting in the evening sunlight, making long streaks across the sky. But the news is dreadful; a civilian bunker has been bombed and they say masses of Iraqis were killed.

Then at two pm, Martin Bell told me there was going to be an announcement in Baghdad, so we listened intently as CNN told us Saddam Hussein was going to withdraw from Kuwait. What a feeling of euphoria and joy! The delight on faces was quite extraordinary.

We then drove forty kilometres west to our new positions at Ray, the last before we go in. But none of us believed we would be going in, with all fears of NBC forgotten. I was suddenly trying to think about how I was going to get people back to normal life ... and, oh ... millions of things.

Robin Watt
War artist

I heard the news that Saddam Hussein had called for peace as we arrived at Ray, after a grim, freezing night travelling in the back of an APC full of equipment, ammunition and dust. We suddenly felt safe, knowing we'd rejoin our families. The greatest worry of all, the chemical threat, had vanished. The younger soldiers were particularly relieved.

But it was they who became the quietest of all when later, the ludicrous and unacceptable details of Saddam's 'peace plan' were rejected by the Allies.

Lieutenant Colonel Arthur Denaro
Commanding Officer, Queen's Royal Irish Hussars

In the dusk at Ray, a feeling of great depression settled on everybody. Our euphoria had in any case been tinged with the disappointment of four months' training for nothing. So as I walked round the laager in the darkness, poking my head under cam nets seeing if the lads were all right, I found most had settled back into the strong feeling of resignation that we will do the business then go home. Back on my tank, my crew cooked a good meal and I slept in a little bivvie in the sand, feeling not too bad really.

Major General Rupert Smith
General Officer Commanding, 1st Armoured Division

At the assembly area, we offered the press off-the-record briefings. I thought they'd like to know what was being planned for them and was very surprised when some refused these briefings, declaring if they couldn't report it, they didn't want to know. Quite a few of them were uncomfortable at being made responsible to us for what we told them. Our embedded journalist system appeared to work quite well, although I don't know whether the relationship would have continued if we'd suffered a lot of casualties, or a disaster.

Lance Corporal Roy Sellstrom
Pioneer Corps, Army War Graves Unit

Somebody kept putting flowers outside the door of the morgue, which I'd kick out of the way; but next day there'd be more. I was angry because flowers weren't going to make this fucking dreadful job any better. Then I saw a young reservist nurse coming out of our compound.

'Are you the one keeps putting the flowers out for us?'

'Are you the one who keeps kicking them all over?'

After that I left the flowers where she put them. With a human face on it, I couldn't be angry and kick them away. This girl was showing me reality, life; that I shouldn't be like that. This was me, Roy, back again, like before.

Lieutenant Colonel Arthur Denaro
Commanding Officer, Queen's Royal Irish Hussars

I'd brought an RSM with me from the SAS, for his 'knife and fork' course with a normal regiment before being commissioned, who taught us prisoner handling and conduct after capture. Nobody was in any doubt that prisoners were to be treated with compassion and respect. I also made the same point about not looting.

Anybody doing anything under my command was totally *my* responsibility. When in the second Gulf War, I learned of instances of the maltreatment of prisoners, I was so ashamed.

Major General Alexander Harley
Assistant Chief of Defence Staff (Overseas) and Deputy Director of Joint Operations, Ministry of Defence, Whitehall

We'd only done the minimum work on prisoner of war handling until, with only a day's notice, the boss of the International Red Cross flew to London demanding a meeting. My boss, Ken Hayr, told me to front up with this, so I got together a team of experts the day before, to work out what we should be doing.

Prisoners of war are a very heavy legal liability. We went through everything, checking that our troops had been given appropriate humanitarian instructions: not to hood prisoners or do any of the bloody things that happened later in Iraq; had we got proper cages and other facilities, did we have a system to publish their names so their families will know where they are? Plus, it was our responsibility to repatriate them. All this had to be smartened up pretty quickly. By the time the Red Cross tweaked us, we had it pretty well squared away, and so it was 'Wonderful, well done Brits.'

The Rt Hon Tom King
UK Secretary of State for Defence

We could only run the air war for a limited time, then we'd have to go in. We couldn't keep three-quarters of a million troops sitting around with temperatures rising.

With the uncertainty of bomb damage assessment, judging when to go in was very difficult. There were also diplomatic considerations; the Russians, Arabs like President Mubarak, then the UN Secretary General and all sorts of politicians, had been trying to persuade Saddam to leave – and also to release the hostages.

Saddam had suddenly released the hostages, so therefore could equally suddenly leave Kuwait. But in the end, it would be a military recommendation to invade, with various political and diplomatic ingredients to be taken into consideration.

Major General Alexander Harley
Assistant Chief of Defence Staff (Overseas) and Deputy Director of Joint Operations, Ministry of Defence, Whitehall

Deciding precisely when to launch the land war depended on weather and other mundane factors. It was entirely up to Schwarzkopf, and we'd be told twelve hours or so in advance.

The more people who knew, the higher the chances of leaks. I had to put together a series of code words, so that just the ten or so people on the list could know.

We now knew that the Republican Guard units were being held back as their counter-strike force. Part of our battle plan was to penetrate the berm defences very fast, then get straight out to find their counter-strike force, aided by air. So now our whole intelligence effort shifted into finding out where they were.

Group Captain Glenn Torpy
Officer Commanding, 13 Squadron, Royal Air Force

We were tasked into Republican Guard areas, centred around the west of Kuwait, to identify their main troop concentrations. The intelligence picture indicated infestations of ZSU-23-4s [radar guided anti-aircraft weapons systems], SAM 7s, and SAM 8s, so there was reluctance to put aircraft in there, and no aircraft had operated in there at low-level.

I went in first with my navigator Tom Perham, escorted by two American harm-shooter Wild Weasels, plus two EF21-11 jammers. We were nervous, especially as five minutes into the trip there was a massive bang, after which we couldn't hear ourselves talk between the two cockpits. It turned out our canopy seal had broken, and the huge noise was turbulence and leakage of air. We flew as fast as the aircraft could go – around five hundred and eighty knots ground speed, with a very bright moon, and saw a huge amount of Iraqi equipment along our routes.

One of the vulnerable moments is at the end of a mission, returning from low-level back up to the sanctuary altitude to avoid being engaged by friendly forces. Pulling up from two hundred feet to twenty thousand is the ideal place for enemy forces to have a pot-shot at you, which was when we detected being locked up by an SA8 and SA6 [low- to medium-level surface-to-air missiles]. These didn't engage, so I guess our jammers were doing their business.

This mission gave our RIC [reconnaissance intelligence centre] guys a lot of material, and so in the build-up to the ground war, looking for the Republican Guard became our bread and butter.

Lieutenant Toby Masterton
A Squadron, The Life Guards, 4th Armoured Brigade

One of the cam nets had broken half-free in a strong wind. I got up and was trying to stake it back down. Everyone else was asleep, and the battle captain, Rupert McKenzie-Hill, got up to help me. As we struggled with this huge flapping net, another bunch of air strikes went in. We stood there watching the horizon light up. When the concussion reached us, it was as if the entire desert floor jumped up a foot or so into the air, and I can't imagine how anybody managed to sleep through this.

This was almost certainly bombing of the Republican Guard, now much closer. I said to Rupert that I felt pity for the poor blokes on the receiving end of all this – no animosity. Soldiers through the ages have felt sympathy over what they're meting out to others. It's true; you don't just read it. You think it and you articulate it.

Major General Alexander Harley
Assistant Chief of Defence Staff (Overseas) and Deputy Director of Joint Operations, Ministry of Defence, Whitehall

In the bombing phase, the Republican Guard headquarters were located and bombed, but by the land war they remained a coherent force. We interrogated some defectors, so we knew they were still ready to fight.

But breaking through the Iraqi berm and minefields was the critical operation for the whole campaign; we were very worried about this and it was planned to the nth degree. We flew a Royal Engineer officer back to London to explain personally to the Chiefs of Staff exactly how this was to be done. He brought the most wonderful maps, incorporating intelligence gleaned from a combination of air photography in the clear desert air, and patrolling. We knew *exactly* where everything was.

RSM Johnny Muir
Regimental Sergeant Major, Queen's Royal Irish Hussars

We'd been hoping the RAF would do the whole job for us. It was very surreal to lie on the desert floor at night, under a cam net having a smoke, watching the fighters circling in the air above while waiting their turn to refuel.

At this time we learned that we were going into Iraq rather than Kuwait. One of our officers was sent back to brigade HQ to pick the new maps.

Lieutenant Colonel Arthur Denaro
Commanding Officer, Queen's Royal Irish Hussars

That night, Division ordered us to send twenty people back forty kilometres at seven o'clock on Sunday morning, to tidy up the areas we'd just left. I refused, as this was disgraceful silliness on the eve of war. I knew my refusal would lead to drama but so what, at this stage?

Maggi Denaro
Commanding Officer's wife, Queen's Royal Irish Hussars

We were doing our best to make sure our husbands wouldn't worry about us. We had a lot of fun, and certainly didn't sit round moping at home. I thought everyone had behaved really well. At the time, it all seemed to go very smoothly. But in reality, as I found out afterwards, some people had behaved disgracefully badly – gone down town, had affairs, and all the rest of it.

Lance Corporal Roy Sellstrom
Pioneer Corps, Army War Graves Unit

We'd ordered body bags but they hadn't arrived. The units had them, but wouldn't give them to us. We preferred getting bodies off the Americans, as they came in proper porous bags you can't see through. From the Arabs, they'd be wrapped in white muslin and in a big see-through plastic bag, which we didn't like. From the Brits, if they didn't make it to the field hospitals, the unit quartermasters weren't using up their body bag stock, so they'd be wrapped in anything they could find.

Instead, we were given six-foot black plastic bin bags. We tried putting our tallest bloke into one. It took eight of us to get him in, as you had to lift him up first, with masking tape around his head to seal it up. A body bag is porous, so inside the bin bags the fluids would be swilling round, turning into soup.

We again asked the units to give us bags – but they didn't want to know. So the only people who really needed body bags – us, didn't have any.

Lieutenant Colonel Arthur Denaro
Commanding Officer, Queen's Royal Irish Hussars

The news was bad; the General himself was irritated by the Irish Hussars' decision not to go and clean up their areas. I was astonished and very disappointed in this hassle. In fact we did send some people off, but against the very essence of good leadership and man management. I wrote to the General that the Irish Hussars was a very good regiment and he should not be irritated with us, ending with a cartoon from Jock to cheer him up. But then I had a very difficult telephone conversation with the Chief of Staff at Brigade, so there was no point sending the letter.

I was seriously irritated by this tiny, totally insignificant piece of beastly staff work, being hassled by Division and to an extent by Brigade. I decided that the next time, I would disobey quietly.

So that was a thoroughly bad day. But I managed to walk over to see A Squadron, who despite their amazement at having been sent rubbish-clearing a few days before going to war, were in very good heart, and I met up with my old mate Trooper Reid. So by the evening, after some very good cards, I was feeling better.

Robin Watt
War artist

The Americans were dropping fuel-air explosives to destroy minefields, B-52s attacking the Republican Guard, and Apache helicopter raids one hundred and fifty kilometres into Iraq. Intelligence believed the biological weapons factories to have been destroyed, but continued to say that chemical attack remained a strong possibility.

Lieutenant Colonel Arthur Denaro
Commanding Officer, Queen's Royal Irish Hussars

At Brigade I found a very depressed Brigadier Patrick, who'd just learned we were on indefinite hold yet again, having had only three days to wait before going in. It wasn't easy bringing the boys up to a peak then letting them down, with everybody's emotions rocking and rolling, facing this very dangerous, frightening unknown. Anyway, it was fun to see people, and I wore my Saddam Hussein mask, which brought a few laughs.

The Brigadier seemed to want to chat. He said that actually the Irish Hussars were still very high in his books, which was nice of him because I'd been pretty beady the day before. But that evening, sadly, I received a phone call to say that AP (one of the wives) has got leukaemia, so we brought HP into our HQ and talked him through it.

Major General Rupert Smith
General Officer Commanding, 1st Armoured Division

UK was worried about us being attacked with anthrax. Then a week before commencing our attack, we were ordered to stab everybody for the plague, but given no reassurance as to the side effects. My excellent divisional medical officer was under great pressure to get on with this, but he was quite clear that we were about to do something to ourselves that we'd regret. There was nowhere to bed people down, so they'd have to get into sleeping bags beside their armoured vehicles until they recovered. So I said 'No'.

This went round the houses a couple of times until somebody very senior explained to me that after an attack, Ministers didn't want to have to tell Parliament that nobody had been inoculated. Again, I refused, as we were then within days of being ordered to attack, with no way of coping with a third of my division being incapacitated.

But Ministers *yet again* insisted that we vaccinate, so I resolved the impasse by sending out a signal saying that anybody could have this treatment, but I as the GOC, wasn't having any of it. I don't know how many people ended up having plague injections, but I, Rupert Smith, wasn't intending to fight a battle that would lead to us being attacked by plague, anthrax or chemicals. But of course the enemy can do unto you whatsoever he wishes.

Lieutenant General Walter Boomer
General Officer Commanding, 1 Marine Expeditionary Force, United States Marine Corps

We were asked to explore the idea of an amphibious attack in the north, then carrying on into Iraq, to Basra.

Studies of the coastal waters showed we couldn't do this; but then Saddam laid mines in the Gulf, damaging two of our ships, requiring much skill and courage from the sailors so we didn't lose them. You can imagine the outcry if we'd lost a ship, with many, many sailors dying. The navy became very concerned, and as we were clearing these mines, General Schwarzkopf asked to meet with Admiral Stan Arthur and I, aboard Arthur's flagship, the USS *Blue Ridge*.

General Schwarzkopf asked about our amphibious operation, then specifically how much collateral damage it would cause to the southern part of Kuwait City, which extends a long way south down the coast. The Iraqis had fortified the beaches, so I knew this would be a tough fight, with significant collateral damage.

General Schwarzkopf said something like, 'We've managed so far to avoid damaging Kuwait City. It's very important that we not destroy the city in order to liberate it, and I'm very concerned about collateral damage. How long will it take you to get the mines cleared?'

I don't remember exactly how many days Admiral Arthur told him, but it was too long. Mines in the ocean are almost as bad as IEDs [improvised explosive devices] on the ground. We were clearing by helicopter – towing sleds behind to explode them, a very painstaking, time-consuming process, and you only have to miss the one.

So having been told that our amphibious attack would take too long and cause collateral damage, General Schwarzkopf then looked down the table at me and said, 'Walt, could you accomplish your mission without the amphibious operation?'

I'm sure there was a pregnant pause there, but ultimately my answer was, 'General, I can – provided we can convince what I believe to be a division of Iraqi troops on the coast, that we *are* going to carry out an amphibious operation, stopping them from reinforcing against us as we go up the centre.'

He said, 'Fine.'

We already had a brigade of Marines at sea aboard the ships, under the navy's command, not mine. They worked very hard to convince the Iraqis we were going to attack from the sea, which in the event succeeded, because those Iraqi troops stayed in their coastal defensive positions until it was too late, then broke and ran to avoid being cut off.

Brigadier Mike Willcocks
Chief of Staff (Land), Joint War Headquarters, RAF High Wycombe
My trip to bring back a copy of the war plan coincided with all the final O groups: Rupert Smith's, 7 Brigade Cordingley's and 4 Brigade Hammerbeck's, which I attended with Peter de la Billiere. The day for the ground war to start – 'Go Day' – was provisionally in a few days' time, so these took place around G minus 4 and 3.

Rupert Smith was his usual charming self, laid-back, relaxed, with a light hand on everything. But the two brigade commanders were completely different. Somebody made a remark about the Iraqis, and even though Peter de la Billiere was sitting there, Hammerbeck snapped back, 'Don't you denigrate the enemy. You must never denigrate the enemy...' Patrick Cordingley on the other hand seemed more laid-back.

But the boys were superbly trained. You got this smell of really, really fit, keen, raring-to-go guys – the wonderful feeling of a combat-ready formation.

Lieutenant Toby Masterton
A Squadron, The Life Guards, 4th Armoured Brigade

Our squadron gathered in a large square. General Rupert Smith appeared, gave us a stirring speech, then asked for questions. Captain Rupert McKenzie-Hill, surrounded by all our soldiers, asked him how long he thought we'd be fighting for, and how fierce he thought it might be. The General gave a very diplomatic response, but didn't answer the question. My friend reiterated his question, but got no real answer, to which General Smith eventually said, 'OK...well done. Top marks for perseverance and not letting me off the hook... This is my wild guess... I think we'll be fighting hard as long as our vehicles and combat supplies allow. This is why we're concentrating on key objectives and bypassing everything else, conserving ourselves and moving on. Afterwards, there may also be a need for units to rotate out here as an occupying guard force.' We went away thinking this was a pretty monumental task.

A little later, Brigadier Hammerbeck came to our battle group and gave us his motivational speech. Rupert Smith was a hard act to follow, having many more credentials, but it was effective and he seemed concerned for us.

Lieutenant General Walter Boomer
General Officer Commanding, 1 Marine Expeditionary Force, United States Marine Corps

The Saudis were on my left, and so I had to work through the battle plan with them, which was a trial. I was concerned about operational security – not that they might tell anybody anything deliberately, but I knew they weren't well-trained in communication security. I tried to be careful, telling them only enough so they could operate. But they complained to General

Schwarzkopf, who chastised me, saying, 'Look, I confide in them, so you will too. Get over it.' So I did.

There were many similar issues: I was, for example, allegedly flanked to my immediate left by the Syrian division, but I never saw them, coordinated or liaised with them – or even talked to them. So what the hell were the Syrians going to do? They're still the 'Ghost Syrians' to me. That's why it was so important for me to have my own armoured brigade on my left flank, which I felt was totally exposed.

Lieutenant Colonel Arthur Denaro
Commanding Officer, Queen's Royal Irish Hussars

On a cold morning with a keen wind, we gave formal orders for Operation Desert Storm. Quite an historic event, but as we'd rehearsed many times already, there was nothing new or startling in my orders. We were due to cross the berm on G+1.

After a new Soviet initiative, Hussein was to talk to the nation. I walked round our position at dusk, the sun reflecting very pinkly on the clouds, people getting more and more tense awaiting the announcement. When Hussein turned the whole thing down, a serious gloom descended upon me. I suddenly realised that we really *were* going to go in now. I'd never truly believed we would.

Lieutenant General Walter Boomer
**General Officer Commanding, 1 Marine Expeditionary Force,
United States Marine Corps**

I had two marine divisions to get through the one minefield breach – a huge amount of people and equipment, which was going to take a long time. But we couldn't see another way of doing this; and the date for the attack was set. General Keys [William M. Keys], who commanded the 2nd Division, came up to me and said, 'You know, neither of us are particularly enamoured of this plan. We think it will work, but it's going to take a long time to get both divisions through the breach.'

We knew that putting both divisions through the same breach meant more time exposed to chemical attack. With two breaches, we'd be through in at least half the time, less exposed to their artillery and chemical units. So I said, 'Yeah, you're right, Bill, but you haven't been here as long.'

I then asked him, 'In the few days we've got, could you make your own breach through that barrier, without taking a huge number of casualties?'

He said, 'Yes I can.'

I said, 'Then you should.'

He said, 'Absolutely.'

I'd known General Keys for a long time. We'd fought together in Vietnam. We were friends, and I knew if he said he could do this huge task, he would do it. So I changed my plan to attack with my two divisions abreast.

I had then to go back and convince General Schwarzkopf, who decided to support the plan. He then had to tell Colin Powell and the president, that the Marines, having been there for longer than anyone else, had changed their mind at the last minute and devised another plan, which he supported.

But to give time for us to shift 2nd Marine Division's huge amounts of supplies and equipment delayed the entire attack. Vast detail went into the planning: from air, artillery, to breaching of the obstacles – you name it. When I look at this today, I wonder how the Marines accomplished it. My decision was based on friendship – that if General Keys said he could do this, he would do it.

Lieutenant Colonel Arthur Denaro
Commanding Officer, Queen's Royal Irish Hussars

Having gone to bed the previous night quite clear that we were now going into war, we woke to hear the news that Iraq had accepted the Soviet resolution and peace plan. However, within half an hour, we were told this was still G-2 and we were rolling, the Americans determined to go in, and us with them.

Robin Watt
War artist

Two more packets of NAPS tablets were issued per man, with last-minute admin instructions – that the last outgoing post would be at 0800 hours tomorrow, and bodies were to be placed in sleeping bags then buried beside their vehicles, with burial a sub-unit responsibility. When we reached the reconstitution line, we were to return to collect our dead. We were also told that authority had been granted for temporary mass burial on Saudi soil, for recovery to the United Kingdom in due course.

Major General Alexander Harley
Assistant Chief of Defence Staff (Overseas) and Deputy Director of Joint Operations, Ministry of Defence, Whitehall

The message came through very late in the evening, warning us they'd be going in at dawn the next day. I sent the code words to the prime minister and other key people. It was pretty secure. By the time the media got hold of the news, all the early targets had been engaged and our people were through the berm.

Major General Rupert Smith
General Officer Commanding, 1st Armoured Division

We would attack the moment the bombing damage assessment of Iraqi armoured formations reached fifty per cent – an enormously high percentage. My concern was to stop the Iraqis moving, leaving them in place to run out of water. I was therefore prepared to attack even if they had a much higher percentage.

We'd moved west, no longer with the Egyptians to our right, instead the 1st US Cavalry Division. We then received the order to attack, and the time, and I ordered my final O group to be on G-Day – the next day at 1000, 24 February 1991.

Lieutenant Colonel Arthur Denaro
Commanding Officer, Queen's Royal Irish Hussars

I spent the morning going through communications on my tank, and chatting with the crew, then bade farewell to the squadrons, taking with me Martin Bell who had a big delicious cake which he shared with the troops. I then spent time with Tim Buxton, the 17th Lancers troop, and then on to D Squadron who had their flag flying and were having a communion service, chatting to all the boys, including Trooper Robinson whose mother had been sending me mass cards.

It was all pretty calm by the evening; we had a good supper and played cards, where I lost lots, then back to my little tent for the last comfy night, and wrote a long letter to Maggs: I had a lifetime to thank her for, and just didn't know how to put that into a last letter. But as I explained to her, it wasn't actually a last letter...

The deadline passed at 2000 hours, and of course there was no sign of an Iraqi move-out, which didn't dismay us.

Lieutenant Toby Masterton
A Squadron, The Life Guards, 1 Royal Scots Battle Group, 4th Armoured Brigade

I'd moved up to live with the Royal Scots battle group headquarters. Their CO, Iain Johnstone, ordered all the windscreens and side-windows of newly arrived trucks and Land Rovers be removed and buried in the sand, to prevent sun reflections, and drivers not hearing incoming fire until too late. This order was very badly received by those who'd signed for these vehicles!

I was summoned to pass on to James that H-Hour [the hour at which combat was to begin] was to be that evening, which is a striking moment in anyone's military career. But then, as I was on wheels, I was told to stay behind with the battle group's rear echelon: 'We'll see you after the war when we do the wash-up...' Not deploying with the squadron offended me greatly.

It was a quiet, still night, and our sub-unit CAM chemical detector went off. Then all across the desert, one could hear detectors in other units going off as well, a kilometre or so away. Some people got up, while others ignored it, remaining in their sleeping bags in the sand beside their vehicles. It was totally dark.

Then some distance off, in another unit, a good old-fashioned sergeant major shouted 'Gas gas gas!' with mess tins being clanged together. Everybody suddenly panicked, putting on respirators, running into tank barrels and bashas, clambering into their rubber boots and gloves. The officers gathered by Rupert's APC, where the signallers were desperately shouting at battle group headquarters, trying to find out if we were being attacked, each being answered, 'Wait out.'

Rupert put a cheap plastic transistor radio on the deck of his vehicle, which suddenly burst forth with the BBC World Service tune – 'Da dullah da da, da dullah daar...' and an announcement that the ground attack on Iraq had just started. A very surreal moment. We don't know what triggered the detectors.

Lance Corporal Roy Sellstrom
Pioneer Corps, Army War Graves Unit

On 23 February, they decided to change over to the same system as the Americans, whose full-time grave registration units stay forward with the fighting troops to remove American bodies as quickly as possible. Enemy dead are fine, as fighting troops are tuned-in for that; whereas seeing your own dead – your friends – affects fighting morale. So our plans went out of the window.

We didn't have enough vehicles to do this, so had to scrounge a four-ton lorry, a Land Rover and trailer, and an eight-ton Bedford TM truck and trailer, plus two twelve-by-twelve and one nine-by-nine tents, plastic surgical gloves and masks, no body bags, a Karcher water spray unit – but no electric generator to run it or jerrycans for the water. So we went off robbing jerrycans, returning with twenty-odd. We scrounged rations as we didn't have any, but never did acquire any ammunition.

At the last minute, two young lads turned up from the RCT [Royal Corps of Transport], plus an RAMC [Royal Army Medical Corps] medic, our subunit ending up a total of twelve.

We moved from Al Jubayl to the forward area, with orders to go with 7 Brigade's war graves team when they breached the minefield and entered Kuwait.

Brigadier Mike Willcocks
Chief of Staff (Land), Joint War Headquarters, RAF High Wycombe

I flew back in an HS125 jet with the war plans on the hard drive of my laptop. Over France I was standing behind the pilots. Heathrow air traffic control ordered a big route diversion and delay. Our pilot said, 'Negative. I've got a guy here with the Gulf War plans and we need to get straight in.'

Air traffic control came back immediately, 'Why didn't you say so? Continue on your current heading,' clearing the airways and we flew straight into Heathrow without even having to turn. A helicopter was waiting beside the runway, and I was whipped off to High Wycombe.

I really hadn't wanted to come back from the Gulf. The feeling in Rupert Smith's division was incredible – they were well and truly up for it. Being there with them had been a wonderful feeling.

CHAPTER 7

COALITION BLITZKREIG

At 0300 hours on G-Day, 24 February, the ground offensive began with the two US Marine divisions of General Boomer's 1st US Marine Expeditionary Force attacking up the coast, and 18 (US) Corps led by 82nd (US) Airborne battalion (3/325 The White Falcons), under the command of the 6th French Division going in as protection for the far north-west flank. That morning, to the left of 1 (BR) Division, the 101st (US) Airborne Division (the Screaming Eagles) put in another deep flank assault, of three hundred transport and assault helicopters carrying two thousand men, vehicles and artillery, which by midday had established a forward operating base fifty miles inside Iraq. Fifteen hours ahead of schedule, 18 Corps launched a devastating attack towards Basra.

At 0100 hours on G-Day, the US Marines began their breaching operations, prior to attacking the most heavily defended enemy positions.

In the centre, on 1 (BR) Division's right, the Arab Joint Force Command East (JFCE) – two Egyptian divisions and one Syrian division – were preparing to go in once the flanks were secured, twenty-four hours later, at G+1.

A week earlier, 1 (BR) Division had moved from its training area with the US 1st Infantry Division, into assembly area Ray, ready to move forwards on G+1 into huge staging areas twenty to thirty kilometres south-east of the minefield breach, in preparation for being called forward according to the type of battle required to be fought on the other side of the minefield. General Smith held his last Orders group at 1000 on G-Day. Their move was scheduled for the early hours of G+2, once the minefield had been breached by the US 1st Infantry Division.

But the speed of the US Marines in the south, and 18 Corps in the north, led General Schwarzkopf to bring forward the US 7th Corps' second breaching operation by twelve hours. B-52 bombers, Apache strike helicopters and artillery preparatory fire were already attacking Iraqi positions around the minefield breach position, for this the most critical of all the attacks, in which 1st US Infantry Division, field engineers to the fore, cleared the eighteen lanes through which the main force would motor.

1st US Infantry Division began the breaching operation at midday on G+1, which they completed unexpectedly quickly in just one hour and twenty minutes. That afternoon and over the first night, the breach head was consolidated, and US 1st and 3rd Armoured Divisions advanced north, while 1 (BR) Division abandoned plans to move their tanks by transporter and completed the tricky passage of lines through the 1st US Infantry Division.

Sandy Gall
ITN television reporter

We knew the ground war would start the following morning. I had a rather crazy cameraman, so we decided we would pretend we were part of the coalition forces. We put inverted 'V' markings on the vehicle and wore charcoal-lined NBC protection suits which journalists weren't supposed to wear unless there was a chemical attack. But thinking we looked official, we decided to drive to the border, and be ready the next morning for when the attack started.

Major General Rupert Smith
General Officer Commanding, 1st Armoured Division

We'd moved into assembly area Ray on 16 February, where we conducted our bit of the Artillery Raids – a preparatory phase of the operation. We'd then been told when G-Day was to be, and the 7 Corps H-Hour. However, our H-Hour was to be on call, because we did not know how long 1st US Infantry Division would take to establish the breach head. Thus we had to move up into a staging area by a stated time after 1st US Div started their attack and be ready for whenever our H-Hour was ordered by 7th Corps, a stated time after 1st US Div started their attack.

Sandy Gall
ITN television reporter

My cameraman chanced his arm at the roadblocks, and wouldn't be flagged down. I assumed that with the war starting tomorrow they'd be on high alert, but with typical Saudi incompetence we were allowed through.

The town of Khafji, which had been fought over, was completely empty with a dead camel in the road, the hotel's plate glass windows shot out. The road did a U bend, then went to the border itself, which had a huge ornate arch. We returned to Khafji and stopped just the other side at a deserted petrol station, where dozens of brand new cars had been left, probably by Kuwaitis fleeing south from Kuwait city.

We decided to bed down in the car and wait to see what would happen at eight the next morning.

G-DAY – SUNDAY 24 FEBRUARY

Lieutenant General Walter Boomer
General Officer Commanding, 1 Marine Expeditionary Force, United States Marine Corps

The 1st Marine Division launched at 0430, and the 2nd at 0530. My mobile command post moved up to the Saudi–Kuwait border between the two divisions, closest to the 2nd. Their attack was pretty uneventful, despite coming under fire as they fanned out towards to Al Jubar airbase.

Sandy Gall
ITN television reporter

We were woken in the middle of the night by a terrific barrage of rockets going over on to the Iraqi forces. At 7am a maroon 4x4 came at high speed along the deserted road past the petrol station. The cameraman said, 'They must be journalists, so why don't we follow them?'

'OK,' I said. 'Why not?'

Following the fast-moving maroon 4x4, we drove out of the petrol station into Khafji and out the other side to the border, where they did a U-turn off the dual carriageway on to a slip road into the desert then disappeared. We were going so fast we nearly ran into them on the other side where they'd stopped. But instead of journalists, four Saudi officers stepped out in uniform. One of them said, 'What are you doing here?'

'We're British,' I said.

'British what?'

'British television...'

'You shouldn't be here.'

So I said, 'Oh... yes...'

They didn't seem to know what to do, so while they were talking with each other, I told the cameraman to quietly reverse then drive away. I was sure they'd arrest us, but they were so busy talking, they let us go.

We drove back on the track towards the dual carriageway through a thick morning mist, with lines of tanks, and armoured personnel carriers coming towards us. Saddam had talked about creating a huge berm which he'd fill with oil and set on fire. We realised that we were on this berm, but it had already been bulldozed flat in one place, ready for Saudi vehicles to cross. As nobody was attempting to stop us, we went back a couple of hundred yards and started filming the waiting troops, one guy doing a sort of dance, shouting they were going to kill Saddam and other typically Arab things.

After half an hour they crossed the berm into Kuwait along the bulldozed track. We followed along, behind half a dozen tanks, a couple of infantry lorries and a petrol tanker, for ten or fifteen miles into Kuwait.

Lieutenant General Walter Boomer
General Officer Commanding, 1 Marine Expeditionary Force, United States Marine Corps

I was insulated from everything except what was going on in front of me. I knew the Corps mission was taking place to the west, that it would be an armoured battle, but was pretty sure it wouldn't spill over into my area. Although taking place at the same time, they were two separate things, so I wasn't following what was going on to the west. But we moved quicker than the others expected – although *slower* than I'd hoped.

But when General Schwarzkopf saw we were getting ahead of his plan, he decided to move everyone else early. This was pretty disconcerting for them, because when you change the timetable for an entire Corps, you're messing with a very complicated piece of machinery that really can't respond at a moment's notice. I don't know what went on between General Schwarzkopf and General Franks, but I do know that General Schwarzkopf was concerned that things on the western side weren't moving fast enough.

Major General Rupert Smith
General Officer Commanding, 1st Armoured Division

I held my final O group in the morning of 24 February. Not long after we finished, we were told the Corps H-Hour was to be bought forward. Thus our move to the staging area had to be brought forward, which meant that the divisional march had to start some three and a half hours earlier than planned. The staff reworked the divisional movement order and 7 Brigade hardly paused in its staging area before being called forward by the regulating HQ into the lanes through the breach.

At the time I wasn't aware of the tension this had generated between Schwarzkopf and Franks, due to the former having a better view of the battle-field due to American intelligence from JSTARS, which indicated things were happening over the other side and the Iraqis were starting to move back. We [at 1 (BR) Division] weren't told why the attack was being brought forward.

Bringing your H-Hour forward – especially by such a long time – is not something one wants to do because of the organisational confusion that can follow, particularly with large formations being moved. But that's what happened, and we managed it, thanks to a clever staff officer and the laptop computers we'd bought in, enabling our movement order to be restructured very rapidly. With the greatest credit to our divisional military police, we got everyone moved into the harbour areas on time.

We were also helped by the desert being flat; this would not have been possible in Europe.

Sandy Gall
ITN television reporter

We came to the first Iraqi outpost. The Saudis had arrived a couple of minutes earlier, there'd been some shooting and an Iraqi soldier had been shot in the leg. The rest were surrendering with their hands up. The wounded man was trying to kiss the Saudi soldier who was looking after him.

We got a bit of filming of all this, then thought we'd better start back to Saudi. We were a long way out – fifteen miles into Iraq; they'd invaded with little opposition and we had the story, so we had to get it back. The allied build-up on the track was now very considerable – we presumed because of mines, which worried me.

Heading back into Saudi, we were now driving against a terrific press of traffic. The story meant nothing unless we could get it back to London. At one point, we were hailed by a guy in a pick-up truck wearing jeans and a bandana. 'You guys could get blown away,' he shouted.

Another guy with a beard in the back of the pick-up was pointing a huge machine gun at us. They were wondering why we were driving in the wrong direction. He had an orange cloth flying from his aerial, which he ripped in half and gave to us: 'Display that for God's sake!'

Robin Watt
War artist

G-Day came with a fierce wind and driving rain. At our regimental O group, Colonel Denaro observed that when the 8th Hussars advanced at El Alamein it was also pouring with rain. As part of the administration section of the orders, we were told that if casualties are light inside Iraq, bodies will not be buried but recovered to a brigade rendezvous, to be dealt with by the War Graves Unit, then taken back to Saudi Arabia.

Sandy Gall
ITN television reporter

We continued against the tide until we reached the border, then rushed back to the hotel to edit and transmit the story. Back in London it was Sunday lunchtime. The lady producer told us they would hold the lunchtime news for our report. So after twenty minutes of editing, we got it to London and on to the air, as the first pictures of the ground war.

Robin Watt
War artist

The Commanding Officer finished by saying, 'Remember we will be in enemy territory. Crews must not stray from vehicles on foot at any time, and never forget the danger of mines. Vehicles must not bunch. A2 echelon vehicles must zigzag, not laager in neat lines. The tank squadrons are to keep going whatever the task, and be aggressive to minimise casualties.'

His final words were 'The best of luck and God bless'. There was much handshaking as officers and men wished each other '*bonne chance*', and then quickly dispersed.

Sandy Gall
ITN television reporter

Once we'd got our report transmitted back to London, the lady producer told me Schwarzkopf had imposed a twenty-four-hour news curfew, so none of the pools got anything out. Five minutes later our footage went out on CNN. A Saudi colonel saw it on his room television and came bursting into our room. 'Where did you get this story? How are you putting it out? You're not allowed to put this story out!'

He demanded to hear it again, so we ran it for him, and when we got to the bit when I said, 'And obviously the next stop is going to be Kuwait City,' he shouted, 'Stop! You can't use that!'

'It's too late. It's already been broadcast.'

We had difficulties with Saudi authorities for the next few days.

Lieutenant Colonel Arthur Denaro
Commanding Officer, Queen's Royal Irish Hussars

I drove from Ray to the assembly area with my second-in-command Mark O'Reilly. We made it in seven hours, and talked about a million things – the war, whether we would be frightened or not, our wives, life in the regiment, what life was going to be like afterwards.

We arrived about midnight, having passed the whole of 1st Armoured Division, thousands and thousands of vehicles. I jumped into my sleeping bag in the back of a Land Rover, and slept quite well.

RSM Johnny Muir
Regimental Sergeant Major, Queen's Royal Irish Hussars

One of the other Ferrets broke down, so with no spares to fix it I had our REME cut off its turret and welded it on to mine. It gave me much better shelter, but not from anything more than a rifle round.

Brigadier Patrick Cordingley
Commander, 7th Armoured Brigade

So off we went at the rush, me trusting to luck that everyone would get to where they were supposed to be.

I arrived in the assembly area very late at night wondering what should I do next. My command vehicle had broken down, so there was nowhere for me to go and look at the maps or relax – which you can't do in a tank. So we put up shelters beside the tank and went to sleep.

G+1 – MONDAY 25 FEBRUARY

Major General Rupert Smith
General Officer Commanding, 1st Armoured Division

The recce screen vehicles started to go through the breach. They reported we'd got clear space beyond so I decided to lead with 7 Brigade, which went into the breach and out the other side in short order. I then got the artillery through so we could begin the deep attack [with artillery raids]. 4 Brigade would then follow.

Brigadier Patrick Cordingley
Commander, 7th Armoured Brigade

I'd received radio orders while on the move confirming we'd be leading the way through the breach, with an artillery group following behind us. Eventually I received confirmatory orders, which didn't tell us anything new beyond pinpointing further enemy positions. I decided to bring in all the commanding officers, which in fact was unnecessary, particularly as they were very busy and John Sharples didn't arrive, as he got lost.

Lieutenant Colonel Arthur Denaro
Commanding Officer, Queen's Royal Irish Hussars

I had to get up to go over to brigade orders; the Americans were moving faster, and breaching the enemy defences was not proving as difficult as had been predicted. Intelligence assessed that the Iraqis would fight, and were deliberately giving ground to lure allied forces into their killing zones.

Brigadier Patrick Cordingley
Commander, 7th Armoured Brigade

We moved forward to the staging area, where we waited for ages, looking at a bloody great berm built by the Iraqis, and American Humvees displaying huge signs marking the beginning of the cleared lanes through the minefield. Then one of the Staffords was shot. I had the terrible business of listening to people over the radio trying to get an American helicopter to take him away. You want to do something, but know it's better to keep out of it and let them get on with the job.

Lieutenant Colonel Charles Rogers
Commanding Officer, Staffordshire Regiment

While we were waiting to cross, one of my soldiers had a negligent discharge shooting another through the chest. They were trying to clean their weapons. I got really very cross – in desperation. It was bad enough going to war, without shooting your own side... I really ripped into the platoon commander, but then we had to go, which was just as well really.

Corporal Darren Wilson
MILAN Platoon, C Company, Staffordshire Regiment

We'd been sitting there for several hours, and I was in front of my vehicle ready for orders. Then a shot went off, and I turned to see Nobby fall on to the ground. It's something you can never describe – ever; the way it happened and our reaction. It was complete and utter shock – and so close to going in.

Captain Chris Hughes
Adjutant, Staffordshire Regiment

We were due to leave in thirty minutes, so were desperately trying to get a casevac helicopter in. We could see the bloody thing five kilometres away, but there were an awful lot of vehicles so we must have been very hard to identify, so it didn't land in the right place.

We let off Firefly strobes and coloured smoke, chasing it on the radio. This, for me, was the first time operations were about to override a serious casualty. In Northern Ireland, somebody would stay with the guy. But we were going to have to leave; it was very difficult.

Captain Tim Sandiford
MILAN Platoon Commander, C Company, Staffordshire Regiment

The medics were already working on young Taylor, who'd been shot through the chest and shoulder. He was horribly yellow and waxen. Corporal Wilson was holding his head and I was shouting at him, trying to keep him talking. He was slipping back and wasn't saying anything coherent, then they pumped him full of something and he started to come round a bit. As there was nothing I could do, I went to find the rest of the section.

It was rather unpleasant, as I couldn't just sit them down for a cup of tea and a chat. I was actually saying, 'Right, you're *now* going to do this and then you're going to do that...'

I wouldn't let the lad who'd shot him or another guy who'd been to school with him go round to see him. They were fairly cut up as it was, and I didn't really know what state he was in. It was a hard decision to make. So after ordering them all around, I went back to Taylor and shouted at him, 'Farewell. I'm off. I'll see you after the war.' He responded I thought coherently, so I left feeling he would survive.

But just before we drove off, the medical officer said, 'I don't think he can make it,' which rather knocked me back, but at least I was prepared for it.

Captain Richard Gale
Medical Officer, Staffordshire Regiment

He had an entry wound on the left side of his chest, with the exit just under his collarbone, conscious when I got to him, and the company medics had already got a drip in. I put in a chest drain and took a litre of fluid off his chest virtually immediately. He was doing well while we waited on a helicopter.

Then just as the American medics turned up, he suddenly went off into cardio-respiratory arrest. As I was intubating him they were saying, 'Let's go, let's fucking go,' so I said, 'Let's just fucking wait, shall we?' – it being difficult to intubate somebody in a helicopter.

Lieutenant Colonel Charles Rogers
Commanding Officer, Staffordshire Regiment

The protocol of crossing a breach is that the unit responsible for the breach – the Americans – provides medical support, so we had to go through brigade HQ, up through division to the American 1st Division. Eventually a helicopter arrived, and while our doctor was desperately trying to save the guy's life, the American medics came rushing in wearing sunglasses and told everyone to get out of the way – rather brutally, we thought. Our doctor hadn't really believed he could save the guy, but was trying desperately to do it.

Captain Richard Gale
Medical Officer, Staffordshire Regiment

He was effectively dead when we put him on the chopper, although the resuscitation continued. I wandered off for about twenty minutes, pretty pissed off. The sergeant major came up and said, 'Get a grip sir, we still have a job to do.' He was absolutely right, of course.

Captain Chris Hughes
Adjutant, Staffordshire Regiment

The helicopter lifted him literally two minutes before we were due to cross the start line. Could we have left an ambulance behind to look after him? An ambulance is a big asset to a battle group just about to go to war. If the helicopter hadn't come, I don't know what we would have done.

Lieutenant Colonel Charles Rogers
Commanding Officer, Staffordshire Regiment

So the guy was flown away rather unceremoniously, still alive. I had no feeling for what then happened to him, and it wasn't until after the war had ended that we found out he'd died. I had the same problem with some of our wounded, which still upsets me even today. When you write to parents to say 'Your son got shot', you can't say 'but I don't know what happened to him.'

Corporal Darren Wilson
MILAN Platoon, C Company, Staffordshire Regiment

Another guy arrived from the reserve [to take Nobby's place]. He met our detachment, then we got into the vehicles and drove off.

I was sitting in the turret thinking, 'Everybody should know what's happened because Nobby was such a good guy.' We'd all been crying, and were shook up and in bits. None of us wanted to talk about it. We believed that Nobby was going to be OK – that after the war was finished we were going to visit him with a bunch of flowers, grapes, Lucozade, in hospital. We all said, 'When we go and see Nobby...', or 'Wait till we've finished, I'm going to go and tell Nobby about this.' It was as if he'd sprained his ankle and was sitting on the sideline. But in the back of our minds we must have thought he might be dead. But it was only when it was finished, once we'd done all the fighting and they came up to us and said, 'We got some bad news.' That's when it really hit us.

Major Tim Gatfield
Headquarters, Staffordshire Regiment

The breach was marked with only two strands of wire, through a minefield only one hundred metres deep. The engineers were placing TNT on top of the mines they'd uncovered and, as we went through, stopped the traffic to explode them.

Some Iraqi positions had been attacked then destroyed by driving along the trenches. The remaining trenches were pathetic; no bends and no real shelters. Apart from a few destroyed vehicles, it was just another bit of desert – not the big obstacle we'd expected.

Brigadier Patrick Cordingley
Commander, 7th Armoured Brigade

Once through the breach, we had to drive some thirty kilometres further on, to give the huge numbers of people behind us enough room to come through as well.

Lieutenant Colonel Charles Rogers
Commanding Officer, Staffordshire Regiment

It was a traffic jam through the marked lanes – stop, go, then into another assembly area, after which we broke out and swept round. By this time it was getting dark and starting to rain.

Brigadier Patrick Cordingley
Commander, 7th Armoured Brigade

I didn't have a lot to do, until eventually I rumbled forward in my tank. But when I got into the breach itself, I realised it was ridiculously badly marked, and became convinced we were being led off in the wrong direction – not north, but west. So, not knowing where the markers were taking us, we struck off on our own without really knowing if we were in the minefield or not. We passed quite a lot of Iraqi equipment destroyed by our artillery fire, so decided this *wasn't* the minefield.

Robin Watt
War artist

It was dirty, smelly and exhausting. We didn't know what was going on, or what was going to happen. We'd expected to be hit with chemicals going through the minefield breach, so we wore all our NBC kit, which was bloody uncomfortable and horrible. By having a map and monitoring the artillery's radios, I knew what was going on, but only at squadron level. Sometimes we stopped, got out and had a look around – at one time for seven hours, waiting while the other brigade moved through us. But I wasn't aware of anything beyond our battle group. We had Martin Bell travelling with us, and because he didn't have a story, he got me in front of the camera, talking about my drawings.

Brigadier Patrick Cordingley
Commander, 7th Armoured Brigade

We finally arrived safely in forming up area Blue, which wasn't marked, but we were confident it was the right place. I told Rupert Smith, 'We're ready, so when do you want us to go in?'; he replied, 'When do you want to go?'

So I said 3pm, but then Charlie Rogers said he had to refuel so wouldn't be ready until three-thirty. I decided to set the QRIH off at three-fifteen, as I needed to get them out in the front of us with the medium reconnaissance screen. As the second hand of my watch ticked around to three-thirty, I was worrying yet again about whether our training had been enough, and the hundreds, possibly thousands, of people who were going to die. I wondered what on earth to say to everyone as they launched.

John Sharples solved the problem for me, coming up on the radio as if beginning a shoot on the ranges: 'We are ready. Permission to take on Hards?' This broke the tension, which had been quite palpable – bless him, and off we went.

Second Lieutenant Alistair Watkins
Grenadier Guards, 3 Royal Regiment of Fusiliers Battle Group, 4th Armoured Brigade

When it had been, finally, our time to move, after 7 Brigade, we'd been put into lines ready to enter the minefield channels, our battle group spread out as far as the eye could see. A lot of artillery and MLRS fire was lighting up the sky. We'd slept the night in our NBC gear in the sand beside the vehicles, eventually passing through the minefield the next day at 1300 hours [G+1].

Captain Tim Purbrick
Commanding 4 Troop, D Squadron, Queen's Royal Irish Hussars

In FUP [forming-up point] Blue we shook out in preparation for taking up the advance. Four kilometres further on, we were to take over the advance from the Americans. The Quartermaster Sergeant Major gave most tanks a squirt of diesel.

The ground around us was rolling desert with scrubby bushes. As night came on, rain rolled in and our thermal pictures degraded such that we could just about make out the tank in front. It was only due to our satellite navigation systems that we could maintain any kind of movement.

Major General Rupert Smith
General Officer Commanding, 1st Armoured Division

7 Brigade was out, with my next step-up HQ behind them. The artillery was already out and firing, with 4 Brigade due to move through in order to be attacking their first object just before dark.

Lieutenant Colonel Mike Vickery
Commanding Officer, 14th/20th King's Hussars, 4th Armoured Brigade

By the time we'd went through the breach, the lanes would be seriously churned up, so we could only take tracked vehicles. Our own resupply vehicles were wheeled, so we were given lots of American M113 tracked vehicles, carrying five jerrycans for each tank, enough fuel for a sip: plus tank and machine gun ammunition resupply. Carrying both on the same vehicle is totally illegal… but that's war.

As the timings began to drift, we sat lined up like traffic on the docks at Dover, as the squadron's six-wheeled Stalwart fuel bowsers moved down the lines giving each tank a last top-up. This would have been impossible without air superiority – which greatly simplifies desert warfare.

Lieutenant Toby Masterton
A Squadron The Life Guards, 1 Royal Scots Battle Group, 4th Armoured Brigade

Going through the minefield breach was a disappointment, with none of the expected fireworks, and only a rather pathetic little berm with big signs,

'Courtesy of The Big Red One, you are now entering Eye-rack…' I later saw that the berm the US Marines had breached beside the coast was very much more significant, presumably as that was where the Iraqis were expecting our main thrust.

We were lined up with our battle group's wheeled vehicles, plus the medium-recce Scorpions and Scimitars, their duties taken over by the much faster, better-protected Challengers. Listening to our battle group radio net, I heard ranging fire, then Pip Earle, the troop commander on the right flank. I remember looking across to Trooper Doyle and saying, 'Doylie, we're going to fucking miss all this – being stuck here with all these jokers.'

I wrote out a short declaration on a bluey, that 'I, 524339, Lieutenant Toby Masterton, and Trooper Doyle, being of sound mind and without any coercion, are hereby proceeding to the front line.' We both signed and counter-signed it – it was absolute rubbish, of course.

We then drove out of the line to the front to see the motor transport officer of the Royal Scots. He said, 'What the fuck are you doing? You're out of order.'

So I said, 'Will you please accept this?' giving him the bluey.

'What's all this? You're out of order. Get to fuck.'

I said, 'No I'm serious. We're doing this. You're absolved of responsibility and I'm not accepting your orders. My squadron will need all sorts of things that we can do – there'll be prisoners, wounded… I'm not missing this. Where did they start from?'

He was furious, effing and blinding at me, until eventually he pointed to where the squadron started and said, 'Go off and get yourselves killed.' So we found where the tank tracks started, and drove up them like railway lines, off into the desert.

Lieutenant Colonel Arthur Denaro
Commanding Officer, Queen's Royal Irish Hussars

Off we went, with helicopters above telling us what's in front, rolling into the unknown. And to start with, we met absolutely no resistance. We risked bypassing some positions, and then reached phase line Larch, about thirty kilometres in. We were fastest by miles, so slowed down a bit. I was extremely keen not to take silly risks.

Brigadier Patrick Cordingley
Commander, 7th Armoured Brigade

I stood up on the seat of my tank and looked around. The QRIH were too far away to be seen or heard, now motoring flat out into Iraq. My tac headquarters comprised my tank, an AFV 436, and my artillery Commanding Officer Rory Clayton in his Warrior. The engineers, close air support, supply, etc. were on radio call at my main HQ, which travelled a short distance behind us, to join us whenever we stopped for more than an hour.

Lieutenant Colonel Charles Rogers
Commanding Officer, Staffordshire Regiment

The other two battle groups had managed to replenish with fuel, which we hadn't because my A1 echelon had been routed into a minefield, damaging some of my vehicles. But at 1525 we kicked off, following the 16th/5th Lancers' recce and QRIH, at a hell of a rate.

Unfortunately Warrior and Challenger go very much faster than medium-recce vehicles and have much better optics, so we kept bumping into the recce that afternoon and evening. The tanks, which were entitled to open fire, saw them as hotspots through their TOGS [Thermal Observation Gunnery Sights] at four kilometres, but couldn't differentiate them from enemy.

Brigadier Patrick Cordingley
Commander, 7th Armoured Brigade

At 1628, Arthur Denaro transmitted the first contact report, of an Iraqi trench position about four miles in front of our first objective, Copper. After machine-gun fire, these positions surrendered. With the light fading, I ordered the QRIH to push on towards objective Zinc, but be careful not to engage the 16th/5th Lancers' recce screen. But irritatingly, at precisely seven o'clock, the GPS navigation system went down, so rather than move too fast and maybe attack our own forces in the now darkness, I ordered a fifteen-minute halt for the QRIH and Staffords.

RSM Johnny Muir
Regimental Sergeant Major, Queen's Royal Irish Hussars

That night, as dusk was upon us, after the rest of the regiment had crossed over, I led our wheeled echelon convoys to the start point. I was never too sure how many miles to the gallon my Ferret consumed. It was petrol driven, and I kept two jerrycans strapped to the louvers on the back, which probably wasn't the most sensible place, but I used all that spare fuel in driving backwards and forwards getting our convoys lined up ready to cross. As they went through we sat having a smoke, the aircraft still doing sorties overhead, as American Humvees drove back, escorting prisoners of war.

The Rt Hon Tom King
UK Secretary of State for Defence

Once the troops were launched, we ran early-morning briefings in the Chiefs of Staff's facility. After considerable 'fog of war' initially, as we appeared to be advancing quite easily, we were very worried that Saddam might unleash a 'scorched earth' policy with chemical weapons, or that we'd have some major setback.

Lieutenant General Walter Boomer
General Officer Commanding, 1 Marine Expeditionary Force, United States Marine Corps

On day two, my 1st Marine Division was subject to determined Iraqi counter-attacks from east to west, from behind burning oilfields they'd torched off to cover them. The place was like hell. This was beaten back by 1st Division, and was the last of what I would call the major opposition. Pockets of Iraqis did continue fighting, and each of our units experienced this. Seventy-five per cent of the Iraqis who didn't run, gave up; the rest fought. This was confusing for our troops.

I'm not so naïve as to say there were no atrocities, but to this day I'm not aware of one. So I would say that to their everlasting credit, our troops managed this very well; at great risk to themselves handling the Iraqis that wanted to fight, and taking the surrenders of twenty thousand POWs. Can you imagine that? And I had to provide the bastards with food and water.

Major General Rupert Smith
General Officer Commanding, 1st Armoured Division

My HQ was set up five hundred metres from the US 1st Infantry Division's tac HQ, so we could coordinate the two divisions passing through each other. In daylight now, our vehicles were nose-to-tail in the lanes. I went over to be with the US divisional commander, Major General Tom Rhame, when the Corps Commander Fred Franks flew in, and took me to one side:

'I've been told to get another division into the attack, and the only way I can do this is to use the Big Red One. But with you still moving through the breach, they're stuck here until you're through. How can we do this?'

The three of us stood round the map. I now had to get through as quickly as possible to allow Tom Rhame to get free and running, but also to give them space the other side, I had to get out into the blue even faster, which made defeating the tactical Iraqi units even more imperative than originally.

So I proposed that once my artillery and 4th Brigade were through the breach, I'd give Tom all the lanes – cutting my division off from its wheeled logistic units. I could do this because my fighting units were carrying everything they needed for several days' fighting: three days at standard rates of fighting, plus more of specific types of artillery ammunition.

My artillery group were through already – a very considerable fighting force; an eight-inch regiment, MLRS, three general support regiments, plus an American National Guard artillery brigade of two eight-inch regiments and more MLRS. I did, however, ask to retain the most easterly lane in both directions so I could bring back casualties.

I'd made a very rapid calculation, based on our pre-calculations – plus deciding to myself that we could do it, reckoning I'd get my back end through in twenty-four hours. But the look on my chief of staff's face when I told him, after the five-hundred-metre walk back to my HQ, indicated that he wasn't quite so certain.

I wasn't comfortable until lunchtime the following day, when my logistic umbilical was joined up once more.

RSM Johnny Muir
Regimental Sergeant Major, Queen's Royal Irish Hussars

We'd worn full NBC kit while crossing the minefield, but on the other side, took off the respirators. It was very cold, as the Ferret had no heater, so at that stage the NBC suits were useful rather than uncomfortable. The guys in the tanks had excellent heaters and boiling vessels. My boiling vessel was beside my seat, so sometimes my rear end was rather too warm.

We regrouped at the other side of the breach, and C Squadron went off to the Staffordshire battle group. Every time we stopped, even for a short time, we dug shellscrapes. I remember as I was digging, hearing over the radio that Iraqi tanks were headed towards us. It seemed crazy to be digging in rather than getting out. But we stuck to the routines, while remaining flexible in our thoughts.

Lieutenant General Walter Boomer
General Officer Commanding, 1 Marine Expeditionary Force,
United States Marine Corps

I told General Keys I was pulling up behind his divisional HQ with my 1 MEF [Marine Expeditionary Force] headquarters. It was dark, and I didn't want us to be in any danger. I was talking to him about this on the radio, saying I wanted him to be careful where he located.

He said, 'OK, but I think we've got a bit of problem.'

I said, 'What the hell is that?'

'There are Iraqis all around me.'

'Keys, I told you not to get too far forward.'

But that's how he likes to fight – from the front, so I took a quick look around, and there were indeed a lot of Iraqi soldiers all around us, but I decided most of them were confused, or looking for somebody to surrender to.

I received criticism about this afterwards, for being too close. I didn't really intend to be *that* close ... but I did intend to be in Kuwait. Communications were not that good in those days, and being close meant I could meet with both divisional field commanders, gather round the map and talk through what we were going to do. It's the best way to fight in my opinion. I don't think the critics know what they're talking about.

Lieutenant Colonel Arthur Denaro
Commanding Officer, Queen's Royal Irish Hussars

A very big enemy position [Copper North] was firing at our helicopters. I wasn't keen to let the young squadron leaders push through that without first taking a close look myself. So the Staffords passed by on the top and we continued to push on as darkness fell and the rain came down. It was very, very dark. Again we kicked on.

Brigadier Patrick Cordingley
Commander, 7th Armoured Brigade

At 1930 G+1, in pitch darkness and driving rain, the Scots DG came across an Iraqi radio communications position at Copper, defended by tanks. The weather was so murky that in peacetime helicopters would not have been allowed to fly, but we had a Gazelle flying out in front of the QRIH. The tanks' thermal sights were affected by the cold and wet, producing only a blurred image. Only the satellite navigation system allowed us to move at all. I was quite a long way off, so could only listen to radio reports.

John Sharples asked for artillery, but Rory Clayton advised that a small position like this one wasn't worth unmasking [revealing the positions of] our guns, particularly as we didn't yet know what the Iraqi counter-battery capabilities were like. Our Scorpion recce vehicles had good illumination rounds, which would be easier to control, so they got on with it.

But as they were lining up, one of their three tanks broke down; then the second tank was ordered to move south toward a reported enemy counter-attack. Second Lieutenant Richard Telfer in the remaining tank led the Stafford's Warrior vehicles into the enemy positions, where he sat very exposed for forty-five minutes using his thermal sights to guide the infantry and give covering machine-gun fire.

Major Simon Knapper
Commander, A Company, Staffordshire Regiment

It was black as pitch with only our red tail lights showing. Sudden reports of enemy on our open flank, of isolated groups of men. We were ordered to clear the position. Marrying up one platoon with a tank, we ran in and debussed, but failed to close with the enemy. Frustrated and dissatisfied, the order to re-embuss was given. Almost immediately D Squadron identified what turned out to be an Iraqi divisional headquarters and communication site, defended by an infantry company. The company moved through the darkness to join the tanks.

My radio orders were brief. Then the enemy vehicles were hit by HESH rounds from the tanks, illuminating the objectives with flame. The Challengers ground forward, the Warrior drivers throttling back to avoid getting ahead of their protection. At eight hundred metres, 3 Platoon peeled off right to their objective, tracer from the fire support tanks guiding them on to the Iraqi position. At three hundred metres, the Challengers slowed, the seven lead Warriors surged forward, their chain guns pouring fire to suppress the enemy, at maximum speed across the last stretch of ground.

'Debus, debus' on the intercom, the armoured door swings slowly open, to cold, wet blackness. A scramble to get out, the thunder of the chain gun filling the air, and cracking bursts of 30mm on automatic. A step into the darkness, a second step then round the corner of the vehicle, lines of tracer cut the blackness, head hunched into your shoulders as you sprint to join the vague outlines of your section. Then slow down, safety catch off, a desperate search for targets: a flash, a shape, the enemy?

On the left, 1 Platoon cleared through the area of the mast and burning vehicles, then gave covering fire for 2 Platoon to assault the depth position. On the right, 3 Platoon fought their way into the bunker area. The enemy fire was sporadic and the sections cleared the bunkers with grenades.

An additional enemy position was identified further to the right. 1 Platoon re-embussed and moved to clear it with a Challenger in support. 2 Platoon secured the depth position, taking the company's first prisoners. 1 Platoon discovered a complex of command bunkers, which they cleared using grenades, eventually taking twenty-seven prisoners.

Captain Jack Ferguson
Second-in-Command, A Company, Staffordshire Regiment

I've seen nothing like it before. It's fine when you go to BATUS and see a firepower display, but when you see the tracer coming the other way towards you it's something else again.

Corporal Melvin Downes
C Company, Staffordshire Regiment

I said to my section, 'I'll be the first man out, and I expect you to follow me. If you don't and I make it back, I'll shoot whoever stayed behind.' I meant it as well. But having lived and worked so close together for five and a half months, nobody would have done that.

Private Andrew Kelly
A Company, Staffordshire Regiment

I ran to the front of the vehicle, saw all the enemy positions, shat myself and returned to the rear of the wagon. The section second-in-command shouted, 'Get your fucking arse to the front and give us covering fire.' So I went back round and started firing, then we moved towards the bunkers.

Private Mark Eason
A Company, Staffordshire Regiment

The LSW gunner got out first and I followed him. There wasn't time to think. I started firing and we moved forward. The training made this automatic. I shot at the muzzle flashes I could see, then Corporal Heaven got out of the vehicle in the middle of us. We moved forward one bound, then on the second bound a flare went up. I saw a flash go off in front and I got hit.

I was lying there, the whole of my side gone numb, thinking I'd been shot through the chest. Then after a few seconds I realised a round had hit my jacket, split my combination tool [for rifle cleaning], and the magazine in my pocket, where it stopped. I was badly bruised, but that was all.

Major Simon Knapper
Commander, A Company, Staffordshire Regiment

The casualties were loaded into Warriors and brought back to a central position before being transferred into an ambulance, which headed off into the blackness. How the hell the ambulances ever found where to go then got back to us without satnav, I don't know.

A further position was identified by D Squadron, so 3 Platoon got into their vehicles and moved back to the mast area to marry up with their intimate support tank. While waiting for them, the Challengers and Warriors engaged enemy vehicles and bunkers. A MILAN missile tore through the darkness, a pause, then a vehicle exploded in the distance. The immortal words come over the air, 'I don't know what it was, but we killed it,' later identified as a Gaz box-bodied truck.

Private Andrew Kelly
A Company, Staffordshire Regiment

We took cover while some grenades were thrown, and then Corporal Heaven was hit. He laughed at first, then looked down and saw blood gushing out of his chest. He said, 'I've been hit,' then coughed up some blood. We could see blood start to stream out of his arms and legs as well. He was in bits. They gave him morphine, then the medics took him away.

Major Simon Knapper
Commander, A Company, Staffordshire Regiment

The company regrouped swiftly. A Company cleared two more positions in this area, taking numerous prisoners, before meeting more opposition in a final set of bunkers, which were cleared with grenades and small arms.

Lieutenant Colonel Charles Rogers
Commanding Officer, Staffordshire Regiment

During that night we'd fired a lot of artillery, especially the MLRS. I was worried that people might have got displaced, and that we might be laying down all this fire on them. We never knew where our medium-recce were either, which was a great worry, as they kept appearing where we didn't expect them. They weren't on our radio net, and my greatest fear was that the tanks would see them and open fire.

Lance Corporal Roy Sellstrom
Pioneer Corps, Army War Graves Unit

Everyone in the brigade had gone through the minefield gaps, but this head-quarters officer wouldn't release us to go with them. Armoured column after armoured column went through. When he finally let us go, we were miles behind where we were supposed to be. We eventually reached 4 Brigade, then spent the first day and a half driving mile after fucking mile in this long column, trying to find the Royal Scots battle group, as well as getting to know the two young Royal Corps of Transport lads we'd just been given – across this enormous Iraqi desert.

Lieutenant Colonel Mike Vickery
Commanding Officer, 14th/20th King's Hussars,
4th Armoured Brigade

7 Brigade had moved through the breach first, then in darkness we had to follow an American tank regiment, which was a touch worrying in the dark, as we knew they were trigger-happy. But we got though the minefield and the American holding brigade very quickly, then shook out into formation in open desert and began advancing, north, then very quickly turned east.

But just as we got motoring, we were stopped dead by a line of more than a hundred ammunition and fuel trucks – 7 Brigade's echelon, in the wrong place – the first really major fuck-up of the war. I don't how they got there, or why they crossed the gap before we did.

In an argument between tanks and trucks, we win. So as we could see the trucks through our thermal imaging sights, I ordered the boys to crack on. They couldn't see us, so we used flashing lights, and despite a lot of bad temper and swearing, nobody was shot and we got through.

Lance Corporal Roy Sellstrom
Pioneer Corps, Army War Graves Unit

We reached an Iraqi position. Their vehicles were still smouldering so we can't have been too far behind the Royal Scots. We then reached their first echelon, where in the cookhouse tent their female assistant adjutant demanded to know who we were. I tried saying 'AWGS' quietly, but she insisted knowing what that was – really pushing it. So when I did tell her, the whole fucking place went dead quiet – like the Grim Reaper had arrived. As we were eating, Lieutenant Parry said we had to leave immediately. We piled back in and joined a huge column, moving forward to the Royal Scots first echelon, arriving pretty late.

Second Lieutenant Alistair Watkins
Grenadier Guards, 3 Royal Regiment of Fusiliers Battle Group, 4th Armoured Brigade

We left at 2000 hours for our first objective, Bronze, moving forty-eight kilometres through the night. For a while I commanded ØC, allowing John a rest in the back. We cleared Bronze and took our first prisoners: one hundred and thirty-nine in total including five officers. It was totally bizarre and unreal to see enemy soldiers.

Our guys were massively calm and professional. There was quite a lot of screaming and shouting from the prisoners, who'd been told we'd shoot them. Some looked like young boys. One spoke perfect American English and had been to Sandhurst! He said, 'It's really great to see you guys.' Another prisoner spoke perfect English and was an architect – only a couple of weeks previously he'd been in his office in Baghdad.

They were all starving, but we didn't know how long we'd have to go before resupply, so people were giving them stuff they didn't want; lots of tins of margarine and pilchards being scoffed with evident delight.

Major General Rupert Smith
General Officer Commanding, 1st Armoured Division

The Corps was now working together for the first time. My artillery commander Brigadier Ian Durie had set up a remarkable system, controlling all the air power as well as all the guns. Everything was integrated; the American artillery commander could fire all the British guns and *vice versa*, and as we continued, I became enormously confident in how he'd stitched all the artillery together to fight the deep battle.

The Iraqis only once tried to attack us with their considerable artillery, immediately receiving a complete MLRS regiment. Our guns were set back, driving forward into range to fire. I don't think the Iraqi artillery tried anything serious again.

After I'd cut my division from its logistics, I needed to fly forwards to my HQ on the other side of the breach. The weather closed in, preventing me going by helicopter, so we set off in the rover group, using our GPS. With no hills, the curvature of the earth very quickly stopped VHF radio transmissions using only normal aerials. So we'd arranged to stop every hour, put up the twenty-seven-foot radio mast, contact HQ, find out what was happening, then carry on. My ADC had drawn a straight line across the map because that's how GPS takes you, and we'd made two or three stops. Fortunately he'd told me where we were, and I'd written the grid reference across the top of my map.

It's my habit to monitor the forward radio nets of my brigades, to follow what's going on – a form of liaison. My rule to myself is that I never come up – just listen. 7 Brigade were getting further ahead and fading, so I switched to 4th Brigade, which were on their start lines, ready to go. I then heard their leading battle group calling a target, and quickly realised this was me, my ADC having got us right across the front of 4th Brigade's attack. So I started breaking my rules, hoping to God that the fucker didn't ask for authentication codes, as I had no idea what they might be.

I came up on to their net with the appropriate 'Your divisional commander is joining you callsign x', and luckily the squadron leader recognised my voice. I said, 'I am the target you are calling, y number of vehicles moving from south to north.'

He said, 'Roger,' and I could then hear him getting all his callsigns to acknowledge this. And so we trundled on, with me having bitten virtually through the ADC's leg in the turret above me. And my vehicles weren't up-armoured.

Brigadier Patrick Cordingley
Commander, 7th Armoured Brigade

With our advance continuing, at 2314 hours, an Iraqi counter-attack of T-55 tanks and armoured personnel carriers was spotted advancing in line. John Sharples ordered all fourteen of his tanks to open fire, reporting five destroyed along with six APCs. Sharples requested stopping the assault as he believed an Iraqi hospital was in the depth positions – a logistic area. I ordered in a US psychological operations team to help encourage the rest of the Iraqis to surrender, and halted the Scots DG until first light.

The Staffords and QRIH were now observing Objective Zinc. I hadn't realised that slowing down could affect 4th Brigade's ability to manoeuvre behind us. But as Zinc seemed like a brigade position, it seemed more sensible to wait until first light when I'd have the Scots DGs back. However, division told us they were quite keen for us to do something about position Zinc, so the QRIH got into a position where they could support the Staffords going in from the west.

But the rain and darkness were so bad I couldn't even see Rory Clayton's Warrior's tail lights. It was difficult to know whether to press on with only two battle groups and risk another counter-attack, so I radioed Rupert Smith and told him it might be worth pausing until first light when we could assess it properly. His calm reply, after a short pause was, 'That would be disappointing.'

Major General Rupert Smith
General Officer Commanding, 1st Armoured Division

My two brigades were closing up with each other. 7 Brigade asked me if they could pause. I told them I'd be disappointed if they did that, and wanted them to have reached a certain line by dawn – so that was the end of that discussion.

Brigadier Patrick Cordingley
Commander, 7th Armoured Brigade

I decided I wasn't going to let Rupert Smith down, so called Rory Clayton over to find out what we'd got artillery-wise. He said, 'What do you want? We've got five British regiments, plus an American artillery brigade – with more forepower than Monty had at the battle of El Alamein.'

I sat down and worked out some simple orders, then Rory Clayton brought over a fire plan using ten regiments. At 2330 I gave radio orders, with the artillery scheduled to start at 0100 hours for thirty minutes [G+2]. We then heard that Private Shaun Taylor of the Staffords had died the first death in 7th Brigade, plus Private Kelly and Corporal Heaven had taken serious injuries during the communications site assault.

The attack on Zinc went ahead, and I'll never forget it; we were fairly close and it was extraordinary. Just before 0100, the radio net crackled to say the guns had fired and the shells were in the air. Then on the dot of one, the ground to our front erupted. I just prayed we'd got our grid references correct.

Lieutenant Colonel Mike Vickery
Commanding Officer, 14th/20th King's Hussars,
4th Armoured Brigade

We'd been told at the final orders group there'd be nothing in our way until first light, when we were to do an assault on Copper South. Yes well... in fact at one in the morning, I received our first contact report from B Squadron leader Richard Shirreff.

Commanding from my tank, I could drive right up to the front line – not to get in the way, as at this point Richard was fighting the battle, but because my most important job was knowing when to throw in the reserves.

I arrived to find tanks, and people firing at us with machine guns [from near Bronze]. We passed our own contact report up to brigade headquarters, which said we'd hit the enemy brigade HQ they'd been expecting. I was pretty irritated at them not telling me this earlier.

I brought up A Squadron on the left and we moved forward, stopped, fired, moved on two hundred metres then fired again. With stabilised guns, we could have fired on the move, but there was no screaming hurry, and it's easier to be accurate if you're standing still.

After about three of these stops and volleys, we could see through our thermal sights that the enemy were waving things from the top of the bunds, so the squadron leader ordered everyone to stop firing. However, despite this order, I could see firing continuing from the left, so I asked the squadron leader to explain why. He replied that all his squadron had stopped firing, but another Challenger was still firing.

I radioed the brigade commander and asked if he was the tank still firing at the Iraqis. He said, 'Yes, I'm up with your squadron.' I had my mouth open and was about to… at which point my adjutant, from below in the loader's position, grabbed my knee. I took a very deep breath. 'Roger,' I said, now rather calmly. 'Please join the squadron radio net which you're supposed to be on. And actually they've already given the Check Fire, so will you please also stop firing.'

After taking a good look through the night sights, I ordered the artillery to lob up some star shell, which revealed that the Iraqis were indeed surrendering, so I ordered Grant Baker and The Queen's Company in to take the prisoners, while we moved to mop up the outer edges of the position. Hearing the company sergeant major marching the Iraqis off into the night with a parade ground 'Left, Right, Left, Right!' and urging them on to smarter drill gave a surreal twist to our first regimental engagement since World War Two.

While moving through the Iraqi position, I had the epic excitement of putting a HESH round into a fuel tanker, which was just wonderful and lit the place up for a while – serious hooligan activity, but seemed like a good idea at the time.

Martin Bell
BBC Television

By the end of the first day we'd stopped, which was when the MLRS rocket launchers were deployed. We stood there watching, the earth shook, and one couldn't help feeling sorry for the poor buggers at the other end. It was a known defensive emplacement. I don't know if we knew this at the time, but all their officers had fled, leaving their guys there to get slaughtered. Came the dawn, there was a big round-up. The only Iraqis we ever saw were surrendering ones.

Lieutenant Colonel Mike Vickery
Commanding Officer, 14th/20th King's Hussars,
4th Armoured Brigade

As an armoured regiment you don't have any spare people or vehicles. In a desert, making attacks over eight or so kilometres, the next objective will be fifteen kilometres further on. There's no water or shelter of any sort, and it's bloody difficult trying to cope with prisoners.

Geneva Convention rules require prisoners to be held outside the ranges of direct and indirect fire weaponry – which means at least twenty miles behind the fighting. But how the hell do you get them there? Up on the front line, we hadn't made plans for such huge numbers. We hadn't realised it would be like this.

Later that day I came across a couple of undamaged Iraqi tank transporters, which my soldiers got running. You could get two hundred and fifty prisoners on each, so I radioed brigade to come and pick them up. Now after every attack, we found we were losing a large part of the battle group just looking after them.

One of an RSM's jobs is looking after prisoners, so I discussed this with him. He reckoned the Iraqis to be delighted to have survived and surrendered. So I decided to take a risk, and leave the RSM, a couple of cooks and three trucks full of rations, with orders to feed them. As we drove off, the RSM had hundreds of them lined up, waiting for a breakfast of tinned pork sausages, which was all we had.

RSM Johnny Muir
Regimental Sergeant Major, Queen's Royal Irish Hussars

You don't worry too much about the ones screaming with pain, as they're not in imminent danger of dying. It's the ones who've gone quiet you have to look at first. As I was moving forward towards a group of about fourteen surrendering Iraqi soldiers, my driver became very unsettled by all the dead bodies lying around the position. He said, 'Please sir, don't make me touch a dead body,' and explained that it was the first time he'd seen one since his father died.

I replied, 'Don't worry. I'll do all that.'

I went through the position and tried to stir the ones that weren't showing any movement, to make sure they were dead. Some were starting to decay, a stench that will stay with me as long as I live. There were eleven injured so I asked RHQ to send two ambulances. We searched the injured to make sure they couldn't give us any harm, but when we picked one up who couldn't help himself, his body literally fell apart in our hands. I thought they'd been ripped up by machine-gun fire, although it could have been artillery airburst.

It looked like these poor sods had either been put into an open position they couldn't get out of without armoured cover; or if there had been tanks, they'd deserted them. Many of these positions were surrounded by mines, so the Iraqis in the trenches couldn't actually get out. An anti-personnel mine exploded under one of the ambulances, and an eighteen-year-old ambulance soldier showed great courage and common sense, which I later reported to his squadron commander.

Sergeant Shaun Rusling
Medic, Parachute Regiment, 32 Field Hospital

When the first ground war battle casualties came in, we were also dealing with RTAs and other casualties anyway, so as they arrived we brought everyone on duty. Soon after that, helicopters delivered all the classic war injuries we'd been trained to deal with: shrapnel injuries, head wounds, bilateral traumatic amputation to arms and legs – really horrendous things. Fortunately, initially there weren't so many British.

First in, before we got any fighting casualties, were a tremendous number of Iraqis, then some Egyptians who'd driven through a minefield, then a group of Syrians who'd copped it quite badly.

Brigadier Patrick Cordingley
Commander, 7th Armoured Brigade

The rockets streaked across the darkness, bursting apart over Zinc with a bright flash, showering hundreds of lethal bomblets, the ground boiling with fire as they exploded.

After twenty-six minutes, Rory Clayton came on the air saying, 'Rounds complete, end of mission.' And then we went in.

Lieutenant Colonel Arthur Denaro
Commanding Officer, Queen's Royal Irish Hussars

After the firepower demonstration, we pushed on four kilometres through the objective [Zinc], forcing our way through various exploding bomblets and pit holes but seeing no enemy. Major David Swan's tank had its external fuel drums punctured by the explosion of an MLRS bomblet. Further back, some enemy surrendered using white flags, then more walked towards us.

It was then that the Brigadier's nerve gave up, and he decided to call a halt after a couple of kilometres. I'm glad it did, because quite frankly we were sitting in a hell of a position, outnumbered, in the midst of an Iraqi brigade, in the pitch dark; and with no infantry, we were very vulnerable.

G+2 – TUESDAY 26 FEBRUARY

Lieutenant Colonel Arthur Denaro
Commanding Officer, Queen's Royal Irish Hussars

I got twenty minutes' sleep, until 0330 when D Squadron, in the centre, reported fourteen vehicles coming down towards us.

By the time I was fully awake there were more hotspots – thirty, thirty-five, forty of them … an Iraqi counter-attack.

Brigadier Patrick Cordingley
Commander, 7th Armoured Brigade

Phase line Lavender was only three miles east of us, and as we had until dawn to get there, I felt we should slow down. We'd been counter-attacked once and fought it off, and I was expecting another. If by first light we were close enough to Lavender to cover it even though not physically occupying it, I reckoned that would comply with our mission.

I ordered the battle groups to slow down, consolidate and await the dawn. The division's main effort then switched to 4 Brigade, giving us a chance to replenish and rearm.

At 0330 Arthur Denaro reported multiple contacts across his front. His D Squadron had come up the back of a slope, and just over the rim picked up some fourteen thermal contacts. They opened fire immediately at almost maximum range, at what was almost certainly a counter-attack. For ninety minutes squadron leader Major Toby Madison took on more Iraqi tanks as they appeared behind the initial contacts. But without night vision the Iraqis were at a terrible disadvantage, out of range and only able to fire back at muzzle flashes.

Major General Rupert Smith
General Officer Commanding, 1st Armoured Division

Our phase lines [e.g. Larch, Lupin, Lavender] were designed to tell us how far we could fight before having to stop and replenish, and were placed in between the metal-named groupings of enemy.

If enemy formation Lead had driven towards the corps attack, we knew we'd have to destroy it. But because they didn't move, we attacked them like a row of stepping stones; but this wasn't how we'd conceived the battle being fought.

We weren't allowed to cross a specific line (of exploitation) until the Corps had reached a certain point and the Egyptians had come up – to avoid getting in their way. But I wanted to get in as deep and as quickly as I could. My recce and the deep attack were one hundred kilometres in by dawn, having made a really excellent, quick move. We were still dealing with enemy close to the breach, plus picking up enemy coming towards us from much further out.

A group of enemy was detected moving near this line of exploitation – exactly what I was looking for. With just my recce out there, as planned, I'd attack them with the artillery and aviation, so my next big decision was to move the guns forward within range of this moving enemy, which would mean being in front of everyone else – and also out of range of being able to support 4th Armoured Brigade. Also, my whole division was now so extended in depth that we'd also lost contact with our logistic tail.

I was breaking my own rules.

Sergeant Shaun Rusling
Medic, Parachute Regiment, 32 Field Hospital

When casualties were flown in, we divided them up into categories P1, P2 and P3. If we got a lot at one time, we'd put the much more serious P3s to one side and concentrate on the ones we could get sorted and back to the battle. But if we weren't so busy, we could treat everyone without having to triage them like that.

Every serious casualty had three medics: one at the head with a footpump sucking out the airway, one at the middle giving medication, and the other at the feet making observations. Everything was manual; pressing with fingers in the groin to estimate blood pressure, with none of even the most basic electronic equipment we were used to from our civvy hospitals back at home.

To start with, we received Iraqi casualties who were in a terrible state of deterioration: infested, smelly with diarrhoea and serious bowel problems, emaciated with their eyeballs sticking out. Some were in sandals with bad feet; doshed out in all sorts of bits of make-do kit, aged from fifteen to sixty-five.

But after being cleaned up, reclothed and given suitable medication, hydration and food, and a couple of days on the wards, these guys perked up very quickly. Then we got wounded Republican Guards, with brand-new, modern Russian webbing, good clothing and weapons. They were on the ball, very well equipped and, apart from their wounds, in very good condition.

Lieutenant Toby Masterton
A Squadron, The Life Guards, 1 Royal Scots Battle Group, 4th Armoured Brigade

We pitched up at the first objective. There were various knocked-out Iraqi tanks and dead soldiers, the squadron sooty-faced and blackened from cordite fumes inside the tank – most lying asleep on the engine decks.

As we drove up, several of them shouted 'Fucking hell, boss. What are you doing up here?' As I got out of the Land Rover, some AK rounds rang out, as an Iraqi section that had been missed, brassed us up. Some people returned fire, then James Hewitt appeared. I said I was sure there were things we could do, and he said, 'OK, crack on, but we have to go.' I knew I was in for some future bollockings, but nobody said anything at that stage.

Major General Rupert Smith
General Officer Commanding, 1st Armoured Division

According to the prisoners we interrogated later, the Iraqi 'attack' turned out to be their response to our crossing the breach. They'd been marching down to reinforce the area, and then to make a counter-attack to catch us in the breach – to fight a battle that was already over, with us a hundred kilometres further on than their commanders assumed.

Lieutenant Toby Masterton
A Squadron, The Life Guards, 1 Royal Scots Battle Group, 4th Armoured Brigade

James Hewitt was bypassing lesser Iraqi positions and really cracking on, so we were frequently left behind. We investigated some enemy positions, in one discovering a kettle of water still boiling, a lit cigarette still smouldering, but nobody there. This was very spooky, so we got out rapidly. Another was clearly a major headquarters, with a marble entrance and solid stone steps down into a shelter, a smart main ops room, and a large bedroom.

The squadron worked through its twelve objectives, some putting up stiff resistance, others none at all. The tanks were shooting at approaching double the ranges of the Iraqi tanks, in pitch darkness, very accurately. One of our tanks even tried a speculative shot at maximum elevation, hitting the target at around five kilometres.

We were taking huge numbers of prisoners, and were soon overwhelmed. An Iraqi T-55 tank had been hit, killing all the crew except its driver, who was trapped inside as it burned. The turret had been knocked out of its ring and over the top of his escape hatch.

We ran forward to see if we could rescue him, but it was too hot to get anywhere near. His hand kept waving out of the hatch, screaming as he burned to death, an absolutely gruesome death, the first I'd witnessed at close hand. A Channel 4 photographer arrived and took lots of photos.

One of our Challengers drove over two guys. I don't know if this had been on purpose or not. One of the Iraqi's face had been shot off by the turret machine gun, both totally flattened into the sand – very strange; completely flat human beings, which is totally shocking and disorientating, like a lilo that you'd think could be re-inflated, with entrails exploded to both sides. An unreal experience.

Sergeant Shaun Rusling
Medic, Parachute Regiment, 32 Field Hospital

Because our field hospital's casualty handling procedures weren't being properly carried out, we were taking the clothing off casualties inside the hospital – sometimes actually in the operating theatre. You could see dust floating around in the air, which we were breathing in.

As we later discovered, especially with Iraqi tank and armoured infantry casualties, some of this dust was the highly radioactive particles of depleted uranium rounds that had hit their vehicles. Because the casualties weren't being treated as dirty, we were getting a face full of crap every time. It had nowhere to go inside the tent, so the toxins were effectively being concentrated in this one place.

Brigadier Patrick Cordingley
Commander, 7th Armoured Brigade

4 Brigade's commander Christopher Hammerbeck gave me an urgent call saying he'd been unable to stop a company of T-55 tanks from breaking clear, which were now heading north into our area, straight for our own small headquarters position. I sent Richard Kemp to drive my tank towards them, to be our only defence. At the same time, Rory Clayton gave the same orders to his Warrior crew, leaving us alone without the fighting vehicles.

Every man in the headquarters was now manning a trench, armed with whatever anti-tank weapon he could find. The drivers were in their vehicle cabs, ready to drive off at a moment's notice. In the back of my own command vehicle, Mark Shelford was kneeling with a torch in his mouth trying to read the instructions on a 66mm anti-tank rocket launcher, which he hadn't fired since leaving Sandhurst.

I remained in the back of my command vehicle, monitoring sporadic contacts from both the QRIH at Zinc, and the Scots DG back at the supply point. The filthy weather continued as it got light, but the T-55 tank attack never materialised. Either 4 Brigade had been wrong, or the enemy took a different route.

To our front it looked as though Lavender was clear.

Captain Tim Purbrick
Commanding 4 Troop, D Squadron, Queen's Royal Irish Hussars
We'd knocked out ten or so enemy vehicles using a mixture of fin [armour piercing] anti-tank rounds and HESH explosive rounds. As dawn came half an hour later, we saw T-55 tanks, hull down, pointing towards us. Our initial engagement began with HESH, which we'd loaded ready for the night battle. After firing off the HESH, we loaded fin.

Our first round went into the berm behind which an Iraqi tank was hiding. Our second round entered its glacis plate and exited through the gearbox at the rear, igniting its ammunition and destroying the tank at a range of three thousand six hundred metres. We then hit an unidentified vehicle at four thousand seven hundred metres, causing the vehicle to explode in a massive fireball, which burned for the next hour.

Lieutenant Colonel Arthur Denaro
Commanding Officer, Queen's Royal Irish Hussars
In these new and various contacts, five T-55 tanks were killed, then other vehicles were detected moving south towards us, and also engaged. By about seven o'clock in the morning, we had destroyed several tanks, taken lots of prisoners and all of us were intact.

Captain Tony Hood
5th Royal Inniskilling Dragoon Guards, attached to B Squadron, Queen's Royal Irish Hussars
The weather was utterly filthy with heavy rain driven on a high wind. Some Iraqi soldiers were warmly clothed in three or four layers of clothing, others

were thinly clothed, and some had no shoes. The casualties were soaked through with rainwater or blood. We found eight Iraqi dead, and fourteen injured, three dying later from severe injuries caused by bomblets from MLRS, their bodies peppered with shrapnel wounds. One of those three had an eye hanging from its socket, and a hole the size of a golfball in the back of his head.

The uninjured element of this group made no attempt to administer first aid to their fellows. This may have been in keeping with the Iraqi policy of treating their wounded after, but not during battles. Consequently some soldiers had simply bled to death, to which they seemed resigned.

Lieutenant Colonel Mike Vickery
Commanding Officer, 14th/20th King's Hussars,
4th Armoured Brigade

Six kilometres away from our expected big battle group objective [Copper South], I realised that B Squadron had fired twenty-five per cent of its ammunition, whereas D Squadron, in reserve, hadn't shot any, so I changed them round, something I'd never even considered during any exercise in Germany. With thirty tanks at night, it's very difficult to do. But at our standard of training and in the desert using GPS, it was terribly easy. I told them of the change; immediately B Squadron commander announced that on moving, he'd drive half right for one kilometre so D Squadron could take his place.

Immediately the timings went adrift. The Royal Scots were to go in first, but they'd also been held up by having to attack somebody else, on an objective several kilometres across. They'd assaulted, destroying Iraqi weapons, to be told by the Life Guards using their night sights of further objectives eight hundred and nine hundred metres away. The tanks fired HESH rounds to indicate exactly where in the darkness, and while their Warriors were driven in for them to remount, they'd walk towards the flashes – all of which took a very long time.

But there was no real reason for me to attack at my ordered H-Hour, when we'd only be given half the artillery. Our enemy was static, we weren't going to surprise them, and they didn't seem likely to attack us, so it was better to wait. Our divisional artillery commander Brigadier Ian Durie had persuaded everybody to use as much artillery as they were given – the big lesson of the Falklands War. So I put my attack off for an hour, and then for a further hour until 1000 hours, when I knew I'd get maximum artillery. We were parked in pretty thick fog, but thanks to GPS knew exactly where we all were.

RSM Johnny Muir
Regimental Sergeant Major, Queen's Royal Irish Hussars

On our way back to the front line, another file of prisoners walked towards us, flying white hankies on pieces of stick. Their leader spoke excellent English with an upper-crust accent – a doctor, the major commanding an Iraqi medical unit. They had no weapons but we searched them, gave them water and oatmeal biscuits, then drove the two kilometres back to A1 echelon with them sitting on the back of the Ferrets. They had no weapons and were wearing flip-flops, and some only T-shirts. The doctor told me he thought we were going to shoot them. I assured him we were not barbarians.

This intelligent medical gentleman had been abandoned by their supposedly elite Republican Guard. One of his soldiers was only fifteen – the same age as my daughter, the others much older than anyone in our army. I felt utmost sympathy for them, and how lucky we were that our officers would always stay with us, regardless what happened.

CHAPTER 8

CRACKING ON

At the end of the morning of G+2 the 101st Airborne, deep inside southern Iraq, had cut Highway 8, the Basra to Baghdad road, then seized the airfield at Nasiriyah. The Egyptians and Syrians to the east had breached the minefield and taken their first objective while the US Marines, despite being delayed by large numbers of prisoners and fog along the coast, were advancing towards Kuwait City. Seven Iraqi divisions had been destroyed, with more than twenty-five thousand prisoners taken.

1 (BR) Division had then motored through the minefield breach, led by 7th Armoured Brigade, its artillery, then 4th Armoured Brigade. Both brigades had attacked enemy brigade locations already identified and labelled by General Smith using the names of metals: Bronze, Copper, Brass, Zinc and Steel.

Smith's two brigades had been used in turn as planned, the one not attacking being resupplied with fuel and ammunition. The division's artillery had been conducting its own deep attacks, using the recce screen and strike helicopters. Massive use of artillery was ensuring that the two brigades' advancing tanks and armoured infantry received only sporadic and indeterminate fire, with determined Iraqi resistance in only a few instances.

However, the enormous speed of the division's advance had led to General Smith taking calculated risks with bringing his artillery forward in front of his tank formations to attack the vital Iraqi depth positions, leaving behind his logistics tail which, being wheeled, travelled slower than the armour, in vulnerable soft-skinned vehicles. Huge numbers of prisoners were an unexpected and were serious logistic problem.

The Iraqi high command appeared still to be unaware of 7th Corps' huge armoured left hook attack to the north and west of Kuwait, thanks to the continuing 1st (US) Cavalry feint attacks in the south along the Wadi al Batin.

1 (BR) Division, protecting the 7th Corps' flank, was now poised on report line Lavender. Their recce screen – the 16th/5th Lancers with a squadron of Queen's Dragoon Guards tanks, were attacking Lead with MLRS fire and air strikes. The division dominated its area, and were now poised to attack the major Iraqi position Platinum, followed by lesser positions Tungsten and Lead, before crossing the border from Iraq into Kuwait, and attacking objective Varsity.

On the afternoon of G+2, CENTCOM intelligence reports indicated the enemy to be withdrawing rapidly northwards, and that to prevent them escaping, pursuit would have to be very swift. At this point, in 1 (BR) Division's battle, objective Tungsten still had to be taken by the 4th Brigade (which they were to achieve at 0600 on G+3), while General Smith ordered his division to make best speed eastwards into Kuwait, towards objective Varsity.

Brigadier Patrick Cordingley
Commander, 7th Armoured Brigade

At 0600 hours I reported to division that we were firm on report line Lavender, ready to move in ninety minutes. Immediately, General Smith delivered his next set of orders, which was to move the division's medium artillery regiment forward so they could support us, and then for us to take over the lead from 4th Brigade. We were to destroy the main force of the Iraqi 12th Armoured Division in Platinum, followed by Lead, and then to deploy forward to phase line Smash.

Platinum was over twelve miles deep and ten miles wide, with little intelligence as to what it contained. Euan Loudon and I decided to split it up. The main eastern section we labelled Platinum 2, contained a brigade, with Platinum 1 the less well-defended western half.

Being only a brigade attacking a division, Euan made the point that the required text-book superiority ratio of three to one was now irrelevant. But nevertheless, we still needed to attack each Iraqi position one at a time, in three phases to apply maximum force to each: the QRIH into Platinum 1, stopping at the boundary of Platinum Two; then firing in support of the second phase; as the Staffords swept through Platinum Two, with the Scots DG going through the middle to attack Lead.

But first I needed to move a company of infantry from the Staffords to the QRIH, to take out the expected trench positions.

I was told that while we were attacking Platinum, our next objective, Lead, would be attacked by the 16th/5th Lancers, artillery and American A-10 aircraft.

RSM Johnny Muir
Regimental Sergeant Major, Queen's Royal Irish Hussars

We got the Iraqi doctor and prisoners back, where I explained that they were medics prepared to help the injured people we'd already got; that they were hungry and needed food, had been thoroughly searched, had behaved impeccably, and were no threat.

We hadn't eaten, so I got a tin of warm beans out of my boiling vessel, some very stale bread and made us a sandwich. But as we were about to head off, I heard shouting: obscenities hurled at these prisoners. I've since thought very deeply about this incident. I'd very carefully briefed this officer about this group of prisoners and their English-speaking major – and I was the regimental sergeant major, which should count for something. I went back and remonstrated with him, advising him that if he didn't treat the prisoners correctly, I would report it. We then had to leave for the front line, but I did take a degree of relief from knowing that the prisoners would not remain long with echelon. Later, I reported this incident to the Commanding Officer.

Sergeant Shaun Rusling
Medic, Parachute Regiment, 32 Field Hospital

Even though we had very many enemy casualties, there were no armed guards on the hospital wards. I did see an RAMC captain lose the plot with an old Arab prisoner who was sitting cross-legged in Evacuation wearing a dirty dishdash, hardly any teeth, his face covered in stubble. I think they'd found a grenade on him – but he hadn't pulled the pin or anything; just a confused old man, conscripted in by the Iraqis. And in any case, they should have searched him properly right at the very start.

The RAMC captain, bright red in the face, was shaking the old man in a way that made me think something was wrong with the captain, behaving in a bizarre manner for an officer.

Brigadier Patrick Cordingley
Commander, 7th Armoured Brigade

While we refuelled I had a wash and shave, and Richard made some cheese and jam sandwiches. They tasted of diesel and sand but were very welcome, the first food we'd had since the war started some twenty-two hours previously.

Then Arthur Denaro's B Squadron reported a new enemy position at the far end of Objective Zinc, beyond an area devastated by the artillery barrage. Large numbers of appallingly injured people were surrounded by unexploded MLRS bomblets. Further on was a much larger position with numerous vehicles, some apparently intact. The enemy were neither fighting nor surrendering, so B Squadron took no chances and destroyed the tanks.

Lieutenant Colonel Charles Rogers
Commanding Officer, Staffordshire Regiment

Iraqi tanks appeared near to my tactical headquarters. My MILANs took out fifteen of them, including one at two hundred and fifty yards, which was rather good as its guidance system doesn't really kick in at such close range.

With everybody moving around in open desert, Iraqi tanks would suddenly appear, and so we had to make sure we were always balanced enough to take them on. My tanks were always out front. They could fire on the move, and also being higher up, could see better, whereas my Warriors had to stop to fire. Whenever we came across Iraqi positions, the tanks would sweep down firing, then the infantry would drive in, get out to secure the area and sort out the prisoners, with the tanks around the edges keeping them safe. Engineers followed along behind to blow out the barrels of unmanned Iraqi tanks and artillery.

Brigadier Patrick Cordingley
Commander, 7th Armoured Brigade

The Staffords attacked with C Squadron of the QRIH leading, from the north in a sandstorm. The enemy were facing the wrong direction and were taken by surprise, the tanks leading the Warriors through the heart of the position. The infantry stopped on the far side, debussed and began to clear the trenches. By 1100 hours the position was clear, the Iraqi wounded evacuated and their weaponry destroyed.

Lieutenant Colonel Arthur Denaro
Commanding Officer, Queen's Royal Irish Hussars

Platinum One looked like a brigade position, with two battalions plus tanks. C Company of the Staffords with my B Squadron made a preliminary attack to clear my FUP, which was overlooked by Iraqi infantry positions defended by T-55 tanks. The sand started to blow almost horizontally. I've never seen a storm like it. You couldn't even put your head out of the turret without your helmet literally being blown off.

Brigadier Patrick Cordingley
Commander, 7th Armoured Brigade

The large number of prisoners was once again a problem. To get his ambulance as near as possible to the wounded, Captain Tony Hood, of the 5th Royal Inniskilling Dragoon Guards, attached to the QRIH, cleared a path through hundreds of live unexploded MLRS bomblets using a shovel.

The attack on Platinum One was still scheduled to run from midday. I asked my three commanding officers for an assessment of the Iraqis' morale. After the battle the Scots DG had fought, John Sharples believed the Iraqis would still fight, but the Staffords felt they'd broken. I insisted they take no chances, treating all enemy tanks as hostile to be destroyed on sight, and attacking artillery and anti-aircraft guns. I could see problems if half of an Iraqi position wanted to surrender when the other half didn't, so I urged them to tell their soldiers to be careful.

We then launched the attack into Platinum One with more heavy winds and another sandstorm. The artillery fired, but we held back with the MLRS. The only threat came from a battery of artillery defended by a platoon of three T-55 tanks.

Lieutenant Colonel Arthur Denaro
Commanding Officer, Queen's Royal Irish Hussars

I preceded our attack with twenty minutes' artillery fire then an A-10 air strike. HELARM sat on the ground in the FUP with us, then flew forward and to the flanks to determine the enemy position's depth. We moved fast in very bad visibility with only a few contacts; mainly on to B Squadron from its right, which we took out using HELARM, who were also dealing with the depth targets. The whole area had been well splattered by artillery,

262

so resistance was light. When we reached report line Tory, I stopped A and B Squadron.

But as D Squadron moved, they were engaged by two T-55 Iraqi tanks from their right. I thought they'd lost a tank, but they came back up on the radio to say both enemy tanks had been destroyed.

Lieutenant Tim Buxton
17th/21st Lancers, attached to B Squadron, Queen's Royal Irish Hussars

We advanced towards Objective Platinum One with our own Lynx helicopters firing missiles over our heads combined with artillery. The sky was clear, but a vicious wind was whipping sand up to the level of the gunners' sight, making the visibility poor.

We stopped two and a half kilometres short of the objective and engaged the enemy. 4 Troop destroyed four Iraqi tanks, then pushed six hundred metres further forward, in front of the squadron, to look for depth positions.

Brigadier Patrick Cordingley
Commander, 7th Armoured Brigade

At 1230 Arthur Denaro reported Platinum One secure; also that as the local Iraqi commander had ordered his men to surrender, we wouldn't need artillery on Platinum Two. I decided to carry on as planned; it could be a ruse, although I doubted it.

Lieutenant Colonel Charles Rogers
Commanding Officer, Staffordshire Regiment

We'd captured quite a lot of people, with many badly injured, and so brought our medical teams right into where the action took place, a new idea, which worked well.

We then did a battle group attack through Platinum Two. Because we were coming in from the Iraqi right flank, we weren't attacking their front line with all its barbed wire and mines. Much further to our right, the US Marines were having to do that. Instead, we were hitting the Iraqi tactical reserve, which was facing the wrong way so wasn't dug in to defend against what we were doing.

But then the fog came down and the GPS froze, which thankfully some-body spotted. So we sat there until it came back on.

Brigadier Patrick Cordingley
Commander, 7th Armoured Brigade

The second attack [on Platinum Two] started at exactly 1245, and it wasn't long before we realised there was no fight left in the enemy. I received reports of hundreds of Iraqis wandering around the centre of positions, not fighting, smoking fags. When we fired at tanks behind them they scattered, but a few minutes later drifted back again. I told everyone to minimise enemy casual-ties, but that their armour remained a threat and so must be engaged.

I ordered the Scots DG to move through the Staffords toward Objective Lead.

Lieutenant Colonel Arthur Denaro
Commanding Officer, Queen's Royal Irish Hussars

We'd started at 1200 hours, and the whole attack was wrapped up by around 1430 hours. We'd been on the go for forty-eight hours without any rest. We settled down, put up the tents and bivvies, with orders for no move before 0300 next morning.

Lieutenant Tim Buxton
17th/21st Lancers, attached to B Squadron,
Queen's Royal Irish Hussars

We reached Platinum Two with little resistance, so continued on north, halting just south of line Smash, where we resupplied with fuel and ammo, and took a few hours' sleep. The drivers got out of their cabs for the first time in two days.

Captain Tony Hood
5th Royal Inniskilling Dragoon Guards, attached to B Squadron,
Queen's Royal Irish Hussars

Twenty-two enemy surrendered to B Squadron during the attack on Plat-inum Two, coming forward carrying a large white flag – a parachute from a British artillery para illuminating round. Four Iraqis could speak English. All declared strongly against Saddam Hussein, delighted to have become POWs.

Four had no shoes. They had plenty of cigarettes but no lighters, delighted with matches from our compo rations – and boiled sweets.

We sent them walking down the axis towards the POW cage, but they returned and gave themselves up again, so we loaded them onto and into our Warrior and drove them to the cage. They said they were thirsty; we gave them water, then they ran off happily to see the other prisoners. An Iraqi doctor said he'd not washed or changed his clothes for forty days, and the shortage of water was so severe soldiers were drinking IV [intravenous] drips.

Lieutenant Toby Masterton
A Squadron, The Life Guards, 1 Royal Scots Battle Group, 4th Armoured Brigade

We again caught up with the squadron. It seemed that some of the conscripted Iraqi soldiers were firing as British units bypassed them – not as attacks, but to say 'Please don't leave us here', apparently not understanding how we'd react.

I talked with one tank commander, a senior NCO, who was very upset. In bad weather, he'd interpreted a speckled TOGS image as a camouflage screen shielding a tank, and had fired at it using the ranging machine gun. But when the troop moved forward, they discovered a group of Iraqi soldiers who'd left their weapons behind in their prepared position, who'd been waving a white large flag. This tank commander now felt he'd murdered half a dozen Iraqis, which as an honourable professional soldier, he was taking very badly.

Lieutenant Colonel Mike Vickery
Commanding Officer, 14th/20th King's Hussars, 4th Armoured Brigade

We had over two thousand prisoners – an enormous logistic problem. The moment any one crew member gets out of a tank, it can't work any more. This means you can't get out to search prisoners. And at night in the desert, it was pitch black, and once the enemy start surrendering, we needed to be able to see – starting with the instantaneous magnesium flares fired by my recce troop, then by popping up mortar rounds, but finally the artillery providing continuous light by firing two huge parachute flares at a time from their much larger star shell rounds.

When we had to move off again, I had far more prisoners than I could deal with, but this time I really needed to take my infantry with me. But I left half of my Grenadier Guards' Queen's Company with a sergeant major and officer to get the prisoners back the five or six kilometres to the brigade prisoner handling unit. We were due to do an attack at dawn, and I thought the Grenadiers would be back with us by then. We wrecked as much of the Iraqi positions as we could above ground, driving over trenches and bunker entrances, and blowing things up.

Sergeant Shaun Rusling
Medic, Parachute Regiment, 32 Field Hospital

The youngest casualty I treated was an Iraqi lad of about fifteen – a very, very frightened young man. This poor fellow had pulled the pin of a grenade but hadn't thrown it. He had shrapnel wounds all over his body, and his hand was completely shattered.

Brigadier Patrick Cordingley
Commander, 7th Armoured Brigade

At nine minutes past two, a very irate Charles Rogers came up on the command net shouting at John Sharples that one of his Scots DG tanks had fired a machine gun and then a HESH round at the Stafford's alternate headquarters. The Staffords had a wounded officer with two broken legs.

Charles was quite certain that this was one of our tanks, so I spoke to John Sharples, who had no idea how this could have happened. I told him to get on with the job, and that I would take over sorting it out.

Lieutenant Colonel Charles Rogers
Commanding Officer, Staffordshire Regiment

My alternative HQ was marshalling prisoners when one of the Warriors was hit. We never really discovered how this happened, but my young officer's leg was very seriously mangled.

Thank God for Chobham armour. They'd fired a HESH round at the Warrior, but the Chobham armour absorbed all the impact. The officer had been outside the vehicle, taking some of the splinters from the impact.

Brigadier Patrick Cordingley
Commander, 7th Armoured Brigade

I called Euan Loudon, who ordered a helicopter to remove the wounded. I felt very sorry for the commander of the Scots DG tank. There was a sandstorm blowing and he thought he was deep in enemy territory. He saw what he thought was an enemy vehicle so he shot it. I never wanted to know his name.

Lieutenant Colonel Charles Rogers
Commanding Officer, Staffordshire Regiment

My officer was evacuated by Canadian medics, back to their field hospital. With these sorts of wound, you're supposed to open it all up, clean it, then leave it open for a couple of days. Unfortunately, the Canadians sewed it up, leaving inside the remains of some phosphorus [from a machine gun tracer round]. My officer was extremely unwell for some time, and I was only able to find him much later, when it was all over. He was very bitter about this. As you might understand, there was also quite a bit of acrimony between the Scots Dragoon Guards and us.

Brigadier Patrick Cordingley
Commander, 7th Armoured Brigade

Manoeuvre warfare is a very risky business. To move one battle group across the back of the other, as I did with the Scots DG, is a calculated risk, and the modern battlefield does not have neat front lines. Soldiers must be ready to find the enemy almost anywhere, so I might have expected the Scots DG to fire on the Staffords if they came across them. There is only one person who should be blamed for this, the man who gave the orders for the manoeuvre. Me.

Sergeant Shaun Rusling
Medic, Parachute Regiment, 32 Field Hospital

Our hospital's interpreters were mostly Kuwait university boys, who showed a great disdain for the wounded Iraqis, blaming them for having invaded their land. I think if your country had been raped and pillaged, you'd probably have a similar opinion. But they stayed with the Iraqis and talked to them, having to tell some of the more frightened ones that the heathen white man wasn't going to eat them and so on.

Lieutenant General Walter Boomer
General Officer Commanding, 1 Marine Expeditionary Force, United States Marine Corps

Kuwait was now ready to be liberated, so we stayed out of it and let the Arab forces move in. We were prepared to move in if the Iraqis decided to fight. But we didn't have to do that. I'm happy the Iraqis decided not to fight in the city.

The air force was getting very good pictures showing streams of Iraqis fleeing in significant numbers from the front of the divisions and from Kuwait. Meanwhile, my army [armoured] brigade had come up right behind Keys's [2nd Division], then moved round and was now protecting my left flank.

Lieutenant Colonel Mike Vickery
Commanding Officer, 14th/20th King's Hussars, 4th Armoured Brigade

While the Fusiliers did an assault, we filled up with fuel, fed the boys and got some sleep. I was busy planning the next move, going round seeing everyone, keeping my finger on the pulse.

In combat, the stopping, starting and accelerating used up over one hundred gallons of fuel per tank each day. Our six-wheeled Stalwart fuel bowsers were constantly driving the twenty kilometres to and from the brigade fuel dump. In each engagement, we fired fifteen to twenty of our forty rounds of main gun ammunition, plus machine-gun ammunition, which was resupplied in packs, then broken down and loaded into the turrets, which takes a long time, and has to be done absolutely correctly otherwise the crew can't fight; poorly stowed shells and propellant endanger the tank.

We were now in the swing of it; very superior in terms of firepower and at night we completely had them, as they couldn't see further than four hundred metres using their 1960s infrared technology. They weren't turning on any white-light searchlights as they knew bloody well they'd get a round down their noses if they did; it was just the same to us if they turned on their infrared search lights, so they didn't much use that either.

But people were getting tired; a gunner caught his foot in the traverse of a tank, breaking his ankle. My Land Rover driver Corporal Cavens announced, 'This is where I leave you, Colonel. We need to take this man back, then I'll take over in his tank as gunner.' There was no asking, and the squadron leader had a new gunner almost before he knew he'd lost one. People were seeing what was needed and just getting on with it.

Brigadier Patrick Cordingley
Commander, 7th Armoured Brigade

Our 16th/5th Lancer medium-recce broke up an Iraqi counter-attack, using MILAN anti-tank missiles. But the Scimitar's light armour gives only questionable protection against a machine gun, let alone a 100mm tank gun, so they'd been forced to withdraw, suffering two fatalities when a T-55 tank sprayed their REME 548 tracked carrier with machine-gun fire.

Before nightfall, at around 5pm, I wanted us all to be in Objective Lead, so there wasn't much time. The Scots DG were to attack Lead as soon as possible, followed by the Staffords and QRIH as soon as Platinum Two was cleared. But this took until 1730, because of the huge number of prisoners – including a brigadier and two full colonels. I would have liked to meet the Iraqi brigadier, but there was no time.

Lieutenant Colonel Mike Vickery
Commanding Officer, 14th/20th King's Hussars,
4th Armoured Brigade

That night, one of my B Squadron tanks was hit by friendly fire. During a foggy, smoky little assault with an infantry battle group, the tank fell into an Iraqi tank scrape. As the driver did a high reverse out, a Warrior crew from one of the infantry battalions misidentified it as an Iraqi tank and loosed off a 30mm cannon shot at it.

Normally this would not have penetrated the armour of a Challenger, but the armour-piercing round went through the sprocket, which isn't armoured and lodged in the drive shaft, bringing the tank to a halt. B Squadron leader Richard Shirreff was furious. No one was hurt and the tank had its final drive replaced and returned to me later that day.

Brigadier Patrick Cordingley
Commander, 7th Armoured Brigade

After a brief firefight for Objective Lead and the destruction of three T-55s, the Scots DG reported it clear of enemy.

I found Lead much as every other part of the desert; flat and featureless with charred and burned-out Iraqi tanks and armoured vehicles. As we drove into our night-time position, through my sights I noticed a single strand of wire, but not thinking anything of it drove straight on. But when I threw open the commander's hatch for a better look around, I could see the unmistakable shapes of mines laid just under the surface. We were in the middle of a minefield and it was a miracle we'd not hit one.

There was just enough light to see our tracks, which were an almost straight line. I ordered Corporal Stevely to restart the engine and drive very slowly backwards, with Richard and I hanging over the side of the turret either side peering at the ground. We crawled the fifty yards back to the wire fence, me praying that these mines were nothing clever, designed to go off the second time you drive over them.

While a further enemy position was surrendering, others tried to resist, an Iraqi firing an RPG 7 rocket-propelled grenade, hitting one of the Staffords in the chest and killing him. Two hours later the shooting was finally over, with nearly three hundred prisoners, of which eleven were severely wounded and were evacuated immediately.

By 1930 we'd secured Lead with a reconnaissance screen out covering all around us. We had thus taken our immediate objective in two days, for which division had planned on ten.

Lieutenant Colonel Charles Rogers
Commanding Officer, Staffordshire Regiment

4 Brigade took over the advance, so we paused in Lead for the night, surrounded by five hundred prisoners. Then one of my companies bumped into an Iraqi battalion, dug in to the south of Nickel, losing one chap killed and a couple more wounded, a very nasty action. There were many bunkers, and with no tank support it took us most of the night to clear.

Armoured warfare was a strange existence for the soldiers, and dangerous. Sitting in the back of a vehicle people switch off, becoming disorientated. Only the section commander has visibility from the turret, and all he can do is pass on what he can see, and what's happening from the radio. It's very claustrophobic, uncomfortable and disconnected, which is bad for infantrymen, who like to be outside using their own senses to work out what's going on. When getting out they fix bayonets as a matter of principle, and cock their weapons. Accidentally stabbing or shooting a friend is always possible.

Brigadier Patrick Cordingley
Commander, 7th Armoured Brigade

At 2030 hours we received orders to move the next morning at 0730 [G+3] to Objective Varsity, to destroy the enemy en route, block enemy routes, then be prepared to attack north.

I'd managed about three hours' sleep in the last sixty, so before detailed Orders at midnight, I decided to get a couple of hours' sleep. I was covered in dust, sand and oil, my eyes stinging with tiredness, the back injury hurting once more, ears ringing with the noise of the radios. But I couldn't sleep. 4 Brigade to the south were carrying out a very noisy barrage, and we seemed to be under the flight path of every American Apache helicopter in the Middle East.

So after two fitful hours, I got up and walked to the headquarters. Euan was still working on the back of the command vehicle, so I told him to go off and get some sleep.

As I sat down at the map board, Sergeant Major Lynch asked to have a private word with me. He'd been walking past the prisoners' cage and had seen the guards making them lie flat on the ground and thought they were being handled very roughly. I asked if they were being hit; he said there was nothing like that going on, but thought they were being pushed around in an unnecessary manner.

I was incensed. Although the prisoner-handling force had a thankless task, and their soldiers would probably rather have been fighting, to mistreat prisoners was utterly inexcusable. I went off to find the prisoner detachment commander, and told him that if I heard of one more instance of a single Iraqi being mistreated I'd have him court-martialled. I stormed back to my HQ, still livid.

Lieutenant Colonel Mike Vickery
Commanding Officer, 14th/20th King's Hussars,
4th Armoured Brigade

We moved for most of that night across the network of oil pipelines. These stuck up about a metre, so in expectation of this crossing, DERA engineers had modified our river-crossing bridges, adding a little up-and-over section, which was quite tricky, especially for tanks using night vision. Anybody falling off on to a pipe would have caused a real mess, which fortunately didn't happen. We moved on from this to a final assault.

We were increasingly expecting a Republican Guard attack, plus an NBC attack. There was, however, a very strong rumour that Saddam had been very quietly told that if he used NBC, Baghdad would be flattened with a mushroom cloud left floating over it. Although we'd stopped wearing respirators after we'd crossed the minefield breach, we were still wearing NBC suits. There was a constant debate about whether we'd be hit by NBC, right up to the very end of the fighting.

We were getting very tired. When I gave [radio] orders, at the end just before saying 'Go', I forced myself to pause and think quickly through whether I'd made any fuck-ups. I'd never deliberately put soldiers into harm's way like this before, knowing some of them would be killed or injured.

We moved up to the Fusiliers' position for a quick brigade commanders' orders group. The 14th/20th were given a break from leading, but because our tanks had good night vision, I had to give each battalion one tank squadron, and received two infantry companies back. The next bit was to be a long march, and after some discussion, my third tank squadron was taken from me to go out ahead [as recce]. So I had a nice quiet night bumbling along with two companies of Grenadier Guards, although the rest of my soldiers had another night of the same.

G+3 – WEDNESDAY 27 FEBRUARY

Brigadier Patrick Cordingley
Commander, 7th Armoured Brigade

Our detailed orders came in at 0243, given by General Smith. If he was as tired as I was, there was no hint of it over the air. We were ordered into Kuwait, with 16th/5th Lancer recce with helicopter support out in front to locate the enemy. To our south, the Egyptians of Joint Arab Command East had similar tanks and vehicles to the Iraqis, so great care would be required. To our north would be the first US infantry division.

I told everyone we'd already suffered one blue-on-blue, and I didn't want any more.

I tried once more to get some rest, but the noise of battle was too much.

Captain Johnny Omerod
Second-in-command, B Squadron, Queen's Royal Irish Hussars

At 0400 hours, our orders came: we were to advance into Kuwait to seize Objective Varsity, moving as soon as possible. We crossed the start line on time, broke into advance formation, married up with the Scots DG and headed for the Kuwait border. To our front were large groups of Iraqis, with many more appearing out of the mist.

Lieutenant Colonel Arthur Denaro
Commanding Officer, Queen's Royal Irish Hussars

As it turned out, we managed a good night's sleep, and were woken at 0534 for a move at 0700.

Brigadier Mike Willcocks
Chief of Staff (Land), Joint War Headquarters, RAF High Wycombe

John Major visited the bunker. He'd no aides, and while I briefed him, sat down in front of my map taking notes on a pad. I'd never seen that before in a prime minister. When I'd finished, he said, 'I've got eight questions,' which he asked all at once, finishing with 'Where are the Belgians?'

This left me thinking, 'Christ, I must try to hang on to these as I've got nothing to write on.'

So I did my best, going through the first seven, but I couldn't remember the last one.

'I'm sorry, Prime Minister. I've forgotten what your last question was?'

'Where are the Belgians?' he repeated. Everybody else started laughing. I was thinking, 'Christ, I've completely forgotten them. Where are they?'

I'd gone completely blank. Where indeed were the Belgians? I didn't know. I was hunting around my map in desperation. Everyone was in hysterics, as the PM was taking the piss. We'd had terrible trouble with the Belgians, who wouldn't sell us any 155mm artillery ammunition. They weren't, in fact, anywhere at all.

Brigadier Patrick Cordingley
Commander, 7th Armoured Brigade

Our rapid advance was causing problems higher up at division and corps. The huge number of prisoners was straining division's logistics, as was the distance our resupply vehicles now needed to travel, with Rupert Smith's engineers furiously laying a road through the desert behind us.

Lieutenant Colonel Mike Vickery
Commanding Officer, 14th/20th King's Hussars,
4th Armoured Brigade

We were put on to two hours' notice to move, so we could reform the battle groups. I was told that all my squadrons would return to me, plus one company of Fusiliers.

The squadron leaders were all very, very tired, needed resupply, and I was getting it in the neck.

When tankers get detached from their own quartermaster, the infantry actually can't look after them. We use up such a lot of resources, and even though the REME does understand, infantry battalions have nothing like the facilities or spares. It's only the people who know us who can look after us.

I told them, 'Quieten down boys. You know the drills. We're going to an RV with the loggies, where there's ammo and we can refuel, with hard standing so you can do some track bashing, and the technical quartermaster's boys with any spares you might need. Just calm down. We *are* thinking about you.'

A captured Iraqi artillery colonel told me that the bombing had brought them down from about ninety-five per cent effectiveness to seventy-five at the end of the month. But then, he said our artillery brought him down to forty per cent within minutes, then our tank attacks finished them off.

Brigadier Patrick Cordingley
Commander, 7th Armoured Brigade

Unlike the previous morning, when the brigade had been chomping at the bit, this morning there was an almost palpable lethargy, a reluctance to face the day. Perhaps it was a feeling our luck could not hold, but maybe it was the inequality of the battle; we were killing a lot of Iraqis, men with little or no will to fight.

Lieutenant Colonel Mike Vickery
Commanding Officer, 14th/20th King's Hussars,
4th Armoured Brigade

Forty-eight hours in, everyone was very tired. But at this point things changed very radically. We were going to have to move much faster. We received coded radio orders, and as we were deciphering, realised they ordered us to move in twenty minutes, with recce to have moved already.

The whole point of giving two hours' notice to move is to allow people to do things that take two hours to complete; topping up the oils in an armoured vehicle takes a full hour and needs to be done as frequently as possible. I was actually having a shower, stark naked with a bucket of water and the radio on a long curly lead.

So, covered with soap, I ordered everyone to move in twenty minutes, with the recce to leave right now. They had to abandon quite a lot of things, some of which we delivered to them later. We didn't complain to brigade headquarters, as obviously this was what was needed so there was no point.

The rest of us drove off twenty minutes later, people wearing only their knickers, rations all over the floors of the tanks, furiously getting dressed, sorting things out as they moved along, disorganised and unbalanced.

At this point, we had 'Contact Wait Out' from A Squadron leader.

Brigadier Patrick Cordingley
Commander, 7th Armoured Brigade

We passed groups of Iraqis seemingly wandering around the desert, who tried to surrender, but I ordered the advance to continue. Several times there were calls for artillery, which I was reluctant to agree. It seemed prudent to conserve our stocks, particularly MLRS ammunition, for when we met the Republican Guard.

The QRIH had to make frequent stops to avoid getting ahead of the Scots DG and Staffords. After yet another stop just short of the border, the QRIH adjutant asked B Squadron why they'd halted. 'There appears to be a problem at Customs,' came the laconic reply from their commander, Major David Swann.

Captain Johnny Omerod
Second-in-command, B Squadron, Queen's Royal Irish Hussars

With Lieutenant Buxton leading as Trimble tank, we entered Kuwait across Wadi Al Batin, and an area of rough ground around a quarry which we named 'moon country'.

The tank troops split as we searched for a route through. If this had been an Iraqi defensive position, we should have suffered badly. We continued to Varsity, which was unoccupied by the time we arrived. We became aware that the oilfields had been set on fire, dark-grey skies in an eerie combination with orange sand.

Lieutenant Colonel Arthur Denaro
Commanding Officer, Queen's Royal Irish Hussars

I was very concerned about our northern boundary, because it wasn't clear who was there or exactly where they were. I had a lengthy discussion with the brigadier about it, and was told to shut up. Anyway we pressed on and all was well, crossing the Wadi al Batin with the Scots Dragoon Guards, pausing to talk to Kate Adie and have a whisky. We then crossed the border into Kuwait, which I suppose was a pretty historic moment.

Brigadier Patrick Cordingley
Commander, 7th Armoured Brigade

At 0930 we crossed the border into Kuwait. I called a halt and had a cup of tea, which seemed the British thing to do.

Lieutenant Colonel Mike Vickery
Commanding Officer, 14th/20th King's Hussars,
4th Armoured Brigade

Two small armoured vehicles were smack in front of us – in my area, so for me to deal with. They appeared on the thermal imager as two blobs, so we couldn't say what they were. You don't fire artillery at two vehicles, so we kept moving. At six kilometres, no threat, but the Iraqis' Russian mobile AT-5 anti-tank system has a range of five kilometres... Nobody was going to give us any artillery, so I badgered brigade HQ, who said there were no friendly vehicles in that position. My Artillery Battery Commander, Andrew Gillespie, had also been asking around on the artillery net.

I even talked personally to the COs of the other battle groups, for which I received a mega bollocking for bypassing brigade HQ – there were times when, frankly, 4th Brigade headquarters irritated me.

So I told brigade HQ these vehicles were now three thousand metres away and asked, 'Could I shoot them?'

They said shoot them.

At two thousand seven hundred metres A Squadron leader decided he wasn't going to wait any longer, so ordered a halt. One shot was fired at the vehicle on the right, which went up in smoke up; then a second shot on the left-hand vehicle. Then we moved on.

Brigadier Patrick Cordingley
Commander, 7th Armoured Brigade

I'd ordered Arthur's battle group to move a little further south as we entered Kuwait, to avoid problems with the Americans in the north. His staff had been badgering mine on this subject, despite constant assurances that the Americans to our north knew where we were, plus we had a liaison officer with them.

Arthur again called me on the radio, asking where the Americans were as he was running very close to his boundary. I relayed the QRIH position to division just to be certain, and asked for confirmation they'd passed it on to the Americans. A little later Arthur called me again, expressing his extreme concern about the northern boundary with the Americans. I told him to worry about the enemy, and let me worry about the friendly forces, then cut him off.

Lieutenant Colonel Arthur Denaro
Commanding Officer, Queen's Royal Irish Hussars

After crossing the Wadi, the boundaries were vague, which I reported to brigade, ordering D Squadron back in to keep us closer together. Then we hit some difficult hilly country, so I moved command troop round to the north. But just as we were going through, there was a contact report from recce on my left rear, and also from command troop, who were very close behind me. I moved fast forward, while deploying some of A Squadron to protect command troop.

As we motored on, I saw 11C's barrel was carelessly pointing straight towards B Squadron. I was horrified then to see two of B Squadron's tank barrels swing round on to him, but couldn't get on the radio because someone else was talking. I could only pray that B Squadron would not blow 11C to pieces. That happily that didn't happen, and I was able to tell him in no gentle terms of his error. And so we came to a halt.

RSM Johnny Muir
Regimental Sergeant Major, Queen's Royal Irish Hussars

We were running and rolling with the Americans on our left flank. Battle group HQ was temporarily halted, with their Ferrets out in front as protection. At 1100 hours, we heard one of our recce Scorpions had been hit. I was instructed to go to this position, and as I was orientating my map, heard bullets whining through the air, hitting the nearby command vehicle, splintering the top of a six-foot table strapped to its side. My driver asked what was happening.

When I told him, he shouted, 'RSM, get your fucking head down. Those rounds are going right over the top of you.' I dropped the seat so my head went down into the turret, very thankful that my driver had spoken to me in such an assertive way – and for my makeshift turret.

Lieutenant Colonel Arthur Denaro
Commanding Officer, Queen's Royal Irish Hussars

A confused report came over the air, that recce troop had been attacked by American M1 tanks, and that callsign 21 had been knocked out. It took quite a long time to unravel what had actually happened.

In the meantime we had fifteen kilometres still to go, so ignoring all this, I got the rest of the regiment balanced. But then I received a sitrep from D Squadron, who'd gone to help recce troop, revealing they had very serious problems.

Our recce troop section had stopped for some prisoners, where they were spotted by two American M1 tanks which fired machine guns and five or six shells, wounding Corporal Lynch and Corporal Balmforth, destroying a Scorpion. The Abrams tanks then saw the rest of command troop going past and sprayed them with a machine gun. Only once they'd done this, did the Americans realise they were firing at British troops.

I have to say the Americans were mind-bendingly stupid, but this is the kind of thing that happens in war. I was so irritated with brigade, who'd said earlier they didn't mind the Americans swanning into our area; and I'd said, 'Well actually, I do mind.'

RSM Johnny Muir
Regimental Sergeant Major, Queen's Royal Irish Hussars

The American tanks stopped firing, and realising what they'd done, kept their hatches battened down. Our command troop staff sergeant, a very big man, made his way over to them, but they remained battened down.

The first Scorpion had been hit by an armour-piercing round, directly in front of the engine beside the driver. The second vehicle was destroyed. The crew received lacerations, but thankfully nothing worse.

Lieutenant Colonel Mike Vickery
Commanding Officer, 14th/20th King's Hussars,
4th Armoured Brigade

My BC Andrew Gillespie said two air defence vehicles had been blown up by mines at a grid reference really too close for comfort to the one we'd fired at.

I stopped the battle group smack in its tracks and told brigade HQ we had a possible blue-on-blue with these vehicles I'd been talking to them about for the last quarter of an hour. I told them I was going personally to investigate this location with the BC. They stopped the rest of the brigade.

I arrived at the scene, to find two air defence Spartans, both burning merrily. One of the BC's sergeants ran to one of the vehicles as he thought he saw a driver moving. But this wasn't the case, so he jumped off before it exploded, and we moved to a safe distance. We'd killed six good men and true from the Royal Horse Artillery.

Brigadier Patrick Cordingley
Commander, 7th Armoured Brigade

The divisional commander's helicopter landed. I climbed out of my tank and walked over to him, wondering who was the more tired. He asked what had happened with the QRIH, then told me people were getting very tired, and so he'd ordered his headquarters only to issue *written* orders, as he considered it now too risky to give out radio orders. 'All it takes is a couple of inaccurate grid references.'

He said American intelligence reckoned there were now less than ten combat-effective Iraqi divisions left in Kuwait, that communications between Baghdad and the front had ceased, we'd taken over forty thousand prisoners, and Saddam Hussein had ordered his troops to leave Kuwait, even though there was nowhere for them to go.

Lieutenant Colonel Mike Vickery
Commanding Officer, 14th/20th King's Hussars,
4th Armoured Brigade

But then six men emerged from behind a nearby hill demanding to know what the fuck did we think we were doing... an air defence troop from 7 Brigade, about six miles south of where they were supposed to be, and absolutely within my boundaries. They'd got lost, then one vehicle had broken down, which was being towed by the other. They'd all got out when some Iraqis arrived on the scene, and only the driver was in the front vehicle. They'd taken the Iraqis prisoner, which they'd got settled down behind the hill.

At this point we'd fired at the broken-down vehicle, at which the driver had bailed out and was in mid air when we hit the second one. A blue-on-blue, but nobody hurt.

This caused huge and very real alarm. The whole of 1st British Armoured Division were heading for a massive blue-on-blue with the American division steaming in from the north-east, which would not have been very funny. So we all stopped, and our move to get round behind the Iraqis ceased, while the American army moved round north and south-east.

Our divisional plan changed, stopping us going north to cut off the Iraqis' Basra pocket, on to a more southerly axis. About this time, air attacks on the Iraqi retreat from Kuwait City were beginning. We remained worried about blue-on-blue, but were told to move on, assured that there wasn't anything in front of us.

But as we moved off again, A and B Squadrons both picked up images in their night scopes of hundreds of trucks moving slowly in front of us. It was now getting dark, the weather dire with very poor visibility, so we couldn't see these trucks using the naked eye, only through thermal imagers. They were moving very slowly. The tanks and artillery were ready to hit them, but I decided we needed these trucks for prisoners of war, and if we presented ourselves, they'd give up.

But as we got nearer and could see them with the naked eye, they had chevrons on the side – and bugger me, it was our old friends 7 Brigade again, the people who should have been being looked after by the air defence people who'd got lost and been hit by us. It makes my blood run cold thinking about how close we were to firing on them.

I reported this to brigade, who said they shouldn't have been there. I said I remained worried about further blue-on-blue, so we all stopped again, while 7 Brigade worked out where all their people were.

Brigadier Patrick Cordingley
Commander, 7th Armoured Brigade

Objective Varsity had been heavily bombed by B-52 raids and our artillery, and was now a moonscape of huge black craters, with only wounded or dead

Iraqis. Allied propaganda leaflets were fluttering in and out of abandoned vehicles. I noticed how dark it was; at first I thought just another cloudy day, but in addition to the smell of cordite and explosives there was now also a more acrid, sulphurous edge that caught in the throat.

Lieutenant Colonel Arthur Denaro
Commanding Officer, Queen's Royal Irish Hussars

It seemed from the news that the war was rapidly coming to an end. We were called into brigade at 1200 for an O group, our first since back in Saudi four days ago, and it was good to see the Commander and the others.

The Brigadier and I walked off into the sand for a good heart-to-heart about my questioning the boundaries, the blue-on-blue and our differences on the air, smoothing and sorting it all out. It seemed we weren't to do any more fighting, and that our two wounded chaps would survive.

Brigadier Patrick Cordingley
Commander, 7th Armoured Brigade

Just after midday I called in the commanding officers. Arthur brought Martin Bell with him. Charles and John came in next, all very tired indeed. I told them what I knew about future plans, then spoke about fatigue. Arthur Denaro was worried about tiredness and the probability of more blue-on-blues, so I told them to break out whatever flags they'd got: Union Jacks, the Cross of St George or St Andrew, whatever. I didn't want anyone to mistake us for enemy, and as I knew all the men had got flags, now was the time to fly them.

RSM Johnny Muir
Regimental Sergeant Major, Queen's Royal Irish Hussars

It was funny how quickly the Union flags appeared. The boys were clearly prepared for victory. Colonel Arthur is a quite strong Catholic, from a little village in County Donegal. His crew, however, were Protestants from Northern Ireland, so his tank led us into Kuwait flying the Unionist Red Hand of Ulster.

Captain Johnny Omerod
Second-in-command, B Squadron, Queen's Royal Irish Hussars

Listening to the BBC World Service, we discovered how devastating an operation this had been. We were now desperately enthusiastic to close with the Republican Guard and have a crack at a T-72 tank.

We received a warning order to sweep up to the Kuwait/Iraq border and on, to the Republican Guard, as far as the Euphrates River. But as the squadron adopted its night-time routine, World Service news of a possible ceasefire was met with mixed emotions.

Sergeant Shaun Rusling
Medic, Parachute Regiment, 32 Field Hospital

The field hospital was now too far behind the advance. I was told I'd be flying forward in a Chinook as part of a forward anaesthetic resuscitation team, to provide tailboard treatment on the front line, while 22 Field Hospital was packed up and moved forward.

Major General Rupert Smith
General Officer Commanding, 1st Armoured Division

Our tiredness was becoming dangerous, and as we ran out from under the Ptarmigan net, our communications were getting more difficult.

The Americans, sweeping round to the north, needed more fuel for their tanks. I had a long conversation with the Corps Commander about whether we should turn south, to shorten the logistic route. But he and his staff were very concerned that our national role was to be on the main attack – that we shouldn't be doing a secondary job like opening up a logistic route. But I said if he needs me to open up his logistic routes to get his fuel, then that's what my division does for him.

I wasn't playing a national card and we were in this together, to win. So we started to plan for 4th Brigade and all my road-building engineers to open this route up from the back.

Lieutenant Colonel Charles Rogers
Commanding Officer, Staffordshire Regiment

Ground attack aircraft worried me, and I never had any desire to call them in. American Apache strike helicopters kept appearing on the flanks, trailing us in a rather sinister fashion, as if sizing us up for a strike.

Each vehicle had air recognition symbols on the top, which couldn't be seen from medium-bombing altitudes. I used to carry a mirror in case I needed to indicate where we were to aircraft. We knew they didn't see things very well, and also that laser target marking wasn't necessarily a fool-proof system.

Brigadier Patrick Cordingley
Commander, 7th Armoured Brigade

I heard on the divisional net what appeared to be a blue-on-blue against part of 4th Armoured Brigade – the Royal Regiment of Fusiliers – with two Warriors having been attacked by American A-10 aircraft. General Smith confirmed this, saying there were nine dead with others injured, a couple seriously. He told me to make sure that the men were very careful, and although there would be a ceasefire soon, things would probably become even more dangerous as people would slacken off and make mistakes.

Lance Corporal Roy Sellstrom
Pioneer Corps, Army War Graves Unit

We were in a wheeled vehicle convoy, miles long, with other convoys moving along to either side of us. We could hear the booming of artillery in the background, and the loud 'bang-bang' of shattering explosives and firing nearby. We'd stopped beside an Iraqi position, then at 1615 hours, a despatch rider came up beside us asking for Lieutenant Parry to go immediately to brigade ops.

It was a blue-on-blue. Lieutenant Parry came back saying the 14th/20th with 4 Brigade had hit one of the Royal Regiment of Fusilier's Warriors, and that he needed a recovery section. Lieutenant Parry took the Land Rover and the TM, and went off ahead, leaving us with the four-tonner. They returned an hour and a half later, none of them speaking – literally.

When I asked him what had happened, he said, 'It was a blue-on-blue air attack. I've picked them all up.'

I said, 'No problem sir. How many have we got?'

'There's nine of them.'

'Fucking nine?'

'Yeah nine – and they're not in a very good state.'

'OK, no problem, sir. Let's get 'em out and wack 'em on to the trestles.'

So I got amongst the lads to sort this out. We dragged all our kit out of the four-tonner, and swapped the bodies over from the TM. Then we were ordered to move – and the convoy was off again, like Wacky Races.

Brigadier Patrick Cordingley
Commander, 7th Armoured Brigade

We'd waited in Varsity for much of the day, and I ensured the men got some rest. I drew up plans for a move east to the Objective Cobalt; astride the Kuwait-to-Basra road, this looked a likely objective.

At 1930, division sent us a warning order to get ready for a push south into Saudi Arabia, with us detaching our engineers and a complete battle group to 4th Brigade, who were to open a new supply route to VII Corps. This was a disappointing task.

Lance Corporal Roy Sellstrom
Pioneer Corps, Army War Graves Unit

That night, when we stopped, Lieutenant Parry came in to tell me that three Queen's Own Highlanders were outside saying they'd heard that members of their regiment had been killed and were now with us. I suggested we give them a cup of coffee.

Their pipe major had brought over two of his lads who were relatives of the men they thought dead; a brother and a brother-in-law.

But we'd been told they were all Fusiliers, so I was sitting there convincing these three guys that their relatives were still alive, hadn't been killed and so weren't with us. We only found out later that three of them *were* Queen's Own Highlanders. So while we were talking, these guys' brother and brother-in-law weren't alive at all, but dead, in the back of our four-tonner.

This was poor passage of information. I got the distinct impression that if I ever bumped into these guys again, I was going to get a good leathering.

G+4 – THURSDAY 28 FEBRUARY

Brigadier Patrick Cordingley
Commander, 7th Armoured Brigade

Thankfully, at three in the morning this logistic route-creating operation was abandoned, and replaced by an attack north towards Basra.

General Smith realised that I would want to know our next move, but apart from swinging north and pushing towards Basra – an option he didn't like, his guess was that we'd push towards Kuwait City to cut off any Iraqi movement north.

Major General Rupert Smith
General Officer Commanding, 1st Armoured Division

Later that night, the logistic route operation was called off, and instead we were ordered to get as far into Kuwait as fast as we could, and race to the coast. We already had outline objectives, so could get on with it.

Partly because of fatigue, and because I'd now got a better feel for the enemy, I made the next big and final command decision, which was to start a pursuit of the Republican Guard, with my division broken down into battle groups rather than brigades.

Brigadier Patrick Cordingley
Commander, 7th Armoured Brigade

Shortly after five-thirty in the morning Rupert Smith called me on the secure Ptarmigan system, to tell me that my mission was to attack east to cut the routes from Kuwait City and prevent the Iraqi army retreating north to Basra. We were to attack in column, moving at first light. He said a ceasefire was expected to come into effect at midnight Washington time, which was eight o'clock in the morning here, and so wanted me to be on the Basra road by then.

Lieutenant Colonel Arthur Denaro
Commanding Officer, Queen's Royal Irish Hussars

I went to bed, but my mind was racing and I couldn't get to sleep. I sat working in my command vehicle, and at 0520 hours was warned that orders were about to come in, that we were going to move, and that we had to cross a start line at 0645 hours and so were leaving now in order to get there in time. This was the fifth day.

Brigadier Patrick Cordingley
Commander, 7th Armoured Brigade

Glancing at the map, I guessed this would be about forty miles' driving. It took five minutes to sort out the plans and I gave Orders at 0530, telling everyone to be ready to move at 0630 hours.

Lieutenant Colonel Arthur Denaro
Commanding Officer, Queen's Royal Irish Hussars

I radio-checked with the squadron leaders, asking them if we could be ready to move by 0600 hours. They said, 'Yes,' so I got through to brigade saying we could move at 0600 hours. They said, 'No, don't worry.'

'But we've got to be forty-five kilometres from here by 0800 hours,' I replied. 'We'll never do it if we don't move from here at 0600 hours.'

'No, don't worry,' was the answer.

But then I got through to the Brigadier himself, who said, 'Yes – go.'

Brigadier Patrick Cordingley
Commander, 7th Armoured Brigade

There was no time to give formal orders, but I knew they wouldn't need them. The reconnaissance squadron set off at exactly six o'clock, with the QRIH as point battle group with, I suspected, Arthur leading from the front. This was going to be nothing less than a cavalry charge. We had two hours to get there, and unless we ran into the Republican Guard, or what was left of it, we were not stopping for anyone.

Captain Johnny Omerod
Second-in-command, B Squadron, Queen's Royal Irish Hussars

The artillery produced the goods yet again, giving us their usual sneak preview of the day's tasks. The Iraqis were withdrawing rapidly from Kuwait City and we hoped to cut off their retreat. So thanks to the gunners, by the time orders reached us from regiment, our maps were already marked, and we were able to react very quickly.

We were given fifteen minutes to get across the start line. As orders were being relayed, the squadron instinctively moved into formation and began to advance. Things happened so quickly that it was only after we'd crossed the start line that the full details of our task were passed down.

Lieutenant Colonel Arthur Denaro
Commanding Officer, Queen's Royal Irish Hussars

And go they went, absolutely like smoke. D Squadron were some way behind because of their position in the overnight formation, and eventually caught up. We must have gone about fifteen kilometres when suddenly the Trimble went down.

Second Lieutenant Alistair Watkins
Grenadier Guards, 3 Royal Regiment of Fusiliers Battle Group, 4th Armoured Brigade

Next day was very grey, grim and overcast, and we stopped the battle group to have a memorial service. There were a lot of very upset soldiers. Nine people is quite a lot, and as the padre gave his speech, there was crying, then ironically, an enormous thunderstorm with rain and lightning which seemed quite fitting.

This service ended in bizarre, random chaos when huge numbers of Iraqis appeared. We didn't know if they were surrendering, but they were.

Lieutenant Toby Masterton
A Squadron, The Life Guards, 1 Royal Scots Battle Group, 4th Armoured Brigade

4 Brigade was to cut off the Republican Guard's escape back into Iraq via Safwan and Basra – their two MSRs. The desert was much harder and flattish so we could keep up. Pennants fluttering, it was like Wacky Races, past tons and tons of burned and blown-up stuff.

Lots of Iraqis were surrendering to us, including in one group a very senior Iraqi officer who'd removed his badges of ranks to avoid being noticed by us. His troops were still respecting of his rank. He was an arrogant twat, and spoke some English. Once he'd realised we weren't cannibals, he became all macho again. For ease of supervision and their protection, we put them into a large tank scrape, but rather than segregate him the guys chucked him in with the rest of the Iraqi *jundis* [arabic for 'soldier']. They descended on him like a pack of hounds at a fox, so a couple of guys had to jump in to get him out before they tore him to shreds.

The Iraqis told us how they were treated: poor food, frequently left for weeks by their officers, having been told they'd be shot if they didn't fight. Others told of officers standing behind them, shooting anybody who wouldn't fight. They couldn't read maps, had no radios; some looked like fourteen-year-old boys, others old men. One very Iraqi-looking soldier asked for a cigarette in a broad Scouse accent. He'd been on holiday with his family in Iraq when it started, and got conscripted.

Lance Corporal Roy Sellstrom
Pioneer Corps, Army War Graves Unit

We drove all through that night, pulling up again at first light. I told Lieutenant Parry we should process the bodies. He'd told me we'd got nine, and the previous night I'd physically counted nine. They were inside NBC casualty bags, which we'd been told was forbidden, as it meant we were supposed to treat them as if they were contaminated. Lieutenant Parry assured me we didn't have to treat them as contaminated, but we did need to transfer them into something else, even though we had only the six-foot bin bags.

I went on to the back of the four-tonner and counted, but could only find eight, plus various other bags full of what I assumed were the guys' equipment and stuff. I did another count, then told Lieutenant Parry we'd lost a body. One of the new RCT lads came round from the front of the wagon and told me a body was half hanging out of the canvas. It had rolled out of the trestle framework during the night, thankfully not falling on to the ground. So we pulled all the bodies out of the trestle framework, and decided there and then to get rid of it. It would be safer just to pile them all on the floor of the truck.

Captain Johnny Omerod
Second-in-command, B Squadron, Queen's Royal Irish Hussars

We covered forty-five kilometres in the first hour. The satellites went down, so we reverted to compass, which worked remarkably well.

Lieutenant Colonel Arthur Denaro
Commanding Officer, Queen's Royal Irish Hussars

Johnny Omerod leapt out of his tank, took a magnetic compass bearing, then kicked on once more. We were meant to be travelling with the Staffords to our left and the Scots Dragoon Guards to our right, but the Staffords had started some fifteen kilometres behind us, and the Scots Dragoon Guards had been asleep on the start line, so we were now some fifteen kilometres ahead of everybody else, going like smoke.

Lieutenant Colonel Charles Rogers
Commanding Officer, Staffordshire Regiment

We'd fought four or five actions from Lead onwards, with a net total [for the Staffords] of five wounded and two dead – with one dead and one wounded as a result of blue-on-blue.

Between Nickel and Varsity was a race with not much else happening, to cut off the Basra Road.

Brigadier Patrick Cordingley
Commander, 7th Armoured Brigade

The deeper into Kuwait we went, the more scenes of devastation, the remains of an army not just defeated but utterly routed, in a semi-darkness created by the ever-thickening clouds of burning oil. Suddenly Corporal McCarthy shouted on the intercom from the gunner's position, 'Contact, T-55 slightly right.'

I saw it too, behind a sand berm, barrel pointing straight at us. 'Hard left,' I shouted to the driver, then gave fire orders to the gunner.

'Fin, tank on.' Corporal McCarthy pushed open the cover on his control stick, flipping the switch initiating the firing circuits. The laser-cooling fan kicked in. Richard rammed one of the bright orange fin charges up into the breech so its cupped end mated with the tail of the depleted-uranium fin round already there. Corporal Stevely brought the tank to a swift halt behind the sand berm, just as Richard slammed shut the breech.

'Loaded.' Another quick look at the T-55. Did I need to destroy it? It looked lifeless, but could I take the risk?

'Fire.'

'Lasing,' shouted Corporal McCarthy.

There was a whine as the laser fired at the T-55. A fraction of a second later the range flashed up: two thousand one hundred metres. Another fraction later our twenty-two ton turret slewed hard as the computer-driven motors put the gun in the exact position for the first shot. 'Firing now!' Corporal McCarthy squeezed the red trigger. The tank was thrown back violently. Through the sight I saw a blinding white flash as the round smashed through the Iraqi tank.

'Target,' said Corporal McCarthy.

'Target, stop,' I replied.

Arthur Denaro came up on the brigade net:

'I'm very concerned about what lies to our front. We could be badly wrong-footed at this speed.'

'Just crack on, best speed,' I snapped back and was immediately angry with myself. We were all very tired and tempers were short. He had a fair point, but Hamish was to our front, and telling us nothing was there.

Lance Corporal Roy Sellstrom
Pioneer Corps, Army War Graves Unit

We got set up with the four-ton trucks parked back to back, our tent in between joining them together, surrounded by canvas screens to process the bodies.

For me this was now very different, because when a bloke has a car crash and is killed, you can blame the car crash, or call him a dickhead. But on a battlefield, you can't blame anyone. It was like my security blanket was suddenly gone.

I felt *raw*, because who could I blame? I'm doing it for fucking real now, with bombs and small-arms fire going off all round me at night. And I've got the end result in front of me: nine dead bodies, all killed by some form of explosive for which you can't blame anything or anyone.

One of the lads came into the processing tent while we were doing this, and said a big queue of people was forming outside. I said, 'Tell them to fuck off.' He came back in to say they thought we were the cookhouse. They didn't believe him, so I went out and asked them what the problem was. We had no water for washing so I was covered with shit and blood. I suppose they thought I was the butcher.

Then Lieutenant Parry came out and told them we were a medical team, and to go away. But then a couple of them said, 'Oh, we're unit medics. We'll give you a hand.'

People hung around our group of vehicles, wondering what we were doing – just being there. They hadn't done anything or seen any action, but we could all hear the bombing, shelling and firing. They knew there'd been people killed in the blue-on-blue, but I don't think they realised the bodies were still in amongst them.

We'd just started on the fifth body when we got the order to move yet again.

Captain Johnny Omerod
Second-in-command, B Squadron, Queen's Royal Irish Hussars

At one point we were nine kilometres ahead of the regiment. In different circumstances this might have been rather risky, but the race was on and the colonel was just behind us.

Brigadier Patrick Cordingley
Commander, 7th Armoured Brigade

At seven o'clock it looked as if we weren't going to make it. Rupert Smith came on the air, asking where we were. 'Still some way off,' I answered.

'It would be good if you could be there by the ceasefire,' he replied.

Lance Corporal Roy Sellstrom
Pioneer Corps, Army War Graves Unit

We really needed to backload the bodies, as now being in the bin bags, fluids were building up. Every time the wind changed, we had to move our tents around so the smell didn't affect other people. Lieutenant Parry booked a helicopter.

In daylight now, we laid out a heli pad and a Chinook landed, diverted to us on its way back from the front. We carried the first bodies up to the rear door, and the air loadmaster said, 'We've come in for casualties. What the fuck have you got here then?'

I said, 'There's no casualties, mate. All these are dead.'

'What do you mean they're fucking dead? You're not mixing live casualties with dead.'

'They're all in bags,' I said.

'Fucking hell,' he said. 'Just quickly get them on.'

As we carried the bin bags up the rear ramp, we could see he'd got an aircraft full of casualties with all sorts of dreadful injuries. He said to me, 'I thought they were fucking bodies?'

'They are,' I replied.

'Are they fucking dwarfs?'

At the time, I didn't think this was funny, but looking back I can understand what he meant. With no time to match up the arms, legs and things, three of them were just a load of bags. Some of the casualties began laughing, lessening the pain for themselves, as we dragged the rest up the rear ramp.

Lieutenant Colonel Arthur Denaro
Commanding Officer, Queen's Royal Irish Hussars

Our objective was to either side of the main Basra to Kuwait City highway crossroads, so it was important for us to cut off any withdrawing Iraqis, particularly as the weather was making it very hard to see anything.

A helicopter landed beside my tank and told me our bit of the main road appeared unoccupied, with a T-55 tank, an MTLB [Russian armoured personnel carrier], transporters and various other vehicles, apparently abandoned. This meant we had plenty of time, so could slow down and advance carefully, whilst awaiting some form of direction as to what we should do when we got there.

Lance Corporal Roy Sellstrom
Pioneer Corps, Army War Graves Unit

We cleaned ourselves up as best we could, then got driving again, for miles through Iraqi positions. Five Royal Military Police Land Rovers and a four-tonner were leading, with us just behind them. We were now very tired, all our reactions extremely slow.

The RMP vehicles in front stopped, then everyone piled out and ran off into the sand. I had the boogie box playing very loudly, and thought to myself this wasn't correct convoy drill. Then I saw the sand making swirly sidewinder-snake movements, quite close, the desert sort of shifting in front of us. As I heard some metallic 'ting-ting' noises, I realised we were getting hit.

I jumped out of the wagon and ran round the back, as Lieutenant Parry shouted, 'Debus, Debus. Ambush drills.' Our blokes were sleeping in the back. I hid behind one of the four-tonner's back wheels. Rounds were ricocheting off the metal. I had a careful look and realised we were in the middle of an occupied Iraqi position.

These Iraqi heads were popping up, like that computer game 'Hit the Twat'. Lieutenant Parry dodged over with his pistol saying he'd left his rifle in the truck. I said, 'Me too, so I've got nowt.'

Dave Bagley had his rifle, but having been asleep and then jumped out the back of the wagon, couldn't understand why we were shouting at him. His sleeping bag cover had caught in the back of his webbing, trailing behind like a wedding dress.

Then we heard very loud revving sounds and a pounding, and these Warriors came through the convoy, then a REME repair tank followed by a Challenger, which stopped right next to us and let rip. The whole of the fucking area moved like an earthquake as it fired, sand everywhere, then it roared off. The Warriors' Rarden cannons were firing for a while, then off they went too.

C Coy I Staffords
assaulting the buildings
and bunkers of an Iraqi
position

A Staffords' Warrior later
in the same attack, with
some of the 100 Iraqi
prisoners of war taken
by C Company being
marched away under the
light from 81mm mortar
illumination flares

A Royal Artillery MLRS
battery firing by day

© CHARLES ROGERS

Oil flowing into the sea across the desert from sabotaged pipelines, burning behind the remains of Iraqi defensive positions just off the Basra Road

Men of the Staffordshire Regiment treating Iraqi wounded: this man looked seventy, but was aged only twenty-five. The medics suspected his injuries had been caused by the man's own officers

© CHARLES ROGERS

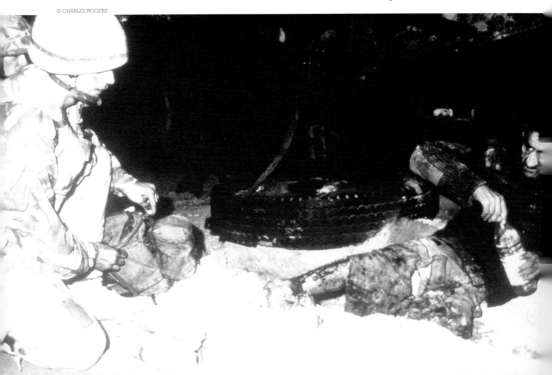

Soldiers of The Staffords guard
Iraqi prisoners, with an Iraqi tank
burning in the background

Lines of Iraqi prisoners
filing from the front line
back to safer rear areas

Guardsmen firing Russian-
made assault rifles captured
from Iraqi troops as they wait
for orders to return to Germany

Inspecting Iraqi defensive positions after
the ceasefire: Major Andrew Ford, Officer
Commanding, Number Two Company, 1 Grenadier
Guards, is at the centre of the photograph

© ARTHUR DENARO

© RICHARD KEMP

Lieutenant Colonel Arthur Denaro's tank flying the regimental flag alongside the Red Hand of Ulster, as their identification marks

7 Brigade HQ vehicles on the Basra Road after the ceasefire

© ALISTAIR WATKINS

The command Warrior of Number Two Company, 1 Grenadier Guards. Left to right: driver Lance Corporal 'Lester' Pigott, second-in-command Captain John Walters of the Australian Army, and Guardsman Henson

The most densely packed part of the Basra highway from Kuwait City to Basra in Iraq on Thursday 28 February 1991, following air strikes. The occupants of most of these vehicles appeared to have escaped to safety after the first attack, but grim photographs of those unfortunate enough to have been caught initially led to a high level decision to curtail the land war [© PA PHOTOS]

Newly appointed Prime Minister
John Major talking to troops at
Camp Four, in Saudi Arabia

Lieutenant General Sir Peter de
la Billiere (right) and Defence
Secretary Tom King at the
Ministry of Defence in London

© PA PHOTOS

A coffin, draped with the Union flag and
containing the body of a British soldier killed
in the Gulf War arriving at RAF Brize Norton
on 8 March 1991, one of seventeen bodies
returned home on that day

The Staffords reuniting
with their families at their
base in Fallingbostel

© CHARLES ROGERS

My ears were really stinging, and I couldn't hear anything at all. Lieutenant Parry told us to get moving again, and we drove through the Iraqi position that had opened up on us.

Brigadier Patrick Cordingley
Commander, 7th Armoured Brigade

Thirty minutes later I spotted a line of pylons I was certain must mark the road. We headed towards them. Fifteen minutes to go and Hamish was speaking.

'I can see the objective.'

'Very good; kick on,' I replied.

And then just before 0750, with pride in his voice, Arthur came up on the air, 'Time 0750 hours. We have Cobalt.'

Ten minutes later the ceasefire came into effect.

Lieutenant Colonel Arthur Denaro
Commanding Officer, Queen's Royal Irish Hussars

We arrived in position by eight o'clock, and I reported to the Commander, then formed a tight perimeter.

Into the centre of all this suddenly trundled the whole of the Brigade. I suppose I was rather sharp and not as polite as I could have been on the air about this, and so I was given a pretty short and sharp response from the Brigadier, which undoubtedly I deserved.

Lieutenant Colonel Mike Vickery
Commanding Officer, 14th/20th King's Hussars,
4th Armoured Brigade

The night before, my adjutant had turned to me and said, 'Colonel, shut the fuck up and go to sleep. I will wake you in three hours' – a direct order from the captain of my tank!

I'd had three hours' kip, which others hadn't. That doesn't mean I wasn't making stupid decisions, but the sleep at least allowed my mind to keep working.

4 Brigade HQ was whipping us on, so I decided to slow down. We moved more steadily that night, and across the Iraq border the next morning.

We stopped at a couple of Iraqi bunkers. They were very well dug in, and having been there rather a long time, had made themselves very comfortable;

a brigade headquarters we entered had beds, chairs, desks, with wriggly tin walls, maps and so on, all underground with sand dunes over the top.

We received the order to stop while we were crossing the Wadi al Batin, then an hour later, the ceasefire. At this actual moment, I looked down from my tank, to see I'd stopped smack in the middle of a minefield.

Sergeant Shaun Rusling
Medic, Parachute Regiment, 32 Field Hospital

Someone came into resus and say they'd stopped advancing and were negotiating. And then it was ENDEX. It was that abrupt.

Lieutenant Colonel Mike Vickery
Commanding Officer, 14th/20th King's Hussars,
4th Armoured Brigade

I started screaming down the radios, ordering people not to get off of their vehicles until they'd very carefully checked where they were, and that I personally was in a minefield. I was very, very worried. I just couldn't countenance anybody dying or being badly injured after the ceasefire, having come through all this without any serious casualties.

We reversed backwards, following our tracks very carefully, then I drove over to the brigade commander's tank, climbed straight on to it, shook his hand, and congratulated him. I also asked him if my confidential report might perhaps now be a little better my having led his brigade all the way through without disasters. He reassured me that all was going to be fine!

The Rt Hon John Major
Prime Minister

The ground war was very successful and mercifully brief. My principal recollection is of the reports coming back. Every casualty is one too many, but to my immense relief, casualties turned out to be infinitely lower than we'd anticipated. We'd over-estimated the strength of the Republican Guard, and hadn't anticipated that they'd withdraw their serious soldiers, leaving children and old men to fight on the front line towards the end of hostilities. It had become what one American commander called a 'turkey shoot', with the most advanced and sophisticated weaponry of American and British forces facing almost defenceless children and others.

The Rt Hon Tom King
UK Secretary of State for Defence

The ground war went better than we could possibly have hoped. The British part of the left hook had run out of fuel. In keeping them going, we'd expended all our supplies. On the fifth morning, we held a War Cabinet meeting. We'd succeeded in accordance with the UN resolution, which was to eject Saddam from Kuwait.

The speed of the land campaign had taken us all by surprise. Nobody had quite got round to asking, 'What do we do when we win?' There was a bit of a gap.

We agreed that we should immediately talk to the Americans; John Major with George Bush, I would speak with Dick Cheney, David Craig with Colin Powell, and Douglas Hurd was in Washington so would speak with Dick Baker. But we all got the same response from their staff – that they were over in the White House in a meeting with the president, and would get back to us when they returned.

This was the meeting where Colin Powell walked in with the photographs of the Mutla Ridge and told George Bush, 'It's really just a turkey shoot now, Mr President.' Somebody else is alleged to have said, 'Well, you could call this the Hundred Hours War – which is a good slogan.' George Bush, like us all, had worried that things could have gone worse with significant casualties, felt a great sense of relief, and decided to stop.

Up until that moment, we'd been kept very closely informed by the Americans, with close consultation in all the decisions. But this one decision was taken solely by them.

Lieutenant Toby Masterton
A Squadron, The Life Guards, 1 Royal Scots Battle Group, 4th Armoured Brigade

After the ceasefire there was a sandstorm and we drove into a belt of mines, reversing gingerly out along our tracks. Later that day, Rupert went over two anti-personnel mines in his 432, which put great shards of metal into his tracks, but he was able to continue. Doyle and I were running along to one side of him in our Land Rover. We felt like John Travolta and Samuel Jackson in the film *Pulp Fiction*, surrounded by whistling bits of metal that peppered and shredded our CARM cover, ripped off our hessian windscreen cover, pinged off the metalwork, but left us amazingly unscathed. We were told to stop for an hour or so – or maybe overnight. Three weeks later we were still there.

Second Lieutenant Alistair Watkins
Grenadier Guards, 3 Royal Regiment of Fusiliers Battle Group, 4th Armoured Brigade

Our company 2ic was an Australian, John Walters, so we were the only vehicle in the Gulf flying an Ozzie flag. At ENDEX, we were inside Iraq, so had to get out very rapidly before anyone accused us of invading.

There were now feelings of anti-climax, 'Is that it?' mixed with all the emotions of losing the nine guys in our battle group. And now nothing else to do except wait to be flown out.

Lance Corporal Roy Sellstrom
Pioneer Corps, Army War Graves Unit

That first day it was fucking barking. The whole of 4th Brigade was spread out with its armoured battle groups in front. We could hear this distinctive rumble which went on for hours – the sort that only armour makes, as the Iraqi Republican Guard were allowed to escape.

Our job was to deal with British bodies plus, rather strangely, the bodies of Allies taken prisoner. But with the huge numbers of Iraqi bodies lying all around, once the other units realised there was a war grave team in the convoy, they started trying to make us deal with these bodies – rather than deal with the problem themselves, which is what they're supposed to do. We couldn't even do our own job – without having to do everybody else's.

CHAPTER 9

HIGHWAY OF DEATH

Over the previous sixty-six hours, 1 (BR) Division had advanced two hundred and ninety kilometres, destroyed three Iraqi armoured divisions, taken seven thousand and twenty-four prisoners including senior commanders, captured more than four thousand vehicles, weapons systems and tanks, and two thousand small arms.

One thousand three hundred Kuwaitis had been killed in the first three days of the Iraqi occupation, and seventeen hundred after that. Two hundred and twenty-three coalition troops had been killed in the ground war, including twenty-five British.

The number of Iraqi soldiers killed was never determined by the Iraq regime. Between ten to twelve thousand are thought to have died in the air campaign, with various reports claiming between ten thousand to twenty-six thousand Iraqi fatalities in the land campaign, and up to seventy-five thousand wounded. The Iraq government said that two thousand three hundred civilians were killed by coalition bombs.

But it was press photographs of the bombing – by American A-10 Warthog ground-attack aircraft – of Iraqi military vehicles escaping north on the road to Basra that had the greatest impression on the public back in the US and other western coalition countries. The media line was of outrage that fleeing Iraqis were being unnecessarily slaughtered in cold blood, prompted by grim photographs of what looked like a massacre of enormous magnitude. This had taken place before the ceasefire, and had a very significant effect on military decision-making.

On 28 February, the Iraqi government would tell the UN that it would comply with all Security Council resolutions. On 3 March, coalition and

Iraqi commanders met and agreed procedures for the release of prisoners of war, to provide information about minefields, and arrangements to prevent future clashes.

British troops assisted the Kuwaitis with their many logistic problems, for which a number of logistic units remained in theatre. On 6 April the Iraqi government agreed to the ceasefire and a UN monitoring force.

The war had lasted forty-two days, and the land war just one hundred hours.

Lieutenant General Walter Boomer
General Officer Commanding, 1 Marine Expeditionary Force, United States Marine Corps

Our aviators had discovered a column of Iraqi army vehicles escaping north on the main Basra road, and began to work on it. I quickly moved up to where that column was, arriving while the engines of most of these vehicles were still running. There were lines of Iraqi combat vehicles, plus stolen civilian cars and trucks as far as the eye could see, loaded with loot stolen from Kuwait.

The Iraqis weren't stupid. Once they'd realised our air had got them focused in, they'd bailed out of the vehicles and run away from the road, and were now escaping on foot to Basra. There was no one there when I arrived.

Some had been hit in the first air attack and hadn't got out in time: for example a military bus full of charred soldiers, which made horrific pictures. This was headlined THE HIGHWAY OF DEATH, with the story that we were bombing the hell out of them even though they were doing what we wanted and leaving. It wasn't even *nearly* that; but a story that was played up in the press all around the world, and made its way even into our own White House, and certainly the Pentagon.

There's a tiny parallel with Vietnam here, over the extent to which the media influenced the decision to stop. They focused on the couple of buses and other vehicles that contained charred Iraqi soldiers, extrapolating that the same thing had happened up and down this column for miles. Which made it a one hell of a good story, complete with horrific pictures.

And having created this story, they created the next story as well, asking, 'Kuwait is liberated. Why aren't you letting these guys go home?'

Major General Alexander Harley
Assistant Chief of Defence Staff (Overseas) and Deputy Director of Joint Operations, Ministry of Defence, Whitehall

Our air photography made us aware of the Mutla Ridge situation well before the media picked it up, restarting the MoD debate about whether we should go further. However, this stopped as soon as the press pictures came in. Then Schwarzkopf very sensibly said he hadn't planned any operations into Iraq, and wasn't going to do it. Fortunately that common sense prevailed, so for us the next stage was securing the borders of Kuwait, tidying up the place and getting the oilfields going again.

Lieutenant General Walter Boomer
General Officer Commanding, 1 Marine Expeditionary Force, United States Marine Corps

By the end of Day Three, I was sitting in north-western Kuwait, with the city liberated, and no more fighting taking place. I gave Schwarzkopf an update, and told him we were poised, ready to move forward towards Basra as ordered.

He said, 'I'll get back to you.'

The next thing I heard over the command channel – not personally from General Schwarzkopf – that it *was* over. We were done. I thought 'OK, that's all right'; I've accomplished the mission, Kuwait is free, citizens out in the streets cheering, Kuwaiti flags broken out. I didn't question it. So we immediately began to plan on how we could get the hell out of there as quickly as the Kuwaitis could be ready to take it over.

But I've been asked a thousand times since, why didn't I just go ahead right then and take Iraq? With hindsight, doing some Monday morning quarter-backing of my own actions, in another three days, Freddie Franks could have finished off the Republican Guard, and we could have policed-up the rest of the Iraqi soldiers in our sector and their armour, relatively quickly. They might perhaps have fought harder defending Iraqi soil – I don't know, but at that point they were pretty demoralised.

It would have been terrific if we could have continued for another three days.

The Rt Hon John Major
Prime Minister

The decision not to go into Baghdad had been discussed and agreed with President Bush. We were both resolute on this point. We'd gone to war under a UN mandate to evict Saddam Hussein from Kuwait, not to go into Baghdad and drag him out by the heels. If we'd given in to pressure to do that, we'd have lost the whole of the Arab coalition and, after going to war to *uphold* international law, we'd have ended the war *breaking* international law.

It would have been a very long time before countries in the Middle East or the wider coalition would have again trusted the word of a British prime minister or an American president. So a ceasefire was agreed, and the war came to a sudden end.

Brigadier Patrick Cordingley
Commander, 7th Armoured Brigade

By 27 February the majority of Iraqi soldiers were already on their way back to Baghdad. By 28 February it was clear that General Schwarzkopf's plan to annihilate the Republican Guard with a left hook through Iraq had failed. So I remain convinced the ceasefire was called at the optimum moment.

In any case we would have had difficulty pushing on to Basra without at least a day's break. We were extremely tired and making mistakes, we had very little water, and no water was available in the immediate area. Our field hospitals were a long way behind us.

Lieutenant Colonel Arthur Denaro
Commanding Officer, Queen's Royal Irish Hussars

As the hours went by, it became clear that the ceasefire was sticking, so we went for a look at some T-55 tanks. Then the divisional headquarters drove through us, and General Rupert Smith got out to have a look as well, so we shook hands and he congratulated us on being the first troops to reach the main highway.

Lieutenant Colonel Charles Rogers
Commanding Officer, Staffordshire Regiment

We arrived at the Basra Road, where I went forward on recce. About three miles away, I found a deserted barracks, then drove to the Mitla Pass. The

Kuwait City ring roads and other roads join on to this road, which then goes through the narrow pass, which we'd heard had been bombed.

I was one of the first people to arrive, to find a lot of vehicles, but very few dead people. Some vehicles had tried to escape from the road but became bogged in, until the pass was blocked and nobody could get through. There were also a lot of Mercedes and other civilian vehicles nicked from Kuwait. It was nothing like the bloodbath subsequently reported by the press.

Brigadier Patrick Cordingley
Commander, 7th Armoured Brigade

We'd stopped some twenty miles north of Kuwait City, the highway strewn with vehicles, bodies and other military wreckage, with black smoke from the oil wells over us. The ceasefire was temporary and uncertain, the lack of sleep dampening any euphoria.

We then received orders from division for our sappers to clear a route through the Mutla Pass, and for the rest of us to bury the Iraqi dead. This was far from the ideal note on which to finish.

Lieutenant Colonel Arthur Denaro
Commanding Officer, Queen's Royal Irish Hussars

By midday the other regiments had arrived. We were then summoned to a brigade orders group. I must admit I was a bit miffed because the brigadier had been rude to me. He was just as miffed about me being rude to him, so instead of a joyous welcome, he and I had another walk in the sand to clear the air. He said I was trying to be too powerful, which I wasn't really; I just wanted to protect my regiment from unexpected attack. I apologised, he apologised; we both almost had a little weep, and shook hands.

I was petrified at the thought of mines and booby-traps, and spent the afternoon shouting at people who were not being disciplined. Corporal Jack very kindly put up my tent in a howling gale – sand blowing everywhere and the darkest, darkest of days, so overcast, almost like Armageddon.

Sandy Gall
ITN television reporter

By the time journalists arrived in Kuwait City, the Iraqis were gone. Nobody had anything terribly exciting to tell us: a nurse claimed to have killed twenty hospitalised Iraqi soldiers by injecting them. I did the story for ITN but I don't know that I believed it.

I stayed in Kuwait City for a week with the ITN team, investigating how the Iraqis had behaved. Anyone suspected of working for the Kuwaiti resistance had been arrested, tortured and killed, with the bodies left outside their relatives' houses to frighten them.

Lieutenant Colonel Charles Rogers
Commanding Officer, Staffordshire Regiment

In the usual way, we did 'area cleaning' of everything around us, which involved a lot of body-burying, clearing of booby traps, dodgy ammunition and huge amounts of weaponry. The vehicles blocking the roads had to be cleared, plus a lot of prisoners to be fed, watered, then sent back. I searched Iraqi bunkers, finding unfinished meals and other signs of hurried withdrawal, untouched by the bombing.

I had one soldier I couldn't account for, so I searched all the way back across the desert by helicopter, trying to find out if he was dead, lost or wounded, eventually discovering he'd been taken back by somebody else. We'd been moving at such a pace, you just didn't know.

Lieutenant Toby Masterton
A Squadron, The Life Guards, 4th Armoured Brigade

Rupert managed to persuade James Hewitt that we should go for a bit of an explore, so we went bumbling off into the desert with his APC's mortar hatches open, through a huge American Army unit, then to where we could see across to the very dramatic sweep of the Kuwait City bay. We were laughing, as it was very exciting to have survived and to be seeing Kuwait City at last. Rupert was videoing the scene when the wind direction changed slightly, bringing the most disgusting smell. This changed our mood like a light being turned off. We drove down to the Mutla Pass road, where American military police told us to fuck off.

Martin Bell
BBC Television

I found myself regretting not having drawn the short straw of covering the amazing scenes at Mutla Pass. Kate Adie was at divisional headquarters and much closer to the satellite truck than me, so she did it. When I drove past the scene, I wondered how on earth I would have presented it. The scene of carnage was the key image of the whole war, and raised all sorts of Nuremberg-trial type questions. I still wonder how I might have covered it.

Brigadier Mike Willcocks
Chief of Staff (Land), Joint War Headquarters, RAF High Wycombe

With the Basra Road secured, our reconnaissance was observing groups of Iraqi military vehicles moving north into the waterways; small packets with three or so tanks, dribbling away from the battlefield, which didn't seem very significant. At this time, the press were hyping up the situation on the Basra road, and so a conscious decision was taken to let them go – not killing for the sake of killing.

But what we didn't realise was that these Iraqi forces weren't just escaping, but had been re-deployed north by Saddam to take the Kurds apart. Their Russian tanks may not have been much of a match for ours, but were lethal against largely unarmed Kurds. With hindsight, this was an error. We should have cut them all off, but we didn't – partly because the slaughter on the Basra highway seemed so awful. These tanks and other Iraqi units were subsequently enough to tip the balance in Saddam's battle with the Kurds.

Sandy Gall
ITN television reporter

Media interest in the 'Fall of Kuwait City' story lasted only twenty-four hours, until the hungry beast wanted something new. Our office wanted to cover the Shia rebellion in Basra, further north in Iraq, where apparently somebody had let all the prisoners out of the jail.

Lieutenant Toby Masterton
A Squadron, The Life Guards, 4th Armoured Brigade

At six in the morning it was still dark. People needed sleep, so assuming our watches were wrong, we stayed in our sleeping bags until mid-morning, seeing trucks driving on full headlights, wondering what was happening. These dark days were often very cold. With the sun completely shielded by burning oil wells, people were quite badly affected. This happened on four or five occasions, when the weather conditions put the smoke in the right direction and there was no wind. There'd be arguments, which instantly erupted into fist fights. The understanding and compromise just went out of everyone.

RSM Johnny Muir
Regimental Sergeant Major, Queen's Royal Irish Hussars

I had two JCBs which we used to dig the graves, making sure they were aligned with Mecca. I remember one body, in a three-quarter prone position, with a very severely damaged right leg. Then I saw he'd been shot through the forehead; whether as an act of mercy before he died, or from incoming fire, I'll never know.

One particular body had no clothing on the lower half, so I got an old blanket to give it some dignity, while the JCB driver had finished digging the grave and I checked the rest of the area. But when I got back, I found a certain officer had removed the blanket, uncovered the body, and was taking photos of it. I was very, very upset about this. I suggested to the officer that if he didn't stop taking photographs and recover the body, I would take an appropriate action. He sneered and laughed at me. So I told him that if he didn't, the appropriate action would be that I would shoot him. He suggested that I might be court-martialled, so I told him to make sure he reported it, as I would definitely be doing that.

Lieutenant Colonel Arthur Denaro
Commanding Officer, Queen's Royal Irish Hussars

This officer was high on my list for an award, having done a really good job throughout. But I now had to change my mind emphatically in the light of this distressing behaviour; which was very sad. How simple life was before, and suddenly how complicated.

Lance Corporal Roy Sellstrom
Pioneer Corps, Army War Graves Unit

On 1 March, we were told to go down to the Basra Road, where Tommy Hulls and his section were cleaning up. Hundreds of cars were crammed into two highways, and the concrete bollard central reservation had T-54 and T-55 tanks, cars and lorries hanging over it. They'd used tanks with dozer blades to clear a lane each way.

We were told to clear the bodies off the main road. Between us and the Americans, we collected no more than one hundred and fifty.

Lieutenant Toby Masterton
A Squadron, The Life Guards, 4th Armoured Brigade

People needed to talk. I was told of tanks doing neutral turns over the top of occupied trenches; people driving through Iraqi positions casually tossing grenades out to either side like fireworks. Whether these stories were apocryphal or not, I couldn't verify, as I'd not been in one of the tanks. But during the fighting I'd been surprised at how the blood got up in some people, and less so in others. Some were really gung-ho; and it was soon clear that others had been very definitely marked by the experiences.

Even during the fighting, there'd been a lot of rumours within the squadron and battle group, about people who'd enjoyed it a bit too much, the rumours straying into war crimes allegations. Not that we really knew what 'war crimes' were. That expression hadn't yet entered my vernacular at that stage of my career and life. These allegations continued afterwards.

There were fist fights, after people said, 'You shouldn't have done that. They'd clearly surrendered,' and younger soldiers saying they weren't going to work with a particular sergeant again because, 'He's an evil bastard – there was no need to have killed those guys.'

These sorts of accusations had been voiced immediately after actions, but also afterwards; but subsequently never got much airtime. It's difficult to know what to do, as you don't want to peddle second-hand rumours. But I heard a lot of these stories first-hand, from people who said, 'I saw so-and-so do this.' and were clearly very exercised by it. Other stories were more like rumours, some involving senior people. We talked a lot about it afterwards, but I've never seen anything come out about it officially.

Brigadier Patrick Cordingley
Commander, 7th Armoured Brigade

After the blue-on-blue when six Fusiliers and three Queen's Own Highlanders were killed by an American A-10, 4th Brigade had problems, but had pulled themselves together and got on with it. But as soon as the fighting was over, both our brigades were inundated with medics, psychologists and psychiatrists, who caused us a lot of problems.

Outsiders coming and telling soldiers what they should be feeling, and so on, was not what they needed; rather their own mates, NCOs, officers – and, of course, the chaplain, who knew them all.

Lance Corporal Roy Sellstrom
Pioneer Corps, Army War Graves Unit

Lieutenant Parry said, 'Let's take a look round Kuwait City.'

We entered through a Kuwaiti resistance checkpoint, where armed resistance guys were shouting at people. Then a couple of vehicles ahead of us, the resistance guy stood back, raised his Kalashnikov and fired into this red car. Someone in our vehicle shouted, 'Load your weapons boys,' so I cocked my rifle. I don't know if they also threw a grenade, but this car was pushed on to the verge and set on fire.

We were waved forward by a guy with less teeth than me, who shouted, 'You OK boys – English. You go chase Iraqis.'

It was wild, with gunfire and the Kuwaiti Resistance executing anyone they thought less than them. People lined up in the streets for water. Some guys in a hotel didn't believe we were British Army, but then made us coffee and showed us round the basement of a health centre next door, which they said had been used as a torture centre. There were shackles on the beds, blood everywhere. They were so pleased to see us they gave us two crates of Heineken beer. It was our first beer for months, which didn't do us any fucking good...

Brigadier Mike Willcocks
Chief of Staff (Land), Joint War Headquarters, RAF High Wycombe

I flew back to Saudi Arabia immediately the land operation ended to organise the recovery of all our forces; then, as a private venture, hitched a lift in a Special Force Hercules from Riyadh to Kuwait. Nobody else was flying at that stage, and the Hercules crew flew so low, it scared the life out of me.

We were the first aircraft to land at Kuwait City international airport. All the houses outside the city had been trashed – an epic of wanton destruction. All the beaches had to be cleared of mines, which the French did later, and everything was booby-trapped. But none of it had been fought over, so it was pure vandalism and looting. We became very worried about the health hazard of the burning oil.

Brigadier Patrick Cordingley
Commander, 7th Armoured Brigade

We'd not thought through the immediate effects of the ceasefire: some soldiers were still spoiling for a fight, others were disturbed by what they'd seen or done. Fortunately the majority were just relieved to be alive and delighted by the result. Then there was the problem of loot – and the understandable desire of soldiers to return home with a souvenir. Putting aside the legal requirements, the danger of collecting the spoils of war is immense, in an area strewn with unexploded mines and bomblets, where deserted bunkers and even some dead bodies were booby-trapped. Our control measures were not popular.

Lance Corporal Roy Sellstrom
Pioneer Corps, Army War Graves Unit

From 1 to 8 March we were burying Iraqi bodies every day, hand-digging holes and throwing them in. At night we came back to 4th Brigade, where nobody wanted to know us. They even asked us to move our tents away, with separate feeding times to everyone else. We felt bad, and if I'd been given an option to leave the army there and then, I'd have gone.

When we arrived at a new position, I let the lads go looking around for a bit, for booby traps, and to see if there was anything interesting. We had a strict rule of not taking wedding rings, watches or anything personal from the bodies. That belonged to them. Cap badges, bayonets and military stuff were fair game. We soon discovered they didn't really have anything.

They also didn't have dog-tag IDs like we do. For torsos without heads, we'd collect ID documents from the pockets, putting them in our own pockets as we didn't have any sandbags, which we'd then put in a big plastic bag and bury – so we were walking round with pockets stuffed with things.

The press turned up when we were working on one position, from *The Times*, *Telegraph* and *Independent*, escorted by a young Coldstream Guards officer. They took photos of our pockets bulging with wallets and stuff. The first question they asked was about this stuff. Their second question was whether we were burying them facing Mecca. The Coldstream Guards officer then told me he didn't like my attitude, which made me burst out laughing:

'Do you really think I'm fucking bothered?'

'Excuse me?'

'Do you really think I'm bothered about what you think of my attitude? Fuck you. Do me, and get me posted out of this fucking horror.'

When we went back to HQ, I reported him to the DCOS, who chewed him out as there were strict orders not to take the press anywhere near us. Later some Coldstream Guardsmen, who were roaming the battlefield collecting Kalashnikovs and anything else they could find, pointed out a group of Iraqis who'd been executed: three were tied up together, shot in the back of the head.

Sandy Gall
ITN television reporter
A British friend took me round Kuwait City. The Sheraton, as other buildings, had been partly burned out. The Iraqis did awful things, which was surprising as they'd regarded Kuwait as a province of Iraq. He took me to what he described as a working palace, 'like Buckingham Palace' quite near the sea. They'd used one of the upper rooms as a lavatory, despite there being lavatories and a perfectly good garden. He thought they'd done it out of disrespect. The throne room had huge mirrors and mosaics, which they'd trashed. Why did they need to behave like this, especially if they considered it to be their property?

The British Consul told me their looting was organised, in three waves: initially the soldiers who took whatever they saw; then more efficient sprees organised by Saddam and Iraqi officials to take special cars, racehorses and precious articles; then criminal gangs, also with official approval, to take away huge quantities of computers, fridges, and so on. I think the Iraqis behaved terribly badly. Now [2009] I feel sorry for the Iraqis. But I liked the Kuwaitis, and felt sorry for them. They'd had a bad time.

RSM Johnny Muir
Regimental Sergeant Major, Queen's Royal Irish Hussars
Two old prisoners stayed with us in battle group headquarters for a couple of days. The oldest was fifty-nine, and told me they'd spent five years on the Iranian front with no option, as if they didn't, their wives and daughters would be raped, their families taken away. When it was time for them to leave, they didn't want to go, and were crying and hugging us. It was so sad, and made me think back to my own family.

Maggi Denaro
Commanding Officer's wife, Queen's Royal Irish Hussars

Once we'd realised there was to be war, days had passed with nothing actually happening, so we'd just waited, becoming calmer about it. Then when it did happen, it was so quick – we held our breaths for forty-eight hours and it was all over. There was no communication from the boys, or from the army. We got to know about what was happening through the news media; but then out of the blue I received a phone call from Arthur saying, 'We're here, we've done it, and it's all over.'

Lance Corporal Roy Sellstrom
Pioneer Corps, Army War Graves Unit

On 3 March Lieutenant Parry was told by 4th Brigade's DCOS to clear a one-kilometre grid square. He asked, 'Where are the bodies?' to be told, 'Iraqi bodies have been reported there. Go and find them.' There were no proper orders, just verbal instructions to 'clear them' – throw them into a hole.

We had to crawl in under the overhead cover of trenches to pull them out – some seeming like they'd melted into their sleeping bags. We found others by following blood or diarrhoea trails; one poor guy had run out of water and had been drinking blood plasma bottles.

With a tank, we'd pull the bodies out, bury them, then put any personal items in a bin bag, walk eighteen paces from the tank and bury it, marking the place by sticking the tank's radio antenna into the ground. But there were too many of them even to bother doing this, so using picks and shovels, we just dug holes and put them in.

Robin Watt
War artist

I visited an abandoned Iraqi tank position, thirty tanks spread in a vast circle, each separated by about six hundred metres. The diameter of the position was about a mile, the farthest tanks appearing as indistinct specks, with the command bunkers in the centre linked by landline.

Tanks had their turrets blown off, while others appeared intact, but on closer inspection their gearboxes or engines had been smashed to tiny fragments. Everywhere was equipment: clothing, small arms, wire, rotting food

– mainly rice, dates and flour – and ammunition, some still in its boxes. There were masses of boots, parkas and coveralls, mostly wrapped in plastic bags. Their abandoned NBC equipment looked very basic: a green rubber cape, very basic-looking respirator and long yellow boots that reached to the knee.

Most bunkers were well constructed with overhead cover of corrugated iron, steel pickets and concrete blocks covered with sandbags. Some had been hit, with everything from coffee pots, cooking oil, mattresses and sandals blown everywhere. A pack of feral dogs moved through swirls of countless pieces of paper.

Lieutenant Colonel Mike Vickery
Commanding Officer, 14th/20th King's Hussars, 4th Armoured Brigade

It was bloody dangerous until the very end; only one hundred hours, but during that time it might have lasted forever, we just didn't know. Each Iraqi position had tanks, with the powerful Republican Guards divisions in reserve – and NBC. The more we cornered the rat, the more likely he was to use it. In *blitzkrieg*, the German Panzer dictum was 'More speed, less blood'. The way of doing things wasn't to hold back, but to get three squadrons up front and smack them. I know from prisoners that we frightened them absolutely, which is why they didn't react. We hit them really hard with overwhelming force, to stop them hitting us back.

RSM Johnny Muir
Regimental Sergeant Major, Queen's Royal Irish Hussars

Clearing the enemy positions was when I knew the soldiers might be stupid; one lot found what they thought a Frisbee, and used it as one – until it exploded. Tiredness was mixed with elation and relief. I ordered squadrons to keep a tight rein while we cleared this brigade position, which had a lot of underground bunkers. But I couldn't do it all myself, so had to trust others to be careful, not take risks and ensure others were careful too. Maybe I was being over-cautious and too controlling, but this 'making safe' phase was very dangerous indeed.

Major David Potts
SO2 Army Logistics, Quartermaster General's Department, Whitehall

From our gilded-ivory MoD tower, getting the troops back was easy. We went on to the Baltic Exchange, hired the ships, which sailed to the Gulf and brought things back – pretty smooth. Egypt had been very anti at the beginning, but came round, so using the Suez Canal wasn't a problem in the end.

But out there on the ground, it was an absolutely monumental task. Apart from everything else, we'd shipped out over a billion quid's worth of ammunition, so the stuff that hadn't been fired was going to have to be reconditioned, packed up, then brought back safely.

Lance Corporal Roy Sellstrom
Pioneer Corps, Army War Graves Unit

We came to an obliterated Iraqi field hospital beside the road, with big red crescent markings, but bodies all over the place – the nightmare scenario once again; arms, legs, heads and stuff all over the place. We pulled out the bodies by hand into large mounds all over the position – twenty on each.

It was weird how after explosions, one bloke would be totally naked with his clothes blown off, others with boots missing, yet others dressed and seeming unaffected. The ground was shallow sand with bedrock a foot or so down, so we asked for engineer plant to help us. But the diggers could only get down a metre, so we put them in, then tipped sand over the top. There was no marking as we had no GPS. It was all we could do.

Sergeant Shaun Rusling
Medic, Parachute Regiment, 32 Field Hospital

Despite the ending of fighting, nothing much changed at the field hospital. Horrendous battle casualties continued coming in, slowly reducing to clumps of twos and threes that hadn't been collected earlier. But we still remained busy with all the stupid accidents that take place in vehicles, aircraft and so on. We were operational until 10 March. Then everything was burned.

Lance Corporal Roy Sellstrom
Pioneer Corps, Army War Graves Unit

An American graves registration unit arrived and offered to help us. They said they had an Iraqi *Imam*, so we suggested he do a service. They dragged this bloke out – like a dog, as he was wearing chains round his ankles and handcuffs, shaking himself. They had a debate about whether they should remove the handcuffs.

There were two tanks-worth – seven or eight blokes, judging from all the bits. We put them into proper American body bags, then the Americans produced a compass and said we had to bury them facing Mecca. We didn't even have a compass.

Robin Watt
War artist

We did PT with Captain Tony Hood's troop, playing rugger, using a rock as the ball and a sand berm as the touchline. One soldier gashed his head on a boulder while scoring a try.

Brigadier Mike Willcocks
Chief of Staff (Land), Joint War Headquarters, RAF High Wycombe

The SAS went to our embassy in Kuwait City, which they thought had been booby-trapped, so they stood well back, blew the door off, then cleared it. The American Special Forces guys watched all this, then flew to their embassy by helicopter, abseiled down from the roof, but used so much explosive the entire roof blew off, leaving their embassy completely unusable.

RSM Johnny Muir
Regimental Sergeant Major, Queen's Royal Irish Hussars

I was waiting beside a bunker that was to be cleared by a Royal Engineer bomb team, when a sergeant major and couple of his men came out, in disobedience of my instructions. He'd been leading junior men into danger. I considered arresting and reducing him to the ranks. However, deciding I didn't want to ruin a career, we had a one-to-one; he knew I wasn't pleased. As warrant officers, we lead by example, which cascades right down to the rank and file. When soldiers lower their standards, the outcome can be quite drastic, especially under these circumstances.

The Rt Hon John Major
Prime Minister

Soon after the war was over, I flew to Kuwait. The sky was black and thick with smoke after the Iraqis had set fire to the Kuwaiti oil wells. There was no difference between the middle of the day and the middle of the night. As I flew over the desert in a helicopter, it was a dark and forbidding sight.

Quite apart from the enormous ecological damage caused by the Iraqis' destruction of the oil wells, Kuwait City itself was in a terrible state. One wondered, on seeing the wreckage, how long it would take to rebuild the homes and lives of so many.

RSM Johnny Muir
Regimental Sergeant Major, Queen's Royal Irish Hussars

Above ground, there was a lot of war debris – artillery pieces, tanks, guns and so on. One of our checking teams drove back to battle group headquarters in a Russian tank, which was quite funny, but worried me. Putting people's lives at risk for something that doesn't need to be done just wasn't sensible – or funny. It could have been booby-trapped then exploded. But maybe I was over-cautious.

Brigadier Mike Willcocks
Chief of Staff (Land), Joint War Headquarters, RAF High Wycombe

On returning to High Wycombe, I desperately needed a low-satellite pass across all the oilfields the Iraqis had set alight, so we could get a handle on which wellheads were burning. JARIC [Joint Air Reconnaissance Intelligence Centre] asked me whether the imagery I wanted was actually that important.

I said, 'Of course it bloody well is! Why are you asking?'

They replied, 'Well we've been waiting for the last three years to get our offices redecorated. The painters have just arrived, and if we have to do this job for you, we'll have to stop them working. Could you delay your request for twenty-four hours, please, until they finish?'

RSM Johnny Muir
Regimental Sergeant Major, Queen's Royal Irish Hussars

An Iraqi brigade headquarters position was amazing; bunkers reinforced with building blocks, and senior officers' areas containing three-piece suites, beds, mattresses, chairs and kitchenettes. They'd been very industrious, and had gone in a huge hurry, so it was all as they'd left it. But these Iraqi officers were quite vain. I found for example little manicure sets, with scissors for nasal hair, and moustache dye. My memories of all those little details will stay with me for the rest of my life.

Brigadier Mike Willcocks
Chief of Staff (Land), Joint War Headquarters, RAF High Wycombe

Paddy Hine called me in to ask if the people in the bunker should be given medals. I said, 'Oh yes certainly, Joint Commander. I came in the other day. Bloody icy on the steps and I very nearly injured myself.' He said, 'OK, I've got your message.'

In fact I felt a bit guilty about this, as they'd all been working double shifts for months, with no windows or fresh air; and then they gave medals to people in Cyprus.

Lieutenant Colonel Arthur Denaro
Commanding Officer, Queen's Royal Irish Hussars

Honours and Awards are so difficult. How hard we worked to try to make it fair; Patrick was brilliant as he knew all about it, but at the next level up, all our best-laid plans were thrown out of the window when only one or two were picked. I'd put in one of my attached 17th/21st Lancer troop leaders for an MID, and I really regret he didn't get it – but we only got two MIDs in the whole regiment.

Group Captain Glenn Torpy
Officer Commanding, 13 Squadron, Royal Air Force

Once the ground offensive kicked off, we didn't do much flying. My last flight was on the 28th, so we became bored and keen to go home. So we sat around for a while, and I wrote a lot of medal citations. We weren't very experienced in this. A lot more people deserved awards than got them. For example, I ended up with a DFC, but my back-seater didn't get anything, which I didn't think was right.

Brigadier Mike Willcocks
Chief of Staff (Land), Joint War Headquarters, RAF High Wycombe

I was on top of the whole honours and awards process. We set deadlines for people to submit their lists of names and citations for honours and awards.

The MoD decided there'd only be one DSO awarded, and a limited ration of other awards. I felt rather bad at having done the classic army thing of pooh-poohing the bunker awards, when people in Cyprus were awarded them. The citations came through us, then with Commander-in-Chief's recommendations, went on up to MoD.

Lieutenant Colonel Mike Vickery
Commanding Officer, 14th/20th King's Hussars, 4th Armoured Brigade

I put one of my REME corporals in for a Military Medal after he'd come unbidden to the front line and repaired Richard Shirreff's TOGS while under fire.

We later discovered that 7 Brigade had got all the commanding officers together to consolidate a brigade bid for awards, the DCOS then sitting with each, helping him write the citations. They did the same amount of business as we did and got lots of awards... whereas with 4 Brigades' list not having been properly collated, when it reached divisional headquarters, it would have looked so much less sensible than 7 Brigade's, so our bunch of goodies was considerably less than anybody else's.

Lieutenant Colonel Charles Rogers
Commanding Officer, Staffordshire Regiment

Writing the medal citations was fighting the real war... when those with the fine pens won *their* battles. It got very political, and you start thinking maybe you were letting your own boys down and should have written yours up a bit stronger. I really didn't like it. Then we heard that RAF ski instructors in Cyprus were being put up for awards because they happened to be where aircraft were flying to and from Saudi.

I also wrote lots of letters to the families of the men who'd been killed and injured.

RSM Johnny Muir
Regimental Sergeant Major, Queen's Royal Irish Hussars

Once the battle areas were cleared, we regrouped at battle group HQ, cleaning up our equipment, and working out how to de-bomb the tanks, which would be left behind. St Patrick's Day was approaching, and we'd been sent the traditional shamrocks. However, Customs thought they were illegal recreational plants and they were impounded.

Brigadier Patrick Cordingley
Commander, 7th Armoured Brigade

Two Huey helicopters suddenly arrived in the middle of my headquarters, and out stepped Major General Mike Myatt of the 1st US Marine Division, who'd spent hours searching for us. His visiting us demonstrated what had been so special in the relationship between his marines and my brigade.

Lieutenant Toby Masterton
A Squadron, The Life Guards, 4th Armoured Brigade

We heard a loud bang from half a kilometre way, near one of the Royal Scots sub-units. I thought it was a mine – a crump sound. Everyone knew instinctively that someone had been hurt. Our ambulance got caught in its cam net as it tried to reverse out, as was the squadron corporal major's pristine new Land Rover. But my ridiculous 'bush' wasn't, so I grabbed Jock, the medic who'd shaved my head earlier, and shot across to the Royal Scots.

At the Royal Scots, some really, really young Toms were looking ashen-white, crying and shaking. A couple of older-looking soldiers had their arms round them, comforting them. I remember feeling strangely proud that they should be doing this. We asked, 'Where's the casualty?' but got no answers from these stunned-looking people. Eventually one of them said, 'Over there, sir, around the corner.'

A commotion of dust and smoke was still hanging in the air, which seemed ridiculous five minutes after the explosion. Twenty metres around the other side of a Warrior, a young guy was lying against the tracks. Allegedly, he'd been doing something with his webbing, trying to clean it or sort it out, when suddenly 'Bang' and he'd flown through the air. Later stories went round that he'd been doing something with a CLAW grenade

Jock knelt down in the sand beside him, and I went round to the top end. You could recognise his boots and trousers from the waist downwards, but there wasn't much left of his face, and he was smouldering.

The guy was moving around and twitching, and we were touching him – you want to clasp him to you and say, 'It's OK, mate.' Jock and I then had a flaming row as we couldn't work out what to do.

I said, 'Fucking give him some morphine,' which was ridiculous as he'd got a serious head wound. Jock shouted back, 'Where should I fucking put it?' Then I seem to remember an NCO arriving and getting incredibly upset, running around screaming and shouting, pointing his rifle at everyone, upset and shocked. He was calmed down and the rifle taken off him.

Then a full colonel in the Army Medical Corps arrived, and I asked him, 'Is he alive? Could we have done anything for him?' He said, 'No. He won't know anything. This is just a body going through its final thing. You've done all you can. There's nothing you could have done about it. Thank you for what you've done. The soldiers say you were very reassuring,' a stream of nice words to make us feel better.

We walked back to my Land Rover and sat there, without turning on the engine.

I turned to Jock and said, 'I don't feel sick or disgusted or traumatised… I just feel absolutely FANTASTIC.' Jock turned to me and said, 'I feel the same way.'

This was a bizarre emotion; light-headedness, elation. Bizarre…

Lance Corporal Roy Sellstrom
Pioneer Corps, Army War Graves Unit

We were really down in the dumps. All the things I believed about the army and the armed forces had gone as the result of doing this fucking horrible job. Although inside our team we still had respect and discipline, for anyone outside, it had completely gone. We weren't taking orders, and didn't care two fucks for anyone outside the team. What could anyone do to us that could be worse than what we were doing now?

We got back in that afternoon about four pm, then heard this huge explosion. We thought 'Oh fuck… there's another one.' We were now so used to death we couldn't take anything seriously. Ten minutes later we were told to send a team to the Royal Scots, to pick up the body. Me, Dave Bagley and Lieutenant Parry jumped in the vehicle, and drove the couple of hundred metres.

All the Royal Scots Warriors were deserted, battened down. Somebody shouted that we were in a minefield, so we walked in along the tracks made by the Warriors towards a huge black cloud. For some reason in the desert, clouds linger.

My immediate thought was 'Why have they got a black bloke in a Scottish regiment?' His hair was all curled up, his body black with burning, giving off small puffs of smoke. I asked for a jerrycan of water, and we lifted him up on to a six-foot table.

He was wearing NBC trousers and boots, untouched from waist downwards. The Warrior's camouflage nets were still burning. The Quartermaster arrived and said, 'We think it was a mine.'

I reckoned this was bollocks, and while we were waiting for the water, I said to Lieutenant Parry, 'You know, sir, I think he's been hit by something – probably something like a CLAW grenade launcher.' By all accounts the infantry had problems with the CLAW. Maybe he'd been trying to service it or something. We poured water over him. Then this huge Scottish lad turned up and said, 'That was my mate. Can I give him some stuff?' I said, 'Go and talk to him if you want.'

I wasn't taking the piss. I actually really did mean 'Go and talk to your mate'. It was his fucking friend. He said, 'We've been told to stay in our vehicles, but he's my best mate. Can I really go and talk to him?'

'He's your mate, so you go and speak to him, but he's not a sight you're going to like.'

He went over and had a chat, then asked if he could bring him some stuff. I said 'Yes', and he returned with a copy of *Follow Me*, the Rangers Football Club magazine, which we put into his trousers side pocket. 'He'd like that,' the big guy said. We then zipped him up, put him into our vehicle and took him off.

Lieutenant Toby Masterton
A Squadron, The Life Guards, 4th Armoured Brigade

We got back to the squadron and told James and the other officers what had happened. Immediately, everyone was ordered on to the vehicles and to stay there – even though we couldn't see a single mine.

Jock went off to brief the junior soldiers, and I was told later that exactly the same happened to him. As I was talking to everybody, they said my face seemed to crumple. All I could feel was a stinging sensation, and instantly I fell into uncontrollable sobbing. Rupert grabbed me and threw me under his 432, where we'd dug out a little underground gym, telling me to stay there until I'd sorted myself out – which was the right thing to do.

I fell apart. I couldn't understand why I couldn't control this. My face felt like it was made of rubber. Then, after fifteen minutes or so it quietened down and stopped. As I came out, having put it all into the sand, I felt so incredibly relieved. I stood beside Rupert, who'd been standing looking away, but listening as I did what I needed to do. I'd been aware of some of the boys coming up to him and asking, 'What's happening with Mister M?' and Rupert saying to them, 'It's fine. Thanks for your concern, but he'll be fine.' We looked at each other and didn't say anything – that was it – it was done.

Jock, who's a shaven-headed, tattooed-to-fuck, toothless Glaswegian medic who's seen a lot of things, was halfway through explaining to the boys when the same thing hit him. He'd crawled underneath his armoured ambulance, curled up like a foetus and bawled his eyes out for fifteen minutes. It was probably very therapeutic for us to have had this reaction then, rather than later.

Brigadier Mike Willcocks
Chief of Staff (Land), Joint War Headquarters, RAF High Wycombe

As of 8 March, we'd lost thirty-two people dead, of which sixteen were killed in action, nine of which were from blue-on-blue incidents: one on a mine, two in the 16th/5th vehicles, one truck accident, three Special Forces and five aircrewmen missing in action – who were later returned as prisoners. Five died before the war started, and eleven in accidents. We had six infantry battalions [almost four thousand men] ready as battle casualty replacements. We destroyed the army's medical services in that Gulf War, but learned nothing – as there'd been virtually no casualties.

Lieutenant Colonel Charles Rogers
Commanding Officer, Staffordshire Regiment

No sooner had the war finished, than immediately a whole lot of silliness crept in: counting the compasses, demanding to know where everything had got to, the quartermasters insisting kit be handed back in – all the boring administration which soldiers don't particularly like. I'd lost my compass somewhere…

Major General Alexander Harley
Assistant Chief of Defence Staff (Overseas) and Deputy Director of Joint Operations, Ministry of Defence, Whitehall

The surrender was set up by Schwarzkopf and his generals, but all that time the debate about whether we should continue fighting still rumbled on, before everybody realised that Schwarzkopf's refusal to continue was right. The surrender parley was general-to-general.

Lieutenant General Walter Boomer
General Officer Commanding, 1 Marine Expeditionary Force,
United States Marine Corps
I wasn't involved with the peace negotiations. I've never talked about the war with General Schwarzkopf, but I've always wondered why those negotiations weren't handled by the state department. We have skilled negotiators, who could have been parachuted in, so to speak, to assist. I still don't understand why they told Schwarzkopf to negotiate it.

The Rt Hon Tom King
UK Secretary of State for Defence
What followed were the less-than-satisfactory ceasefire negotiations at Safwan, with Norman Schwarzkopf, Saudi Joint Commander Prince Khalid and Peter de la Billiere. They hadn't been given an agreed brief on this, which led to the unfortunate decision to allow Saddam to continue to fly helicopters, which became of considerable significance later on.

The Rt Hon John Major
Prime Minister
Britain and America were keen to impose the no-fly zone but, morally, I would have found it very difficult to have denied Saddam the use of helicopters in support of his people on humanitarian grounds. Iraq had an extremely difficult humanitarian problem: we had comprehensively destroyed his military, and did not wish to be repressive to the people of Iraq. We did not believe Saddam would survive in office, and there was therefore an air of magnanimity in the peace negotiations.

The Rt Hon Tom King
UK Secretary of State for Defence
The failure to deny Saddam use of helicopters then combined with a statement by George Bush that the future of Saddam Hussein was 'up to the Saudi people', which was taken by Iraq's Shia to indicate American encouragement to rise up against Saddam with coalition support – which wasn't an accurate

interpretation of what the president had meant. The ensuing uprising led to very severe loss of life on the Shia side, in which those extra Republican Guards divisions proved a critical factor in Saddam's survival.

My not-very-helpful view is that we would have been justified under the UN resolutions in continuing to advance for another twenty-four hours or so, to ensure not only the liberation of Kuwait but its continued future security. We should have done this, and this was a mistake.

Brigadier Mike Willcocks
Chief of Staff (Land), Joint War Headquarters, RAF High Wycombe

The actual reason for our not pushing on into Iraq was that the very clear strategic and political objective of the Foreign Office and Prime Minister was to keep Saddam Hussein in post. He was considered the lesser of two evils, compared to the Iranian Shiite threat.

The official objectives for the next stage of the campaign against Saddam were listed formally on 5 March 1991, having been very clearly understood very much earlier than that:

The Abandonment of Aggressive Foreign Policy;

Restore Law and Order;

Presume the Ba'ath party will Stay in Place;

International Rehabilitation;

Economic Recovery.

The Kurds' aspirations for a Kurdish state had been greatly encouraged by the Gulf War and Saddam's crushing defeat. I'm pretty convinced that US pressure led the Kurds to think they could overthrow Saddam. We weren't involved in this 'encouragement', which I suspect was probably largely American 'Black Op' operations – although possibly the Foreign Office might have been involved.

After the Marsh Arabs and Kurds revolt, there was to be an awful bloodbath inside Iraq, which was made possible by two key decisions: allowing Iraqi forces to escape from the 'Basra Pocket'; and the 'You Fly, You Die' rules of engagement not being enforced against Iraqi helicopters.

These two decisions enabled Saddam to survive – which was British government policy, from before the crisis, and reiterated in the government objectives listed on 5 March 1991: that the Ba'ath party was presumed to remain in power, with the next objective being the international rehabilitation of Iraq.

The Rt Hon John Major
Prime Minister

I know of no one, in the immediate aftermath of the war, who thought it remotely likely that Saddam Hussein would survive in power.

Stringent conditions were to be set by the international community with regard to sanctions, but these proved to be very leaky. We – and the Americans – were hugely frustrated by the weakness of much of the international community in observing sanctions to which they had solemnly agreed. It was a poor performance, and did much to prop up Saddam Hussein and his hideous regime.

Hashim Ali
Iraq freedom fighter

I remember very well the call of President Bush senior for the Iraqi people to rise up against Saddam's dictatorship. I remember the misery of the Kurdish people, and the people in the south. Fourteen of the eighteen district governorates rose up. This was the voice of the people – a sort of democracy really – the right of the people to be supported. Of course, many of those uprising people were not angels. There were a lot of atrocities and scoring back on the people who had initiated the problems.

Lieutenant General Walter Boomer
General Officer Commanding, 1 Marine Expeditionary Force, United States Marine Corps

In retrospect, another three or four days, with his army finished, might perhaps have been enough to topple the entire Saddam Hussein regime – perhaps. But it didn't happen, and I was never critical of that. But we'd left Saddam enough forces to be able to put down the uprising in Basra with great brutality, to remain in power and control that kind of uprising.

The Rt Hon Tom King
UK Secretary of State for Defence

Subsequently, a certain myth has developed; that we should have gone all the way to Baghdad, which would have obviated the need for the Iraq invasion and the current war in Iraq, and was a bad tactical mistake. Some quite surprising people who hadn't been in favour of the original campaign became supporters of that argument.

RSM Johnny Muir
Regimental Sergeant Major, Queen's Royal Irish Hussars

Civilian vehicles were starting to come back south along the Basra Road from Iraq, Kuwaitis returning home. As we prepared the tanks for going home, some of them stopped and came over to shake our hands, saying 'Thank you for giving us back our country'. This gave a nice feeling, which in some ways justified it.

We de-bombed back at Al Jabayl, where it could all be reconditioned back into storage.

Lance Corporal Roy Sellstrom
Pioneer Corps, Army War Graves Unit

On 8 March we married up with the other war grave teams, then drove back to Al Jubayl.

The atmosphere in our unit was terrible. I found out that some of the others had been taking jewellery. There were lots of arguments, and people I didn't speak to after that. I had a constant headache like someone was driving a nail into my brain, tears running down my face, and I was dead inside – no emotions. I'd been in a war, seen people killed, but now I could go out and buy a burger… and my unit was near to mutiny. I went sick at the med station; sitting there crying that I couldn't do the job any more. The doctor major referred me to the forward psychiatric unit.

Brigadier Mike Willcocks
Chief of Staff (Land), Joint War Headquarters, RAF High Wycombe

Brigadier Rob McAvie, our man in the air headquarters in Riyadh, told us that the aircrew needed to be got out rapidly: 'They're full of self-confidence, battle-proven but there's nowhere for them to train or go on R&R, and they need amenities like telephones. The G3 [operational planners] are now wound down, and the G2 [air intelligence] are licking their wounds after not having got it right. They had wildly over-estimated [the effects of the bombing] and had made predictions based their own philosophy. The spooks have collected a lot of kit.'

Lance Corporal Roy Sellstrom
Pioneer Corps, Army War Graves Unit

Around 11 March, the Americans had collected the bodies of the SAS guys

323

from Bravo Two Zero and the RAF pilots who'd crashed, from inside Iraq. When our chain of command told us we had to process these bodies, a lot of people refused, so in the end, me, Tommy Hulls and a couple of others, agreed to do it. I wasn't well, but the job had to be done.

These bodies were fucking stinking. The pilots had been sitting in planes – some since 17 January, out in the desert, baking under the canopies, some eaten by animals, and one had a huge head that had inflated somehow. Our job was to clean them up as best we could, put them into clean body bags, then into a zinc-lined coffin which was welded shut, then into a transit coffin which is what you see when they're brought back to the UK.

We brought in welders from the Royal Navy, Royal Engineers and REME. The last airlift we did had twelve guys on board, and when the welders were brought in, nobody'd told them what they'd be welding. Lying about it made an unpleasant job even worse. When we admitted what it was, they'd flip up their helmets and do it, then leave as fast as possible. We had to let the air out of the bags just before the lid went on, which smelled terrible. You could see them like they were on tilt – on the very edge of collapsing through nausea.

Squadron Leader Phil Smith
Royal Air Force

It was fairly certain to us all some of the crews we'd lost were dead, but until the prisoners were returned, nobody could be certain. Seeing those who'd survived was like them returning from the dead. The bodies were flown back home, the funerals taking place during leave.

I still get very emotional about it, even now; certain music from those times still chokes me up. The funerals were like normal squadron funerals after peacetime training accidents, really powerful.

Brigadier Patrick Cordingley
Commander, 7th Armoured Brigade

The prime minister on his visit had impressed everyone by promising it would not be long before we went home. General Peter de la Billiere had been more realistic, causing consternation. But by 8 March, much quicker than expected, the recovery plan was issued and morale soared. The tanks were transported to Al Jubayl and the soldiers started to fly out on the 11th.

Six days later, on Sunday 17 March, St Patrick's Day, I returned to Germany with the Irish Hussars.

Lieutenant Colonel Charles Rogers
Commanding Officer, Staffordshire Regiment

The only time Arthur Denaro and I fell out was over which unit should go home first. Arthur insisted the Irish Hussars should go home first, in time for St Patrick's Day. I disagreed, as we'd lost men killed and wounded, and I could see my families being pretty unimpressed with us poor infantry in amongst the smart cavalry, not getting a fair deal. In fact, in a judgement worthy of Solomon, Patrick Cordingley decided that the Scots Dragoon Guards would go back first.

Lieutenant Colonel Arthur Denaro
Commanding Officer, Queen's Royal Irish Hussars

A good, good day – as we learned the date we fly out. Charles Rogers came over in the afternoon and we made up!

Brigadier Mike Willcocks
Chief of Staff (Land), Joint War Headquarters, RAF High Wycombe

Some of the people had been out in the desert a long time, and there was no question of their remaining to garrison the place or anything like that. They invariably asked me, 'How soon are you going to get us home?' – with a pause, and then 'Sir'.

We started repatriating on R-Day, and got all forty-five thousand guys back by R+35. Getting the kit back, however, took months. A giant black American sergeant guarding a huge park of Iraqi tanks offered me a T-72 for my beret. I imagined myself coming home hatless, but with my own tank… tempting.

Group Captain Glenn Torpy
Officer Commanding, 13 Squadron, Royal Air Force

Mine was the last four-ship to leave Dhahran, when our second tanker went unserviceable. We were bringing everything back, the aircraft loaded with four tanks and Sidewinder missiles. Working out all the fuel and headwinds, we reckoned we should just be able to make Cyprus in one go, so I opted for a change of scenery. Having a night in Cyprus provided a good break, and we flew on to Honnington the next day, 9 March, landing about nine pm. The station commander welcomed us back in his DJ from a dinner party.

Getting home was very nice – but an anti-climax. Everybody went on leave for a couple of weeks, and I was keen to get back to work by the end of it. I was very lucky as a squadron commander, as we didn't lose anybody, nor did we have any domestic problems – so it was pretty boring in that respect, which is how one wants it to be!

I was worried about the guys flashing around the UK at a hundred feet. In fact they'd had more than enough excitement, and slotted back into life back at home with remarkable ease, and a lot more experience under their belts.

Lieutenant Colonel Charles Rogers
Commanding Officer, Staffordshire Regiment

While our vehicles were parked up in Al Jubayl port ready for shipping back to UK, they were broken into and kit stolen, probably by the British soldiers guarding the park. I hate to say that, but there was no one else there. This left a very sour note.

Lance Corporal Roy Sellstrom
Pioneer Corps, Army War Graves Unit

The psychiatric unit laid on a group session. I found this really difficult and embarrassing, with Lieutenant Parry, Sergeant Robson and all the others sitting there, with me an NCO, crying and feeling so weak. I then booked an individual session with the psychiatrist I'd seen, Major Gilham, but when I turned up was told he'd gone back to UK.

I told our Staff Sergeant I couldn't do this job any more, but he told me, from the powers that be back in UK, I could either stay out here and carry on, or go straight back to Northern Ireland – no going back to Northampton or seeing a psychiatrist. Lieutenant Parry told me not to worry as he'd sort it out back in UK. I wasn't fit enough to be in the army, let alone Northern Ireland.

Lieutenant Colonel Mike Vickery
Commanding Officer, 14th/20th King's Hussars,
4th Armoured Brigade

After 7 Brigade left, we remained for over three weeks. This was a really bad time for the soldiers and for me, listening to news reports of Saddam Hussein taking revenge on the Marsh Arabs, and the Kurds in the north. They were spitting mad, wanting to go to Baghdad and duff Saddam up. We'd done the job, and yet the madman was still abusing his people.

We thought maybe the politicians had said to all the anti-Saddam people, if you rise up then we'll support you, but then didn't... we were pretty disgusted with ourselves, and our government. So, despite having a won a war in double-quick time, all the shiny whoopee we'd felt initially disappeared.

Brigadier Mike Willcocks
Chief of Staff (Land), Joint War Headquarters, RAF High Wycombe

General Schwarzkopf was concerned at the speed of the British withdrawal from theatre, so we had to agree to leave a battle group out there. We also had to work out what to do with the Iraqi equipment: tanks, complete weapon and communication systems; how much to bring back to UK, and where it would go. The political imperative was to get everything back as fast as possible.

Sergeant Shaun Rusling
Medic, Parachute Regiment, 32 Field Hospital

By the time the field hospital was burned, there was a sense of anticlimax, and a strong desire to get out of there. We waited there for a week or so, before a coach to Dhahran for flights back to good old South Cerney.

We were met at three in the morning by some brigadier who said that nobody was allowed to go home in uniform. We had visions of being issued with some sort of demob suits, as all our civvies were back in Plymouth. But no... we were given navy-blue acrylic British Home Stores tracksuits with white and red stripes, and no shoes. So there we were, one hundred and twenty of us shivering in the darkness and cold of the station platform, wearing big boots, with no hair and the best tans you could wish for. It was completely obvious who we were and where we'd been. If the IRA wanted to blow us up, we were a totally obvious target. A ripple of laughter went down the platform as we realised this.

RSM Johnny Muir
Regimental Sergeant Major, Queen's Royal Irish Hussars

The cabin staff served alcohol, which after five months, had an immediate effect. I had a quiet word with the senior cabin steward. She wasn't in the military, and politely questioned who did I think I was. After a twenty-second briefing on British Army rank structure, I told her the guys' families were waiting at Hannover along with the press, and two hundred drunken soldiers would not be appreciated. Copious amounts of coffee and sandwiches were served for the rest of the flight.

As the Tri-Star touched down, I remembered the commitment I'd made to that staff sergeant and his family. We'd had some injuries, but I'd got them all back home. That was very important to me.

Lieutenant Colonel Charles Rogers
Commanding Officer, Staffordshire Regiment

The staggeringly good-looking stewardesses on our Lufthansa jumbo opened the bar. Soldiers just never seem to lose it. I was upstairs with the RSM, but could see soldiers wearing stewardess's uniforms; one chap was even in with the pilots, helping fly the plane. I told the RSM we couldn't have drunken chaps rocking off the plane at the other end, so please could he do something about it?

So there came an announcement from the flight deck, that we were flying across Turkey, a strict Muslim country, so the bar was to be shut. Luckily most were asleep by that time, and only one soldier was still drunk by the time we arrived. We slipped him off from the other side of the aircraft after everybody else had disembarked.

RSM Johnny Muir
Regimental Sergeant Major, Queen's Royal Irish Hussars

A British Frontier Force Customs officer was waiting at Hannover Airport – a former Irish Hussar warrant officer, Terry Hurst, who waved us through. The Commanding Officer gave interviews to the press. Coaches took us to Fallingbostel, driving past the most incredibly green fields with budding trees and beautiful sunshine.

I started to have doubts about meeting my family. How will they find me? Had we changed? Like everybody else, I'd lost two stones, which wasn't a bad thing. Travelling those last few kilometres, I suddenly felt dirty. We hadn't had a proper wash for months, and our uniforms were worn and dirty too. I felt uncomfortable.

Sergeant Shaun Rusling
Medic, Parachute Regiment

I was met at Hull station by my family. They'd a party organised, with more family; they're all ex-military or police, nurses… But although I was grateful to them for being there for me, I didn't feel comfortable with it. I was pretty much exhausted, and sort of lost, unable to cope with the calm of it.

Lieutenant Colonel Mike Vickery
Commanding Officer, 14th/20th King's Hussars,
4th Armoured Brigade

The Quartermaster brought up big tents, and ran central cooking with fresh vegetables every day. Parcels and letters arrived. We had vehicles, instructors and bugger-all to do all day, so we trained the drivers as gunners, and both as signallers, which helps them with promotion. We ran a village fete with slippery pole competitions; then were given the task of surveying the battlefield out in front, to bring in Iraqi vehicles and report ammunition and fuel stores.

Enormous amounts of ammunition needed to be got rid of, blowing it up in huge piles. We took T-55 tanks and lots of ammunition, blocked off a piece of desert and had a gunnery camp, ending with shooting at the Iraqi tanks. Anybody who came visiting us got a go in an Iraqi tank, including the American Army Chief Rabbi, our Chaplain General, the Prime Minister, the Chief of the General Staff and so on.

RSM Johnny Muir
Regimental Sergeant Major, Queen's Royal Irish Hussars

At Fallingbostel, everyone was waiting for us, including the guys who'd already returned. I was last off the last bus, and with all the hugging and greeting going on, couldn't find my wife and daughter. So I put my RSM voice to good use and asked if anybody wanted to hug and love *me*!

Entering the house with my wife and daughter felt very uncomfortable. I'd not lived in an enclosed environment for a long time; all we'd touched was sand, oily vehicles and weapons. For quite a few days I preferred to be in the garden. But I'd also to get used to my family, who I love very much. I could detect a special bond between them, and all of a sudden here was I, a third person breaking this bond. Rona was fifteen-and-a-half and had become very close to her mother. Being that age can be very difficult, but she was very courteous to me. It must have been very difficult for them. We had a week sorting things out in Fallingbostel before going on extended leave, which gave us time to get used to being back together.

Major General Alexander Harley
Assistant Chief of Defence Staff (Overseas) and Deputy Director of Joint Operations, Ministry of Defence, Whitehall

The air campaign against Iraq had to continue, as did the intelligence operation so we could monitor the insurrections in Basra and subsequent events inside Iraq – a lot of killing. Then we had to set up a UN inspection regime.

We decided to over-fly Iraq every day, a serious operation which the Iraqis would challenge, using their SAMs. Everything from helicopters upwards were to be taken out: fast-jet bases, airfields and other related targets, with four squadrons flying all the time. The Americans, French and ourselves committed an enormous amount of aircraft, including U2 spyplanes, to impose southern and northern no-fly zones.

The Rt Hon Tom King
UK Secretary of State for Defence

We established no-fly zones over Iraq, firstly in the south and then in the north for Operation Provide Comfort for the Kurds. We were to deploy a commando actually inside Iraq, protecting the Kurds from Saddam's forces. The Peshmerga [armed Kurdish fighters] could look after themselves on the land, but still needed protection from Saddam's helicopter gunships, which had permission to fly [under the terms of the Safwan ceasefire].

Group Captain Glenn Torpy
Officer Commanding, 13 Squadron, Royal Air Force

We patrolled over Iraq continually for the next nineteen years, containing the Iraqi regime in a way that was politically acceptable to the international community, at minimal financial cost (compared to ground operations), and without losing anybody. People tend to forget about this.

Coalition aircraft were targeted throughout these missions, and occasionally Saddam would shoot at us and we'd respond. We flew with recce guys, bombers, fighters and jammers, building up a very good picture of Iraqi air defences. By the end, the only area with any serious air defences left was what we called the 'Baghdad Super-MES' – missile exclusion zone. We didn't fly in there, as there were other ways of watching it, plus we didn't want to give Saddam the kudos of shooting down one of our aircraft.

Major General Alexander Harley
Assistant Chief of Defence Staff (Overseas) and Deputy Director of Joint Operations, Ministry of Defence, Whitehall

The whole programme cost billions of pounds each week. Although heinous things were still happening on the ground, Iraq's expeditionary ambitions were being thwarted by America paying through the nose. But how could it end? There was no extraction plan. The French pulled out after a couple of years, and we reduced to a couple of squadrons, but ten years later, we and the Americans were still there. This was to continue until 9/11, which Bush II used to get off the hook of this constant, very costly, over-flying of Iraq.

The Rt Hon John Major
Prime Minister

The Iraqis were murdering Kurds in the North. The 'Safe Haven' policy was thought up and planned in the Foreign Office and Downing Street, and on a plane to an EU Council meeting in Brussels, with Stephen Wall, my foreign affairs private secretary, who had succeeded Charles Powell.

After speaking to Jacques Santer, Chairman of the Council, I had private meetings with Mitterrand, Kohl and Delors, at which I asked for European Union support. Diplomatically, unless we secured European agreement, it was going to be almost impossible to pull the international community together, hence bringing in Kohl and Mitterrand at an early stage.

Helmut came in and straight away said, 'Yes, I agree with John.' Mitterrand looked up from signing postcards, which was invariably his habit at meetings like this, and supported it; and Delors said he thought it important – and that was it.

The European Union backed the plan without dissent. Our ambassador to the UN, David Hannay, immediately began to seek support for it.

The Foreign Office were drumming up Commonwealth support and, having achieved European agreement, we then approached the Americans. They were reluctant at first, having borne the principal burden of the war. Unsurprisingly, the thought of another – much longer – commitment in northern Iraq didn't instinctively appeal to them.

But George Bush is a great humanitarian. Once he'd focused on what was happening in northern Iraq, American agreement came quickly and comprehensively. This was a president who is not only one of the nicest men I've ever met, he's also a true citizen of the world.

The Safe Haven policy saved thousands of lives and was very much a British démarche. We also played a principal role in the no-fly zone operation. Other nations less so, which was another cause of great frustration.

Major General Alexander Harley
Assistant Chief of Defence Staff (Overseas) and Deputy Director of Joint Operations, Ministry of Defence, Whitehall

The Kurds have a large following in the UK, in two different sects which don't always see eye to eye. The Kurdish community in UK demanded that we do something, as their families back in Iraq were being persecuted by Saddam. As the Kurdish population is spread over Turkey, Iraq and Iran, there was scope for serious problems.

One of these sects was setting up a 'Free Kurdistan' state, which was anathema to Turkey with its long-standing problem over Kurds drifting to and fro across the border. We thought a Kurdish state would be destabilising of a potentially unstable area.

Brigadier Mike Willcocks
Chief of Staff (Land), Joint War Headquarters, RAF High Wycombe

My next task was as Chief of Staff (Land) for the British part of Operation Provide Comfort – the Kurdish relief operation. It was mounted very quickly. We were still doing our recce in the north of Iraq when the main body of 45 Commando flew in.

Major General Alexander Harley
Assistant Chief of Defence Staff (Overseas) and Deputy Director of Joint Operations, Ministry of Defence, Whitehall

UK – I thought surprisingly – took the decision to mount a British-led operation, sending 3 Commando Brigades' four thousand troops into the north of Iraq. We don't often take the lead in that sort of way. It's rather a beautiful area, and we came across two of Saddam's summer palaces where he went to escape the hot weather.

It was a very well-run operation, coordinated with air power out of Incirlik. There were several firefights, but I don't think anybody was killed on our side.

Second Lieutenant Alistair Watkins
Grenadier Guards, 4th Armoured Brigade

Eventually we received a departure date. Another battalion had come in to take the vehicles from us, wearing brand-new combats and pasty-white. It was weird to be leaving the vehicles that had been our homes for so long. The soldiers hid a lot of war souvenir weapons in the fuel tanks of the Warriors. When the vehicles arrived back, some of these were found, but a lot weren't.

Sergeant Shaun Rusling
Medic, Parachute Regiment, 32 Field Hospital

The civvie hospital I worked in – Beverley Westwood – was closing down, so I came home to a redundancy notice. However, as I'd not spent anything for three months I wasn't short of money. But I wasn't well. The effects of NAPS tablets were still giving me very bad night sweats, pains in my joints, and fevers – and even back home, these were still really bad. (I've got the same problems now, twenty years on.)

Lieutenant Toby Masterton
A Squadron, The Life Guards, 4th Armoured Brigade

On the day I left the Gulf, there was another suspicious death associated with the CLAW grenade. Apparently, a Fusilier was firing a CLAW grenade from an SA80, but instead of the SA80 round striking the base of the grenade and firing it off down the range, it had exploded on the firing point. There was a theory that all the banging around inside the Warriors for months had somehow made it possible for the CLAW grenade to become armed without being fired.

A couple of months later, I asked a Skill-at-Arms Corps warrant officer about these two CLAW grenade incidents. He told me firmly that neither of these incidents took place. I wasn't sure whether he meant that the grenade wasn't at fault or whether it was all still being investigated. He said simply that both incidents had never happened, leaving me to think I'd imagined them both...

Second Lieutenant Alistair Watkins
1st Battalion Grenadier Guards

We were flown home by a British airline, with some drinks and lots of fun. They showed the film *Ghost*, at which all these grizzly, leathery-brown senior NCOs had a quiet weep. It was a grey, rainy, north German morning when we landed, the fir trees dark and gloomy.

The married guys were totally delighted, seeing their children and being back, whereas we young unmarried officers got off the coach, collected our kit, and headed off to the mess. Getting into a proper bed for the first time in three months, having a shower and using a clean towel, not having sand into everything, or flies in tea, were so luxurious. We had all sorts of trouble with mad piss-ups. Our poor old Commanding Officer had been on his own for three months, and thought it best to send us off on leave pretty quickly.

RSM Johnny Muir
Regimental Sergeant Major, Queen's Royal Irish Hussars

We had a delayed St Patrick's Day parade on 22 March, wearing desert uniforms, with two rehearsals as we hadn't done any foot drill for six months. It was time to start forgiving and forgetting those who didn't go for whatever reason, accepting we're all different, and get the family back together again. I told all the sergeants major not to single out anybody for any reason. There was some banter, but nothing serious. This reintegration happened very quickly, with total acceptance.

Everyone paraded, those who didn't come with us wearing their Europe combat kit. Brigadier Patrick Cordingley came and took the salute, then during a light lunch, we presented him with a blackthorn. We then headed off on disembarkation leave.

CHAPTER 10

AFTER-EFFECTS

With the Middle East safer and more secure than it had been before the land war, and coalition forces melting away, Britain and the US began collecting their IOUs for the enormous cost of the war – in excess of $80bn. Saudi Arabia, Kuwait and other Gulf states paid up some $50bn; Germany and Japan, which sent no troops, some $16bn. A US Congress report estimated that the US – which provided almost three-quarters of the combined force – actually paid only twelve per cent of what the cost of the war would have been without the subsidy from the allies. The UK was saved a similar proportion of its costs. This financial support enabled the very rapid response, which deterred Saddam from invading Saudi Arabia, and the success of the removal operation.

The extreme speed of the ground war, and the rapidity with which Brigadier Willcocks and his Joint HQ team got the troops back from the Gulf, were disorientatingly successful. People returned from six months of living in the grease and sand of their tank or armoured personnel carrier, to winter weather and the comparative luxury of normal life to find their families exhausted by media exaggeration and hype, and Army colleagues and superiors who were jealous or dismissive of their experience. Senior officers denigrated the Gulf veterans' achievement as 'the war that never happened'; returning troops found themselves irritated by the unnecessarily rapid imposition of petty peacetime administration and regulations.

For another group of people, various serious health problems were to emerge, which although now recognised medically as Gulf War Syndrome, still remain the source of much debate. The US Government Research and Advisory Committee on Gulf War Veterans' Illnesses report published in 2008, says that one in six of the 679,000 US veterans of the First Gulf War are suffering from Gulf War Syndrome. Symptoms are complex, with no effective treatments, and differ fundamentally from trauma and stress-related syndromes reported after other wars.

The MoD say that the same pattern of ill-health suffered by Gulf War veterans is also suffered by UK military personnel who did *not* deploy to the Gulf in 1990–91, but that those who did deploy suffer more of the symptoms, more severely. The MoD also says that 'a large number of non-specific, multi-system, medically unexplained symptoms have also been reported'. Many Gulf War veterans believe the MoD to be avoiding taking responsibility for health problems caused by war service.

The Rt Hon John Major
Prime Minister

The pay-off came in various different ways. Some nations asked for favours on other fronts later, with the subliminal reminder of their contribution [to the Coalition] hanging in the air. But that's politics – and also life.

It was sometimes quite difficult to round up the cash. The Treasury was mainly involved with that, but we certainly had problems with some countries. I can't remember the defaulters, but seem to recall we only received token contributions from some EU countries; far less than we anticipated. This was very disappointing.

But the second aspect of this was the nations who'd contributed troops afterwards feeling that little closer to Britain and America – in many cases more so to Britain. America is so big, that people relate to it almost as a sort of 'Big Brother'; whereas we've been in the Middle East for so much longer, people felt closer to us.

The Gulf states, in particular, were very grateful that we'd gone there.

Lieutenant Colonel Mike Vickery
Commanding Officer, 14th/20th King's Hussars,
4th Armoured Brigade

Although we'd cleaned them up as best we could, after months sitting on the docks at Al Jubayl and the voyage back, our tanks were in complete shit order. While on leave, the Royal Armoured Corps Centre at Bovington telephoned, really angry over the state of three Life Guards' tanks that for some reason had been delivered to them. I was ordered to come off leave and sort them out. I refused.

'But there's a rotten sandwich in one of the turrets...!'

Lieutenant Colonel Charles Rogers
Commanding Officer, Staffordshire Regiment

I sent everyone on five weeks' leave, which was too long. We needed to focus on the next event, rather than having our people floating round the UK causing problems. They do tend to misbehave after operations, and afterwards we had to sort a few of them out.

Returning to the Germany peacetime routine was dull; handing back equipment to other units, quibbling over details. My own Warrior miserably failed its 'Fitness for Role' inspection, and our vehicles were heavily criticised for being dirty... We had a new brigadier, and to be honest, having done it for real, I wasn't really interested in going back to all the pettiness. I was a bit flat, and it was rather a good thing that I left the regiment a few months later.

The soldiers were looking at another Northern Ireland tour, plus amalgamating, so their horizons were rather different. And, of course, the 'Options for Change' defence cuts process started up again. We whipped up a huge campaign, involving MPs like the chairman of the Defence Select Committee, Bruce George. One newspaper even alleged that we were mutinying. In the end, we avoided being amalgamated, but overall, half the number of soldiers in Germany were axed.

The Rt Hon Tom King
UK Secretary of State for Defence

After drawing breath, we shifted back to the 'Options for Change' defence cuts. I think there was plenty of military support for the package. But I'm afraid it was cutting infantry and cavalry regiments that became the most overwhelming issue. When I made the statement in the House, it was the naming of these regiments that had all the MPs jumping up and down in their seats. The proposal to cut the Staffordshires led to particularly great excitement.

The Rt Hon John Major
Prime Minister

There was a great deal of pressure on me to hold what some crudely called a 'Khaki Election', taking advantage of the military victory. I thought this idea absurd and, actually, morally wrong. The 'Options for Change' defence review had been interrupted by this war, and afterwards the Soviet Union was even weaker. We re-evaluated the threat (and our response), which is what 'Options for Change' was all about.

Lieutenant Colonel Arthur Denaro
Commanding Officer, Queen's Royal Irish Hussars

That summer was not all fun. The government's defence cuts to the army were announced on 24 July 1991: forty thousand soldiers to be made redundant over four years, with cuts of many famous regiments, including the Queen's Royal Irish Hussars. This was the saddest day of my military career.

RSM Johnny Muir
Regimental Sergeant Major, Queen's Royal Irish Hussars

We'd hoped that the war would save us from disbandment. But it didn't. I felt we'd been let down, a disillusionment that's stayed with me to this day.

We'd also thought the government would provide us with everything we'd need to do the job, but didn't realise just how poorly provided for we were. When we were amalgamated with the Queen's Royal Hussars in 1993, we moved to their base in Hohne, to find all their Challengers *still* just shells sitting on blocks. What was the point of it all?

Lieutenant Colonel Mike Vickery
Commanding Officer, 14th/20th King's Hussars,
4th Armoured Brigade

After leave, we settled back into normal life with a resoundingly dull thud. People came to inspect our equipment and found things were missing: 'And where are the Special Armour Packs 3, 7 and 16 from the following tanks?'

'They fell off in the middle of the desert.'

The unfortunate Commanding Officer of the Royal Scots had removed the windows and windscreens of all his trucks and Land Rovers lest they be seen by the Iraqis' Hind helicopters in the sunshine at over ten kilometres.

He buried them in the sand. People were after him for these, so he gave them a grid reference.

Second Lieutenant Alistair Watkins
1st Battalion Grenadier Guards

My parents were split up, but got together for a family dinner, sitting together at the same table for the first time in ten years, which was a bit bizarre. I then went on holiday to Crete with my girlfriend, but after a couple of days we split up. In retrospect that was terrible, and I can't believe I did it. I felt so guilty. Two or three of the other guys also binned their long-term girlfriends. We all had a bit of an issue adjusting to normal life.

It hadn't seemed such a bad experience. We'd lost nine soldiers, which was tragic, but hadn't happened right next to me. As young blokes, we were so pumped up that normal life was dull. Maybe if we'd been a bit older with more responsibility we'd have reacted differently, or if we'd had a much worse time.

There was a mad energy about everyone. That summer, skydiving was the big thing and everyone was off to Florida; or buying motorbikes and doing crazy things. We were a tight-knit bunch – all searching for the next thing to do.

Lieutenant Colonel Mike Vickery
Commanding Officer, 14th/20th King's Hussars, 4th Armoured Brigade

I'd put my regiment in for quite a few awards, so on the day the awards were announced, I thought I'd organise a little parade of the regiment, to congratulate people. But then I wasn't sure how many awards we were going to get, and in any case there was plenty of time to organise something before lunch.

So off I went off to brigade headquarters, to discover that I'd been given an OBE – and that was that. Nobody else got anything at all. I was livid, absolutely spitting.

Sergeant Shaun Rusling
Medic, Parachute Regiment

I thought my mood swings were part of settling down. My wife said I was like a cat on a hot tin roof, but I didn't think I was that bad. The idea of not being able to cope isn't something a Para would ever admit. But it all got worse and worse, and by January 1992 my wife and I were divorced, for my 'unreasonable behaviour'. I had no patience, had lost my sense of humour, and was a different person. My physical and mental health degenerated. I still had pain from parasthesia in my hands and feet, which felt like someone sticking red-hot needles through my hands and the balls of my feet, plus pains in my left flank, from when we'd been given the NAPS tablets and vaccinations. But the worst thing was the constant fatigue. I was trying to resist the pain, but it all built up until I had what the doctors described as 'a complete physical and mental breakdown'. I was diagnosed with PTSD [post traumatic stress disorder], which didn't seem like something I could suffer from. I thought maybe I'd not been prepared right in the training, or something. But on the other hand, PTSD would explain my mood swings and the other problems I was having.

Lance Corporal Roy Sellstrom
Pioneer Corps, Army War Graves Unit
I had a week at home, then was sent to Kineton, where they'd gathered a stack of psychiatrists from the army and RAF. I felt like a guinea pig.

Tommy Hulls shouted at them, 'Why weren't there any fucking body bags?' They said they weren't there to discuss our admin problems, and he said, 'That's why we're ill, you fuckers.'

Other people were shouting as well, and we wanted to be allowed to go home.

RSM Johnny Muir
Regimental Sergeant Major, Queen's Royal Irish Hussars
We hadn't seen the television news, so never realised what our families were being put through by its unreal drama and exaggeration. We talked to journalists, but never saw the end product, or even thought about what we'd said or how it might look.

When somebody'd been killed and the MoD hadn't yet released the name, the way it was presented and the way the units were mentioned made our families think it was us – their father, their husband. And the way the reports were presented were very automated and formal. My God, we thought we were at the sharp end, but our families went through hell.

Lance Corporal Roy Sellstrom
Pioneer Corps, Army War Graves Unit

I was sent back to Northern Ireland on 18 May, suffering terrible nightmares about being buried alive, scratching away. I'd asked for help, and ended up in Northern Ireland, so I thought if I asked for help here, things would get even worse for me.

Tommy was on the other shift, and other guys were there too – all of us having nightmares. We were spending our twenty-four hours off in our rooms drinking, because if I thought about what I'd done, all I wanted to do was blow my fucking brains out. I don't know why I didn't do it. The lads in the guardroom wondered why all the sleeping bag zips were broken. They were like a body bag, and in my nightmares, I'd be fighting my way out.

I forced myself to go sick in August, but the doctor looked through my documents and told me there was no record of my having been out in the Gulf, and to pull myself together. I didn't know what to say to him. On leave, I spent the time while my wife Deb was at work drinking, with the curtains drawn. She asked me to put out the bins, and came home to find me struggling with these black bin bags.

Maggi Denaro
Commanding Officer's wife, Queen's Royal Irish Hussars

There was a honeymoon period for six months, before problems started to emerge. We were a very open bunch of people. I might be being naive I suppose, but our children didn't seem to have any serious problems – and we did talk openly as a family about it. But some families had bigger problems; wives become dependent on drink, their husbands having been dry all that time; and young wives who'd left for the UK finding it difficult to return to the regiment and life in Germany.

We didn't seem to have Gulf War Syndrome problems, but that could be because Arthur wouldn't let them have all the injections – and is a very moot point.

Lieutenant Colonel Arthur Denaro
Commanding Officer, Queen's Royal Irish Hussars

We had so much bloody stuff pumped into us that I wouldn't be remotely surprised if some people reacted badly. We had almost no instances of GWS in our regiment. One 17th/12st officer had a Down's Syndrome child, and wondered if that's what it was. But I was strict about the bloody injections; a couple I refused to let the Regiment have. The risk of getting plague or anthrax wasn't worth the effect of the injections themselves.

Lance Corporal Roy Sellstrom
Pioneer Corps, Army War Graves Unit

I went back to Ireland, but after a couple of days I was RTU-ed [returned to unit]; my missus had told them I shouldn't be out there. The OC told me I should leave the army; but then he also told me that I hadn't been to the Gulf, and refused to believe that I had. I threw his big fucking table across his office. They took me to the med centre in Northampton to see the doctor wearing handcuffs! I ended up travelling down to the psychiatric department at Woolwich three times a week as an outpatient.

Second Lieutenant Alistair Watkins
1st Battalion Grenadier Guards

My mate Charlie and I really struggled on the platoon commanders' battle course, having hoped we might not have to do it. There was lots of time on exercise, being attacked all the time by a couple of instructors. I was twenty-one, a Second Lieutenant with a Gulf War medal, at a time when other much more senior officers didn't have any medals at all. You could see them thinking, 'You little shit.'

Lieutenant Toby Masterton
Life Guards

I became a UN military observer in the demilitarised desert zone of southern Iraq, spending a cathartic couple of months back in the desert. I found a shot-down American pilot and his aircraft, and revisited the battlefield, where winds blew the sand away to reveal and rebury mummified Iraqi corpses, whose wounds and facial expressions could still be clearly seen.

I got to know Kuwait really well, and learned from people just what a terrible, really brutal time they'd had during the Iraqi occupation, being shown the many places used to torture people, and the gothic-horror, medieval instruments. There was a beach club, in which one of the unused cabanas was discovered to be full of severed fingers.

Lieutenant Colonel Mike Vickery
Commanding Officer, 14th/20th King's Hussars

I suggested we skip the scheduled September gunnery camp. But they insisted we do it, so we did the training and I planned a much more interesting camp than usual, which surprised the gunnery school.

But our boys hadn't fired a tank since the Gulf, with some of us, me included, getting quite twitchy. I was listening to the Three Tenors in the bath – which I'd listened to all the time in the desert. I had a complete collapse, burst into tears and found myself in a very odd state. I talked it through with my missus, who said she'd thought this was bound to happen and had rather been waiting for it.

Some of the soldiers, especially those who'd done things like driven tanks over people who might or might not have been dead at the time, had serious problems. Come September, I knew they really did need somebody. The regimental doctor, a very approachable Irish woman who we all loved dearly, and the brigade padre, had been out in the Gulf with us. I decided to talk to them about my worries, and asked if they'd come to our firing camp, to work with the boys as part of the team.

After the ammo bashing, the doc and padre reported that the boys had done a lot of talking and chatting, remembering; and even more on Day Two after we'd fired the guns, with all the smell of cordite and so on. In the messes and pubs that night, with no girls, kids or families around, it was just us and the tanks once more. We hadn't talked about it – the horrors and worries of actually killing people, and needed to relieve the pressure, which had been building up. One of my REME sergeants committed suicide.

There was quite a lot of going out and getting pissed, but nothing terribly notable. Having time to chat about it afterwards and depressurise was very important. But during the live firing, my lot simply didn't get pissed, as they knew they couldn't operate a tank properly in the morning. On one of the evenings, there'd been an enormous fight in a beer hall. The Royal Military Police major came in to see me next morning: 'Your boys were involved there last night…'

'Oh God,' I said, 'so what's to be done now?'

'Nothing, but I just thought you'd like to know. People were hitting each other over the heads with chairs and all the rest of it, so after fighting their way out, your soldiers walked home together. We gave a lift to half of them because they were good boys.'

The gunnery staff found our performance interesting – the boys were awfully good! But they worried that our fire orders and various other procedures weren't very formal; the boys were saying things like, 'See that?'

'Yes.'

'Hit it.'

'Loaded!'

'Fire!' Bang!

'Got it!'

The Gunnery Staff were saying, 'They're extremely fast and very accurate, but they don't use proper fire orders.'

Maria Rusling
National Gulf Veterans and Families Association

We've noticed a huge difference between guys who were in the Territorial Army, and those in the regular units. The TA guys came home, went back to work and thereafter were on their own; whereas the regulars stayed together in their units when they returned. The TA guys are much worse affected by everything they experienced, and receive much less help and support.

Lieutenant Colonel Mike Vickery
Commanding Officer, 14th/20th King's Hussars,
4th Armoured Brigade

We were a very small percentage of the British Army: only three armoured regiments, three infantry battalions, three gunner regiments – plus extras. Only a very small percentage of the army went. It was also the first armoured war since the Second World War – real armoured warfare, which nobody else had done. But when we got back, the rest of the army was *spittingly* jealous – I could not believe it. They were *green…*

Brigadier Patrick Cordingley
Commander, 7th Armoured Brigade

I worry about the effects of the media on modern warfare. Reporters wanted to know all about our fears and emotions, an intrusion which they justified as being caring and in the public interest. Under this examination, we confessed to being frightened.

And the reporting of the very clinical nature of modern weapons systems and the effects of these systems on the bunkers and buildings in Baghdad led the public, particularly the American public, to lose touch with the reality of the war, which was a grim, ghastly bloody affair. At the same time, sensationalist reporting heightened public concern over casualties.

Sensationalism and dramatisation of war is a dangerous media preoccupation when a war is being fought – which the media follow for their own profit and benefit. I worry if commanders in the television age can be ruthless enough to pursue the enemy to the limit? Half-measures don't win wars.

Lieutenant General Walter Boomer
General Officer Commanding, 1 Marine Expeditionary Force, United States Marine Corps

The idea that this was somehow a 'non-war' is totally wrong. It was, for example, the largest deployment of the US Marine Corps under one command in the history of the United States. In the beginning we were vastly outnumbered. By the time we completed our build-up, I had almost all of the entire US Marine Corps – and if you looked at the Iraqi order of battle, we absolutely needed all that.

But because of good planning and execution, at the end it seemed as if we hadn't needed all those troops. But we did need them, and we didn't know how it was going to be until the very end. It could all have gone very differently.

Lieutenant Colonel Mike Vickery
Commanding Officer, 14th/20th King's Hussars

Our Divisional Commander back in Germany, who'd run all the training but didn't go out to the Gulf, was very angry at not going. From the day we returned, it was business as usual, as if nothing had happened; no study days, talks, lectures or post-operational debriefing sessions.

I was really quite shocked by this; but also in the full realisation of how we'd been so ridiculously short of soldiers, and all the desperate problems with the tanks and our equipment; the whole British Army being able to raise only two brigades by destroying the rest of what was supposed to be a corps of nine brigades. And then the incredible jealousy.

Sergeant Shaun Rusling
Medic, Parachute Regiment

I was being given bizarre diagnoses from the doctors – of things like fibromyalgic chronic fatigue, irritable bowel syndrome and so on. I reckoned it would be statistically unlucky to have one or two of these conditions, but not to have the whole lot!

I reckoned it began with the vaccinations; nothing particular, but from having been given too many of them in too short a space of time. After much effort and time, I was given a war pension, but then they took it away from me, because I hadn't been formally discharged from the TA.

I was then formally discharged from the army with spinal injuries and PTSD on 1 December 1995, then sent to the medical assessment programme. They told me there was no such thing as 'vaccine damage', so told me to list every symptom, resulting in a separate tribunal for each one: PTSD, depression, chronic fatigue, irritable bowel, fybromyalgia, osteoporosis and so on. This annoyed me, and took a very long time. I discovered they'd done the same to every other veteran – a process apparently designed to put you off making your claim, and the effect on many people, who were in a bad way to start with, was just that.

In the meantime I got myself tested privately for depleted uranium poisoning: two twenty-four-hour urine samples to Morrell University in Canada, and two samples to the UK, all independent of each other. They came back positive for U234, U235, U236 and U237 – all four isotypes. U236 can only come from either a nuclear fission facility or the battlefield. I saw a US Army doctor who'd written papers on depleted uranium exposure, who peer-reviewed my tests and confirmed my exposure.

Second Lieutenant Alistair Watkins
1st Battalion Grenadier Guards

I'd started out as a social soldier, but the Gulf made me really interested in doing the skills as well as possible. So although the platoon commander's course was a complete pain up the arse, it made me determined to be as good as I could be.

Back in Germany was chaos, with no vehicles or spares, the whole of BAOR having been ripped out to put the show on the road. We moved back to UK in 1992, then I was a platoon commander in South Armagh for six months, which arguably was more stressful than the Gulf, after which I tried for SAS selection, but came off with an injury, then left the army. The idea of countless meaningless exercises on Salisbury Plain was a massive turn-off. I was hugely grateful for the experience but it was time to move on and experience the next challenge in life.

Maria Rusling
National Gulf Veterans and Families Association

I met Shaun in 1995, and he was already ill, but we didn't know why. I married Shaun in 1996. In January 1998 we went to a medal handing back demonstration at the MoD in Whitehall. Shaun didn't want to hand his medal back, but to support those who did. Going to the MoD gave me immediately the essence of what was really going on. The whole thing was really rushed, like they wanted to get us out of the building as quickly as possible. I realised that these were not kind people.

Afterwards Shaun and a couple of others were arguing about sharing the information they'd got about people being ill, and writing to the MoD. With another wife, we decided to set up a northern branch of the Gulf Veterans charity and run an open day to get the interest going. It all snowballed from there.

Sergeant Shaun Rusling
Medic, Parachute Regiment

In 1994 I'd also claimed for Gulf War Syndrome. In 1998 the MoD appealed against this, and so I had to go to Leeds Crown Court. The judge, Mr Justice Newman, stopped the proceedings and asked the MoD QC if he believed I was ill from the Gulf War. He replied, 'Yes, undoubtedly, my lord, but we believe this is with signs and symptoms of ill-defined conditions.'

'Who diagnosed this?' asked the judge.

He replied, 'I'm sure it's there in the file somewhere, my lord.'

So I said, 'Nobody's diagnosed me with this, my lord. I've now got a war pension for something I haven't got, which was imposed on me by the MoD on policy because they didn't want to accept Gulf War Syndrome.'

The osteoporosis, depleted uranium poisoning and so on, which the MoD hadn't wanted to consider, and had prevented being heard by the court, were all on file. And yet, bizarrely, the MoD lawyers were telling the High Court they didn't know why I was ill.

Many times I've questioned my own sanity. In the army, we're the sort of people who sort ourselves out, and it's very hard for us to admit we can't cope. The MoD makes it as hard as possible for veterans, hoping they'll go away.

Maria Rusling
National Gulf Veterans and Families Association

The MoD took the case to appeal, for which we received legal aid, turning into a huge job, with vast amounts of paperwork all over our conservatory floor for months. We had to make several trips to the court. The MoD QC was very aggressive to the tribunal judge, and so each member of the tribunal ended up having their own QCs – a big long line of them sat there.

The last hearing was very tense. Shaun couldn't sleep and was certain he'd lost. We had a conference with our lawyer at seven that morning, then when we actually went into the High Court, it was so quick I didn't have time to take it in. The MoD barristers weren't there, even though the court was full.

As we sat down, our solicitor whispered privately to me that we'd won on every point, but couldn't tell Shaun until the judge delivered the judgement. Shaun was sitting crying, repeating, 'I know I've lost. I've lost, I've lost…'

Lance Corporal Roy Sellstrom
Pioneer Corps, Army War Graves Unit

I slowly regained my desire to be a soldier, but the drinking remained. The nightmares were less frequent, but I didn't dare go to bed until the small hours, until I was tired enough to sleep. I had flashbacks every day; like for example, glimpsing a person on the street, and the angle of their nose or something reminding me of one of the bodies I'd dealt with – or the whiff of a smell like a barbecue; or the smell of fuel, like the Basra Road.

I did another Northern Ireland tour, then Bosnia, and a NATO Bosnia tour, with Falklands, Cyprus and Belize in between. Sometimes I'd need help, but by 2000 I was doing OK. After an incident when I saved a recruit after he'd had a heart attack, I couldn't sleep and was banged on to anti-depressants, which were terrible. At another camp, the constant smell of fuel made me very bad tempered and got me drinking again. The anti-depressants made me worse, and another psychiatrist, Brigadier Wycombe, told me it was all because of my childhood experiences. My son was born in 2000, which they *then* said was the cause of my problems. They weren't listening.

Then, after a very unhappy time as Provost Sergeant at Deepcut Barracks, where recruits were killing themselves, in August 2004 I was posted to 10 Gurkha Transport Regiment. They'd been told [in contravention of medical confidentiality] of my medical problems so they made me rations storeman – a very demeaning job for someone of my rank. Part of this required me to handle goat and sheep carcasses, which I found I couldn't do. So, after much difficulty, in October 2005 I was medically discharged from the army with PTSD.

Sergeant Shaun Rusling
Medic, Parachute Regiment

We'd always been taught in our army medic training that we'd know when we were under chemical attack because people would be dropping around us, with dilated pupils, frothing at the mouth, jerking about and so on. But as we were soon to realise, in reality this isn't what happens. The body can cope with a certain amount of chemical exposure. An enzyme called PON1 enables some people to take in more toxins than others. Low-level doses of chemicals don't set off alarms or have much immediate effect, so no one realises they've been exposed or contaminated. The MoD has admitted that we at 32 Field Ambulance were exposed for one day, after the end of the war, when the weapons bay at Khamisiyah Depot was destroyed.

Others believe we were also exposed to low levels of chemical agents throughout the war, which is why the NAIADS were going off all the time. There were Scud attacks when all the NAIADS went off, sometimes four or five times a day.

We now know that many of the casualties, especially Iraqis from armoured vehicles hit by coalition-fired depleted uranium rounds, were covered in very fine DU contaminated dust. Unless you were wearing a respirator when you cut the clothes and equipment off them, you'd be breathing in this stuff – which is what we did, with everybody needlessly contaminated. You could see all the dust floating in the air. If we'd stuck to the correct SOPs [standard operating procedures], when casualties arrived as the NAIADS were sounding, we'd have put them into casualty bags, decontaminating them before bringing them into the hospital for treatment.

The MoD knew all about the chemical threat; there were Joint Service publications detailing the standard operating procedures, but the MoD failed to inform the troops. According to Porton Down, the NAIADS warning devices are totally reliable and only go off in the presence of the designated chemicals. But somebody gave the order to ignore them and carry on working.

Maria Rusling
National Gulf Veterans and Families Association

Our charity is still receiving twenty-five new cases each month, and they're awful. We've got over three thousand on our books, and we know there are others who haven't come forward; often because they're unwilling to admit being ill. The MoD are paying war pensions to almost nine thousand ill Gulf War One veterans, the number still increasing at more than fifty every month. Many veterans don't know they can claim a war pension, and the MoD fights against giving these pensions, even though it's only £30 a week – a tiny amount of money and you wonder why on earth they won't just pay it.

But a lot of people have already died; the MoD says in June 2003 the number was six hundred. We think this is more like eight hundred, but the NHS has no record of their military service.

CHAPTER 11

THE LEGACY OF WAR

In deciding to invade Iraq in 2003, it has been suggested that the Bush presidential 'dynasty' became increasingly motivated by regret for a job left undone. Presidents Bush senior and Bush junior were depicted as haunted by the desire for revenge, seeking and being given evidence of Saddam's weapons of mass destruction; or, as British Prime Minister Tony Blair stands accused, of ignoring or misinterpreting evidence to the contrary.

However, the idea of 'Bush regret' creating a legacy of war can only have developed after 1991, and as a function of internal US politics. In 1991, as far as the rest of the world was concerned, President George H.W. Bush senior, the 41st president, had put together a remarkable coalition – uniting the Arab world, sticking absolutely to UN directives and resolutions, dissuading Israel from responding to enormous provocation from Saddam whilst enduring pressure from the very powerful US Jewish lobby – to rid Kuwait of Iraqi occupation without breaking any international laws. Regime change by the coalition was not on the agenda.

The UK's policy was that Saddam should remain in power, for all the same reasons he'd been kept in power throughout the Iran–Iraq war. There's no evidence that the US had changed its mind, or disagreed with the UK on this.

But by 2003, after a decade of human rights abuses, Saddam's taunting, and the enormously expensive no-fly air campaign over Iraq, the Bush dynasty was reported to be desirous of 'closure'. The events of 11 September 2001, although nothing to do with Saddam or Iraq, triggered George W. Bush's call to arms against the 'axis of evil' into which he added Iraq, ostensibly because of its weapons of mass destruction. Unfortunately these had either been destroyed by the bombing of January 1991 or, those that remained, by Saddam himself afterwards.

After the allied invasion of Iraq, and of course the earlier intervention in Afghanistan, the regional balance of power swung very strongly in Iran's favour, where it presently remains (in 2010): the very situation diplomats had worked for decades to avoid, and which Saddam Hussein had at least prevented.

President George H. W. Bush' war of 1991 was a masterpiece of diplomacy, determination and military expertise, with Britain playing the leading role in ensuring its success. The Iraq invasion of 2003 was a politically very different conflict, for both President Bush junior and Prime Minister Tony Blair, especially in the latter's seeming failure to question, urge caution and demand a plan for nation-building before approving the destruction of Iraq.

The Rt Hon John Major
Prime Minister

I don't believe the events of 1991 contributed to subsequent events, or to the second Gulf War, except in one regard: Saddam survived. But I do think that the failure of the sanctions regime removed huge pressure from Iraq, thereby allowing Saddam Hussein to survive. The leaking away of the sanctions regime throughout the Nineties, and the failure of so many nations to impose them, allowed this profoundly bad man to talk of his weapons of mass destruction in order to survive in power. This led to the second war.

There was never any question, or intention, of us moving on from the liberation of Kuwait to the invasion of Baghdad. Under international law, that would have been illegal, and we would never have done it. But the removal of sanctions allowed Saddam to rebuild a power base, and persuade people that he had weapons of mass destruction.

Could we have required Saddam to step down, as a condition of peace? Possibly yes, but we did not. But at that time nobody imagined that he could or would survive beyond the liberation of Kuwait. I think most of us thought that – in the traditions of Iraq – somebody from inside would remove him. But they didn't. There are lessons to be learned from this, as well as from the second Gulf War.

Brigadier Mike Willcocks
Chief of Staff (Land), Joint War Headquarters, RAF High Wycombe

The political objectives of this war were much, much clearer than in the subsequent invasion of Iraq. President Bush senior had played a blinder in foreign policy terms. He'd got together an astonishing coalition: Egyptian, Saudis, Jordanians and so on, acting with total legality. He didn't overplay his hand by trying to set up a democratic government in Baghdad – quite the opposite. The entire thing was much clearer and better handled.

General Sir Alexander Harley
Assistant Chief of Defence Staff (Overseas) and Deputy Director of Joint Operations, Ministry of Defence, Whitehall

Very soon after the surrender, we had to get together a UN inspection regime to monitor Saddam's weapons of mass destruction. The teams were boffins from defence establishments and universities, mostly with beards, and were trained by Intelligence Corps and Dstl [Defence Science and Technology Laboratory] at a couple of secret places in the UK, learning to drive Land Rovers, operate radios and so on. We prepared military plans to get them out, and instructions for what they should do in various areas under various circumstances.

The UN inspection teams visited Iraqi facilities without warning, as part of a pre-determined strategy, backed up by the air armada's constant activities overhead. Despite Iraqi prevarication, they found hundreds and hundreds of barrels of chemicals and biological stuff. But after a while the Iraqis got wise about where they were going next, and the longer it went on, the less they found, until about three years before Gulf War Two, Saddam got cocky and kicked them out. Unknown to anyone else, Saddam then got rid of the rest of his WMD.

The UN inspectors also found out who in the West had been helping Iraq, uncovering audit trails back to Russia, France, Germany and a couple of companies in the UK. The UN inspection teams also found and destroyed bits of the so-called 'Supergun'. There were two of them, aimed at Israel, and I think only one was actually fired but didn't hit anything. I saw one of the trial Superguns, a bloody great long pipe rusting beside a runway in Barbados.

The Rt Hon Tom King
UK Secretary of State for Defence

When I bumped into Kate Adie afterwards, she complained that she'd been in the middle of the action but had seen absolutely nothing. From the press point of view, it wasn't much of a war. There wasn't any fighting, except when the Saudi army took on a small Iraqi cross-border raid. It was rather dull for them. The air campaign provided them with some very interesting films from raids – for example of a lorry crossing a bridge seconds before it was destroyed, to which Norman Schwarzkopf said, 'That's got to be the luckiest truck driver in Iraq.' So in terms of really nasty, dirty war with fighting over a prolonged period of time, the Gulf War wasn't as exciting as others the journalists might have reported.

Lieutenant Colonel Mike Vickery
Commanding Officer, 14th/20th King's Hussars, 4th Armoured Brigade

The logistics of armoured warfare determine the outcome, and are phenomenally difficult. Having the right amount of fuel, ammunition and spares of all the various types, in the right place, is very difficult. We don't take enough time, in peace, to understand how the logisticians do this.

Brigadier Patrick Cordingley
Commander, 7th Armoured Brigade

The logistic effort was Herculean: thirty-five thousand British soldiers deployed with four hundred thousand tonnes of equipment, munitions and freight, and thirteen thousand five hundred vehicles. We moved twenty-three thousand tonnes of ammunition, six thousand and fifty tonnes of rations and nearly two million litres of petrol over two hundred miles to Logistic Base Alpha in nineteen days. During the ground war, each day troops were provided with a thousand tonnes of ammunition, half a million litres of fuel and three-quarters of a million litres of water. We destroyed three hundred enemy tanks and armoured personnel carriers, and took eight thousand prisoners of war.

Lieutenant Colonel Arthur Denaro
Commanding Officer, Queen's Royal Irish Hussars

In terms of operational experience the Gulf War was second to none. When we fought, it was small battles as they counter-attacked, but that wasn't the point. Only the other day [2009], an older, rather bitter fellow in my Regiment said to me, 'Of course, yours wasn't really a proper war.' How does he know? He wasn't there. How can he know how tense it was driving through that sixteen-kilometre minefield gap expecting NBC attacks whilst being channelled into their defences; or when we hit the Iraqi brigade and had to attack it at night?

Hashim Ali
Iraq freedom fighter

I believe in the wisdom that says that three hundred days of talks and negotiations is better than one day of fighting and war. War should be the last resort – it truly *should* be. But people get involved in military operations. When things get started, like any other job it needs to be done rightly and properly.

There is an Arab religious proverb, which says 'Everything in its time is a worship'; that everything can be like worshipping. When you do things in the right time, it's like worshipping God.

They [Saddam's regime] were used to aggression. They sent the army to the Syrian border as they wanted to attack Syria, and they threatened Turkey when they started building a dam that might take water from the Tigris. They thought they could invade and do whatever they like. Such people shouldn't be allowed to stay in power.

Dr Mary McLoughlin

We believed the whole thing to have been a conspiracy generated by the United States. My partner had worked in Saudi Arabia, and knew how closely the Saudi government worked with the Americans. The other Gulf states were in the process of becoming much more independent, as was Iran and Syria. We reckoned that around 1990, America found itself becoming irrelevant to Middle Eastern politics and economics. With Iran and Iraq talking to each other after the war, the Americans were going to become much less powerful in the Middle East. We thought that, in the face of this, some bright spark in America had decided to encourage Saddam to invade Kuwait. The whole thing was contrived by the Americans to change the political landscape of the Gulf states. But I have absolutely no idea what my Iraqi friends might have thought about this. They never talked about it.

Brigadier Patrick Cordingley
Commander, 7th Armoured Brigade

Saddam Hussein and his generals were accused of fighting a defensive battle similar to that of the Western Front in 1916. They did not, however, have many other options. Their defence was centred on Basra, consisting of three layers: the front manned by conscripts but nevertheless well prepared, along the Kuwaiti–Saudi Arabian border. Behind this came the regulars, and then, in reserve, the Republican Guard. Iraqi engineers had built an elaborate network of interconnecting roads, allowing for easy redeployment and logistics supply. But that was their problem. Whenever a vehicle moved, the American surveillance system spotted it and the resultant onslaught from the air was devastating.

It was only later that I came to the conclusion that Saddam Hussein probably did not care what happened to any of his forces, except the elite Republican Guard. Most of the huge number of conscripts were expendable; his army was far too large, and he was having trouble feeding and paying it. Their loss was a small price to pay, whereas the Republican Guard was essential to his survival.

Lieutenant Colonel Arthur Denaro
Commanding Officer, Queen's Royal Irish Hussars

I didn't want to go to war. I wasn't frightened for myself at all, but for my lads; and frightened of letting the team down myself. We [commanders] had to think about everything – even about what information I'd pass on to my officers, or to the soldiers, or keep to myself. We went from euphoria and relief, to huge disappointment. It was intellectually challenging, and I found it quite testing.

The Rt Hon John Major
Prime Minister

Historically, Britain is a warrior nation. We revere great leaders who have engaged in warfare and have emerged as victors. But when it's a *personal* involvement – and if you have any sort of sensitivity – you see things through very different eyes. For me, the first Gulf War was always seen through the eyes of those young soldiers I'd seen from the top of that Challenger tank. This image never left me throughout.

It was always very clear in my own mind that the victims of that war were sons, daughters, fathers, mothers – not just in our own and the Iraqi armed forces, but civilians too. Iraqi soldiers were simply obeying instructions – as ours were; and although Saddam's regime was a wicked one, Iraq was not – and is not – a wicked nation. I was concerned about the destruction of so much of the Iraq infrastructure. But, in warfare, such things are inevitable.

The first Gulf War made me very cautious about military involvement. When you see war at close quarters, especially when coffins are brought back home due to decisions that you, yourself, have made, it brings things down to a very human level. Throughout the war, my personal concerns ran in constant parallel with a quite dispassionate political judgement that the war was justified. This political judgement never wavered, but nor did my concern over the human element.

Had I been in government at the time of the second Gulf War, I would have been more cautious before commitment. I don't think I can put it any better than that since I have no knowledge of what information would have been available to me at the time. Consequently, notwithstanding the reservations which I raised at the time, I supported that war. I believed what Prime Minister Blair told us was true.

Robin Watt
War artist

It's terribly important for a war artist to show the balance between all the terrible destruction, and normal life which, even in war, still goes on: the lovely Bedou cross the desert with their camels; the plants and birds recover from the pollution and oil fires. But war artists don't often do this. I wasn't actually the official war artist, who was from the Imperial War Museum. It seems to me that when a civilian artist comes out to a war, they just cover the death and destruction, as they don't understand enough about what they're seeing to know that it's only part of the story. If you have more experience of life, you can see this. Soldiers are familiar with violence and death, regarding it as part of the job they do – sad though it is.

Dr Mary McLoughlin

The Iraqi people I knew, I can definitely say, didn't give a single damn for the Ba'ath party's idea of Iraq becoming the leading country in the Arab world.

They only cared about ending the war, and then having a normal life. They had no ambitions at all. They'd say, 'Now the war is over, how good it is to have peace.' They said many, many times that they wanted peace, 'Pray for us, pray for peace.' They just wanted to get on with life, and I really don't think they cared whether they were the first or the last in the Arab world. They just wanted to have a life again, which had just begun to happen at the point at which Saddam invaded Kuwait.

Brigadier Patrick Cordingley
Commander, 7th Armoured Brigade

Many of us felt embarrassed about the City of London's welcome home parade, with thousands of us marching the traditional route along Finsbury Pavement, Moorgate, past Bank into Cheapside and then to the Guildhall. The Queen would take the salute at the Mansion House, and the Prince and Princess of Wales would join us for lunch. It all seemed a little un-British.

At midnight on Wednesday, when the streets of the City were empty for our rehearsal, we felt foolish. But nothing prepared us for the sensations of the actual event. As we left Armoury House and turned into the City Road, we were engulfed by a cloak of emotion. Thousands of Britons, standing five deep in the drizzle, were waiting to greet us. You could sense the same people, in spirit at least, who'd supported and encouraged us every day for the previous six months. As I marched towards the City Marshal on his grey horse, I knew I'd not remember the correct words to ask his permission for us all to enter the City. But, for the first time in many months, it probably didn't matter if I made a mistake.

Brigadier Mike Willcocks
Chief of Staff (Land), Joint War Headquarters, RAF High Wycombe

Fighting a ground war at divisional level against an armoured army of the size of the Iraqis but suffering only fifteen dead, was unbelievable.

People afterwards said, 'Oh well, the Iraqis didn't fight.' Well, that's because of everything that was put in around the Iraqis to stop them. It was *immensely* successful. In the second Gulf War, the Americans seemed to have learned the lesson; and so before it started, told the Iraqis to lay down their arms – and they did. But *then* what did the Americans do? Disbanded the Iraqi army! This is obviously another story – but was completely crazy.

RSM Johnny Muir
Regimental Sergeant Major, Queen's Royal Irish Hussars

I still question was this a right war? I never felt victorious. I'm proud of the regiment, the soldiers and the officers, but became very disenchanted. All we did was put a few pieces of the jigsaw puzzle back together again. Maybe we should have done more. I wouldn't say it was an unjust war, but I question the point of what we did. Afterwards Saddam was free to murder the Kurds and Marsh Arabs. Within two years of coming back, the Irish Hussars ceased to exist. What was the point?

Lance Corporal Roy Sellstrom
Pioneer Corps, Army War Graves Unit

Even now [2010], I can remember the names of every single one of the blokes I looked after: their ages, what killed them, what they looked like. It's a weird – a terrible burden. It's like they're sitting on my fucking shoulder. When it was all over, and I was trying to get on with my life, they were all still there. But I was the last person who saw them. If I still remember them, then they're not forgotten.

That job destroyed me. I loved the army. It was everything to me, the only thing I ever wanted to do with my life. But this job showed me a horrible, different part of the army.

It's not called 'Army War Graves Team' any more now. 144 Squadron in 23 Pioneer Regiment run it now, and they're called 'assistant morticians'. I was asked to go and give a talk to them, but I decided I wouldn't, as after talking to me, they might not be able to do that job any more. When I go to Tesco and carry a plastic shopping bag home, in my mind I'm carrying a head by its hair. They're heavy. You try carrying one by the hair for a couple of hundred metres... that was my normality. Now, to survive, I take mood stabilisers, Temazepam, and a morphine patch every seven days.

Major David Potts
SO2 Army Logistics, Quartermaster General's Department

Now, with people like General David Richards [in 2010 CGS – chief of the general staff], the army does at last understand expeditionary warfare. But we're now going into another resource-constraining review. In three years' time, I imagine we'll still be tied down in Afghanistan, but how well poised will we be for something we haven't predicted?

I'm now posted to Kenya as Defence Attaché [as a brigadier], so I'm hoping the UK and MoD will put more resources into soft power and prevention, which isn't fluffy, and can make a huge difference if you can get it right.

Hashim Ali
Iraq freedom fighter

We can't put a blame on any one person, the events were history, but if we are to find what is the right side, we have to look to the sanctity of human life. We should protect and respect life, whether we are a soldier, a woman or a boy… life is the most holy thing of all. But unfortunately life in Iraq became so cheap. The government and police used to say, 'You will cost me only a bullet to get rid of you.' It was normal every morning to see new corpses lying on the street. These are the morals that dominate in Iraq after waging many wars, seeing so many corpses.

I attended the birth of my son thirteen years ago. Iraqi men don't enter the birth room at all – it's not a masculine thing. But what I saw in the birth room I felt was a miracle. We need to keep this miracle and not waste it in fighting… This Gulf War was the biggest crime committed against the Iraqi people at the hand of the irresponsible Iraqi regime. And then after all that, they withdrew back to the border, and crushed the uprising of the people. As they say, all the rest is history.

ACKNOWLEDGEMENTS

A great many people do a lot of work to get a book like this into the public domain. Most important of all are the contributors, who had to remember back twenty years, to events they'd very often not thought about in a long time. For my military witnesses, many of these events were things they preferred not to think about. In the process of their efforts to ensure what they told me was accurate, many stirred up memories they'd tried very hard to forget. A very tiny minority of my contributors had an eye for their own reputations; but most were concerned that future generations of soldiers might understand the realities of this war – and in the process, the taxpayers, their families and friends, to whom most hadn't told their full and unexpurgated story. Very many thanks.

I apologise to all my contributors for the many important parts of what they so painstakingly told me, that I've been forced to edit out. I much hope I've done justice to them, their views – and their and their unit's considerable achievements in this remarkable war. I make particular mention of General Sir Rupert Smith, who has also been kind enough to write this book's most erudite foreword; and also Hashim Ali, who now lives in the UK, with the hope that Iraq may find its way back to the civilisation of its glorious past, and the tolerance that once existed between its remarkably diverse religious and ethnic groups.

My literary thanks must begin with Ebury publisher Jake Lingwood, whose championing of what one might describe as 'oral history', allows the thoughts and characters of real people caught up in momentous events to take precedence over the views of historians – at least that's how I regard this genre of history. The tides of history are rarely affected by individual Canutes no matter how influential, but swelled by wave upon wave of ordinary people whose first-hand testimony tell us what really happened; source material for historians once we are all dead...

Thanks also to commissioning editor Charlotte Cole for perseverance in getting this project under way in times of economic reduction; to editor Liz Marvin as we shoulder-charge the printer's deadlines whilst striving to avoid error amid a nightmare of detail, and copy editor Bernice Davison. After all this, I claim any remaining mistakes. I would also like to thank in advance of her main effort on this book, publicity manager Caroline Newbury, and also in retrospect for her sterling efforts with my last Ebury book; plus also for his professional input to these *two* books, former cavalry officer Roger Field.

By publication date, my friend and literary agent Barbara Levy and I will have been together for a quarter of a century – she the youngest slip of a girl when we first began. So as ever, my thanks to Barbara for so much wise advice, help and support, over time that's flowed like water.

Hugh McManners
Little Venice, London,
September 2010

GLOSSARY

ACDS – Assistant Chief of Defence Staff

ADC – aide-de-camp

AFV 432 – an armoured fighting vehicle, more strictly known as FV432. A tracked armoured personnel carrier produced from 1961 to 1971, still used by British Army supporting arms

AK-47 (also known as 'AK') – the standard Russian automatic assault rifle

APC – armoured personnel carrier

APDS rounds – armour-piercing discarding sabot: high velocity, kinetic energy anti-tank penetrator projectiles fired from tank guns. Largely superseded by 'Fin' or APFSDS

AR-5 – aircrew NBC hood respirator

AWGS – Army War Graves Service

B-52 – 'Stratofortress' long-range, subsonic American Air Force high latitude strategic bomber, in service since 1955

BAOR – British Army of the Rhine

BATUS – British Army Training Unit Suffield, in Canada

BC – artillery Battery Commander

berm – a ridge or embankment

blue-on-blue – when friendly troops accidentally fire at each other (from military maps showing friendly forces using blue markings)

bluey – free airmail letter

Bravo Two Zero (B20) – the callsign of an SAS patrol partially (and famously) captured in the very early days of the war (and the title of a book by one of its captured members)

brew, a brew up – army slang for a tank catching fire

BRIXMIS – British Military Liaison Mission, an intelligence unit for observing Soviet exercises and collecting data on Soviet equipment

bund – a protective embankment constructed around a defensive position

BW – biological warfare

CARM – chemical agent resistant material (camouflaged tarpaulin under camouflage nets)

CASEVAC – casualty evacuation

CDS – Chief of the Defence Staff

CENTCOM – US Army Central Command

CGS – Chief of the General Staff

Challenger – the main battle tank of the British Army

CLAW – close light assault weapon (a grenade launcher)

CO – Commanding Officer (of a regiment or battalion)

compo – British Army combat rations

CRAV – Challenger recovery tank

DCOS – Deputy Chief of Staff

DERA – Defence Evaluation and Research Agency

DFC – Distinguished Flying Cross (a gallantry medal)

DMPI – desired mean point of impact (for bombing raids)

DOAE – Defence Operational Analysis Establishment

'dozer – bulldozer

DSO – Distinguished Service Order (gallantry medal)

DU rounds – (ultrahigh density) depleted uranium long-rod penetrator tank rounds, with much longer effective ranges than normal APDS or AFPDS rounds

ECM – electronic counter-measure

ENDEX – end of exercise

EW – electronic warfare

FCO – Foreign and Commonwealth Office

Ferret – type of scout car

'Fin' round – tank ammunition. Short for APFSDS armour-piercing 'fin-stabilised' discarding sabot

FUP – forming-up point

G2 – military intelligence

G3 – military operational planning

GCHQ – the UK Government Communications Headquarters (a British intelligence agency)

Glacis Plate – sloped (and very thick) front armour section of the hull of a tank

GOC – General Officer Commanding

GPMG – 7.62mm general-purpose machine gun

GPMG SF – general purpose machine gun in sustained-fire role (with tripod)

GRU – the Russian Red Army's main intelligence directorate

Gulf Cooperation Council – political and economic grouping of Gulf states.

GWS – Gulf War Syndrome

HARM – High Speed Anti-Radar Missile

HELARM – helicopters firing rockets and guns

Hercules (aircraft) – C130 medium transport aircraft.

HESH – high explosive squash head (tank ammunition rounds)

HR – Human Resources (personnel)

HUMINT – human intelligence

Humvee – US large four-wheel drive vehicle

IED – improvised explosive device

JACIG – Joint Arms Control Implementation Group

JARIC – Joint Air Reconnaissance Intelligence Centre

JIB – Joint Information Bureau

JSTARS – Joint Surveillance Target Attack Radar System (or Joint STARS). A US radar ground vehicle (and helicopter) tracking system using (in 1990–1) two Boeing 707s

jundi – Arabic word meaning 'soldier'

laager – tank or vehicle defensive position

LAW 80 – anti-tank weapon

LSL – landing ship, logistic

LSW – light support weapon: 5.56mm machineguns used primarily by infantry sections

MEF – Marine Expeditionary Force (US Army)

MID – Mentioned in Dispatches – a gallantry award, denoted by an oak leaf on the campaign medal ribbon

MILAN – guided anti-tank rocket

MLRS – artillery Multiple Launch Rocket System

MoD – Ministry of Defence

MREs – Meals Ready-to-Eat, US Army combat rations

MRTs – media reaction teams

MSR – main supply route

MTLB – a Russian armoured personnel carrier

Mujahideen – Arabic for 'struggler', 'freedom fighter' or 'justice fighter', from the word 'jihad' meaning war. Many different Muslim groups around the world describe themselves as Mujahideen

NAIAD – Nerve Agent Immobiliser Agent Detector, an alarm that warns of the presence of nerve agents

NAPS – nerve agent pre-treatment tablets

NATO – North Atlantic Treaty Organisation

nav – aircraft navigator

NBC – Nuclear, Biological, Chemical

NCO – non-commissioned officer

NOTICAS – notification of casualty (messages and system)

OC – Officer Commanding (usually of a company or squadron)

O group – orders group

Operation Desert Shield – the overall America name for the initial coalition deployment to defend Saudi Arabia

Operation Granby – the British name for their part of the operation

Operation Provide Comfort – the protection of the Kurds in northern Iraq, after the Gulf War ended

Patriot – American surface to air aerial interceptor missile and radar defence system, used to defend against Iraqi Scud missiles

Porton Down – the Defence Science and Technology Laboratory, the UK's chemical and biological warfare research establishment

Ptarmigan – British Army communications system

PTSD – post traumatic stress disorder

PWO – Prince of Wales's Own Regiment (infantry)

QM – quartermaster

QDG – Queen's Dragoon Guards (a cavalry regiment operating tanks)

QMG – Quartermaster General: the MoD-based (in those days) general in charge of all supplies

QRIH – Queen's Royal Irish Hussars (cavalry regiment operating tanks)

R&R – rest and recuperation

RAMC – Royal Army Medical Corps

RCT – Royal Corps of Transport

recce – reconnaissance

REME – Royal Electrical and Mechanical Engineers

reservist – a member of the Territorial Army and Volunteer Reserve

resus – resuscitation

RHQ – Regimental Headquarters

RIC – reconnaissance intelligence centre

RMP – Royal Military Police

RPG – rocket-propelled grenade

RSM – Regimental Sergeant Major

RTA – road traffic accident

RTU-ed – returned to unit

RV – rendezvous

SA8, SA6 – low- to medium-level surface-to-air missiles

SA80 – British Army standard assault 5.56mm rifle

SAM – surface-to-air missile

SAS – Special Air Service

SBS – Special Boat Service

Scots DG – Royal Scots Dragoon Guards (a cavalry regiment operating tanks)

Scud – long-range surface-to-surface guided missile, fired from a mobile launcher by Iraqi military in Gulf War One

2ic – second-in-command

SOP – standard operating procedure

SSVC – a registered charity set up to entertain and inform Britain's Armed Forces and their families around the world, operating television and radio stations and providing entertainment facilities for troops on operations

T-55 – Russian tank

T-62 – Russian tank

T-72 – Russian tank

TA – Territorial Army

tac HQ – tactical HQ. A small command unit with which a Commander moves around the battlefield

TIALD – thermal imaging airborne laser designator

TOGS – thermal observation gunnery sights

Trimble – satellite navigation system

Triple A – anti-aircraft artillery

UAE – United Arab Emirates

UHF – ultra high frequency

USAAF – United States Army Air Forces

VC10 – a 1962 aircraft still used by the RAF for passengers and as an air-to-air refuelling tanker

Warlords – a senior aircrew officer, grounded for an operation, to administer the squadron, allowing its Commander to concentrate on flying.

Watchkeepers – officers on HQ duty 24/7, tasked with monitoring radio traffic, plotting movements and incidents, keeping operations staff alerted

WMD – weapons of mass destruction

WO1 – Warrant Officer Class 1

INDEX